CROWN AND SWORD

EXECUTIVE POWER AND THE USE OF FORCE
BY THE AUSTRALIAN DEFENCE FORCE

CROWN AND SWORD

EXECUTIVE POWER AND THE USE OF FORCE BY THE AUSTRALIAN DEFENCE FORCE

CAMERON MOORE

PRESS

Published by ANU Press
The Australian National University
Acton ACT 2601, Australia
Email: anupress@anu.edu.au
This title is also available online at press.anu.edu.au

National Library of Australia Cataloguing-in-Publication entry

Creator: Moore, Cameron, author.

Title: Crown and sword : executive power and the use of force by the Australian Defence Force / Cameron Moore.

ISBN: 9781760461553 (paperback) 9781760461560 (ebook)

Subjects: Australia. Department of Defence.
Executive power--Australia.
Internal security--Australia.
Australia--Armed Forces.

All rights reserved. No part of this publication may be reproduced, stored in a retrieval system or transmitted in any form or by any means, electronic, mechanical, photocopying or otherwise, without the prior permission of the publisher.

Cover design and layout by ANU Press. Cover photographs by Søren Niedziella flic.kr/p/ahroZv and Kurtis Garbutt flic.kr/p/9krqeu.

This edition © 2017 ANU Press

Contents

Prefatory Notes vii
List of Maps ix
Introduction 1
1. What is Executive Power? 7
2. The Australian Defence Force within the Executive 79
3. Martial Law. 129
4. Internal Security 165
5. War 205
6. External Security 253
Conclusion: What are the Limits? 307
Bibliography 313

Prefatory Notes

Acknowledgement

I would like to acknowledge the tremendous and unflagging support of my family and friends, my supervisors and my colleagues in the writing of this book. It has been a long journey and I offer my profound thanks.

Applicable Law

This book reflects the law as it stood up to 28 March 2016.

Terms

'State' and 'Territory' in this book will refer to States and Territories of the Commonwealth of Australia as opposed to nation states and foreign territories.

List of Maps

Map 1. Area of the Territories of New Guinea and Papua under Military Control pursuant to the *National Security (External Territories) Regulations 1942* 153

Map 2. Area of Australia under Military Control pursuant to the *National Security (Emergency Control) Regulations 1941* 154

Introduction

The Australian Defence Force (ADF) has considerable power at its disposal. It is physically more powerful than any other organisation in Australia. This is hardly surprising when it has the task of defending the country,[1] conducting warlike and peacebuilding operations overseas,[2] enforcing maritime legislation,[3] and providing a degree of internal security.[4] Yet only a minor proportion of this activity is authorised by an Act of Parliament.

In fact, some of the more extreme powers currently exercised by the ADF, such as the offensive use of lethal force, deliberate destruction of property, interception of shipping and detention of civilians, are actually contrary to some Acts of Parliament. The authority for such activity lies elsewhere. The scant literature on this topic in Australia would identify the executive power of the Commonwealth as the source of this extraordinary authority[5]—whether it is to invade Iraq in 2003, to conduct warlike operations in Afghanistan since 2001, to bomb Syria since 2015, to board shipping in the Arabian Gulf since 1990, to counter piracy off Somalia since 2009, to fly combat air patrols to protect visiting dignitaries in 2002 and 2003 or to occupy East Timor in 1999.[6] In some senses, executive power as a source of authority for ADF operations is a new question. Australia did not lead an international military operation itself until the

---

1   Department of Defence, *White Paper 2013*, 28.
2   Ibid.
3   Ibid 30.
4   Ibid.
5   See Harold Renfree, *The Executive Power of the Commonwealth of Australia* (Legal Books, 1984): 461–4; H P Lee, *The Emergency Powers of the Commonwealth of Australia* (Law Book Company, 1984): 38–42.
6   These operations are discussed and referenced in more detail in subsequent chapters.

East Timor intervention in 1999.[7] Questions of executive power and internal security have really only come to the fore since the MV *Tampa* crisis[8] and the terrorist attacks on the United States in 2001.[9]

More often than not, any discussion of the legal basis for or limits upon ADF operations concerns international law; where there is ample consideration of the law of armed conflict, the law of peace operations, international human rights law, the international law relating to armed intervention and the law of the sea.[10] The basis in Australian law is not as commonly challenged or discussed. Yet international law does not automatically form part of Australian law;[11] it does not directly define the legal basis for, and limits upon, ADF operations. Within Australia, statute is the usual source of authority under which the ADF conducts fisheries or migration law enforcement, or provides security for major events such as the Commonwealth Games, G20 Leaders' Meeting or an Asia-Pacific Economic Cooperation (APEC) meeting.[12] This is only a limited part of what the ADF does though, and does not account for virtually all of its overseas operations.

To state executive power as the legal basis for an ADF operation does little to explain the limits on that power, or even its character. Citing executive power broadly identifies the constitutional setting of the power. It does not necessarily identify who may exercise the power, where an action is beyond power, whether such an action prevails over an Act of Parliament or whether the exercise of the power is reviewable by a court. Executive power, in itself, is a poorly understood concept even though it extends to the full range of the concerns of government. The most recent High Court cases on the subject of executive power have concerned spending and the tax power,[13] as well as spending on school chaplains.[14] Understanding

---

7   See Commonwealth, *Parliamentary Debates*, House of Representatives, 21 September 1999, 10047–51 (Alexander Downer) reproduced in 'Australian Troops in East Timor' in Rod Kemp and Marion Stanton (eds) *Speaking for Australia: Parliamentary Speeches that Shaped Our Nation*, (Allen and Unwin, 2004) 280.
8   *Ruddock v Vadarlis* (2001) 110 FCR 491 ('*Tampa Case*').
9   Department of Defence, *Submission to Senate Legal and Constitutional Committee Inquiry into Defence Legislation Amendment (Aid to Civilian Authorities) Bill* (2005) 3.
10 Subsequent chapters will address this literature.
11 *Chow Hung Ching v R* (1948) 77 CLR 449, 471; *Bradley v Commonwealth* (1973) 128 CLR 557, 583.
12 See, eg, *Maritime Powers Act 2013* (Cth); *Fisheries Management Act 1991* (Cth); *Migration Act 1958* (Cth); *Defence Act 1903* (Cth) pt IIIAAA.
13 *Pape v Commissioner of Taxation* (2009) 238 CLR 1 ('*Pape*').
14 *Williams v Commonwealth* (2012) 248 CLR 156 ('*Williams*').

the lawful extent of executive power exercisable by the ADF then requires some examination of the nature and extent of executive power generally before considering its specific application to the activities of the ADF.

The aim of this book is to identify the sources of and limits upon the exercise of executive power by the ADF. Even if the limits are not known or defined, they must exist because it is not possible to have limitless power in a system of constitutional government. In any event, the ADF has never exercised executive power as if it were limitless. Any discussion of these limits must be at least partly theoretical because no Australian or English court has ever sought to elaborate a complete doctrinal statement on executive power. Nor is there an exhaustive definition of executive power and its limits, even though there have been some High Court cases on executive power. In fact, there has been a marked reluctance to provide one.[15] Still less has there been any settled doctrinal position on executive power as it relates to the ADF—there have simply not been relevant cases before the courts. This is significant in itself and is the subject of discussion in Chapter 1. The approach of this book, therefore, is to develop a theoretical position on the character and limits of executive power generally before considering the specific powers that relate to the ADF.

The term 'prerogative power' is significant. Contemporary Australian jurisprudence identifies s 61 of the *Constitution* as the source of Commonwealth executive power.[16] This jurisprudence is cautious of the term prerogative power as an English law concept, which informs the content of s 61 but does not provide its limits.[17] This is a debate upon which Chapter 1 will elaborate. For the purpose of this book, however, s 61 in itself provides virtually no guidance as to the limits of executive power exercisable by the ADF. Most case authorities and literature refer to distinct prerogative powers rather than executive power generally. As poorly understood and elusive as the prerogatives are in themselves, at least they are, to some extent, identifiable.

---

15   *Williams* (2012) 248 CLR 156, 226–7 (Gummow and Bell JJ); *Davis v Commonwealth* (1988) 166 CLR 79, 93 (Mason CJ, Deane and Gaudron JJ); *Pape* (2009) 238 CLR 1, 24 (French CJ).
16   See *Pape* (2009) 238 CLR 1, 83 (Gummow, Crennan and Bell JJ), *Williams* (2012) 248 CLR 156, 184–5 (French CJ) and 342 (Crennan J) together with express constitutional provisions such as s 68 concerning command-in-chief of the naval and military forces of the Commonwealth.
17   *Tampa Case* (2001) 110 FCR 491, 538–9 (French J).

For this reason, following Chapter 1, the structure of this book will then be to address, in turn, each of the main prerogatives which relate to the ADF. Chapter 2 will address the prerogative with respect to control and disposition of the forces.[18] This is necessary in order to understand how executive power flows to the ADF, and the principle of military subordination to the civilian government, before considering how the ADF exercises executive power. Chapter 3 will then consider martial law[19] as perhaps the most extreme manifestation of prerogative power as exercised by a military force. Chapter 4 considers internal security,[20] which is distinct from martial law, as troops on the street are a chilling prospect in a modern Australian political culture which almost supposes a constitutional bar to using the ADF for internal security. Chapter 5 discusses war,[21] the most destructive and perhaps best-recognised prerogative, while its substance is one of the least considered in both case law and literature. Finally, Chapter 6 will turn to the external affairs prerogative,[22] which has been the basis for the most extensive ADF operations in recent decades. At the same time, as this prerogative relies significantly upon Act of State doctrine, it is perhaps the most unsettled in Australian case law.

The nature of the prerogatives having some identity and historical context also makes them preferable to a broad invocation of s 61. These prerogative powers are extraordinary and capable of authorising extreme exercises of power. There are more likely to be identifiable limits where there is some content to the power, and this is more likely to be consistent with the rule of law. Even so, Australia's distinct constitutional structure means that it might be necessary to rely upon s 61 alone—particularly the aspect of it known as the nationhood power—in very limited circumstances. This could be the case in respect of internal security where the prerogative with respect to public order rests with the States but the Commonwealth retains significant responsibilities, such as for protecting visiting dignitaries, which might require use of the ADF.

---

18   *China Navigation Company Ltd v Attorney-General* [1932] 2 KB 197, 207 ('*China Navigation*').
19   *Marais v General Officer Commanding the Lines of Communication* [1902] AC 109 ('*Marais*').
20   *R v Secretary of State for the Home Department; Ex parte Northumbria Police Authority* [1989] 1 QB 26 ('*Northumbria Police Case*'); *Republic of Fiji v Prasad* (Unreported, Fiji Court of Appeal, Casey J (Presiding), Barker, Kapi, Ward and Handley JJA, 1 March 2001) ('*Prasad*').
21   *Burmah Oil Ltd v Lord Advocate* [1965] AC 75 ('*Burmah Oil*'); *Joseph v Colonial Treasurer (NSW)* (1918) 25 CLR 32, 46–7.
22   *Al-Jedda v Secretary of State for Defence* [2011] 2 WLR 225, 253 ('*Al-Jedda*'); *Thorpe v Commonwealth (No 3)* (1997) 144 ALR 677, 681.

This book will argue that it is possible to identify sources and limits to the exercise of executive power by the ADF. There cannot be precise limits however because executive power is meant to deal with the unpredictable and the external. It would never be possible to define precisely in advance what circumstances might require of the ADF. Even so, the principle of legality applies to the ADF and those who wish to wield executive power through it must keep this in mind. As Starke J stated in the case which established the doctrine of combat immunity, *Shaw Savill and Albion Co Ltd v Commonwealth* ('*Shaw Savill and Albion Co Ltd*'), in 1940:

> If any person commits … a wrongful act or one not justifiable, he cannot escape liability for the offence, he cannot prevent himself being sued, merely because he acted in obedience to the order of the Executive Government or any officer of State.[23]

---

23 *Shaw Savill & Albion Co Ltd v Commonwealth* (1940) 66 CLR 344, ('*Shaw Savill & Albion Co Ltd*') 353 citing *Raleigh v Goschen* (1898) 1 Ch 73, 77.

1

What is Executive Power?

I Introduction

In the 1988 case of *Davis v Commonwealth*, Mason J said of executive power that it is potentially very broad yet 'its scope [is not] amenable to exhaustive definition.'[1] Executive power is a power with significant content but ill-defined limits. It is not the particular power of lawmaking, or of determining disputes but, rather, the general power to carry out all the other functions of government. In the Westminster tradition, all governmental power derived originally from the Crown[2] and independent legislative[3] and judicial[4] functions were a subsequent development. The *Coronation Charter* of Henry I, the immediate successor to William I and, therefore, the first postconquest king to have a coronation as such, illustrates the breadth of the original power of the Crown (the following excerpts indicating executive, judicial and legislative power respectively):

---

1   *Davis v Commonwealth* (1988) 166 CLR 79, 93.
2   *Magna Carta* 1215 (Imp); *NSW v Commonwealth* (1975) 135 CLR 337, 480, 487–91 ('*Seas and Submerged Lands Case*') (Jacobs J); J H Baker, *An Introduction to English Legal History*, (Butterworths, 2nd ed, 1979) 12–15; John Gillingham, 'The Early Middle Ages 1066–1290' in Kenneth Morgan (ed), *The Oxford Illustrated History of Britain* (Oxford University Press, 1984), 104; Elizabeth Wicks, *The Evolution of a Constitution: Eight Key Moments in British Constitutional History* (Hart, 2006) 3–6; cf *Australian Capital Television Pty Ltd v Commonwealth* (1992) 177 CLR 106, 137–8 Mason CJ discussing 'sovereign power which resides in the people' by virtue of the mechanism for constitutional amendment being a referendum under s 128 of the *Constitution*.
3   *Bill of Rights 1688* (Imp).
4   *Act of Settlement 1701* (Imp).

> 11. To knights who hold their lands by military service (*per loricas*) I grant, of my own gift, the lands of the demesne ploughs … so that … they may the better provide themselves with arms and horses, to be fit and ready for my service and the defence of my kingdom.
>
> 12. I establish my firm peace throughout the whole kingdom and command that it henceforth be maintained.
>
> 13. I restore to you the law of King Edward …[5]

In this respect, executive power might be thought of as the original and residual power of government. This could help to explain why it is potentially so broad and important and yet so ill-defined.[6]

This chapter seeks to establish what the executive power of the Commonwealth of Australia is. It will address the theory, history and doctrine of the concept of executive power. It will then deal with its explicit basis in the *Constitution*, the relationship between executive and prerogative power, the critical relationship between prerogative power and statute, and the implicit concept of nationhood power. It will then put forward an argument on the limits of the executive power of the Commonwealth which is based upon this combination of theory, history and doctrine.

This chapter will rely primarily on case law and legal history because statutorily granted executive power, whilst extensive, ordinarily deals with particular aspects of the power rather than its general nature.[7] This chapter will not draw the connection between executive power and the ADF directly, which will be the subject of Chapter 2.

---

5   Henry I, *Coronation Charter*, (1100) in Carl Stephenson and Frederick George Marcham (eds and trans), *Sources of English Constitutional History: A Selection of Documents from AD 600 to the Present* (Harper and Brothers, 1937) 46–8. Legal instruments issued under prerogative power, such as this charter, letters patent and orders in council, are so obscure that they do not even rate a mention in the *Australian Guide to Legal Citation*.

6   See discussion of flexibility and uncertainty in executive power in Robin Creyke, 'Executive Power – New Wine in Old Bottles: Foreword' (2003) 31 *Federal Law Review* iv.

7   Likewise, despite frequent references to judicial power, statute does not define it either. As to the need to refer to legal history to understand executive power in Australia, it is because s 61 of the *Constitution* is 'barren ground for any analytical approach'. See Leslie Zines, 'The Inherent Executive Power of the Commonwealth' (2005) 16 *Public Law Review* 279, 279, quoting D G Morgan discussing the equivalent position in the *Irish Constitution,* in *The Separation of Powers in the Irish Constitution* (Sweet & Maxwell, 1997) 272.

II A Theory of Executive Power?

> When legislative power is united with executive power in a single person or in a single body of the magistracy, there is no liberty, because one can fear that the same monarch or senate that makes tyrannical laws will execute them tyrannically. Nor is there liberty if the power of judging is not separate from legislative power and executive power ... If it were joined to executive power, the judge could have the force of an oppressor.[8]

What are the limits of executive power? There is no authoritative source that states this so it becomes a theoretical question.[9] This is complicated by the character of executive power as derived from a number of sources so that, as discussed earlier, executive power is not a power in itself but rather a description of power which the Executive exercises.[10] This may be a key to divining some sort of coherent theory of the limits of executive power. As Gageler J stated in *Plaintiff M68/2015 v Minister for Immigration and Border Protection* ('*M68*'):[11]

> The nature of Commonwealth executive power can only be understood within that historical and structural constitutional context. It is described – not defined – in s 61 of the Constitution, in that it is extended – not confined – by that section to the 'execution and maintenance' of the Constitution and of laws of the Commonwealth. It is therefore 'barren ground for any analytical approach'.[12] Alfred Deakin said of it in a profound opinion which he gave as Attorney-General in 1902 that 'it would be dangerous, if not impossible, to define', emphasising that it 'is administrative, as well as in the strict sense executive; that is to say, it must obviously include the power not only to execute laws, but also to effectively administer the whole Government'.[13]

---

8   Charles de Secondat, Baron de Montesquieu, *The Spirit of the Laws* (Anne Cohler, Basia Miller and Harold Stone trans and eds, Cambridge University Press, 1989) Book 11, Ch 6, 156–7 (trans of *De L'Esprit de Lois* (first published 1748)).
9   See Chief Justice R S French, 'The Executive Power' (Inaugural George Winterton Lecture, Sydney Law School, University of Sydney, 18 February 2010) (2010) May *Constitutional Law and Policy Review* 5.
10   See *Pape v Commissioner of Taxation* (2009) 238 CLR 1, 83 ('*Pape*'), (Gummow, Crennan and Bell JJ); *Williams v Commonwealth* (2012) 248 CLR 156 ('*Williams*'), 184–5 (French CJ), 342 (Crennan J) and 373–4 (Kiefel J).
11   [2016] HCA 1, [129].
12   Quoting Zines, 'The Inherent Executive Power of the Commonwealth', above n 7.
13   Quoting Sir Alfred, 'Channel of Communication with Imperial Government: Position of Consuls: Executive Power of Commonwealth' in Patrick Brazil and Bevan Mitchell (eds) *Opinions of Attorneys-General of the Commonwealth of Australia, Volume 1: 1901–14* (1981) 129, 130–1.

The limits of executive power may be more a matter of the limits of executive functions rather than the limits of identifiable legal authority. This may be because executive functions are the residual functions of government left after the more identifiable legislative and judicial functions. As Gerangelos puts it:

> Parliament left such traditional 'executive' powers as foreign relations, declaring war and peace, altering national boundaries, acts of state, conferring honours, pardoning offenders, etc. in the hands of the Crown for essentially pragmatic reasons.[14]

If a matter is not suitable for the legislative or judicial branches of government but it is a matter for government nonetheless, then it could only be a matter for the executive government.[15] As a result, it is not possible to define in advance every matter upon which the Executive may act. This book will, therefore, argue for a theory of executive power which emphasises that it must be flexible and, at its extreme, may only be limited by the written *Constitution* and the doctrine of necessity, but is nonetheless subject to the principle of legality.

The resort to early theorists to explain aspects of the *Australian Constitution* is not novel. The High Court has done so with respect to responsible government, citing J S Mill in *Egan v Willis*,[16] and the separation of powers, citing Blackstone in *Polyukhovich v R*,[17] as well as Dicey and Blackstone with respect to executive power in *Williams v Commonwealth* ('*Williams*').[18] This section will consider the early theorists before considering the modern debate on the theoretical limits of executive power.

---

14   Peter Gerangelos, 'The Executive Power of the Commonwealth of Australia: Section 61 of the *Commonwealth Constitution*, "Nationhood" and the Future of the Prerogative' (2012) 12(1) *Oxford University Commonwealth Law Journal* 97, 117.
15   John Locke, 'An Essay Concerning the True, Original, Extent and End of Civil Government (1690)' in Sir Ernest Barker (ed) *Social Contract: Essays by Locke, Hume and Rousseau* (Oxford University Press, 1946) 137.
16   (1998) 195 CLR 424, 451.
17   (1991) 172 CLR 501, 606.
18   (2012) 248 CLR 156, 185–6 (French CJ).

A The Nature of Executive Power—Early Theorists

Looking at early constitutional theorists does not, of itself, of course provide legal authority for the limits of executive power, but it does provide insight into the values which underlie contemporary constitutional arrangements. Dicey considers Montesquieu to be the origin and strongest theoretical influence on the development of the separation of powers.[19] Montesquieu's book *De L'Esprit Des Lois* of 1748 considered constitutional structures that favour liberty.[20] However, given that Montesquieu receives credit for having the greatest influence on the development of the theory of the separation of powers, he has relatively little to say about executive power. He concentrated more on the balance of powers itself rather than analysing at length the character of each branch of government. As Montesquieu perhaps best explains himself: '[S]o that power cannot abuse power, power must check power by the arrangement of things',[21] and he continued, 'among the Turks, where the three powers are united in the person of the Sultan, an atrocious despotism reigns'.[22] On the character of executive power, and why it must be a separate power, Montesquieu did however state:

> The executive power should always be in the hands of a monarch, because the part of the government that almost always needs immediate action is better administered by the one than the many, whereas what depends on legislative power is better ordered by many than by one.[23]

Blackstone had read Montesquieu and reflected something of this view in 1803 in his own *Commentaries* in the chapter 'Of the King's Prerogative':[24]

> We are next to consider those branches of the royal prerogative, which invest thus our sovereign lord, thus all-perfect and immortal in his kingly capacity, with a number of authorities and powers; in the exertion whereof consists the executive part of government. This is wisely placed in a single hand by the British constitution for the sake of unanimity, strength, and dispatch. Were it placed in many hands, it would be subject to many wills:

---

19 Which he saw as a misunderstood and misapplied doctrine. A V Dicey, *Introduction to the Study of the Law of the Constitution* (Macmillan, 10th ed, 1959) 338.
20 Montesquieu, above n 8.
21 Ibid 155.
22 Ibid 157.
23 Ibid 161.
24 *Blackstone's Commentaries with Notes of Reference, to the Constitution and Laws, of the Federal Government of the United States; and of the Commonwealth of Virginia* (Hein Online reproduction, 1803) 260.

many wills, if disunited and drawing different ways, create weakness in a government; and to unite these several wills, and reduce them to one, is a work of more time and delay than the exigencies of state will afford.[25]

Hume wrote in the 18th century, at the time of the emergence of ministerial government. As much as Hume sought to reduce politics to science, he also wrote that no government 'subsisted without the mixture of some arbitrary authority, committed to some magistrate' and no society could support itself only with the control of 'rigid maxims of law and equity'.[26]

Between these influential writers there is a consistent picture of the qualities of coherence, alacrity and strength needing to reside in the executive branch of government, as opposed to the qualities of deliberation required of the legislature or impartiality in the judiciary. Indeed the inconsistency between these attributes is the reason for the separation of powers and an indication that executive power is meant to be an active function of government. It should be able to respond to requirements as they arise rather than having its function narrowly prescribed in advance.

Fatovic's examination of the influence of these theorists on the American Founding Fathers' conception of executive power also considers Machiavelli. He states that the idea of the need for executive power to deal with contingency began with Machiavelli,[27] observing that:

> Niccolo Machiavelli's insight that contingency is the single constant in politics forms the backdrop for any serious investigation of executive power in modern political and constitutional thought ...[28]

Machiavelli himself stated in his advice to *The Prince* in 1513:

> I hold it to be true that Fortune is the arbiter of one half of our actions, but that she still leave us to direct the other half, or perhaps a little less ... So it happens with Fortune, who shows her power where valour has not prepared to resist her, and thither she turns her forces where she knows that barriers and defences have not been raised to constrain her.[29]

---

25 Ibid 250.
26 Clement Fatovic, *Outside the Law* (John Hopkins University Press, 2009) 83, quoting David Hume, *The History of England from the Invasion of Julius Caesar to the Revolution of 1688 (Continued to the Death of George the Second by T Smollett M D)* (Joseph Ogle Robinson, 1833) 574.
27 Ibid 282, n 22.
28 Ibid 11.
29 Niccolò Machiavelli, *The Prince* (W K Marriott trans, Encyclopaedia Britannica, 1952 (first published in Italian in 1513 and in English 1640)) 35.

This book is concerned with the capacity of the law to respond to *Fortuna* (Fortune) and argues that executive power provides the means to do so, but this must be within constraints. Montesquieu, Blackstone and Hume, in differing degrees, reflect this analysis of *Fortuna*—the capricious nature of fortune—in their own attempts to find a way to have an executive that could respond to contingency.[30]

Consistent with this, the influential commentator on the *Australian Constitution*, Harrison Moore, writing in 1910, emphasised the importance of executive power to the whole constitutional endeavour and, in doing so, reflected a view of executive power shared by the theorists discussed above:

> In the history of Australia the want of such an authority to speak and to act for the whole was as potent a factor in producing union as the absence of a common legislative power. The authority must be continuous, and not occasional; it must be capable of prompt and immediate action; it must possess knowledge and keep its secrets; it must know discipline. In a word, it must have qualities very different from those which belong to the large representative and popular bodies which in modern times exercise legislative power.[31]

Locke also grappled with *Fortuna*, even if he did not name the phenomenon of contingency. Locke wrote around the time of the Glorious Revolution of 1688 and, despite experiencing horrific excesses of executive power, stated:

> This power to act according to discretion for the public good, without the prescription of the law and sometimes even against it, is that which is called prerogative; for since in some governments the law-making power is not always in being and is usually too numerous, and so too slow for the dispatch requisite to execution, and because, also it is impossible to foresee and so by laws to provide for all accidents and necessities that may concern the public, or make such laws as will do no harm if they are executed with an inflexible rigour on all occasions, and upon all persons that may come in their way, therefore there is a latitude left to the executive power to do many things of choice which the laws do not prescribe.[32]

---

30 Fatovic, above n 26, 18–20.
31 W Harrison Moore, *The Constitution of the Commonwealth of Australia* (Maxwell, 2nd ed, 1910) 292.
32 Locke, 'Essay Concerning the True Original, Extent and End of Civil Government', above n 15, 137; Oren Gross and Fionnuala Ni Aolain, *Law in Times of Crisis: Emergency Powers in Theory and Practice* (Cambridge University Press, 2006) 119–23 state that Locke greatly influenced the Founding Fathers of the United States.

Despite the idea of acting against the law, Gross and Aolain argue that Locke's theory actually accommodates the ability for the executive to respond to contingency as part of the constitutional order, rather than being extraconstitutional.[33] This is important because this book argues that, in an extreme situation, it may only be an exercise of executive power that can preserve constitutional government in the face of anarchy and chaos. If such action is necessary, the authority for it can be a part of the legal order, not contrary to it. This chapter will return to this point.

The consistent theme in these early theorists then is that there is a need for an executive power to be available continually, not only occasionally, and to respond to the unexpected, *Fortuna*, which may even be necessary to maintain the very existence of constitutional government. Legislative bodies are not suited to this task for various reasons, such as: being deliberative and, therefore, unable to respond to emerging situations quickly; being corruptible, if they have the power to make as well as to execute the laws; or being open and accommodating of different views. They do not, therefore, possess the qualities of discretion, secrecy and consistency or unity of purpose required for such functions as maintaining order, foreign relations and the conduct of war. For the most part, therefore, the theorists determined that there had to be a field of action left to executive authority. This could not be narrowly defined or precisely limited because it had to be able to respond to the unexpected, *Fortuna*. None of the theorists, therefore, describe a precise theoretical limit to executive authority but, rather, in one way or another, set up a structure to contain it in the form of the separation of powers.

B Early Theorists and the Limits of Executive Power?

Before turning to the separation of powers, it is important to acknowledge that the ancient maxims, *inter armes silent leges*,[34] among the arms the laws are silent, and, *salus populi est suprema lex*, the welfare of the people is the highest law, represent recurring ideas in the writings, whether implicitly[35] or explicitly.[36] As can be seen above, Locke states that prerogative power

---

33 Gross and Ni Aolain, 121.
34 Montesquieu, above n 8, 159.
35 See Fatovic, above n 26, 36.
36 Locke, 'Essay Concerning the True Original, Extent and End of Civil Government', above n 15 (art 158) 117.

can authorise acting against the law. In his words: 'This power to act ... without the prescription of the law and sometimes even against it.'[37] As the American Founding Father Thomas Jefferson put it:

> Should we have ever gained our Revolution, if we had bound our hands by the manacles of the law, not only in the beginning, but in any part of the revolutionary conflict? There are extreme cases where the laws become inadequate even to their own preservation, and where the universal resource is a dictator, or martial law.[38]

This is perhaps the point of greatest discomfort for all of the writers on this issue. If constitutional structures are meant to create the rule of law and protect liberty, how can the executive have authority to break the law? Excesses of executive power, indeed, led to the Glorious Revolution as well as the American Revolution.

It may be appropriate for the executive not to break the law but to have an authority to act, which creates exceptions from the ordinary application of the law in certain circumstances. In extreme situations, the executive may need to act to preserve the constitutional order. Montesquieu suggests that there are times when executive power might expand to encroach more upon liberty than is usual in order to take account of threats to the state itself. This is to be temporary only and for the purpose of preserving liberty in the longer term:

> But if the legislative power believed itself endangered by some secret conspiracy against the state or by some correspondence with its enemies on the outside, it could, for a brief and limited time, permit the executive power to arrest suspected citizens who would lose their liberty for a time only so that it would be preserved forever.[39]

This is an abstract and highly subjective measure of when the executive may act under an exception to the law but Blackstone provided some guide. He distinguished the 'ordinary course of the law' from

---

37 John Locke, *Two Treatises of Government* (Mobilereference.com, first published 1689, 2008) (Article 160) 118.
38 Fatovic, above n 26, 204, quoting Thomas Jefferson, 'Letter LXXI to Doctor James Brown, Washington, October 27, 1808' in Thomas Jefferson Randolph (ed) *Memoirs, Correspondence and Miscellanies from the Correspondence of T Jefferson* (F Carr, 1829) 3, 115.
39 Montesquieu, above n 8, 159.

those extraordinary recourses to first principles, which are necessary when the contracts of society are in danger of dissolution, and the law proves too weak a defence against the violence of fraud or oppression.[40]

These extraordinary recourses are limited however as:

[T]he king is irresistible and absolute, according to the forms of the constitution. And yet, if the consequence of that exertion be manifestly to the grievance or dishonour of the kingdom, the parliament will call his advisers to a just and severe account. For prerogative consisting (as Mr Locke has well defined it) in the prerogative power of acting for the public good, where the positive laws are silent; if that discretionary power be abused to the public detriment, such prerogative is exerted in an unconstitutional manner.[41]

Blackstone raises two distinct but related limitations which are very significant for this book. The first is that the ministry, even if the king himself can do no wrong, is responsible to the Parliament for its actions in response to extraordinary events.[42] The second limitation is that the exercise of prerogative power is bounded by the constitution. It is not open to use executive power to change the constitutional order itself, noting the imprecise and unwritten character of the English constitution in Blackstone's time. This is a more precise consideration with Australia's written constitution today, which is therefore arguably more amenable to Blackstone's limits. It comes now to consider how more modern theorists have addressed this issue before turning to Australian constitutional doctrine, then putting it together with this legal history and theory to propose limits on the executive power of the Commonwealth.

C The Nature of Executive Power—Modern Theorists

It is important to place the early theorists against current writing on executive power, particularly that which emerged in the context of the heightened concerns over terrorism post-2001. Craig and Tomkins in

---

40 *Blackstone's Commentaries*, above n 24, 251.
41 Ibid 252.
42 For a rejection of the 'grandiose claims about the "rule of law"' which, instead, locates public law within 'a wider body of political practices' see Martin Loughlin, *The Idea of Public Law* (Oxford University Press, 2003) 156–7. This is consistent with Blackstone's view, and that of this book, that the executive is limited through political accountability to Parliament, but the author of this book is not willing to reject the rule of law as a fundamental principle which should guide the use of executive power through the ADF.

their introduction to *The Executive and Public Law*,[43] a 2006 collection of essays on executive power in various Western liberal democracies, emphasised that the role of the executive is to *do*. It is also to fulfil all the other functions of government which the legislative and judicial branches do not perform.[44] All of the essayists had difficulty defining and theorising the limits of executive power in the nations which they considered. The written constitutions they examined all said very little about executive power.

For example, Tomkins stated of the British executive that:

> Just as in Britain there is no constitutional definition of the executive, neither is there an authoritative list of executive functions … Perhaps the nearest that domestic British law gets to an understanding of what are executive functions is in its recognition of prerogative powers …[45]

Having identified a number of prerogative powers Tomkins goes on to state:

> All that can be gleaned from such lists of powers is that the executive acts in a bewilderingly wide array of policy arenas and subject matters. No general or over-arching principle that is defining or determinative of executive functions can be distilled by listing the powers that are conferred upon the executive by either statute or prerogative.[46]

This is consistent with the theorists discussed above in that executive power is a function rather than a clear set of powers. The interesting addition to this is that there is a general theme of executive power growing with respect to the power of the other branches.[47] Alternatively, it may be that the power of the legislative and judicial branches has also grown because the role of government generally has grown. Therefore, as the role of the state has increased over the centuries since Machiavelli advised the Prince,

---

43 Paul Craig and Adam Tomkins (eds), *The Executive and Public Law: Power and Accountability in Public Perspective* (Oxford University Press, 2006).
44 Ibid 1.
45 Adam Tomkins, 'The Struggle to Delimit Executive Power in Britain', in Craig and Tomkins (eds), *The Executive and Public Law: Power and Accountability in Public Perspective* (Oxford University Press, 2006) 16, 24. From an Australian perspective, Evans detailed executive accountability and echoed Tomkins to some extent in concluding that there was an inherent tension in constitutionalism between the need for accountability and the 'need to allow [public power] to be exercised effectively for the public good'. See Simon Evans, 'Continuity and Flexibility: Executive Power in Australia', in Craig and Tomkins (eds), *The Executive and Public Law: Power and Accountability in Public Perspective* (Oxford University Press, 2006) 89, 123.
46 Tomkins, above n 45, 25.
47 Craig and Tomkins, 'Introduction', above n 44, 1–2.

so it appears that the role of the executive has increased with it. This, perhaps, supports the view that the executive will act where there may be uncertainty as to whether the other branches can or should perform a governmental function.

Dyzenhaus wrote in 2006 on British and American failures to maintain the rule of law in response to terrorism. Drawing heavily on Dicey's concept of the rule of law, he rejects the idea that there is 'authority, within or without the law, to authorize the state to act outside the law'.[48] Dyzenhaus explains that Dicey accepted that there were times when 'the Ministry may break the law and trust for protection to an Act of Indemnity' but it was essential for the 'maintenance of law and the authority of the Houses' that extra-legal action receive at least the retrospective authority of statute.[49] Without this authority such action remains unlawful and subject to legal sanction. Dyzenhaus's point appears to be that while retrospective acts of indemnity or prospective statutory equivalents are contrary to the rule of law in themselves, such statutes can bring executive action within the scrutiny of Parliament and the courts. This process can help to reassert the rule of law over action that is inherently against the rule of law.[50] On this view, Dyzenhaus, together with Dicey, would reject any extended view of prerogative or executive power to preserve the constitutional order in times of emergency. This view would significantly constrain the lawful scope of executive power in an emergency and would be difficult to reconcile with views like those of Locke.

If the concern is to bring executive action within the scrutiny of the Parliament and the courts, then prospective legislation, with all the benefits of considered deliberation in calmer times, could achieve this more effectively than an act of indemnity. Even then, this book argues— particularly in Chapter 4—it is not possible to provide in advance for every contingency. There needs to be a mechanism within the law for the executive to act 'for the public good, without the prescription of the law'.[51] These mechanisms can be found within executive power and can

---

48   David Dyzenhaus, *The Constitution of Law: Legality in a Time of Emergency* (Cambridge University Press, 2006) 200.
49   Ibid 196, quoting Dicey, n 19, 412–13. Dicey gave no examples but an Australian one is the *Martial Law Indemnity Act 1854* (Vic) which followed the Eureka Stockade incident, discussed in Chapter 3.
50   Dyzenhaus, *The Constitution of Law*, above n 48, 196.
51   Locke, 'Essay Concerning the True Original, Extent and End of Civil Government', above n 15, 137.

operate within the *Constitution*. The view of Dicey and of Dyzenhaus is also unsatisfactory insofar as it requires the executive to break the law in response to a contingency. It does not adequately address the consequences of armed forces personnel breaking the law, both for the individual members of the armed forces that might face prosecution or suit nor the broader issue of armed forces being disciplined and obedient. As this book will argue in Chapter 2, this may undermine the duty of obedience of ADF members.

There is further scholarly debate on the question of whether the authority to deal with an exceptional situation exists inside or outside the law. For example, the 2008 book *Emergencies and the Limits of Legality*[52] collects essays on this question from a range of authors, responding in many respects to the view of Nazi philosopher Carl Schmitt that the state cannot respond to violent emergencies and remain 'faithful to the demands of legality'.[53] In it, Gross argued for a limited capacity for public officials to break the law in emergencies, so as to preserve the legal order.[54] However, Dyzenhaus continued to look to the judiciary or legislature to uphold the legal order after the event:

> Following Dicey, I accept that as a matter of fact when individuals are faced with what they perceive to be necessitous circumstances, they will act as they see fit, which might result in illegality. But also with Dicey, I think there is no distinction here between public officials and private individuals and that those who so act should be subject afterwards to the tribunal of law and, if they are found not to have met the requirements of the defence of necessity, to the tribunal of politics … A successful defence does not legalise a past illegality but finds it not to be illegal.[55]

---

52 Victor Ramraj (ed), *Emergencies and the Limits of Legality* (Cambridge University Press, 2008).
53 Victor Ramraj, 'No Doctrine More Pernicious: Emergencies and the Limits of Legality', in Victor Ramraj (ed), *Emergencies and the Limits of Legality* (Cambridge University Press, 2008) 4, citing Carl Schmitt *Political Theology: Four Chapters on the Concept of Sovereignty*, trans George Schwab (University of Chicago Press, 2005) 12.
54 Oren Gross, 'Extra-legality and the Ethic of Political Responsibility' in Victor Ramraj (ed), *Emergencies and the Limits of Legality* (Cambridge University Press, 2008) 62–3.
55 David Dyzenhaus, 'The Compulsion of Legality' in Victor Ramraj (ed), *Emergencies and the Limits of Legality* (Cambridge University Press, 2008) 33, 54.

By way of contrast, in the same book, Campbell does not see Gross or Dyzenhaus as offering an acceptable choice[56] and argues that:

> In principle, the emergency measures authorised in a state of emergency ought to be as formally correct as other laws specifying government powers and should be laid down in the particular piece of emergency legislation with justifiable precision, rather than expressed in the broad terms of indeterminate meaning.[57]

Notably for this book, he cites Part IIIAAA of the *Defence Act 1903* (Cth), discussed in more detail in Chapter 4, as an example of such legislation. Campbell also accepts that there may be appropriate circumstances for 'broad powers of executive legislation and wide discretion of minor officials being given power to issue particular binding commands'.[58] This is a more attractive position which seeks to provide positive authority for executive action in advance, whilst still acknowledging that it is not always possible to legislate for every eventuality.

Fatovic, although acknowledging Dyzenhaus, takes quite a different view. He concludes that, despite the growth of a range of statutory powers to deal with emergencies in the United States, such statutes still might not deal with the 'sudden and unexpected', which inherently defies definition but includes existential violent crises such as invasion.[59] Prerogative, to Fatovic meaning extra-legal action, remains an 'indispensable option'.[60] As to the limits of extra-legal action, he does not define a time period but, drawing on Locke, suggests that such action could continue until it is possible to convene the legislature. Even then there are risks in a legislature hastily convening and passing poorly considered legislation. Indeed, legislation may unacceptably normalise what should be extraordinary.[61] Fatovic's view may be more consistent with some of the earlier theorists but still does not satisfactorily resolve the question that the resort to extra-

---

56 Tom Campbell, 'Emergency Strategies for Prescriptive Legal Positivists: Anti-terrorist Law and Legal Theory' in Victor Ramraj (ed), *Emergencies and the Limits of Legality* (Cambridge University Press, 2008) 201, 228.
57 Ibid 212.
58 Ibid 212–3.
59 Fatovic, above n 26, 255–6.
60 Ibid.
61 Ibid 261–4.

legal powers begs: what are the limits? He seems to leave this point in the same way that many other theorists do—in the need for virtuous leaders.[62] This is a question of politics rather than law.

Dyzenhaus reviewed Fatovic's book along with two others on this question in 2011 and disagreed with him on the basis that:

> [A] liberal democratic state must adopt a liberal-legalist approach to emergencies, one which requires not only that all executive action be authorized by law, but also that all executive action is subject to the control of the rule of law.[63]

This is the position of this book as well. Consistent with this and from an Australian perspective, Lee quoted Winterton to this effect:

> Once the realm of extra-constitutional power has been entered, there is no logical limit to its ambit; only the constitution can fix the boundaries for the lawful exercise of power. Once the constitution is removed as the frame of reference for the lawful exercise of authority, the only substitute is the balance of political – and, ultimately, military – power in the nation.[64]

Winterton was concerned to ensure that arguments in favour of necessity justifying otherwise unlawful actions to prevent a breakdown in the legal system do not then become 'employed to legitimate a coup d'état'.[65] Lee places this quote in a discussion of 'striking a balance' between the need to protect society as a whole while still preserving individual liberty.[66] Arguably, this balance is much more difficult to achieve through extra-legal or extraconstitutional measures as power is no longer constrained by law.

---

62   Ibid 274–6; Ernest Abbott, 'Law, Emergencies and the Constitution: A Review of *Outside the Law: Emergency and Executive Power*' (2010) 7 *Journal of Homeland Security and Emergency Management* 1, 3.
63   David Dyzenhaus, 'Review Essay: *Emergency, Liberalism and the State: Outside the Law: Emergency and Executive Power* by Clement Fatovic' (2011) 9(1) *Perspectives on Politics* 69, 70.
64   H P Lee, '*Salus Populi Suprema Lex Esto:* Constitutional Fidelity in Troubled Times' in H P Lee and Peter Gerangelos (eds), *Constitutional Advancement in a Frozen Continent: Essays in Honour of George Winterton* (Federation Press, 2009), 54 quoting George Winterton, 'Extra-constitutional Notions in Australian Constitutional Law' (1986) 16 *Federal Law Review* 223, 239.
65   Winterton, 'Extra-constitutional Notions in Australian Constitutional Law', above n 64, 239.
66   H P Lee, '*Salus Populi Suprema Lex Esto*', above n 64, 54.

As far as the High Court of Australia is concerned, the principle of legality, discussed below, assumes that the executive can only act in accordance with the law. For this reason the resort to extraordinary executive powers needs to be part of the law, and not outside of it. An executive power with identified limits, even if they are not precise, is better than no power at all. Campbell, discussed above, makes an attractive argument for seeking to put such powers on a statutory footing before they might be required, while still acknowledging that it is not possible to provide in advance for every contingency. While wide and flexible grants of statutory power can be desirable, the purpose of this book is to explore the authority for and limits upon the ADF being able to act where the Parliament has not provided such powers. It is to explore the extent to which limits on the exercise of executive power by the ADF in circumstances of martial law, internal security, war and external security operations can arguably be found in law. The question of some extra-legal authority for the ADF to act in such situations is a different question concerned more with political and social theory, which is not the subject of this book.

Modern theorists illustrate that the debates of the 17th and 18th centuries are alive today, and are no closer to settling the limits of executive power. Even so, both early and modern theorists do much to illustrate the character of executive power in a way that points to some limits, such as necessity, the separation of powers and the need to preserve the constitutional order. It comes now to consider these limits in more detail.

III The Nature of the Executive Power of the Commonwealth

Section 61 of the *Constitution* is titled 'Executive Power' and provides:

> The executive power of the Commonwealth is vested in the Queen and is exercisable by the Governor-General as the Queen's representative, and extends to the execution and maintenance of this Constitution, and of the laws of the Commonwealth.

Section 61, itself, does not describe what the executive power of the Commonwealth is. It merely states that the executive power 'extends to the execution and maintenance' of the *Constitution* and the laws of the Commonwealth, without limiting the executive power of the Commonwealth just to these functions. It clearly connects the executive power of the Commonwealth to the Crown, by vesting it in the Queen, without necessarily stating that this power includes the powers of the Crown. Mason J found in *Barton v Commonwealth* in 1974 that the executive power of the Commonwealth does include those powers of the Crown exercisable without the authority of Parliament, known as the prerogative powers, relevant to the Commonwealth and capable of exercise in Australia.[67] The majority of the High Court in *Cadia Holdings Pty Ltd v NSW* ('*Cadia*') stated that:

> The executive power of the Commonwealth of which s 61 of the *Constitution* speaks enables the Commonwealth to undertake executive action appropriate to its position under the *Constitution* and to that end includes the prerogative powers accorded the Crown by the common law.[68]

It is important to note here the distinction between executive and prerogative power. As this chapter will elaborate below, executive power is a broader concept and may, at least arguably, derive from prerogative, statute, the existence of the Commonwealth as a polity or the capacities of the Commonwealth common to legal persons.[69]

Other provisions of the *Constitution* grant specific executive powers to the Governor-General, such as command-in-chief of the naval and military forces (s 68), or to the Governor-General in Council, such as the appointment of ministers (s 64), justices (s 72) or civil servants (s 67). By convention, the Governor-General exercises these powers on the advice of relevant ministers.[70] Whilst s 61 does not elaborate on the nature of the executive power of the Commonwealth for which it provides, it is significant because it makes executive power an explicit constitutional power rather than a power found only in common law and statute. The intention of the drafters appears to have been only to provide for who may exercise executive power, as well as to confine it

---

67 (1974) 131 CLR 477, 498. McTiernan and Menzies JJ agreed with Mason J, 491. Barwick CJ, 488, and Jacobs J, 508, appear to assume that the external affairs prerogative had passed to the Commonwealth, without referring to s 61. Prerogatives with regard to such subjects as the Church of England and Royal Swans are clearly not applicable.
68 (2010) 242 CLR 195, 226 (Gummow, Hayne, Heydon and Crennan JJ).
69 *Pape* (2009) 238 CLR 1, 83; *Williams* (2012) 248 CLR 156, 184–5.
70 *FAI Insurances v Winneke* (1982) 151 CLR 342, 400–401 (Wilson J).

to the sphere of Commonwealth responsibility within the federation,[71] rather than to address the nature of executive power itself.[72] Despite this, the explicit constitutional character of s 61 has had implications for its relationship with other structural elements of the *Constitution* such as federalism and judicial power, as well as 'nationhood power' which this chapter discusses below.

To place s 61 in the context of Australian constitutional commentary, Winterton analysed executive power in terms of breadth and depth:

> s 61 having two components which may appropriately be termed 'breadth' and 'depth'. It was argued [previously by Winterton] (following, inter alia, the views of Mason and Jacobs JJ in *AAP*) that the subjects in respect of which Commonwealth executive power can be exercised (breadth) are those on which it can legislate, including matters appropriate to a national government, which should be seen as falling within s 51(xxxix) in domestic matters and s 51(xxix) in foreign affairs. But the question then arises as to what activities the government can undertake with regard to those subjects (depth). It was argued that, apart from 'executing' the *Constitution* and laws of the Commonwealth, the government is limited to those powers falling within the Crown's prerogative powers. In other words, the government can 'maintain' the *Constitution* and laws of the Commonwealth only to the extent allowed by the Crown's prerogative powers.[73]

---

71   On this point, French CJ in *Williams* (2012) 248 CLR 156, 188–9 referred approvingly to the following passage in *AAP Case* (1975) 134 CLR 338, 378–9, where Gibbs J stated, 'According to s 61 of the Constitution, the executive power of the Commonwealth "extends to the execution and maintenance of this Constitution, and of the laws of the Commonwealth". These words limit the power of the Executive and, in my opinion, make it clear that the Executive cannot act in respect of a matter which falls entirely outside the legislative competence of the Commonwealth.' In the same paragraph French CJ also stated, 'Barwick CJ said that the Executive "may only do that which has been or could be the subject of valid legislation" [at 362] ... The content of executive power as Mason J explained it "does not reach beyond the area of responsibilities allocated to the Commonwealth by the Constitution" [at 396]'; and to similar effect 229–32 (Gummow and Bell JJ), 271–2 (Hayne J), 302–308 (Heydon J), 364, 371 (Kiefel J).
72   John Quick and Robert Garran, *Annotated Constitution of the Australian Commonwealth* (Legal Books, first published 1901, reprint 1995) 701–702.
73   George Winterton, 'The Limits and Use of Executive Power by Government' (2003) 31(3) *Federal Law Review* 421, 428, citing George Winterton, *The Parliament, the Executive and the Governor-General* (Melbourne University Press, 1983) 29–30, 40–4. On Winterton's view of the scope of Commonwealth executive power see Peter Gerangelos, 'Parliament, the Executive, the Governor-General and the Republic' in H P Lee and Peter Gerangelos, *Constitutional Advancement in a Frozen Continent: Essays in Honour of George Winterton* (Federation Press, 2009) 190–8.

Winterton's approach separates the subject matter of Commonwealth and State executive power, that is, its breadth. This is important for a government of limited powers in a federal system.[74] Breadth is distinct from the extent to which the Commonwealth can then exercise that power in respect of a particular subject, that is, its depth. This approach has merit but, as discussed below, it is not consistent with *Williams*,[75] which does not neatly discern depth from breadth. It does not support a view which would see the breadth of Commonwealth executive power as coextensive with Commonwealth legislative power. This case postdates Winterton's quote above of 2003. Another difficulty is that Winterton limits depth to prerogative power only. *Williams* also states that nationhood power is a source of executive power distinct from prerogative power. This is a point to which this chapter will return.

A The Founding Fathers and the Nature of Executive Power

It might be hoped that the Founding Fathers of the *Australian Constitution*, through their Convention Debates,[76] would shed some light on what they thought they meant by executive power and its limits. There is not much to find in the debates though. The Founding Fathers did consider executive power[77] but it was no new constitutional concept by then. There was no bloody upheaval at the time, such as the American Revolution or the Glorious Revolution, to prompt a deep questioning of the powers of the executive. While they did draw upon the example of the *Constitution of the United States*[78] in addition to the Westminster tradition with which they were already familiar, the Founding Fathers did not adopt the American separation of powers slavishly or uncritically, or arguably even

---

74 Winterton, 'The Limits and Use of Executive Power by Government', above n 73, 428.
75 *Williams* (2012) 248 CLR 156. However Gageler J refers in approving terms to this concept in *Plaintiff M68 v Minister for Immigration and Border Protection* [2016] HCA 1 ('*M68*') [130]–[131].
76 'Convention Debates' refers to the Official Record of the Proceedings and Debates of the Australasian Federation Conference, 1890, Melbourne; Official Report of the National Australasian Convention Debates, 2 March – 9 April, 1891, Sydney; Official Report of the National Australasian Convention Debates, 22 March – 5 May 1897, Adelaide; 2–24 September 1897, Sydney, scans of the published records of the debates at <www.aph.gov.au/About_Parliament/Senate/Powers_practice_n_procedures/Records_of_the_Australasian_Federal_Conventions_of_the_1890s>.
77 *Williams* (2012) 248 CLR 156, 194–206 (French CJ); French 'The Executive Power', above n 9, 9–12.
78 *Official Report of the National Australasian Convention Debates*, Sydney, 2 March – 9 April, 1891; 18 March 1891, 464–5 (Richard Baker); *Official Report of the National Australasian Convention Debates,* Adelaide, 22 March – 5 May 1897, 17 April 1897, 766 (Edmund Barton).

at all.[79] The intention and effect appears to have been to adapt the British traditions of parliamentary and responsible government to a federal system with a powerful judiciary.[80] Their main concern appears not to have been to understand the theory underlying executive power but to fit it within the new constitutional structure.

The judgments in *Williams*,[81] discussed below and which consider the Founding Fathers, bear this out. The drafting history of s 61 primarily concerns distinguishing between Commonwealth and State executive power and, to a lesser extent, between Commonwealth legislative and executive power.[82] As French CJ put it:

> There is little evidence to support the view that the delegates to the National Australasian Conventions of 1891 and 1897–1898, or even the leading lawyers at those Conventions, shared a clear common view of the working of executive power in a federation. The Constitution which they drafted incorporated aspects of the written Constitutions of the United States and Canada, and the concept of responsible government derived from the British tradition. The elements were mixed in the Constitution to meet the Founders' perception of a uniquely Australian Federation. In respect of executive power, however, that perception was not finely resolved.[83]

---

79   Fiona Wheeler, 'Original Intent and the Doctrine of the Separation of Powers in Australia' (1996) 7(2) *Public Law Review* 96, 104.
80   *Official Record of the Debates of the Australasian Federal Convention*, Melbourne, 20 January – 17 March 1898, 8 March 1898, 2033 (Sir John Downer) & 2065-7 (Edmund Barton); 10 March 1898, 2180–1 (Isaac Isaacs); *Official Record of the Debates of the Australasian Federal Convention*, Melbourne, 20 January – 17 March 1898, 2 March 1898, 1724–5 (Josiah Symon), 1731 (Frederick Holder); This is consistent with the view expressed by Gageler J in *M68* [2016] HCA 1 [115]–[119]. On responsible government, judicial oversight and the British tradition, see Evans, 'Continuity and Flexibility: Executive Power in Australia' above n 45, 89–93, 112–6, 123. On the paucity of the historical record to demonstrate a strong separation of powers intention among the Founding Fathers see Wheeler, 'Original Intent and the Doctrine of the Separation of Powers in Australia', above n 79, 99–104. On the lack of a doctrinal approach to the separation of powers among the Founding Fathers see Fiona Wheeler, 'The Separation of Judicial Power and Progressive Interpretation' in Lee and Gerangelos (eds), *Constitutional Advancement in a Frozen Continent: Essays in Honour of George Winterton*, n 73, 237, 237–8. In praising the understated yet profoundly democratic and federalist character of the *Constitution*, Craven identifies responsible government and the High Court as central to the Founding Fathers' concerns but not the separation of powers, Greg Craven, *Conversations with the Constitution: Not Just a Piece of Paper (Law at Large)* (University of New South Wales Press, 2004) 28–30.
81   (2012) 248 CLR 156; On this case generally see George Williams, Sean Brennan and Andrew Lynch, 'Supplement to Chapter 11' (2012) to Tony Blackshield and George Williams, *Australian Constitutional Law and Theory* (Federation Press, 5th ed, 2010); Leigh Sealy, '"Adrift on a Sea of Faith": Constitutional Interpretation and the School Chaplain's Case' (Paper presented at the Gilbert and Tobin Centre Constitutional Law Conference, Sydney, 15 February 2013).
82   *Williams* (2012) 248 CLR 156 194–206 (French CJ), 296–300 (Hayne J), 362–3 (Kiefel J).
83   Ibid 202–203.

Quick and Garran were participants in the creation of Australia's *Constitution* and considered the separation of powers in their *Annotated Constitution of the Australian Commonwealth*.[84] They described the 'Tripartite Separation' and primarily cite American judgments and commentaries to explain the concept, which in turn refer to Montesquieu.[85] They also discuss the concern of the drafters with making a vague separation of powers operate with the system of responsible government.[86] This suggests that the separation of powers—even if not executive power specifically—was a consideration in the development of the *Constitution*, but possibly not much of one. As Harrison Moore described, the prevailing conception was: '[E]xecutive power is so closely allied to the legislative that it may be impossible to draw any other line than that which expediency and practical good sense commend'.[87]

It appears then that the Founding Fathers' concern was that the executive was responsible to the Parliament and they did not articulate a theory as to the limits of executive power beyond that. Any particular Australian understanding of executive power in the *Constitution* must then come from post-Federation jurisprudence and scholarship.[88] It comes then to consider the cases.

B Doctrine

Two recent cases have together taken the jurisprudence on executive power further than the Founding Fathers might have envisaged. As will be discussed below, they have reasserted a more federal sense to constitutional interpretation in constraining executive power in relation to the States. These two cases have also firmly asserted parliamentary supremacy over the executive, particularly in relation to spending.

1 *Pape v Commissioner of Taxation*

Pape v Commissioner of Taxation ('*Pape*') concerned the validity of payments made to taxpayers under the *Tax Bonus Act 2009* (Cth).[89] The payments were part of a Commonwealth Government fiscal stimulus package designed to counter the effects of a global financial

---

84 Quick and Garran, above n 72.
85 Ibid 380–2.
86 Ibid.
87 Harrison Moore, *The Constitution of the Commonwealth of Australia*, above n 31, 98.
88 The value of practice in determining lawfulness is discussed further in Chapter 6.
89 (2009) 238 CLR 1, 51.

crisis. Mr Pape's unsuccessful challenge concerned whether s 61 of the *Constitution*, in combination with the incidental power under s 51(xxxix), authorised the legislation. Although a topic well removed from the use of force by the ADF, *Pape* is very important to the concept of nationhood power, discussed further below. It also has significant implications for executive power more broadly, which it is important to discuss at this point. Gummow, Crennan and Bell JJ, in finding for the Commonwealth, commenced their consideration of the executive power of the Commonwealth by considering the place of s 61 within the text and structure of the *Constitution*.[90] Their conclusions on executive power likewise emphasised interpreting s 61 in this way:

> The content of the power provided by s 61 of the *Constitution* presents a question of interpretation of the *Constitution*. That power has at least the limitations discussed in these reasons, but it is unnecessary in the present case to attempt an exhaustive description. A question presented in a particular controversy as to the existence of power provided by s 61 may be determined under Ch III of the *Constitution* with appropriately framed declaratory and other relief.[91]

Their Honours stated that the executive power of the Commonwealth could not be as extensive as the executive power of the United Kingdom because of the limits of federalism: 'There could … be no doubt that the polity which the *Constitution* established and maintains is an independent nation state with a federal system of government'.[92] The earlier thinking that the Commonwealth could spend 'for the purposes of the Commonwealth' by virtue of s 81 was mistaken as that section of the *Constitution* concerned parliamentary appropriation of funds for particular purposes, rather than a power for the executive to spend.[93] It was also not the same as the power of the Crown in the United Kingdom to spend for the 'public service'.[94] Further, '[W]hile s 51(xxxix) authorises the Parliament to legislate in aid of the executive power, that does not mean that it may do so in aid of any subject which the Executive Government regards as of national interest and concern.'[95] There had to be a more specific basis for the exercise of executive power, in this case a 'nationhood power' enabled by legislation.

---

90   Ibid 83.
91   Ibid 89.
92   Ibid 84.
93   Ibid 78.
94   Ibid 81.
95   Ibid 87–8.

In this particular case, their Honours drew upon a 'formulation of criterion to determine whether an enterprise or activity lies within the executive power of the Commonwealth'[96] as stated by Brennan J in *Davis v Commonwealth*,[97] which in turn drew from Mason J in *Victoria v Commonwealth and Hayden* ('*AAP Case*').[98] This formulation saw executive power, in this case, as related to 'activities peculiarly adapted to the government of the country and which cannot otherwise be carried on for the public benefit'.[99] This judgment did not seek 'to determine the outer limits of executive power'[100] but made clear that it involved the limits of federalism, as well as being subject to the parliamentary appropriation process and the supervision of courts established under Chapter III of the *Constitution*.

French CJ differed with Gummow, Crennan and Bell JJ on the character of s 81 of the *Constitution* concerning the Commonwealth's power of appropriation.[101] However, on the nature of executive power, his Honour stated:

> Section 61 is an important element of a written constitution for the government of an independent nation. While history and the common law inform its content, it is not a locked display cabinet in a constitutional museum. *It has to be capable of serving the proper purposes of a national government.* On the other hand, the exigencies of 'national government' cannot be invoked to set aside the distribution of powers between Commonwealth and States and between the branches of government for which this *Constitution* provides, nor to abrogate constitutional prohibitions [emphasis added].[102]

---

96 Ibid 87.
97 (1988) 166 CLR 79, 111.
98 (1975) 134 CLR 338, 397.
99 *Pape* (2009) 238 CLR 1, 92.
100 Ibid 87.
101 *Pape* (2009) 238 CLR 1. In brief terms, French CJ saw the text of s 81 as 'words of constraint', 45, as '"[t]he purposes of the Commonwealth" are the purposes otherwise authorised by the *Constitution* or by statutes made under the *Constitution*', 56. Whereas Gummow, Crennan and Bell JJ stated that 'There is no support … for the construction … treating the phrase in s 81 "for the purposes of the Commonwealth" as containing words of limitation of legislative power' as they relate only to appropriation, not a legislative power to spend, 75. Hayne and Kiefel JJ said that 'asking whether a particular appropriation can be described as being for a purpose of the Commonwealth will seldom if ever yield an answer determinative of constitutional litigation in this Court' as the issue would 'turn upon the ambit of power … said to be engaged', 112. Heydon J's position was similar to that of French CJ in that he saw s 81 as limited by s 83 as the 'words "by law", limits the power of appropriation to what can be done by the enactment of a valid law', 214. The majority position therefore would not see any real limitations on the function of appropriation, seeing the case more as a question of a limitation on the power to spend, as discussed further below.
102 *Pape* (2009) 238 CLR 1, 60.

This description is broadly consistent with that of Gummow, Crennan and Bell JJ in that 'proper purposes of a national government' appears to be quite similar to 'activities peculiarly adapted to the government of the country and which cannot otherwise be carried on for the public benefit'.[103] French CJ's description is not put as an essential criterion for limiting executive power but his subsequent limitations of the federal structure, the separation of powers and constitutional prohibitions have a similar effect.

Hayne and Kiefel JJ did not seek to describe or limit executive power as their Honours found the impugned Act, as read down, to be a law with respect to taxation.[104] They did not therefore draw firm conclusions on the limits of executive power other than to state that the 'executive power to spend is not unlimited'[105] and, as will be discussed in more detail below, to criticise the concept of nationhood power. Heydon J, in dissent, also criticised nationhood power as will be discussed below.

The reasoning in *Pape* on limits to the power of the executive to spend together with concerns for the limitations of federalism and the separation of powers laid the foundations for the later judgments in *Williams*.

2 Williams v Commonwealth

The 2012 case of *Williams*[106] is the High Court's more recent consideration of the extent of Commonwealth executive power. The matter was a challenge by a parent to the funding of the chaplain at his children's school by the Commonwealth.[107] It is difficult to conceive of a matter more removed from the use of force by the ADF absent statutory authority. In this case though, not one of the judgments accepted the plaintiff's apparent primary concern for the separation of church and state under s 116 of the *Constitution*. Instead, the case turned essentially on whether the Commonwealth could fund the chaplaincy program by authority of executive power alone and with no more statutory authority than generally worded Appropriation Acts. The majority found against the

---

103 Ibid 92.
104 Ibid 133.
105 Ibid 121.
106 (2012) 248 CLR 156.
107 See the procedural history and factual background as set out in the judgment of French CJ in *Williams* (2012) 248 CLR 156, 180–4.

Commonwealth on this point and the plaintiff was therefore successful. Even though this case concerned a power to spend money, its reasoning applies to executive power more generally.[108]

Key questions most relevant to this book were whether s 61 extends to permit the Commonwealth executive, first, to do anything which any ordinary citizen could do and, second, to do anything which the Commonwealth legislature *could* have authorised the executive to do by an Act of Parliament but even *without* an actual authorising Act. None of the judgments accepted that the Commonwealth could do anything any natural person could do,[109] (although some of the judgments, as discussed below, indicated that it could exercise the powers it has in common with legal persons in matters related to the exercise of its other properly construed executive powers). As Saunders put it:

> In any event, the court denied that conclusions about the scope of Commonwealth power could satisfactorily be derived by analogy from the capacities of legal persons, given the public character of Commonwealth funds, its accountability obligations and the coercive mechanisms at its disposal.[110]

---

108 Ibid 178, 184–5 (French CJ).
109 Ibid 193 (French CJ), 238–9 (Gummow and Bell JJ), 253–4 (Hayne J) 320–1 (Heydon J, insofar as the 'breadth' of Commonwealth power was a limitation, although this involved a question of 'depth' which was not adequately considered), 352 (Crennan J), 373–4 (Kiefel J). Interestingly, Zines foreshadowed this position in 'The Inherent Executive Power of the Commonwealth', above n 7, 283–6, although this case does not refer to this article. French CJ does refer to Zines's *The High Court and the Constitution* (Federation Press, 5th ed, 2008) 349–50 on a broadly similar point relating to the limits to the Commonwealth's power to contract at 213, as does Heydon J in relation to whether the executive power of the Commonwealth extends as far as its legislative power, 308, referring to Zines 346–7, and 310, in Zines (2008) 347 (as well as earlier editions of Zines's book). Heydon J also refers to Zines's 'Commentary' to H V Evatt, *The Royal Prerogative* (Law Book Co, first presented as a doctoral thesis 1924, with commentary by Leslie Zines, 1987), C12, to support the same point, 310–11.
110 Cheryl Saunders, 'The Scope of Executive Power' (Speech delivered at Senate Occasional Lecture, Parliament House, 28 September 2012, Papers on Parliament No 59) <http://www.aph.gov.au/About_Parliament/Senate/Research_and_Education/pops/~/link.aspx?_id=C8C131542382464EB28135A33F9EA201&_z=z>; Shipra Chordia, Andrew Lynch and George Williams share a similar view in '*Williams v Commonwealth* – Commonwealth Executive Power and Australian Federalism' (2013) 37(1) *Melbourne University Law Review* 189, 226–7.

As to Commonwealth executive power extending to doing anything which the Commonwealth legislature could have authorised it to do, the plurality essentially found that it did not.[111] French CJ decided this on the basis that the authorities, particularly in the *AAP Case*,[112] did not go that far,[113] but also because it offended principles concerning the Parliament's control over spending by the executive, an aspect of the central constitutional consideration of responsible government.[114] Consistent with this, Gummow and Bell JJ stated that 'such a proposition would undermine the basal assumption of legislative predominance inherited from the United Kingdom'.[115] Crennan J stated:

> If the fact that the Parliament *could* pass valid Commonwealth legislation were sufficient authorisation for any expenditure by the Commonwealth Executive … the Commonwealth's capacities to contract and to spend would operate, in practice, indistinguishably from the Commonwealth Executive's exercise of a prerogative power. Such a view … disregards the constitutional relationship between the Executive and Parliament affecting spending.[116]

Hayne J decided this point on a different basis. His Honour could not find a hypothetical law which would have supported the school chaplaincy scheme.[117] He saw it as desirable that 'programs of the kind in issue in this case' have a legislative basis but did not wish to conclude that the executive could never spend money without legislative authority.[118] Kiefel J also declined to decide on whether an unexercised legislative power was sufficient because the Commonwealth's legislative power would not have

---

111 See discussion in Geoffrey Lindell, '*Williams v Commonwealth* – The shrinking scope of the Executive Power of the Commonwealth and the increased role of the Australian Parliament in authorising its exercise' (Parliamentary Briefing Paper No 1, Commonwealth Parliament, 6 December 2012) 21; Gabrielle Appleby and Stephen McDonald, 'Looking at the Executive Power Through the High Court's New Spectacles' (2013) 35(2) *Sydney Law Review* 253, 281. In an article which French CJ cites with apparent approval, but not on this point, at 180 of *Williams v Commonwealth*, Saunders appears to have foreshadowed that Commonwealth spending under authority of s 61 alone was 'a generous construction' and 'would have implications not only for the federal character of the Australian system of government, but also for the traditional mechanism for the accountability of government that regulatory legislation represents' in Cheryl Saunders, 'Intergovernmental Agreements and the Executive Power' (2005) 16(4) *Public Law Review* 294, 295.
112 (1975) 134 CLR 338.
113 *Williams* (2012) 248 CLR 156, 187–9.
114 Ibid 205–206.
115 Ibid 232–3.
116 Ibid 358.
117 Ibid 274–81.
118 Ibid 281.

extended to funding the chaplaincy scheme in this case and therefore the Commonwealth's executive power did not extend to funding the chaplaincy scheme.[119]

A majority in *Williams* confirmed that, since *Pape*, the power for the executive to spend is limited and is not to be derived from ss 81 and 83 of the *Constitution*.[120] As put by Gummow and Bell JJ, '[T]he following passage in the reasons of French CJ, Gummow and Crennan JJ in *ICM Agriculture Pty Ltd v The Commonwealth*[121] should be noted. With reference to *Pape*, their Honours said':

> [I]t is now settled that the provisions … in s 81 of the *Constitution* for establishment of the Consolidated Revenue Fund and in s 83 for Parliamentary appropriation, do not confer a substantive spending power and that the power to expend appropriated moneys must be found elsewhere in the *Constitution* or the laws of the Commonwealth.[122]

This reflects a clear concern to ensure that the executive remains subordinate to the Parliament, which is a fundamental principle underlying the relationship between executive and statutory power. Unlike the House of Lords in the United Kingdom, the Senate is able to reject appropriation or tax bills originating from the lower house[123] and therefore deny the government a supply of funds on a particular matter or even generally.[124] This is potentially an important check on the executive government, which may not command a majority in the Senate, and a reason to ensure that spending by the executive government remains under the scrutiny of Parliament. Spending based upon exercising the powers of a natural person or unexercised legislative powers is not consistent with parliamentary scrutiny. By extension, executive power cannot simply derive from these sources (although the extent of the Commonwealth's power held in common with legal persons, such as to contract, is not clear).[125] On this view, the executive must be accountable to Parliament even if for no reason other than to secure funding. It is consistent with Blackstone's view that making the Crown's advisers answerable to Parliament is a check

---

119 Ibid 365–6.
120 Ibid 248, 179 (French CJ), 252 (Hayne J), 341 (Heydon J), 356–7 (Crennan J), 362 (Kiefel J).
121 (2009) 240 CLR 140, 169.
122 *Williams* (2012) 248 CLR 156, 224.
123 *Constitution* ss 53, 57.
124 *Williams* (2012) 248 CLR 156, 184, 205–206 (French CJ), 235 (Gummow and Bell JJ), 260 (Hayne J), Appleby and Macdonald, above n 111, 264–5, do not see this as necessitating a conclusion that executive power to spend must normally find authority in legislation.
125 As noted by Appleby and Macdonald, above n 111, 258, 275.

on the potential of the Crown to abuse its power.¹²⁶ To limit the potential for abuse of executive power then, this book will argue that where the ADF could rely upon either statutory or nonstatutory executive power to do the same thing, it should prefer the statutory power unless necessity clearly dictates otherwise.

Only Heydon J dissented, on the point that the executive power of the Commonwealth under s 61 does extend to doing anything which the Commonwealth legislature could authorise it to do (which he described as the 'Common Assumption').¹²⁷ Echoing Winterton, his Honour said that this was a question of breadth and expressed concern that the Court had not heard full argument on the question of depth, which might include power to contract using properly appropriated funds.¹²⁸ He stated, 'The lack of full argument about the "depth" element in this case is a further illustration of how the circumstances of this case do not make it one in which it is appropriate to narrow the executive power of the Commonwealth.'¹²⁹

For this reason it is difficult to assess the wider implications of Heydon J's broader view of executive power. For the purposes of this book, concerned as it is with more violent and extreme exercises of executive power than government contracting and spending, the view of the majority is preferable for its more constrained view of executive power, particularly in its 'assumption of legislative predominance'.¹³⁰

As much as the case turned upon the executive power to spend, its reasoning is applicable to executive power more broadly because some of the judgments directly considered the sources of executive power more broadly. Also, if a matter is something upon which the executive cannot spend, a relatively benign power, then it would seem less likely that it is a matter upon which the ADF could use coercive powers. As Gageler J put it in *M68*, 'There is, of course, a difference between spending and doing: "The power to make a present to a man is not the power to give him orders"'.¹³¹

---

126 *Blackstone's Commentaries*, above n 24, 252.
127 *Williams* (2012) 248 CLR 156, 295 (Heydon J).
128 Ibid 320–1.
129 Ibid 321.
130 Ibid 232–3 (Gummow and Bell JJ).
131 [2016] HCA 1, [144] quoting Commonwealth, *Royal Commission on the Constitution of the Commonwealth, Report of Proceedings and Minutes of Evidence* (Canberra), 22 September 1927, 72 [396] (Sir Robert Garran).

1. WHAT IS EXECUTIVE POWER?

Although none of the judgments went so far as to state what the actual limits of executive power might be, some of the judgments did make clear what the sources of executive power were and, in so doing, where its limits might be found.

French CJ said:

> Nevertheless, it can be said that the executive power referred to in s 61 extends to:
>
> - powers necessary or incidental to the execution and maintenance of a law of the Commonwealth;
> - powers conferred by statute;
> - powers defined by reference to such of the prerogatives of the Crown as are properly attributable to the Commonwealth;
> - powers defined by the capacities of the Commonwealth common to legal persons [referred to in this book as the 'common capacities'];
> - inherent authority derived from the character and status of the Commonwealth as the national government.[132]

French CJ's judgment suggests that an analysis of any exercise of power under s 61 must find a basis in the list of sources above. It is not enough to find an unexercised legislative power of the Commonwealth.[133] It is particularly important to note the 'powers defined by reference to such of the prerogatives of the Crown as are properly attributable to the Commonwealth',[134] as such power is central to this book.

Crennan J stated that 'despite the establishment of some limits, s 61 is not amenable to exhaustive definition in any single case.'[135] Her Honour also identified sources of executive power as including statute, prerogative power such as 'the power to enter a treaty or wage war' and:

> Powers which derive from the capacities of the Commonwealth as a juristic person, such as the capacities to enter a contract and to spend money when exercised in the ordinary course of administering a recognised part of the Commonwealth government.[136]

---

132 Ibid 184–5 (French CJ).
133 Ibid.
134 Ibid.
135 Ibid 342.
136 Ibid.

Consistent with this, her Honour later stated that moneys appropriated under s 81 of the *Constitution* must be for some governmental purpose, as distinct from contracts entered into by private parties.[137] Her Honour also added, citing Mason J in the *AAP Case*, '[T]hat s 61 is the source of the Commonwealth Executive's capacity to "to engage in enterprises and activities peculiarly adapted to the government of a nation ... which cannot otherwise be carried on for the benefit of the nation"'.[138] This reference is to nationhood power, which is further discussed below.

Kiefel J made clear that executive power extended to 'its prerogative powers, to subject matters of express grants of legislative power in ss 51, 52 and 122 and to matters which are peculiarly adapted to the government of a nation'.[139] Her Honour also stated, consistent with the principle of legality cases discussed below, that:

> The question is not one of the Executive's juristic capacity to contract, but its power to act. Actions of the Executive must necessarily fall within the confines of some power derived from the *Constitution* ... An activity not authorised by the *Constitution* could not fall within the power of the Executive.[140]

Notably, Kiefel J identified virtually the same sources of executive power as those stated by Crennan J but without explicitly identifying 'common capacities' such as the power to contract. Kiefel J's statement that 'the question is not one of the Executive's juristic capacity to contract, but its power to act' would suggest that such powers are not separate but follow implicitly from the sources of executive power which her Honour explicitly identifies. The only powers which French CJ identifies separately but which Crennan J and Kiefel J do not are 'powers necessary or incidental to the execution and maintenance of a law of the Commonwealth', which relates directly to the wording of s 61. Arguably such powers are also implicit in those other powers explicitly identified in all three of their judgments.

In *Williams*, Gummow and Bell JJ did not really add to their consideration in *Pape* of the limits on or sources of executive power other than to reject an argument for 'the assimilation of the executive branch to a natural

---

137 Ibid 352.
138 Ibid 342.
139 Ibid 373.
140 Ibid 373–4.

person and other entities with legal personality'.[141] Hayne J usefully cited with approval the judgment of Gummow, Crennan and Bell JJ in *Pape*, discussed above, as to when an activity lies within the executive power of the Commonwealth.[142] His judgment was primarily concerned with 'the cardinal principle of parliamentary control', as expressed in his joint judgment with Kiefel J in *Pape*, over raising and expenditure of revenue established through Chapters I and IV of the *Constitution*.[143] His Honour looked particularly to the point arising from *Pape* that 'federal considerations limit the scope of executive power',[144] as well as rejecting the notion of the Commonwealth having the same powers as a natural person.[145] Hayne J did however mention that officials might exercise their own powers as a natural person in the course of their duty.[146] This is a point to which Chapter 4 will return.

As to the *Williams* case as a whole, when considered with *Pape*, the effect is to make s 61 the starting point for any consideration of executive power, as part of a distinctly Australian constitutional structure which restrains executive power through federalism and judicial supervision of the written text. As Hayne J put it:

> Significantly for the present case, all members of the Court in *Pape* held that considerations of text and structure, akin to those alluded to or elucidated in earlier decisions, limit the executive power of the Commonwealth, at least in so far as it enables the Commonwealth to spend public moneys.[147]

This structure also includes the supremacy of a Parliament with a Senate which, although relatively weak in respect of appropriations, is powerful in respect of general legislation and in which the government may not command a majority.[148] English authorities and legal history are important to understanding executive power but within a context in which the Commonwealth has more limited powers than the Crown in England.

---

141 *Williams* (2012) 248 CLR 156, 237–8.
142 Ibid 272, although he did not support the reliance upon nationhood power in that case, *Pape* (2009) 238 CLR 1, 121.
143 Ibid 259, citing *Pape* (2009) 238 CLR 1, 105.
144 Ibid 252.
145 Ibid 257–8.
146 Ibid.
147 Ibid 251. Appleby and Macdonald, above n 111, 273, put it that in Australia now responsible government 'means responsibility both nationally *and federally* [emphasis in original]'.
148 As discussed with respect to *Williams* (2012) 248 CLR 156, 179 (French CJ), 224, 252 (Hayne J), 341 (Heydon J), 356–7 (Crennan J), 362 (Kiefel J), 365–6; *ICM Agriculture Pty Ltd v Commonwealth* (2009) 240 CLR 140, 169; *Constitution* ss 53, 57.

(a) Post Williams Cases and Executive Power

(i) Williams v Commonwealth [No 2]

In 2014, *Williams v Commonwealth [No 2]* continued the litigation but primarily concerned the legislative power of the Commonwealth to support the school chaplaincy scheme. The majority of French CJ, Hayne J, Kiefel J, Bell J and Keane J, in finding against the Commonwealth, essentially affirmed the majority views on executive power stated in the first *Williams* case:

> This assumption, which underpinned the arguments advanced by the Commonwealth parties about executive power, denies the 'basal consideration'[149] that the *Constitution* effects a distribution of powers and functions between the Commonwealth and the States. The polity which, as the Commonwealth parties rightly submitted, must 'possess all the powers that it needs in order to function as a polity'[150] is the central polity of a federation in which independent governments exist in the one area and exercise powers in different fields of action carefully defined by law. It is not a polity organised and operating under a unitary system or under a flexible constitution where the Parliament is supreme. The assumption underpinning the Commonwealth parties' submissions about executive power is not right and should be rejected.[151]

As Chordia, Lynch and Williams suggested, '[I]t may simply have been an opportunity for the Court to reiterate the authority of *Williams [No 1]* … with the weight of a joint opinion'.[152]

(ii) CPCF v Minister for Immigration and Border Protection

In 2015, *CPCF v Minister for Immigration and Border Protection* ('*CPCF*')[153] turned on statutory powers under the *Maritime Powers Act 2013* (Cth) but also provided some valuable obiter dicta on executive power. As French CJ put it, the central question in the case was whether maritime powers under the Act, or nonstatutory executive power, authorised the detention and taking of the plaintiff from Australia's contiguous zone to India.[154]

---

149 *Attorney-General (Vic) ex rel Dale v Commonwealth* ('*Pharmaceutical Benefits Case*') (1945) 71 CLR 237, 271–2 (Dixon J).
150 *R v Kirby; Ex parte Boilermakers' Society of Australia* (1956) 94 CLR 254, 267-268.
151 (2014) 252 CLR 416, 465–9.
152 Shipra Chordia, Andrew Lynch and George Williams, 'Case Note: *Williams v Commonwealth [No 2]:* Commonwealth Executive Power and Spending after *Williams [No 2]*' (2015) 39(1) *Melbourne University Law Review* 306, 314.
153 [2015] HCA 1.
154 Ibid [4].

The plaintiff was a Tamil asylum seeker originally from Sri Lanka who had attempted to enter Australia by sea, having commenced the voyage in India.[155]

In separate judgments, French CJ, Crennan J, Kiefel J, Gageler J and Keane J found that the Act authorised the detention and taking of the plaintiff. It was not necessary therefore to decide the question of whether executive power would also have authorised this action. Such comments on executive power as there were in these judgments were therefore obiter dicta but nonetheless significant. Notably, French CJ did not take the opportunity to address the issue of an executive power to expel aliens and its relationship with equivalent statutory power which,[156] as discussed later in this chapter, had been a matter of controversy since he first did so in the Federal Court in *Ruddock v Vadarlis* (the '*Tampa Case*')[157] in 2001. Kiefel J effectively approved the reasoning of Black CJ in dissent in that case and rejected the existence of an executive power to expel aliens.[158] Ironically, Keane J took the position that French CJ had taken in the *Tampa Case*,[159] even though French CJ did not in this case.[160] Crennan J did not address executive power at all[161] and Gageler J agreed with French CJ on the question of executive power.[162] These judgments did not disturb the position on executive power generally taken in *Williams*, although they did address issues of the relationship between prerogative power and statute, prerogative power as an aspect of executive power and an executive power to expel aliens, which arise later in this chapter.

Hayne and Bell JJ in dissent found that neither the Act nor any executive power authorised the action. They provided a strong statement of the need for any exercise of executive power to have a clear source of authority, which is consistent with *Williams* as well as the cases discussed below on the principle of legality:

> To adopt and adapt what was said in *Chu Kheng Lim*, why should an Australian court hold that an officer of the Commonwealth Executive who purports to authorise or enforce the detention in custody of an alien

---
155 Ibid [1]–[4].
156 Ibid [40]–[42].
157 (2001) 110 FCR 491.
158 *CPCF* [2015] HCA 1 [266]–[268], [283]–[286].
159 (2001) 110 FCR 491.
160 *CPCF* [2015] HCA 1 [482]–[483], [489].
161 Ibid [228].
162 Ibid [393].

without judicial mandate can do so outside the territorial boundaries of Australia without any statutory authority? Reference to the so-called non-statutory executive power of the Commonwealth provides no answer to that question. Reference to the royal prerogative provides[163] no answer. Reference to 'the defence and protection of the nation' is irrelevant, especially if it is intended to evoke echoes of the power to declare war and engage in war-like operations. Reference to an implied executive 'nationhood power' to respond to national emergencies[164] is likewise irrelevant. Powers of those kinds are not engaged in this case. To hold that the Executive can act outside Australia's borders in a way that it cannot lawfully act within Australia would stand legal principle on its head.

This statement has significance for the discussion in Chapter 6 of the exercise of coercive powers by the ADF outside Australia in external security operations, which is also the case for the next High Court consideration of executive power.

(iii) *Plaintiff M68/2015 v Minister for Immigration and Border Protection*

In 2016, *M68* also concerned the exercise of coercive powers by the Commonwealth outside Australia.[165] Again, the case turned on the exercise of statutory powers but provided useful obiter dicta on executive power which essentially affirmed the approach taken in *Williams*. The plaintiff in this case was a Bangladeshi national who sought to enter Australia by sea and became a detainee in the Australian-funded immigration detention centre in Nauru under the *Migration Act 1958* (Cth).[166] Commonwealth officials brought her to Australia to undergo medical treatment.[167] The plaintiff sought an injunction and a writ of prohibition to restrain the Commonwealth and relevant officials from returning her to the immigration detention centre in Nauru, as well as orders prohibiting payments by the Commonwealth to a contractor providing services to run the detention centre.[168]

French CJ, Kiefel and Nettle JJ decided that Nauru, and not the Commonwealth, detained the plaintiff and that statutory power authorised the Commonwealth's participation in that detention.[169]

---

163 Citing *Entick v Carrington* (1765) 19 St Tr 1030, (1765) 2 Wils KB 275, 291 [95 ER 807, 817].
164 *Pape* (2009) 238 CLR 1.
165 [2016] HCA 1 [129].
166 Ibid [1].
167 Ibid [14].
168 Ibid [16].
169 Ibid [54].

Their Honours therefore did not see it as necessary to decide whether Commonwealth executive power authorised the detention.[170] Bell J agreed with the answers to the questions of law provided by French CJ, Kiefel J and Nettle J and did not directly address executive power at all.[171] Keane J separately found that the Commonwealth did not detain the plaintiff, statutory power authorised such action as the Commonwealth took to procure the detention and it was not therefore necessary to consider executive power.[172] The judgments of French CJ, Kiefel and Nettle JJ, and also Keane J however stated that the Commonwealth could enter into the memorandum of understanding with Nauru which procured the detention on the basis of 'non-statutory executive power' (rather than prerogative power) to enter into external relations derived from s 61 of the *Constitution*.[173] This point will become significant in Chapter 6 in respect to the exercise of coercive powers by the ADF outside Australia.

Gageler J and Gordon J, however, did squarely address the question of whether executive power could authorise the detention of the plaintiff and made clear that it did not. Gageler J provided a lengthy consideration of executive power, its Australian constitutional history and its limitations. His Honour emphasised a view, consistent with *Williams*, of Commonwealth power under the *Constitution* restrained by considerations of federalism:

> The purpose of s 75(v), as Dixon J put it, was 'to make it constitutionally certain that there would be a jurisdiction capable of restraining officers of the Commonwealth from exceeding Federal power'.[174] … The purpose was to supplement s 75(iii) so as to ensure that any officer of the Commonwealth acted, and acted only, within the scope of the authority conferred on that officer by the Constitution or by legislation.[175]

Notably, Gageler J saw that Australia entering into a memorandum of understanding with Nauru was an exercise 'of its non-statutory <u>prerogative</u> capacity to conduct relations with other countries [emphasis added]', rather than simply as an exercise of nonstatutory power under s 61.[176] He made a clear distinction in nonstatutory executive power between prerogative executive power, being uniquely governmental power 'which

---

170 Ibid [24]–[28], [41].
171 Ibid [102]–[103].
172 Ibid [239]–[242], [265]
173 Ibid [54], [201].
174 *Bank of New South Wales v The Commonwealth* (1948) 76 CLR 1, 363.
175 *M68* [2016] HCA 1 [126], [145].
176 Ibid [178].

is capable of interfering with legal rights of others', and nonprerogative executive capacities, which are nothing more than the utilisation of a bare capacity or permission, which are subject to 'the same substantive law as would be applicable in respect of the act had it been done by any other actor'.[177] This point will be significant in respect of ADF internal security operations as discussed in Chapter 4. Gageler J also saw that there was no prerogative to detain, as there might be in respect of an enemy alien in war or in preventing an alien from entering Australia, which would have authorised the detention of the plaintiff in Nauru.[178] This point will become significant in Chapter 6 in respect of security detention by the ADF in external security operations which are not war.

Gordon J only briefly addressed executive power and, consistently with *Williams*, found that there was no authority to detain the plaintiff under executive power:[179]

> The executive power of the Commonwealth does not itself provide legal authority for an officer of the Commonwealth to detain a person and commit a trespass.[180] Absent statutory authority, the Executive does not have power to detain.[181]

This simpler position would create difficulties in respect of taking prisoners of war, as Chapter 5 will consider, or security detainees, as Chapter 6 will consider.

The significance of *CPCF*[182] in terms of broader doctrine on the executive power of the Commonwealth is essentially to affirm the position in *Williams*. It raises more specific questions in respect of the exercise of the foreign affairs prerogative and the conduct of coercive external security operations by the ADF which Chapter 6 will address.

---

177 Ibid [134]–[135].
178 Ibid [164].
179 Ibid [372].
180 Citing cf *CPCF* (2015) 89 ALJR 207 239–40 [147]–[150], 255–8 [258]–[276]; 316 ALR 1 39–40, 60–4.
181 Citing *Chu Kheng Lim v Minister for Immigration, Local Government and Ethnic Affairs* (1992) 176 CLR 1, 19, 63; *CPCF* (2015) 89 ALJR 207, 239–40 [147]–[150], 255–8 [258]–[276]; 316 ALR 1 39–40, 60–4.
182 [2015] HCA 1.

(b) Conclusions on Williams and Subsequent Cases

Williams and the subsequent cases together indicate that the sources of executive power include statutory power, prerogative power and nationhood power. Powers common to the capacities of legal persons are arguably implicit in the first listed powers. It is from these sources that some limits might be derived, because, consistent with the principle of legality discussed below, for a federal government of limited powers it is necessary to find a source of authority for the exercise of a Commonwealth executive power. It is not enough to argue that the Commonwealth executive has the powers of a natural person or can rely upon an unexercised equivalent legislative power. The principle of parliamentary supremacy over the executive will also be significant in arguing when it is, or is not, appropriate for the executive to act without the authority of an Act of Parliament. This leads to a consideration of the principle of legality.

3 Principle of Legality

The question of the scope of executive power immediately confronts the principle of legality. This presents a profound challenge in any analysis of executive power. The principle that any exercise of governmental power must have an authority in law does not sit easily with a source of authority that is so imprecise and difficult to determine. That the principle of legality derives from cases on excesses of executive power only serves to emphasise the point. In referring to *A v Hayden*[183] and *Entick v Carrington*,[184] which subsequent paragraphs address, Zines stated that 'the courts have leaned against finding a prerogative power to interfere with the life, liberty or property of subjects. Coercion by the executive must be justified by law'.[185] He goes on to state that there is an exception 'to the principle that prerogatives are non-coercive' in respect of war and other

---

183 (1984) 156 CLR 532.
184 (1765) 19 St Tr 1030.
185 Zines, 'The Inherent Executive Power of the Commonwealth', above n 7, 286. There is a debate over the principle of legality in respect of statutory interpretation and parliamentary intention to abrogate fundamental common-law rights and liberties. See, eg, J J Spigelman, 'The Principle of Legality and the Clear Statement Principle' (2005) 79 *Australian Law Journal* 769; Dan Meagher, 'The Common Law Principle of Legality in the Age of Rights' (2011) 35 *Melbourne University Law Review* 449; Stephen Gageler, 'Common Law Statutes and Judicial Legislation: Statutory Interpretation as a Common Law Process' (2012) 37(2) *Monash University Law Review* 1, 13; Brendan Lim, 'The Normativity of the Principle of Legality' (2013) 37(2) *Melbourne University Law Review* 372. This is close to the concerns of this book but distinct from it because this book is concerned with discerning the authority of the executive to act, including statutory interpretation as discussed in Chapter 5, rather than the rights and liberties of citizens, as such, in relation to legislation.

emergencies.[186] This book argues that the prerogatives with respect to war, martial law, internal security and external operations can be coercive but are nonetheless subject to the principle of legality. Also, it is only such prerogatives which can justify action based upon necessity in extreme circumstances.

At this stage it is important to note that this book will refer more often to the principle of legality rather than the more general concept of the rule of law. Whilst not rejecting the rule of law as a constitutional value by any means, the inherent difficulty in defining it and its aspirational quality make it preferable to refer to the principle of legality. The rule of law suggests an absence of arbitrariness, despotism and political violence, or even violence in society generally, as well as government limited by law, which might also be described as constitutionalism.[187] These are worthy aims to aspire to but not necessarily easy points upon which to assess the lawful limits upon the use of force by the ADF in war or other extreme situations. This book, therefore, will usually refer to the loss or potential loss of the rule of law as a justification for the ADF to act rather than the rule of law being a limit upon its action. It will consider examples of the collapse of civilian government in places like Somalia in 1993, East Timor in 1999, Fiji in 2000 or Darwin in 1942. The rule of law, therefore, is more easily invoked in its absence than its presence. The more specific nature of the principle of legality on the other hand, with more precise authority with which to give it content, makes it a better yardstick by which to measure the limits to ADF action under executive power.[188]

As to the principle of legality itself, *Entick v Carrington*[189] is the case traditionally cited, from Dicey[190] to today,[191] to support the idea that official action must have legal justification. With respect to the execution of a warrant which the court found to be issued unlawfully, Lord Camden

---

186 Zines, 'The Inherent Executive Power of the Commonwealth', above n 7, 287.
187 In supporting the rule of law, Evans discusses the debate over the definitional difficulties, aspirational qualities and value of the concept in Simon Evans, 'The Rule of Law, Constitutionalism and the MV Tampa' (2002) 13(2) *Public Law Review (The Tampa Issue)* 94, 94–6.
188 This position reflects Loughlin's criticisms of the rule of law as a concept, but without accepting his conclusions because of the value of the rule of law as an aspiration, in Martin Loughlin, *Foundations of Public Law* (Oxford University Press, 2010) 312–13.
189 (1765) 19 St Tr 1030.
190 Dicey, above n 19, 193.
191 *CPCF* HCA [2015] 1, [150] (Hayne and Bell JJ); David Clark, *Principles of Australian Public Law* (Lexis Nexis Butterworths, 2nd ed, 2007), 73.

1. WHAT IS EXECUTIVE POWER?

CJ said 'one should naturally expect that the law to warrant it should be clear in proportion as the power is exorbitant. If it is law, it will be found in our books. If it is not to be found there, it is not law'.[192]

A key case for this book in respect of the principle of legality and the war prerogative, discussed in Chapter 5, is the 1940 High Court case of *Shaw Savill & Albion Co Ltd*.[193] The facts of the case were that the British flagged merchant vessel MV *Coptic* was sailing from Brisbane to Sydney on a route determined by naval instructions and without lights, also as required by naval instructions. HMAS *Adelaide* was sailing at high speed on a reciprocal course and was without lights as well. The two ships collided, causing considerable damage.[194] The owners of the *Coptic* sued the Commonwealth in negligence for the damage. The Commonwealth pleaded as part of its defence that the matter was not justiciable as the incident occurred in the course of operations against the enemy.[195]

Both Starke J and Dixon J went to some lengths to outline an immunity for the Commonwealth from tortious liability for actions during combat operations, more easily described as a 'combat immunity doctrine'. Starke J referred to the case of *Marais*,[196] and some of the Irish cases[197] discussed in Chapter 3 on martial law, and made clear that matters of war are nonjusticiable, *durante bello*.[198] His Honour also pointedly referred to *Entick v Carrington* and strongly affirmed the principle that, outside of combat with the enemy, the armed forces are as much subject to the law as anyone else:

---

192 *Entick v Carrington* (1765) 19 St Tr 1030, 1066.
193 (1940) 66 CLR 344. Surprisingly, an extensive search revealed very little in the way of Australian journal articles relevant to this book on this case, which perhaps reflects that the principle of legality in relation to the ADF and the combat immunity doctrine has received little attention in Australia. Beasley discusses it in the context of the Commando Court Martial (Transcript of Proceedings, *Sergeant J and Lance-Corporal D*, Australian Defence Force General Court Martial Pre-trial Directions Hearing, Brigadier Westwood, Chief Judge Advocate, 20 May 2011) but that is all. He agreed with both the combat immunity doctrine and its application in the Command Court Martial. Richard Beasley, 'Duty of Care on the Battlefield', *Bar News* (Summer 2011–2012) 53, 56–8. A recent British report considers the application of combat immunity doctrine in the United Kingdom Supreme Court case of *Smith v Ministry of Defence* [2013] UKSC 41 ('*Smith*'). It argues that this case unacceptably narrows the doctrine because it will make military 'leaders focus on the duty of care rather than adaptability and mission success'. See Thomas Tugenhadt and Laura Croft, *The Fog of Law: An Introduction to the Legal Erosion of British Fighting Power* (Policy Exchange, 2013) 31–2. This is discussed further in Chapters 5 and 6.
194 *Shaw Savill & Albion Co Ltd* (1940) 66 CLR 344, 357–8.
195 Ibid 366.
196 [1902] AC 109.
197 *Shaw Savill & Albion Co Ltd* (1940) 66 CLR 344, 356.
198 Ibid 356–7.

> If it be established that the matters complained of were done or omitted in the conduct of war in the sense indicated, the courts cannot and will not interfere: such matters are not justiciable. War cannot be controlled or conducted by judicial tribunals: what is necessary or reasonable in its conduct must necessarily rest with those charged with the responsibility of the operations in whatever theatre of war they take place. But there is authority for the proposition that though the courts of law cannot interfere with the conduct of war, *durante bello,* yet after the cessation of hostilities or the restoration of peace the courts have jurisdiction to inquire and determine whether matters done or occurring during its continuance affecting the rights or properties of the King's subjects were justifiable.[199]

The Court left it for the trial court below to determine whether the facts of the collision between HMAS *Adelaide* and the MV *Coptic* attracted the combat immunity doctrine.[200]

Although it did not refer to either *Entick v Carrington* or *Shaw Savill & Albion Co Ltd,* the High Court of Australia again made a clear statement in favour of the principle of legality in the later case of *A v Hayden.*[201] It concerned an Australian Security Intelligence Service exercise in the Sheraton Hotel in Melbourne in 1983 in the course of which personnel allegedly committed a number of criminal offences. The Victorian Police sought the names of the personnel concerned in order to investigate the incident. The Commonwealth refused to divulge the names on the basis that it had a contract of confidentiality with those concerned.[202] Mason J said:

> It is possible that the promise was given, and the arrangements for the training exercise made, in the belief that executive orders would provide sufficient legal authority or justification for what was done. It is very difficult to believe that this was the Commonwealth's view – superior orders are not and never have been a defence in our law – though it is conceivable that the plaintiffs may have had some such belief.[203]

---

199 Ibid 356–7, Dixon J, 361, Williams J, 366, focused on the narrower question of the application of the duty to take care, rather than the application of the law generally, although the two views are consistent. Rich ACJ, 351 and McTiernan J, 364, agreed with Dixon J.
200 Ibid 357.
201 (1984) 156 CLR 532.
202 Ibid 533.
203 Ibid 550.

Murphy J memorably stated:

> The executive power of the Commonwealth must be exercised in accordance with the *Constitution* and the laws of the Commonwealth. The Governor-General, the federal Executive Council and every officer of the Commonwealth are bound to observe the laws of the land. If necessary, constitutional and other writs are available to restrain apprehended violations and to remedy past violations. I restate these elementary principles because astonishingly one of the plaintiffs asserted through counsel that it followed from the nature of the executive government that it is not beyond the executive power, even in a situation other than war, to order one of its citizens to kill another person. Such a proposition is inconsistent with the rule of law. It is subversive of the *Constitution* and the laws. It is, in other countries, the justification for death squads.[204]

This statement quite emphatically asserts the principle of legality, even if not using that term, and underlines the key values in question; constitutional government and the rule of law. His Honour followed this by elevating the proper response to unlawful orders as being a *duty* to disobey, 'Military and civilians have a duty to obey lawful orders, and a duty to disobey unlawful orders'.[205] In 2010 in *Habib v Commonwealth*, a civil claim by an Australian citizen alleging that Commonwealth officials were complicit in his torture and detention in various places including Guantanamo Bay, Perram J cited this part of Murphy J's judgment, inter alia, in stating: '[Section 61] was conferred for the express purpose of maintaining the laws of the Commonwealth and could not, therefore, be the source of any authority to commit Commonwealth offences'.[206]

Gageler J also referred to *A v Hayden* in *M68* as follows:

> That inherent character of non-prerogative executive capacity is given emphasis by the absence of any prerogative power to dispense with the operation of the general law: a principle which Brennan J noted in *A v Hayden*[207] 'is fundamental to our law, though it seems sometimes to be forgotten when executive governments or their agencies are fettered or frustrated by laws which affect the fulfilment of their policies'.[208]

---

204 Ibid 562.
205 Ibid.
206 (2010) 183 FCR 62, 68–9, 71.
207 (1984) 156 CLR 532, 580.
208 [2016] HCA 1 [136].

As simple and clear as these propositions sound, as Chapter 2 will discuss, members of the ADF have obligations to obey lawful orders that are greater than those of civilians, and the ADF has a long heritage of obedience. When executive power is so hard to define, it will not always be clear whether an order is lawful or not. Nonetheless, this does not change the legal obligation of the ADF member. This highlights the tension between executive power and the principle of legality with which this book is concerned, and supports an approach which errs on the side of the principle of legality.

As with *Entick v Carrington*,[209] the order of an executive official in *A v Hayden*[210] was not a legal authority in itself and makes clear that legal authority for executive action must be found elsewhere. This is a problem when legal authority for executive action can be so hard to determine. It underlines the need to find some content, or depth, to the powers under consideration. This requires a closer examination of prerogative power, being the primary source of nonstatutory authority for most uses of force by the ADF.

IV What is Prerogative Power?

Five of the justices in *Williams* noted the significance of the prerogative as a source of executive power.[211] The wisdom received from Dicey is that prerogative power is 'a residue of discretionary power' left to the Crown which is not exercisable by Parliament or the courts.[212] Winterton made the point that when the Crown exercises the attributes of having legal personality, such as the power to own property, sue, contract, incorporate and so on, it cannot be like any other legal person exercising such powers.[213] The position of the Crown is such that any of its acts are

---

209 (1765) 19 St Tr 1030.
210 (1984) 156 CLR 532.
211 (2012) 248 CLR 156, 184–5 (French CJ), 227–8 (Gummow and Bell JJ), 342 (Crennan J), 373 (Kiefel J); French CJ affirms this in *CPCF* HCA [2015] 1, [42]; Gageler J also notes the significance of prerogative power in *M68* [2016] HCA 1 [133]–[136].
212 Dicey, above n 19, xcix–c, 424; *Council of the Civil Service Unions v Minister for the Civil Service* [1985] AC 374, 398 (Lord Fraser).
213 Winterton, 'The Limits and Use of Executive Power by Government', above n 73, 426. In *Williams* (2012) 248 CLR 156, 193, French CJ cites Winterton with apparent approval on this point, from *The Parliament, the Executive and the Governor-General*, above n 73, 112.

inherently governmental.[214] Another view, attributed first to Blackstone[215] and which Wheeler prefers,[216] is that the prerogative power is that residual power which only the Crown can exercise. This would appear to be the better view as the majority of the High Court in *Cadia* stated in 2010:

> Blackstone described the prerogative as part of the common law of England but, given its nature, as being out of the ordinary course of the common law. The 'prerogative' in the context of the present case concerns the enjoyment by the executive government of preferences, immunities and exceptions peculiar to it and denied to the citizen.[217]

Even if this observation might be limited to preferences and immunities rather than powers, Crennan J also addressed this point directly in *Williams* in 2012 in stating:

> The Commonwealth defendants' primary contention was that the Commonwealth Executive's power to spend is sourced in the Commonwealth's legal capacity as a juristic person to spend moneys lawfully appropriated to be spent, and to enter into contracts ('the wider submission'). In *Davis*, preferring Blackstone to Dicey, Brennan J distinguished between the Crown's unique governmental prerogative rights and powers once enjoyed by 'the King … alone' and the Crown's ordinary rights and powers in its private capacity, described by his Honour as 'mere capacities', which were no different from the capacities of ordinary persons to enter into contracts or to spend money.[218] This restrained approach to the prerogative is consistent with Australia's legal independence from Britain, the constraints of federalism and the

---

214 A view which might support this position is that of Zines, which is essentially that the Commonwealth can only exercise those attributes of legal personality related to governmental purposes, and not all the attributes of legal personality which any person could exercise, therefore the exercise of those attributes of legal personality is inherently governmental. Citing *Attorney-General (Vic) v Commonwealth* (1935) 52 CLR 533 (the '*Clothing Factory Case*'), he argued, before *Williams*, that the Commonwealth executive may be limited to exercising only those powers incidental to the Commonwealth's legislative power, Leslie Zines, *The High Court and the Constitution*, above n 109, 349–58. French CJ noted this in *Williams* (2012) 248 CLR 156, 213.
215 *Williams* (2012) 248 CLR 156, 185–6 (French CJ) quoting *Blackstone's Commentaries*, above n 24, 232.
216 See discussion in Fiona Wheeler, 'Judicial Review of Prerogative Power in Australia: Issues and Prospects' (1992) 14 *Sydney Law Review* 432, 447–8. It is worth noting that if a power is not unique to the Crown, that is that it concerns a power which it shares in common with other legal persons, such as an employment relationship rather than a governmental power, it may indicate that it is a subject more amenable to judicial review, *Council of the Civil Service Unions v Minister for the Civil Service* [1985] AC 374, 399 (Lord Fraser).
217 (2010) 242 CLR 195, 223 (Gummow, Hayne, Heydon and Crennan JJ).
218 (1988) 166 CLR 79, 107–109.

paramountcy of the Commonwealth Parliament, and respect under our democratic system of government for the common law rights of individuals.[219]

The powers which the Commonwealth has in common with any other legal person are not necessarily prerogative powers but are, on this view, ordinary executive capacities. What is important is that, since *Williams*, it is apparent that any Commonwealth executive powers which it shares in common with any legal person are not as extensive as that of any legal person and may be confined to being exercisable only when incidental to its other properly construed executive powers.[220] It is a potentially significant point for ADF internal security operations, which, absent a request from a State government, would normally need to relate to a Commonwealth power. Chapter 4 will discuss this point.

A Relationship to Common Law

Most executive powers not found in statute or the *Constitution* relate to a prerogative identifiable through the common law. There is a question though as to whether prerogative power derives from the common law or is simply recognised by common law. High Court cases often refer to the common-law powers of the Crown when discussing prerogative power. As quoted above, the majority in *Cadia* described the prerogative 'as part of the common law of England but, given its nature, as being out of the ordinary course of the common law'.[221] In *NSW v Commonwealth* (the '*Seas and Submerged Lands Case*') there was a question as to whether the common law could only extend to the low water line given that the

---

219 *Williams* (2012) 248 CLR 156, 343–4. Gageler J elaborates on this point in *M68* [2016] HCA 1, [133]–[136], exploring Brennan J's distinction between a prerogative executive power and a nonprerogative executive capacity.
220 (2012) 248 CLR 156, 192–4 (French CJ), limited discussion of 'ordinary and well recognised functions of government', 234 (Gummow and Bell JJ), s 61 grants a power to spend where authorised by statute or the *Constitution,* 249, recognised power of Commonwealth to inquire which is held in common with every other citizen, 206 (Hayne J), Commonwealth may exercise the capacities of a juristic person 'in the ordinary course of administering a recognised part of the Commonwealth government', 342 (Crennan J), 'an activity not authorised by the *Constitution* could not fall within the power of the Executive', 373–4 (Kiefel J). Other than the reference to French CJ, these references are indirect at best in support of this point but they indicate views which are at least not inconsistent with it.
221 (2010) 242 CLR 195, 223.

power of the Crown extended beyond that.²²² Jacobs J made clear in that case that the prerogative does not necessarily rely upon the common law to exist but the common law may recognise a previously existing prerogative. The common law existed of its own force only within England yet the prerogative power of the Crown extended as far as the Crown was able to assert it.²²³ This is consistent with the historical origin of the powers of the Crown in William I and the development of the common law subsequent to his conquest of England.²²⁴ This is a conceptually significant point for this book because, as Jacobs J noted of the King's prerogative power beyond the realm:

> The breadth or width of his [the King's] assertion from time to time depended on high politics and it varied from time to time depending on considerations of power and of expediency. The history of its changes lies not in legal history but in political history.²²⁵

This indicates that political power and expediency can be as important, if not more important, to prerogative power than legal authority. This leads to the issue of executive power more generally being a description of function rather more than of authority. It is hard to say what executive power is because sometimes it is whatever it needs to be. It is not always possible to ascertain the extent of executive power by an assessment of legal authority. There simply is not an identifiable authority in law for everything the executive does, particularly the ADF. As Locke stated, '[F]or prerogative is nothing but the power of doing public good without a rule.'²²⁶ Nevertheless, despite questions over the legal source of prerogative power, particular prerogatives, such as those relevant to this book concerning martial law, internal security, war and external affairs, are still identified by reference to the common law.

---

222 (1975) 135 CLR 337, 487–91 (Jacobs J). This question is perhaps not as significant now as there have been decisions of the High Court which have accepted that the common law operates beyond the low water line, *Commonwealth v Yarmirr* (2001) 208 CLR 1; *Blunden v Commonwealth* (2003) 218 CLR 330, 335–6.
223 *Seas and Submerged Lands Case* (1975) 135 CLR 337, 489.
224 Baker, above n 2, 11–32 and above n 2 and above n 5 generally.
225 *Seas and Submerged Lands Case* (1975) 135 CLR 337, 489.
226 Locke, 'Essay Concerning the True Original, Extent and End of Civil Government', above n 15, 142.

B Subject Matter

What are the prerogatives then? This chapter does not seek to provide an exhaustive list of all the prerogatives, even if that were possible. Evatt J was of the view in *Federal Commissioner of Taxation v Official Liquidator of EO Farley Ltd (in Liq)* that 'the royal prerogatives are so disparate in character and subject matter that it is difficult to assign them to fixed categories or subjects'.[227] In that case, his Honour referred to his own doctoral thesis[228] in which he had described three broad categories of prerogatives. The first was that of the 'executive prerogatives', which included making peace and war. The second category was that of 'immunities and preferences', which included such things as priority of debts owed to the Crown over other creditors and immunity from court processes. The third category was that of 'property rights', involving rights to royal metals, escheats (usually meaning deceased estates with no beneficiary) and the foreshore and seabed.[229] For Australia, the executive power of each Commonwealth, State and Territory government includes those prerogatives applicable to the functions of that particular government in the federal system.[230] His Honour stated that the more significant prerogatives relevant to the Commonwealth include those with respect to defence and foreign affairs.[231] Prerogatives such as those concerning priority in debts could be exercised at the Commonwealth or State level as applicable.[232] By virtue of the federal division of responsibilities, the States and Territories would more likely exercise such prerogatives as those with respect to metals, escheats, treasure trove and the foreshore.[233]

---

227 *Federal Commissioner of Taxation v Official Liquidator of EO Farley Ltd (in Liq)* (1940) 63 CLR 278, 320.
228 See Evatt, above n 109.
229 *Federal Commissioner of Taxation v Official Liquidator of EO Farley Ltd (in Liq)* (1940) 63 CLR 278, 320.
230 *Commonwealth v Colonial Combing, Spinning and Weaving Co* (1922) 31 CLR 421, 432; Constitution s 70.
231 *Federal Commissioner of Taxation v Official Liquidator of EO Farley Ltd (in Liq)* (1940) 63 CLR 278, 320. To this might be added acquisition of territory, particularly in the maritime domain in more recent years, *Seas and Submerged Lands Case* (1975) 135 CLR 337, 487–91, which Jacobs J said was a prerogative which did not ever pass to the States.
232 *Federal Commissioner of Taxation v Official Liquidator of EO Farley Ltd (in Liq)* (1940) 63 CLR 278, 319.
233 Ibid 321. In *Cadia* Gummow, Hayne, Heydon and Crennan JJ questioned whether this division was appropriate for royal metals, given that the rationale for the prerogative was to finance the defence of the realm, but did not consider the matter further, (2010) 242 CLR 195, 225–7.

C Relationship to Statute

A consequence of a power being a prerogative power is that it may be exercised without the authority of an Act of Parliament. The legal authority is found in the prerogative itself, which common law may recognise. While the prerogative can adapt to new circumstances, such as developments in warfare, as a result of the Glorious Revolution in 1688 it is no longer possible to create a new prerogative: '[I]t is 350 years and a civil war too late for the Queen's courts to broaden the prerogative'.[234] As Jacobs J made clear in the *AAP Case*, the executive is subordinate to the legislature:

> The Parliament is sovereign over the Executive and whatever is within the competence of the Executive under s 61, including or as well as the exercise of the prerogative within the area of the prerogative attached to Australia, may be the subject of legislation of the Australian Parliament.[235]

French CJ endorsed this view explicitly in *Pape*.[236] Statute may regulate or extinguish prerogative power by express words or necessary implication. It may control the exercise of the power without interfering with its source or actually remove the source of a prerogative power and either replace it with a statutory power or abolish it altogether.[237] Either way, as Gummow and Bell JJ stated in *Williams* that 'when a prerogative power is directly regulated by statute, the Executive Government must act in accordance with the statutory regime'.[238] The *Defence Force Discipline Act 1982* (Cth) is a good example of a field in which statute has replaced regulation by prerogative virtually completely.[239]

This preserves the supremacy of Parliament over the executive. The inability to create new prerogatives limits prerogative power to a fixed field of subject matter, even if the limits of the prerogatives themselves are unclear. In some way this acts as a check on potential abuse of prerogative power for despotic purposes. It supports constitutional order and the rule of law. It is also fundamentally democratic in making the actions of the

---

234 *Tampa Case* (2001) 110 FCR 491; Black CJ quoting Diplock LJ in *British Broadcasting Corporation v Jones* [1965] Ch 32, 79. See George Winterton, 'The Prerogative in Novel Situations' (1983) 99 *Law Quarterly Review* 407, 408 as to the capacity of prerogative power to adapt to changing circumstances (as opposed to the creation of new prerogatives).
235 *AAP Case* (1975) 134 CLR 338, 406.
236 (2009) 238 CLR 1, 51.
237 *M68* [2016] HCA 1 [121]–[122]. (Gageler J); See also *Attorney-General v De Keyser's Royal Hotel Ltd* [1920] AC 508 ('*De Keyser's Royal Hotel*').
238 *Williams* (2012) 248 CLR 156, 227–8.
239 See discussion in *Millar v Bornholt* (2009) FCA 637, [16]–[25] (Logan J).

Crown subject to the will of the people as expressed through Parliament, as opposed to the people being subject to the will of the Crown. The effect of this is to have those who exercise prerogative power do so, ultimately, for public purposes rather than in their own self-interest or risk having Parliament extinguish the power.

D Statutory Interpretation

Statutory interpretation, then, is very important because of its rules with respect to discerning the extent to which statute prevails over prerogative power. There is some debate as to how this occurs and the *Tampa Case* exemplified the differences of view on this point.[240] The dissenting judgment of Black CJ was that the *Migration Act 1958* (Cth) by necessary implication extinguished any prerogative with respect to preventing the entry of aliens because it dealt comprehensively with this subject.[241] The leading judgment of French J in that case found no express words or necessary implication in the legislation to extinguish the relevant executive power, as informed by prerogative power, so executive power remained available.[242] (Notably, the prerogative was not the basis of the power to expel aliens without statutory authority. This was found in s 61 alone, being a form of nationhood power, which is discussed below.[243])

Winterton has argued that the 'covering the field' test, which is relevant to inconsistencies between State and Commonwealth legislation under s 109 of the *Constitution*, should be applicable to questions of whether legislation has extinguished a prerogative power:[244]

> In determining whether legislation impliedly intends to alter, regulate or abolish a prerogative power ... There should, at most, be a mild presumption against such intention, especially when the prerogative power is well established and clearly important to government ... The courts should also draw on the extensive jurisprudence relating to a broadly analogous question – inconsistency of Commonwealth and State legislation under s 109 of the *Constitution*.[245]

---

240 (2001) 110 FCR 491.
241 Ibid 507–508.
242 Ibid 540.
243 Ibid 538–9.
244 Winterton, 'The Limits and Use of Executive Power by Government', above n 73, 421 n 59).
245 George Winterton, 'The Relationship between Commonwealth Executive and Legislative Power' (2003) 25(1) *Adelaide Law Review* 21, 48–9. On Winterton, statutory interpretation and the *Tampa Case* see Gerangelos, above n 73, 203–9.

Evans, in arguing for a 'covering the field' test, criticises French J's view in the *Tampa Case*[246] on the basis that 'the history of the executive power since the 17th century demonstrates progressive constitutionalism, moderation and republicanisation, all values which support a presumption of the kind rejected by French J'.[247]

Evans goes on to say that:

> The argument is even stronger if one adopts a version of *democratic* constitutionalism as a standard. Notwithstanding the dominance of the executive in Parliament, enacting legislation requires greater openness, scrutiny and democratic deliberation than the exercise of prerogative powers [emphasis in original] …[248]

A number of the judgments in *Attorney-General v De Keyser's Royal Hotel Ltd* ('*De Keyser's Royal Hotel*'),[249] would also support this view. Black CJ quoted them at length as follows:

> It is uncontentious that the relationship between a statute and the prerogative is that where a statute, expressly or by necessary implication, purports to regulate wholly the area of a particular prerogative power or right, the exercise of the power or right is governed by the provisions of the statute, which are to prevail in that respect: *Attorney-General v De Keyser's Royal Hotel Ltd* [1920] AC 508. The principle is one of parliamentary sovereignty. The question is, what is the test to determine whether a prerogative power has been displaced by statute? The accepted test is whether the legislation has the same area of operation as the prerogative.
>
> In *De Keyser's*, Lord Dunedin said (at 526):
>
> It is equally certain that if the whole ground of something which could be done by the prerogative is covered by the statute, it is the statute that rules. On this point I think the observation of the learned Master of the Rolls is unanswerable. He says: 'What use would there be in imposing limitations, if the Crown could at its pleasure disregard them and fall back on prerogative?'

---

246 (2001) 110 FCR 491.
247 Evans, 'The Rule of Law, Constitutionalism and the MV Tampa', above n 187, 98. Zines supports Evans's view in Zines, 'The Inherent Executive Power of the Commonwealth', above n 7, 291–3.
248 Evans, 'The Rule of Law, Constitutionalism and the MV Tampa', above n 187, 99.
249 [1920] AC 508.

Lord Moulton said (at 554):

> the statutory powers ... are wider and more comprehensive than those of the prerogative itself. [The Parliament] has indicated unmistakably that it is the intention of the nation that the powers of the Crown in these respects should be exercised in the equitable manner set forth in the statute.

Lord Sumner said (at 561):

> It seems also to be obvious that enactments may [abrogate the prerogative], provided they directly deal with the subject-matter, even though they enact a modus operandi for securing the desired result, which is not the same as that of the prerogative.

Lord Parmoor said (at 576):

> [w]here a matter has been directly regulated by statute there is a necessary implication that the statutory regulation must be obeyed, and that as far as such regulation is inconsistent with the claim of a Royal Prerogative right, such right can no longer be enforced.

See also per Lord Atkinson (at 538).[250]

The High Court has not yet explicitly applied a 'covering the field' test to such a question. In 2010, *Cadia* restated the position that stood in the *Tampa Case*:

> Despite subsequent development of responsible and representative government in Britain, and the exercise of prerogative authority only on advice, it remains an orthodox approach by the courts to statutory construction to say that the prerogative of the Crown is not displaced except by express words or by necessary implication.[251]

Nonetheless, French CJ also stated in *CPCF* that explicit preservation of executive power in s 5 of the *Maritime Powers Act* (MPA) could not 'be taken as preserving unconstrained an executive power the exercise of which is constrained by the MPA'.[252] Hayne and Bell JJ as well as Kiefel J came to a similar conclusion.[253] This would appear to amount

---

250   *Tampa Case* (2001) 110 FCR 491, 501–502.
251   (2010) 242 CLR 195, 228 (Gummow, Hayne, Heydon, Crennan JJ).
252   *CPCF* HCA [2015] 1, [41].
253   Ibid [141] (Hayne and Bell JJ); [277]–[286] (Kiefel J).

1. WHAT IS EXECUTIVE POWER?

to a 'covering the field' test, even if not by that name. Keane J however adhered to the view that executive power continues to exist where it is not abrogated, presumably explicitly, by statute.[254]

As Black CJ notes, this is a question of the principle of parliamentary supremacy over the executive. The approach to this aspect of statutory interpretation is a critical point for this book as it argues that the primacy of the legislature over the executive, deriving from the Glorious Revolution and informed by principles of democracy and the rule of law, should determine this question. As stated above, to counter the potential risk of arbitrariness and despotism, executive action should rely on statutory power before executive power on the same subject unless necessity demands otherwise.

E An Extra Step in the Statutory Interpretation Process

Therefore, where the Parliament has provided statutory authority for the executive to carry out its functions,[255] then the executive should rely upon that statutory authority. It is only in extreme circumstances where necessity could justify that the executive should resort to the authority of executive power alone. These are the situations which Blackstone described, as quoted above, which require 'those extraordinary recourses to first principles, which are necessary when the contracts of society are in danger of dissolution, and the law proves too weak a defence'.[256] Even then, it should only be where the prerogative in question (or even possibly nationhood power, as discussed below) actually envisages extraordinary circumstances such as the collapse of constitutional government, war or serious threats to life. This book argues that there is some recognised content to these powers which can assist in determining when to rely upon them instead of statutory power. This means that a statute 'covering the field' should *not*, without express words, automatically extinguish executive power on the same subject. Executive power should remain available because it may be, in an extreme situation, statutory power is not available and executive power is better than no power at all. This book argues for a position, then, that is different to that of French J. A further

---

254 Ibid [2015] 1, [488]–[492].
255 See discussion in Zines, 'The Inherent Executive Power of the Commonwealth', above n 7, 292.
256 *Blackstone's Commentaries*, above n 24, 251.

step of analysis is required to determine whether, in the circumstances of a particular case, the existence of statutory power should preclude reliance upon executive power.

By way of example, in the *Tampa Case,* the issue should not just have been, as in the view of French J, whether the prerogative or broader executive power to expel aliens survived the enactment of the relevant provisions of the *Migration Act 1958* (Cth).[257] It should, instead, have been if the *Migration Act* expressly 'covered the field' in empowering the executive to protect Australia's borders from unlawful arrivals whether it was then necessary to resort to executive power. The authorities on the history and the actual character of the prerogatives themselves recognise the circumstances where necessity would justify relying upon them instead of on a statute which covered the same field. These circumstances did not exist and the prerogative (or nationhood power) to exclude aliens is nothing like the prerogatives with respect to war, martial law or internal security. French J described the power to exclude aliens as follows:

> Absent statutory abrogation it would be sufficient to authorise the barring of entry by preventing a vessel from docking at an Australian port and adopting the means necessary to achieve that result. Absent statutory authority, it would extend to a power to restrain a person or boat from proceeding into Australia or compelling it to leave.[258]

This describes the essentially routine function of border control. French J nonetheless described it in the following terms:

> The power to determine who may come into Australia is so central to its sovereignty that it is not to be supposed that the Government of the nation would lack under the power conferred upon it directly by the *Constitution*.[259]

His Honour did not cite any authority which supported this statement nor any particular reason why, even if border control was so central to sovereignty, that it justified the use of executive power instead of statutory power. There is no suggestion that other matters just as central to sovereignty, such as taxation or citizenship, should rely upon executive

---

[257] (2001) 110 FCR 491, 541–4. As discussed further below, in addition, the prerogative should have been the first point of reference, before referring to the broader 'nationhood power'. Evans's discussion of prerogative power and statutory interpretation in this case generally, and criticism of French J's approach, is above n 187, 96–9.
[258] *Tampa Case* (2001) 110 FCR 491, 544.
[259] Ibid 543.

rather than statutory power just because they are central to sovereignty. This argument could undermine the relationship of subordination of the executive to the Parliament. However, martial law, war and internal unrest threatening life are exceptional situations which can threaten the very existence of constitutional order. They are far from routine. An executive power to exclude aliens is not concerned with such extraordinary situations which could justify action based upon necessity. There was, therefore, arguably no basis to resort to executive power when Parliament intended to cover the field in the *Migration Act*. This approach is more consistent with the theory of the separation of powers between the executive and the legislature, as argued by Black CJ, but with the additional consideration of whether it is necessary for the executive to act without statutory authority.

Black CJ doubted that there was a prerogative.[260] In his view, the legislation empowered the ADF to act but was not properly complied with.[261] If there was no power to be found in these sources, then the executive action was ultra vires. This is in accordance with the principle of legality, the majority in *CPCF* as well as the judgments of Gageler J and Gordon J in *M68*, as discussed above. His Honour could also have considered necessity arising from extreme circumstances but this did not appear on the facts of this case and his conclusion would have been no different.

This book will argue, then, that necessity, in relation to the exercise of particular executive powers, is an important extra limiting factor or justification in determining whether to rely upon executive power where statute already expressly 'covers the field'. Necessity is not necessity in general terms, however; its meaning relates to particular prerogative powers and possibly nationhood power. The circumstances in which necessity might justify reliance upon the prerogatives with respect to martial law, war, internal security and, possibly, nationhood power, are the subject of the rest of this book.

This leads to the issue of the different sources of authority within the executive power of the Commonwealth, particularly as between prerogative and nationhood power. If statutory power is not available and there is no prerogative power on the same subject, recourse may possibly be had to 'nationhood power', although still limited by necessity.

---

260 Ibid 500–501.
261 Ibid 508, 514.

V Nationhood Power

This book does not reject 'nationhood' power completely but argues that it should not be relied upon where there are existing prerogatives, particularly in the case of the extreme exercises of power relevant to the ADF. It comes now to address the issue of nationhood power directly.

The High Court has confirmed, in *Pape*[262] and *Williams*,[263] that some nonstatutory executive powers derive from s 61 of the *Constitution* itself rather than relying on prerogative or common-law authority.[264] On this view, section 61 can be informed by prerogative power but is itself the source of authority. The aspect of nonstatutory governmental executive power under s 61 that is additional to the prerogative powers is known as nationhood power.[265] French J put this view strongly in the *Tampa Case*, seeing the executive power of the Commonwealth as 'measured by reference to Australia's status as a sovereign nation'.[266] As Chief Justice of the High Court, he confirmed his views in *Pape* stating that the short-term fiscal measures to respond to the global financial crisis in that case were 'peculiarly within the capacity and resources of the Commonwealth Government',[267] a view consistent with that of Gummow, Crennan and Bell JJ.[268] There is considerable uncertainty however over the nature and extent of nationhood power which does not relate to any prerogative. It is important to this book overall, because potentially there is considerable scope within it to authorise action by the ADF, but without reference to the venerable prerogatives which traditionally have authorised military action. For this reason it is worth elaborating on the provenance of nationhood power.

---

[262] (2009) 238 CLR 1, 60 (French CJ), 87–8 (Gummow, Bell and Crennan JJ).
[263] (2012) 248 CLR 156, 184–5 (French CJ), 235 (Gummow and Bell JJ), 342 (Crennan J), 373 (Kiefel J).
[264] See Winterton, 'The Limits and Use of Executive Power by Government', above n 73; Bradley Selway, 'All at Sea – Constitutional Assumptions and "the Executive Power of the Commonwealth"' (2003) 31(3) *Federal Law Review* 495.
[265] *Davis v Commonwealth* (1988) 166 CLR 79, 93.
[266] (2001) 110 FCR 491, 542.
[267] (2009) 238 CLR 1, 63.
[268] Ibid 87–8.

A Origins and Development

There were a number of forerunner cases which suggested or described, but did not use the term, 'nationhood power'. They varied as to whether it was an executive or legislative power or both. In the war powers case of *R v Kidman*, Isaacs J held that there was implied executive power for the Commonwealth to carry out its functions. His Honour said it has 'an inherent right of self-protection … [which] … carries with it – except where expressly prohibited – all necessary powers to protect itself and punish those who endeavour to obstruct it'.[269] In another war powers case, *Commonwealth v Colonial Combing, Spinning and Weaving Co* (the '*Wooltops Case*'), Isaacs J also hinted at the protective function of the Commonwealth executive power.[270] It is not clear that Isaacs J saw this as something more than prerogative power or to counter a view that relevant prerogative power might not be available to the Commonwealth via s 61 at that time, resting instead with the King.[271]

In *Attorney-General (Vic) ex rel Dale v Commonwealth* (the '*Pharmaceutical Benefits Case*'),[272] which concerned the Commonwealth's spending power, the whole scheme for the Commonwealth to subsidise the sale of pharmaceuticals failed but, in a passage which Mason CJ, Deane and Gaudron JJ later referred to with approval in *Davis v Commonwealth*,[273] Dixon J stated:

> In deciding what appropriation laws may validly be enacted it would be necessary to remember what position a national government occupies and … to take no narrow view, but the basal consideration would be found in the distribution of powers and functions between the Commonwealth and the States.[274]

This view appears to have developed Isaacs J's view of the Commonwealth as a national, not just a federal, government.

---

269 (1915) 20 CLR 425, 444–5.
270 (1922) 31 CLR 421, 442.
271 Zines contrasts the view of Isaacs J with that of Higgins J in this case, ibid 453–4, to the effect that s 61 was confined to the execution and maintenance of the *Constitution* and laws passed by Parliament, Leslie Zines, 'The Growth of Australian Nationhood and its Effect on the Powers of the Commonwealth' in Leslie Zines (ed) *Commentaries on the Australian Constitution: A Tribute to Geoffrey Sawer* (Butterworths, 1977) 24.
272 (1945) 71 CLR 237.
273 (1988) 166 CLR 79, 93.
274 (1945) 71 CLR 237, 271–2.

Dixon J carried this further in obiter dicta in the sedition case of *R v Sharkey*, quoting with approval this statement from Quick and Garran in order to distinguish the spheres of Commonwealth and State power:

> If, however, domestic violence within a State is of such a character as to interfere with the operations of the Federal Government, or with rights and privileges of federal citizenship, the Federal Government may clearly, without a summons from the State, interfere to restore order. Thus if a riot in a State interfered with the carriage of the federal mails, or with interstate commerce, or with the right of an elector to record his vote at federal elections, the Federal Government could use all force at its disposal, not to protect the State, but to protect itself. Were it otherwise, the Federal Government would be dependent on the Governments of the States for the effective exercise of its powers.[275]

This quote goes more to the point of nationhood power with which this book is concerned, the use of force. It is useful in making a distinction between the respective power of the Commonwealth and the States because, as Chapter 4 will discuss, it is not one which traditional English jurisprudence on the prerogative recognises.

In obiter dicta in *Australian Communist Party v Commonwealth* ('*Communist Party Case*'), Dixon J also referred to the two sedition cases of *R v Sharkey*[276] and *Burns v Ransley*,[277] and stated:

> As appears from *Burns v Ransley* (1949) 79 CLR, at p 116 and *R v Sharkey* (1949) 79 CLR, at pp 148, 149, I take the view that the power to legislate against subversive conduct has a source in principle that is deeper or wider than a series of combinations of the words of s 51 (xxxix) with those of other constitutional powers. I prefer the view adopted in the United States, which is stated in Black's *American Constitutional Law* (1910), 2nd ed, s 153, p 210, as follows: 'it is within the necessary power of the federal government to protect its own existence and the unhindered play of its legitimate activities. And to this end, it may provide for the punishment of treason the suppression of insurrection or rebellion and for the putting down of all individual or concerted attempts to obstruct or interfere with the discharge of the proper business of government'.[278]

---

275 *R v Sharkey* (1949) 79 CLR 121, 151 quoting Quick and Garran's *Annotated Constitution of the Australian Commonwealth*, above n 72, 194.
276 (1949) 79 CLR 121.
277 (1949) 79 CLR 101.
278 *Australian Communist Party v Commonwealth* (1951) 83 CLR 1, 188 ('*Communist Party Case*').

In the same case, Fullagar J also said with regard to the inherent right of self-protection:

> But I think that, if it ever becomes necessary to examine it closely, it may well be found to depend really on an essential and inescapable implication which must be involved in the legal constitution of any polity. The validity of the Act, however, if it could be supported by the power, would not be affected by the fact that its framers had taken too narrow a view of the source of the power.[279]

This is where the jurisprudence takes a more concerning turn as, even though focused upon legislative power, it takes quite forceful ideas, such as suppression of subversion, and bases them upon textual assumptions and implications. It goes against the idea that exercises of executive 'power should be clear in proportion as the power is exorbitant' which underpins the principle of legality.[280] It is one thing to attribute a power to the Commonwealth as opposed to the States but it is another to make it potentially extreme and at the same time merely implied and therefore potentially unlimited.

By way of contrast, in the *Seas and Submerged Lands Case*, Barwick CJ characterised Commonwealth jurisdiction over Australia's maritime zones as a 'consequence of the creation of the Commonwealth under the Constitution'.[281] This is a more benign application of the nationhood power concept as it concerns the respective power of the Commonwealth as opposed to the States and is in essence facultative rather than coercive.

These cases demonstrate that even before the term 'nationhood power' entered High Court jurisprudence, there were significant references to a power of this nature, whether legislative or executive. While the context of the words quoted relate to the division of power between the States and the Commonwealth, as can be seen above, they could also apply readily to a view about Commonwealth executive power more broadly and particularly the use of force. They will be directly relevant to the discussion of internal security in Chapter 4.

---

279 Ibid 260.
280 *Entick v Carrington* (1765) 19 St Tr 1030, 1066.
281 (1975) 135 CLR 337, 373.

B Nationhood Power Cases

As to the cases which identify nationhood power more directly, in the *AAP Case* Mason J stated that executive powers could be 'deduced from the existence and character of the Commonwealth as a national government'.[282] This appears to be the start of the line of authority to support nationhood power, as such, as a source of executive power with the key words being 'the Commonwealth as a national government'.

Although not a case, the Hope *Protective Security Review* 1979 is also relevant because it is the only consideration by judicial writers of the Bowral call-out of 1978, which actually involved an ADF intervention in a State under what appeared to be nationhood power.[283] In his extracurial report, Justice Hope annexed an extracurial opinion of retired High Court Justice Sir Victor Windeyer. Sir Victor stated that the constitutional authority of the Commonwealth to intervene with force in a State to protect its own interests, in this case to protect visiting Commonwealth Heads of Government, was an incident of nationhood:

> The power of the Commonwealth Government to use the Armed Forces at its command to prevent or suppress disorder that might subvert its lawful authority arises fundamentally, I think, because the *Constitution* created a sovereign body politic with the attributes that are inherent in such a body. The Commonwealth of Australia is not only a federation of States. It is a nation.[284]

This example is important because it illustrates that nationhood power is not an abstract concept confined to reports of constitutional cases. It can actually be an authority for military intervention in the most sensitive of contexts, internal security. This book argues in subsequent chapters that it might be necessary to rely upon nationhood power to provide authority for Commonwealth action, as opposed to State action, but the risks in having such an extreme yet imprecise power are such that it should only occur in very limited circumstances.

---

282 *AAP Case* (1975) 134 CLR 338, 397.
283 Discussed in Chapter 4.
284 Justice Robert Hope, *Protective Security Review* (Parliamentary Paper 397, Parliament of Australia, 1979) 'Appendix 9: Opinion of Sir Victor Windeyer, KBE, CB, DSO on Certain Questions Concerning the Position of Members of the Defence Force When Called Out to Aid the Civil Power', 279. Zines does not appear to question this in Zines, 'The Inherent Executive Power of the Commonwealth', above n 7, 289, noting that there was a relevant statute, the *Crimes (Internationally Protected Persons) Act 1976* (Cth).

1. WHAT IS EXECUTIVE POWER?

It is important, therefore, to illustrate that the provenance of nationhood power is contentious. *Commonwealth v Tasmania* (the '*Tasmanian Dam Case*')[285] was equivocal about nationhood power as it had the potential to increase the power of the Commonwealth at the expense of the States. In this case, Wilson J, in dissent, did not see nationhood power as relevant to coercive powers to protect 'a heritage distinctive of the Australian nation', and saw no basis for an inherent legislative power 'independent of any express legislative power conferred by the *Constitution*'.[286] Deane J, in the majority, had a similar view, reviewing the 'nationhood power' cases and confining them to 'areas in which there is no real competition with the States'.[287] He accepted that the Commonwealth, using powers 'not included in any express grant of legislative power' to 'assist what are truly national endeavours', could appropriate money to spend in an area of State activity but did not accept 'drastic' coercive measures which ousted State powers on the basis of an unexpressed nationhood type power.[288] Gibbs CJ,[289] Murphy J[290] and Dawson J[291] did not reject the power but saw it as having no application to the case. Mason J did not address nationhood power.[292]

Davis v Commonwealth,[293] drawing on the *AAP Case*,[294] is a defining case on nationhood power. Mason CJ, Deane and Gaudron JJ saw nationhood power as a power to legislate with respect to the Bicentennial, including power to incorporate a company in the Australian Capital Territory for the purpose,[295] and coercive power to protect the name and symbols of the Bicentennial Authority.[296] Importantly, their Honours saw this power as possibly being an inherent legislative power, operating independently of a combination of s 61, the executive power, and s 51(xxxix), the incidental

---

285 (1983) 158 CLR 1.
286 Ibid 203.
287 Ibid 252.
288 Ibid 252–3.
289 Ibid 109.
290 Ibid 182.
291 Ibid 322–3.
292 Even so, in the same year in *R v Duncan; Ex parte Australian Iron and Steel Pty Ltd*, Mason J took a more expansive view of nationhood power. He said that it extended to authorise agreements between the Commonwealth and the States on matters of joint interest, including joint legislative action, as long as they did 'not contravene the *Constitution*', (1983) 158 CLR 535, 560. Notably, this position was not followed in *R v Hughes* (2000) 202 CLR 535, 583, discussed below.
293 *Davis v Commonwealth* (1988) 166 CLR 79.
294 (1975) 134 CLR 338.
295 *Davis v Commonwealth* (1988) 166 CLR 79, 94.
296 Ibid 97.

65

power, which had been the more accepted position until then.²⁹⁷ Wilson and Dawson JJ did not support this expanded view of an inherent legislative power and saw it as only deriving from s 51(xxxix).²⁹⁸ Brennan J did take a broad view of nationhood power as an executive power though. He stated:

> The end and purpose of the *Constitution* is to sustain the nation. If the executive power of the Commonwealth extends to the protection of the nation against forces which would weaken it, it extends to the advancement of the nation whereby its strength is fostered. There is no reason to restrict the executive power of the Commonwealth to matters within the heads of legislative power. So cramped a construction of the power would deny to the Australian people many of the symbols of nationhood – a flag or anthem, for example – or the benefit of many national initiatives in science, literature and the arts.²⁹⁹

Even with an expansive view of nationhood power, Mason CJ, Deane and Gaudron JJ invalidated aspects of the legislation under challenge on the basis of it being disproportional to the end sought. Protection of words such as '1788', '1988', '200 years' and 'Sydney' with criminal sanction was an 'extraordinary intrusion into freedom of expression ... not reasonably and appropriately adapted to achieve the ends that lie within the limits of constitutional power'.³⁰⁰ Proportionality in this case then was the limit on nationhood power. It has something in common with waxing and waning in the war power cases, which Chapter 5 will address. *Davis v Commonwealth* again favours a facultative approach to nationhood power but takes a constrained view to a coercive aspect to the power, which is consistent with the approach of this book.³⁰¹

The coercive aspect of the power was at its highest in the *Tampa Case*.³⁰² As mentioned above, French J decided that the executive power to prevent unlawful entry of aliens into Australia was effectively an incident of nationhood. As quoted above, he stated:

---

297   Ibid 93, the inherent and independent power is consistent with Dixon J in the *Communist Party Case* (1951) 83 CLR 1, and Fullagar J in the same case, 260.
298   *Davis v Commonwealth* (1988) 166 CLR 79, 101.
299   Ibid 111.
300   Ibid 99.
301   Zines echoes Winterton's criticism of the High Court insufficiently considering depth as well as breadth in this case, in Zines, 'The Inherent Executive Power of the Commonwealth', above n 7, 281, citing Winterton, 'The Relationship between Commonwealth Executive and Legislative Power', above n 245, 31–2.
302   (2001) 110 FCR 491.

1. WHAT IS EXECUTIVE POWER?

> The power to determine who may come into Australia is so central to its sovereignty that it is not to be supposed that the Government of the nation would lack under the power conferred upon it directly by the *Constitution*.[303]

In a view which this author shares and elaborates upon below, Zines wrote of this statement that:

> It is to be hoped that the court does not find any other coercive powers of the executive that are essential to sovereignty and which may be exercised free of any limitations or safeguards in legislation.[304]

Black CJ on the other hand, stated that: 'The Australian cases in which the executive power has had an "interest of the nation" ingredient can be contrasted with those in which such power has been asserted for coercive purposes'.[305]

He then listed a number of examples where nationhood power has not supported a coercive power, stating that it

> has been held not to be available to sustain deportation (*Ex parte Walsh; Re Yates* (1925) 37 CLR 36 at 79); detention or extradition of a fugitive (*Barton* at 477, 483, 494); the arrest of a person believed to have committed a felony abroad (*Brown*); the arbitrary denial of mail and telephone services (*Bradley v Commonwealth* (1973) 128 CLR 557); or compulsion to attend to give evidence or to produce documents in an inquiry (*McGuiness v Attorney-General (Vic)* (1940) 83 CLR 73) …[306]

Black CJ saw that the executive power to expel aliens must come from a prerogative and stated that the continued existence of any such prerogative 'is entirely uncertain' and excluded by the *Migration Act 1958*.[307] As much as the *Tampa Case* stands for a coercive use of nationhood power, as this chapter will discuss further below, it is not widely supported in the case law or the literature and must be treated with some caution.

---

303 Ibid 543.
304 Zines, 'The Inherent Executive Power of the Commonwealth', above n 7, 289.
305 *Tampa Case* (2001) 110 FCR 491, 501.
306 Ibid.
307 Ibid.

1 A Narrowing of Nationhood Power?

Two High Court cases which saw a limiting of nationhood power would appear to support this view. In *Re Wakim; Ex parte McNally* (the '*Cross-vesting Case*'), Kirby J suggested that a cross vesting scheme between State and Commonwealth courts might also find support in nationhood power.[308] Gummow and Hayne JJ, however, explicitly rejected this view as based on 'perceived convenience' instead of 'legal analysis' and 'constitutional doctrine'.[309] In *R v Hughes*,[310] Kirby J rejected the use of nationhood power to support a coercive Commonwealth and State corporations law prosecutions arrangement. Proportionality was an issue and such a scheme could not rely on constitutional implications as 'convenience and desirability are not enough if the constitutional foundation is missing'.[311] Together, these cases suggested a trend in High Court jurisprudence away from nationhood power as a legislative power, reflecting continuing concerns in the earlier cases with respect to interference with the States and the lack of an explicit textual basis for it. Despite this, *Pape*[312] appears to have affirmed nationhood power, even if not in its coercive aspect.

C *Pape*

In 2009 *Pape* confirmed nationhood power as a source of executive power. The majority judgments strongly confirmed the existence of a nationhood power. Gummow, Crennan and Bell JJ went so far as to say that the fiscal response to the global financial crisis was 'somewhat analogous to determining a state of emergency in circumstances of a natural disaster', for which only the national government had the means to respond.[313] French CJ did not go this far but stated, as quoted above:

> While history and the common law inform its content, [s 61] is not a locked display cabinet in a constitutional museum. It is not limited to statutory powers and the prerogative. It has to be capable of serving the proper purposes of a national government.[314]

---

308 (1999) 198 CLR 511, 615.
309 Ibid 581.
310 (2000) 202 CLR 535.
311 Ibid 583.
312 (2009) 238 CLR 1.
313 Ibid 89.
314 Ibid 60.

These statements affirmed that nationhood power was by then clearly part of the High Court's jurisprudence on s 61 but it was limited by its description as 'peculiarly adapted to the government of the country and which cannot otherwise be carried on for the public benefit'.[315] It is this imprecision with which the other judgments, as well commentators, had concern, and which underlines the concern this book has with nationhood power as an authority for ADF action.

Hayne and Keifel JJ found that the fiscal stimulus package could find support in part under the taxation power in s 51 (ii) of the *Constitution* but did not find any support for it, as mentioned above, in

> an exercise of executive power identified as derived from the character and status of the Commonwealth as a national polity or as deduced from the existence and character of the Commonwealth as a national government.[316]

They went on to state that 'words like "crisis" or "emergency" do not readily yield criteria of constitutional validity'.[317]

Heydon J in dissent was forceful in his criticism of the majority approach. It is worth quoting from his judgment at length because he illustrates how an ill-defined power may at the same time grow and yet become more difficult for the courts to review. His Honour described the potential for abuse of nationhood power in this way:

> *No constitutional warrant.* Secondly, there is no constitutional warrant for the supposed power to deal with a national fiscal emergency. There is no express warrant for it. The claim that it exists is entirely novel. Its existence is doubtful because of its potential for abuse. Let it be assumed that, whatever conclusions historians writing in the future may come to, the current economic crisis is as severe as the special case says … the present age is one of 'emergencies', 'crises', 'dangers' and 'intense difficulties', of 'scourges' and other problems. They relate to things as diverse as terrorism, water shortages, drug abuse, child abuse, poverty, pandemics, obesity, and global warming, as well as global financial affairs. In relation to them, the public is endlessly told, 'wars' must be waged, 'campaigns' conducted, 'strategies' devised and 'battles' fought. Often these problems are said to arise suddenly and unexpectedly … Even if only a very narrow power to deal with an emergency on the scale of the global financial crisis

---

315 Ibid 92.
316 Ibid 121.
317 Ibid 122.

were recognised, it would not take long before constitutional lawyers and politicians between them managed to convert that power into something capable of almost daily use. The great maxim of governments seeking to widen their constitutional powers would be: 'Never allow a crisis to go to waste'.

Definitional difficulties. Thirdly, it is far from clear what, for constitutional purposes, the meanings of the words 'crises' and 'emergencies' would be. It would be regrettable if the field were one in which the courts deferred to, and declined to substitute their judgment for the opinion of the Executive or the legislature. That would be to give an 'unexaminable' power to the Executive, and history has shown, as Dixon J said, that it is often the Executive which engages in the unconstitutional supersession of democratic institutions. On the other hand, if the courts do not defer to the Executive or the legislature, it would be difficult for the courts to assess what is within and what is beyond power. It is a difficulty which suggests that the power to deal with national fiscal emergencies does not exist.[318]

If one puts the lack of precise basis for nationhood power in the context of the use of force by the ADF, then Heydon J's concern for unconstitutionality becomes more telling. It is confronting to think that members of the ADF might be asked to take to the streets with the potential to use lethal force on the basis of a power that is so open to question, as occurred with young soldiers with high-powered automatic weapons on the streets in Bowral in 1978.[319] It is very difficult to reconcile with the principle of legality that the 'power should be clear in proportion as the power is exorbitant'.[320]

Twomey shared Heydon J's concern in criticising *Pape* in this way:

> The major problem with the *Pape* case is that the majority relied on an implied executive nationhood power without giving adequate justification for that reliance and without clearly explaining how that power is to be implied from the text and structure of the *Constitution,* and what limits necessarily apply to it. There is little more in the judgments than bald assertions and references back to prior judgments that themselves fail adequately to ground such an implied power in the *Constitution*.[321]

---

318 Ibid 193.
319 Hope, above n 284, 'Appendix 9: Opinion of Sir Victor Windeyer, KBE, CB, DSO on Certain Questions Concerning the Position of Members of the Defence Force When Called Out to Aid the Civil Power', 279.
320 *Entick v Carrington* (1765) 19 St Tr 1030, 1066.
321 Anne Twomey, 'Pushing the Boundaries of Executive Power – *Pape*, the Prerogative and Nationhood Powers' (2010) 34(1) *Melbourne University Law Review* 314, 342.

1. WHAT IS EXECUTIVE POWER?

She went on to note 'the inherent dangers involved in vague, undefined executive powers'.[322] Kerr echoed these sentiments in respect of both the *Tampa Case*[323] and *Pape*[324] in this way:

> If the *Tampa Case* and *Pape* are correct, the Governor-General has undefined arbitrary and discretionary non-statutory powers not known to the prerogative. Taken to their logical conclusion, such cases challenge an aspect of the premise of secure constitutionalism. That aspect is the subjection of the executive to limits imposed by law.[325]

Gerangelos was also critical, asking:

> How is one to determine such a vague and amorphous power in the abstract, without essential resort to the prerogative and historical experience? ... [A]n 'inherent content' view of s 61 cannot be sustained. If one relies on criteria based on 'national' imperatives alone, and without reference to the common law, resort will invariably be had to purely policy considerations.[326]

It is for this reason that this book argues for a very limited scope for nationhood power. Although not a nationhood power case, it may also be that these concerns led to the more conservative approach to executive power in *Williams*.[327]

D Characteristics of Nationhood Power

This survey of the cases suggests a few key characteristics of nationhood power.

1 An Inherent Executive and Legislative Power?

Nationhood power appears clearly to be an inherent executive power. It is cast as being inherent in the existence of Australia as a nation, and in the Commonwealth as the government for the nation. Virtually any

---

322 Ibid.
323 (2001) 110 FCR 491.
324 (2009) 238 CLR 1.
325 Duncan Kerr, 'The High Court and the Executive: Emerging Challenges to the Underlying Doctrines of Responsible Government and the Rule of Law' (2009) 28(2) *University of Tasmania Law Review* 145, 180.
326 Gerangelos, 'The Executive Power of the Commonwealth of Australia', above n 14.
327 (2012) 248 CLR 156. As discussed above, ironically, Heydon J advocated a more expansive view of executive power there, but, apparently, on the basis that the authorities supported such a view in respect of Commonwealth executive power being as extensive as Commonwealth legislative power, at 319.

executive power has to be inherent or implied as s 61 does not describe the executive power of the Commonwealth, rather it only states its existence. Nationhood power goes beyond prerogative power though, in that it does not derive from historical prerogative powers but from the nature of the *Constitution* itself. There appears to be less concern, surprisingly, with nationhood power as an executive power than there does with it as a legislative power. This may be because the nationhood power cases in the High Court have primarily focused upon legislative power. The *Tampa Case*[328] is exceptional as an executive power case but it did not reach the High Court. Even *Pape*[329] dealt with the *Tax Bonus Act* and not executive power alone.

As to the future of nationhood power, the legislative aspect may now be more contained, being confined to a combination of s 61 and s 51(xxxix) rather than being inherent. Gummow, Crennan and Bell JJ in *Pape* appeared to describe the relationship between the two heads of power as it now stands:

> In determining whether the *Bonus Act* is supported by s 61 and s 51(xxxix) of the *Constitution*, it is necessary to ask whether determining that there is the need [which] falls within executive power and then to ascertain whether s 51(xxxix) of the *Constitution* supports the impugned legislation as a law which is incidental to that exercise of executive power.[330]

The executive power of the Commonwealth is still quite imprecise though, and, for this reason, concerning. If the High Court had a purely executive power case before it, particularly one that was more coercive than facultative, it might be more concerned with the implications of nationhood power as executive power. This would be consistent with its more constrained approach to executive power generally in *Williams*.[331]

2 A Facultative Power

Nationhood power finds strongest support as a facultative power; that is, a power to promote, encourage or enable certain activities of a national character. This is usually linked to a spending power so that there is virtually no regulatory function or intrusion into the affairs of the States. This first

---

328 (2001) 110 FCR 491.
329 (2009) 238 CLR 1.
330 Ibid 89.
331 (2012) 248 CLR 156.

appears most clearly in the *AAP Case*,[332] where the various judgments of Barwick CJ, Mason J and Jacobs J gave examples of such things as the CSIRO and exploration as possible activities which nationhood power would support.[333] Brennan J took this further in *Davis v Commonwealth* to not just spending powers but matters such as a flag and an anthem. This facultative aspect of the power is less concerning.

3 A Coercive, Purposive Power

The High Court has expressed most concern with regard to the coercive aspect of nationhood power. In the *Tasmanian Dam Case*[334] Wilson J[335] and Deane J[336] rejected a coercive aspect to the power. Mason CJ, Deane and Gaudron JJ did accept a limited coercive aspect to the power in *Davis v Commonwealth*,[337] but made it clear that nationhood power was a purposive power subject to the requirements of proportionality. Even in *Pape*, French CJ stated, as partly quoted above:

> Future questions about the application of the executive power to the control or regulation of conduct or activities under coercive laws, absent authority supplied by a statute made under some head of power other than s 51(xxxix) alone are likely to be answered conservatively. They are likely to be answered bearing in mind the cautionary words of Dixon J in the *Communist Party Case*: 'History and not only ancient history, shows that in countries where democratic institutions have been unconstitutionally superseded, it has been done not seldom by those holding executive power. Forms of government may need protection from dangers likely to arise from within the institutions to be protected'.[338]

It is the coercive power which creates the most concern for this book as well, and is a theme to which it will return.

E The Approach of this Book to Nationhood Power

It may be attractive for reasons of national sentiment to locate the source of executive power in s 61; which does not rely upon the prerogative powers of the Crown even if it can be informed by them. Independent

---

332 (1975) 134 CLR 338.
333 Ibid 337, 362, 397, 412–13.
334 (1983) 158 CLR 1.
335 Ibid 203.
336 Ibid 252.
337 (1988) 166 CLR 79.
338 *Pape* (2009) 238 CLR 1, 24.

nationhood as a broad concept appears to be the frame of reference for the current majority of the High Court in understanding s 61. As Gummow, Crennan and Bell JJ put it in *Pape*:

> The Executive Government is the arm of government capable of and empowered to respond to a crisis be it war, natural disaster or a financial crisis on the scale here. This power has its roots in the executive power exercised in the United Kingdom up to the time of the adoption of the *Constitution* but in form today in Australia it is a power to act on behalf of the federal polity.[339]

The difficulty is that such an approach may suit nonviolent issues such as the Bicentennial[340] or even the Global Financial Crisis,[341] but the use of armed force in British history has profoundly shaped Westminster constitutionalism itself.[342] It is hard to understand why this weight of legal history should not fully be brought to bear on such profound constitutional questions as raised by the use of the ADF under executive power. This is especially so as the arguments in favour of relying upon s 61 alone rest primarily upon nationalism in a nation with so little history of independent military action. It is also difficult to embrace a s 61 approach when leading writers such as Winterton,[343] Evans,[344] Twomey[345] and Kerr[346] have criticised or questioned it; when Heydon J was so critical of it in *Pape*;[347] and, in the same case, a leading proponent of this approach, French CJ, made his statement on future questions on nationhood power being 'likely to be answered conservatively'. His invocation of Dixon J's famous statement on threats from within the executive could not be more telling for this book. The use of military power on such a questionable basis, especially internally, seems contrary to the principle of legality and the very spirit of constitutional government. This book will argue, then, that 'nationhood power', relying upon s 61 alone and 'absent authority

---

339 Ibid 89. See also *CPCF* [2015] HCA 1 [42] (French CJ); *M68* [2016] HCA 1 [41] (French CJ, Kiefel and Nettle JJ), [201] (Keane J).
340 *Davis v Commonwealth* (1988) 166 CLR 79.
341 *Pape* (2009) 238 CLR 1.
342 Brennan and Toohey JJ describe this history and emphasise its importance in *Re Tracey; Ex parte Ryan* (1989) 166 CLR 518, 556–2 ('*Re Tracey*') where they consider the place of the military within the constitutional settlement in the 17th century as central to understanding that settlement.
343 Winterton, 'The Limits and Use of Executive Power by Government', above n 73, 426–33.
344 Evans, 'The Rule of Law, Constitutionalism and the MV Tampa' above n 187, 98; Evans, 'Continuity and Flexibility: Executive Power in Australia', above n 45, 123.
345 Twomey, 'Pushing the Boundaries of Executive Power', above n 321, 339–43.
346 Kerr, above n 325, 177–8.
347 (2009) 238 CLR 1, 177–93.

supplied by statute', must only be a basis of last resort in authorising action by the ADF.³⁴⁸ Such action must first find its basis in one of the previously recognised prerogatives.

There may be a basis to use the ADF under nationhood power where there is no prerogative available, but this is likely to be only in circumstances where the English character of the prerogative cannot operate within Australia's distinct constitutional arrangements. This is best illustrated by an example. If an earthquake and tsunami were to level Hobart and the Tasmanian State Government ceased to be effective, the Commonwealth Executive, in the form of the ADF, could arguably step in to restore its functioning. Commonwealth action might include maintaining public order and delivering essential services until the State services could do this again themselves.³⁴⁹ This is essentially what occurred in Darwin after Cyclone Tracy in 1974 but, as that was in a Territory, different constitutional considerations applied.³⁵⁰

Prerogative would not readily provide for this because the prerogative did not develop in contemplation of a federal constitution. As Chapter 4 will discuss, under the federal division of executive power, the prerogative for a government to restore order must rest primarily with the States because there is no equivalent legislative power for the Commonwealth to restore order. The Commonwealth, arguably, may act to protect its own functions³⁵¹ but this power does not extend to restoring State government functions. Yet, if a State government effectively collapsed, it would self-evidently be beyond its power to restore itself. It is likely that the ability to restore the Tasmanian State Government would then be 'peculiarly within the capacity and resources of the Commonwealth Government'.³⁵² A 'nationhood power' reading of s 61 authorising the 'maintenance of the *Constitution*'³⁵³ would support this because having functioning States is fundamental to the *Constitution*, as well as having

---

348 Ibid 24.
349 See Michael Eburn, 'Responding to Catastrophic Natural Disasters and the Need for Commonwealth Legislation' (2011) 10(3) *Canberra Law Review* 81, 82, 91; Joe McNamara, 'The Commonwealth Response to Cyclone Tracy: Implications for Future Disasters' (2012) 27(2) *The Australian Journal of Emergency Management* 37.
350 Eburn, above n 349, 83, 90.
351 *R v Sharkey* (1949) 79 CLR 121, 151 quoting Quick and Garran's *Annotated Constitution of the Australian Commonwealth*, above n 72, 194 (Dixon J). Zines supports this view in Zines, 'The Inherent Executive Power of the Commonwealth', above n 7, 289.
352 *Pape* (2009) 238 CLR 1, 63.
353 *Williams* (2012) 248 CLR 156, 184–5 (French CJ).

some basis in the text of the provision itself.[354] Such an approach would also be consistent with a view that preserving the States is implicit in s 119, which obliges the Commonwealth to protect them from 'invasion and violence'.[355] Restoring a State government is also, arguably, a more facultative application of nationhood power, although it may possibly have a very limited coercive aspect to it which would be in proportion to the purpose of the intervention. This example should illustrate that there is a place for nationhood power to support ADF action but it should only be in an extreme case and where prerogative power cannot operate due to Australia's distinct constitutional structure.

VI Conclusion

The range of sources of executive power and their imprecision bear out Mason J's view that executive power is not 'amenable to exhaustive definition',[356] and also reflect the character of executive power as an original and residual element of governmental power. It also reflects the theoretical position that executive power is meant to respond to contingency, *Fortuna*. It can address issues of governmental responsibility for which the judiciary and legislature are not suited. When this imprecise yet extensive power is the main authority for the control and exercise of military power, the implications are significant. Executive power,

---

354 Chordia, Lynch and Williams appear to suggest that, based upon the judgments of Jacobs J and Mason J in the *AAP Case* (1975) 134 CLR 338, this might be all nationhood power was meant to be, above n 152, 33–4. Twomey, above n 321, 332–4, argues that there is a prerogative power of self-protection relying upon *Burmah Oil Co Ltd v Lord Advocate* [1965] AC 75 ('*Burmah Oil*') and so there is no need for a nationhood power source of authority. She does not cite a pinpoint reference in the case, however, and it is difficult to see how it could be authority for a federal government to intervene in a State to protect its own functions. If there can have been no new prerogatives since 1689, when there was no contemplation of a federal Commonwealth of Australia, it is difficult to see how prerogative power could authorise Commonwealth intervention in a State to protect Commonwealth or State functions. For this reason it is, arguably, preferable to refer to the text of s 61 itself, a nationhood power approach, for the source of authority.
355 As Chapter 4 will discuss, this is the quid pro quo for the State's handing over their existing naval and military forces, and the power to raise them in the future, to the Commonwealth under *Constitution* ss 69, 'Transfer of Certain Departments', 51(vi) 'Power to Make Laws … with Respect to the naval and military defence of the Commonwealth and of the several States …' and s 114 'States may not raise forces'. Selway argues that 'the Commonwealth Constitution is predicated upon, and requires the cooperation of, the States and the Commonwealth to a much greater degree than is the case in either Canada or the United States', in Bradley Selway, 'Horizontal and Vertical Assumptions within the Commonwealth Constitution' (2001) 12 *Public Law Review* 113, 114.
356 *Davis v Commonwealth* (1988) 166 CLR 79, 93.

perhaps rather than being a source of power in itself, is actually a general description for power exercised by the executive branch of government, as it derives from several sources.

From this assessment of the sources of the executive power of the Commonwealth, and an appreciation of the theory of executive power as being able to respond to *Fortuna,* this book will argue that its limits are as follows:

1. The federal structure of the *Constitution*. Executive power cannot alter the federal character of the *Constitution*;
2. The separation of powers itself. Executive power cannot normally be the basis for an exercise of the powers of the legislature or judiciary;
3. Following point 2, relevant legislation (although statutory grants of power are mainly relevant to this book as a guide to the limit of executive power);
4. Military subordination to the civilian government (which Chapter 2 will consider but which follows from the principles considered in this chapter);
5. Necessity—the above limitations can temporarily be overcome by necessity. Where necessity requires, a particular executive power can provide power where no other power is available, but only for the period of time required to meet that need. Where Parliament has provided the same power—that is, 'covered the field'—through legislation, then necessity would only justify action where the prerogative power (or possibly nationhood power) in question inherently concerned extraordinary circumstances. It would be necessary to look to the nature of such prerogative powers as those with respect to martial law, war or internal security, or possibly nationhood power as well in respect of internal security, to determine when to rely upon them instead of statutory power;
6. The written *Constitution*, including that:
    a. Executive power cannot effect an enduring change to the *Constitution*;[357]

---

[357] See *Republic of Fiji Islands v Prasad* (Unreported, Fiji Court of Appeal, Casey J (Presiding), Barker, Kapi, Ward and Handley JJA, 1 March 2001) ('*Prasad*') discussed in Chapter 3.

b. The sphere of Commonwealth legislative responsibility and the limits of the Commonwealth's power as a legal person. Executive power cannot exceed the legislative competence of the Commonwealth Parliament, and post *Williams*,[358] does not simply extend to doing anything which the Commonwealth legislature could authorise it to do or any legal person could do;

c. The express constitutional office holders as applicable, for example, where power must be exercised by the Governor-General or the Queen as required. It is unlikely that necessity could ever justify altering these constitutional offices by executive power.

This book will proceed to analyse the exercise of specific prerogative powers by the ADF within this framework of limitations. It will elaborate on the concept of necessity in particular.

To assist the reader, the following definitions used for the purpose of this book may assist:

- Executive power—this will normally mean nonstatutory executive power unless the context indicates otherwise;
- Principle of legality—the principle that any exercise of governmental power must have an authority in law;
- *Fortuna*—the capricious nature of fortune, the unexpected or contingency;
- Necessity—is defined by the particular prerogative, nationhood or ordinary citizens' power to which it relates.

---

358 (2012) 248 CLR 156.

2

The Australian Defence Force within the Executive

> If the legislative power enacts, not from year to year, but forever, on the raising of public funds, it runs the risk of losing its liberty ... The same is true if the legislative power enacts, not from year to year, but forever, about the land and sea forces, which it should entrust to the executive power.[1]

I Introduction

Right at the beginning of the constitutional and legal tradition which Australia has inherited, William I gained and maintained the Crown of England through force of arms; and military power remains at the heart of executive power.[2] In the Westminster system, despite nearly 1,000

---

1   Charles de Secondat, Baron de Montesquieu, *The Spirit of the Laws* (Anne Cohler, Basia Miller and Harold Stone trans and eds, Cambridge University Press, 1989) Book 11, Ch 6, 156–7 [trans of *De L'Esprit de Lois* (first published 1748)] 164–5.
2   Papua New Guinea Constitutional Planning Committee, *Report* (1974) <http://www.paclii.org/pg/CPCReport/main.htm> discusses this point in Chapter 13 'The Disciplined Forces', [1]. Article 2 of *Magna Carta 1215* (Imp) refers to earls and barons holding their tenancy in chief from the Crown by military service. See *NSW v Commonwealth* (1975) 135 CLR 337, 489 ('*Seas and Submerged Lands Case*') Jacobs J, on the prerogative power of the Crown extending as far as the Crown was able to assert it. See also J H Baker, *An Introduction to English Legal History*, (Butterworths, 2nd ed, 1979) 12–15; John Gillingham, 'The Early Middle Ages 1066–1290' in Kenneth Morgan (ed), *The Oxford Illustrated History of Britain* (Oxford University Press, 1984), 104; and Elizabeth Wicks, *The Evolution of a Constitution: Eight Key Moments in British Constitutional History* (Hart, 2006) 3–6 on the constitutional and political history of this period.

years of constitutional development in limiting executive power, there is still a uniquely direct relationship between government and militaries. Military power underlies the integrity of the state and the existence of government.[3] Dicey recognised

> the common law right of the Crown and its servants to repel force by force in the case of an invasion, riot, or generally of any violent resistance to the law. This right, or power, is essential to the very existence of orderly government, and is most assuredly recognised in the most ample manner by the law of England.[4]

The constitutional challenge has been to harness military power to underwrite governmental power whilst ensuring that such military power remains under the control of government.

This chapter considers the relationship between the ADF and executive power. It seeks to establish how executive power is transmitted to the ADF and how the ADF is then made subordinate to the civilian government. It draws a distinction between the ADF as a part of the executive branch of the Commonwealth Government, and the exercise of executive power inside the ADF. It will consider the historical factors which have shaped the current constitutional relationship between the executive government and the ADF. This chapter will then address the consequences of this prerogative authority for the relationship between the ADF and the Parliament, as well as the executive government and the judiciary. It will also consider the awkward interaction between the ADF and the power of the States, being a result of a federal system which historical English principles do not address. This chapter will also address the constitutional relationship between the Crown and members of the ADF.

It is important to see the ADF as a central but distinct part of the executive. It attracts the limits that apply to Commonwealth executive power generally but it also has limits of its own because it is a potential danger to the civilian government which it serves. There is a careful balancing between granting the ADF enough power to perform its function without usurping executive power altogether. The tension within this balancing informs every aspect of the exercise of executive power by the ADF. This discussion, therefore, underpins the remaining chapters.

---

3   See W F Finlason, *Commentaries upon Martial Law, with Special Reference to its Regulation and Restraint* (Stevens, 1867) 74.
4   A V Dicey, *Introduction to the Study of the Law of the Constitution* (Macmillan, 10th ed, 1959) 288.

The chapter will conclude that, whilst there is considerable history behind these constitutional relationships, they are still uncertain and not well understood in some respects. This is perhaps because of their centuries-old character and the relatively recent development of Australia as an independent actor in defence matters. Australia's defining legend is that of ANZAC.[5] The Gallipoli campaign from which it grew and campaigns before the East Timor intervention in 1999 mostly involved citizens in uniform, that is to say, personnel who served for a particular war or intervention as volunteers or conscripts but, mostly, not for a career.[6] Until 1999, Australia also always participated in these campaigns as a junior participant in a bigger force. East Timor was the first major campaign with Australia as the lead nation and with an all-professional contingent of personnel.[7] Arguably then, Australia has not really had to address issues around the constitutional relationship between the military and the executive very often at all. The primary focus on providing citizen forces to fight overseas as part of larger United Kingdom or United States forces has had the result that, when the courts have occasionally addressed these issues, they have tended to apply the inherited English principles without much adaptation.

II The Underlying Danger

The warning of Dixon J, repeated by French CJ and quoted in Chapter 1 is worth repeating here because it points to the underlying danger of executive power to a constitutional democracy, as well as the fact that this danger has been of enduring concern in the High Court. Dixon J stated in *Australian Communist Party v Commonwealth* ('*Communist Party Case*') in 1951:

---

5   See discussion in Marilyn Lake, 'Introduction: What Have You Done for Your Country?', in Marilyn Lake, Henry Reynolds, Mark McKenna and Joy Damousi (eds), *What's Wrong with Anzac? The Militarisation of Australia's History* (University of New South Wales Press, 2010) v, vii–viii; Henry Reynolds, 'Are Nations Really Made in War?' in Marilyn Lake, Henry Reynolds, Mark McKenna and Joy Damousi (eds), *What's Wrong with Anzac? The Militarisation of Australia's History* (University of New South Wales Press, 2010) 1, 1–23.
6   Peter Dennis, Jeffrey Grey, Ewan Morris and Robin Prior, *The Oxford Companion to Australian Military History* (Oxford University Press, 2nd ed, 2008) 155–60.
7   Ibid 191–3.

> History and not only ancient history, shows that in countries where democratic institutions have been unconstitutionally superseded, it has been done not seldom by those holding the executive power. Forms of government may need protection from dangers likely to arise from within the institutions to be protected.[8]

French CJ quoted this statement in *Pape v Commissioner of Taxation* after stating that:

> Future questions about the application of the executive power to the control or regulation of conduct or activities under coercive laws, absent authority supplied by a statute made under some head of power other than s 51(xxxix) alone, are likely to be answered conservatively. They are likely to be answered bearing in mind the cautionary words of Dixon J.[9]

Cases in recent years in the courts of Australia's near neighbours amply illustrate the issue. The Fijian military has staged four coups d'état against democratically elected civilian governments since 1987, two in 1987, one in 2000 and another in 2006.[10] In 2009, the President of Fiji abrogated the constitution altogether and installed a military government under an extraconstitutional legal order.[11] The 2001 case of *Republic of Fiji Islands v Prasad* ('*Prasad*')[12] considered the question of when the military could stand lawfully in the place of the elected government, and also when it had acted unconstitutionally. The 'Sandline' affair in Papua New Guinea in 1997 saw the civilian government contract with a mercenary company, Sandline International, to quell the separatist uprising in Bougainville Province. The then Papua New Guinea Defence Force commander, Brigadier Singirok, made an address to the nation calling on the civilian government to resign and ordered Operation Rausim Kwik, which

---

8   *Australian Communist Party v Commonwealth* (1951) 83 CLR 1, 187 ('*Communist Party Case*').
9   (2009) 238 CLR 1, 24 ('*Pape*').
10 *Constitution of the Sovereign Democratic Republic of Fiji (Promulgation) Decree 1990* (Fiji) ch XIV; *Republic of Fiji Islands v Prasad* (Unreported, Fiji Court of Appeal, Casey J (Presiding), Barker, Kapi, Ward and Handley JJA, 1 March 2001) ('*Prasad*'); *Immunity (Fiji Military Government Intervention) Promulgation 2007* (Fiji).
11 *Decree No 1 Fiji Constitution Amendment Act 1997 Revocation Decree 2009* (10 April 2007); *Decree No 2 Executive Authority of Fiji Decree 2009* (10 April 2009).
12 *Prasad*, (Unreported, Fiji Court of Appeal, Casey J (Presiding), Barker, Kapi, Ward and Handley JJA, 1 March 2001); See discussion of this case in George Williams, 'The Case That Stopped a Coup? The Rule of Law and Constitutionalism in Fiji' (2001) 1(1) *Oxford University Commonwealth Law Journal* 73; and for a critical perspective, Michael Head, 'A Victory for Democracy? An Alternative Assessment of *Fiji v Prasad*' (2001) 2(2) *Melbourne Journal of International Law* 535.

apprehended the mercenaries.[13] This had a destabilising effect, soldiers rioted outside Parliament and the Defence Force faced mutiny within its ranks. These events were, inter alia, the subject of proceedings in 1997 in *State v Enuma*[14] and in 2002 in *State v Dege*.[15] Papua New Guinea came very close to losing a constitutional relationship between the civilian government and the military. As Sevua J said of the Sandline affair in the Court Martial matter of *State v Enuma*,[16] 'Operation Rausim Kwik … almost brought constitutional and parliamentary democracy to their knees'. Remarkably Papua New Guinea addressed these issues through the courts. These events were near to Australia and relatively recent in time. They amply illustrate Dixon J's point.

Militaries can be the ultimate guarantee of the rule of law and also pose its greatest threat. The extended use of executive power through the military, with its potential arbitrariness, is contrary to the idea of the rule of law. Conversely, in some cases only the extended use of executive power through the military can preserve the rule of law. The relationship, then, between civilian governments and their militaries has to be a careful balance between effective military power and subjection to lawful authority.

A The 17th Century and the English Constitution

The events of the 17th century and their effect on the English Constitution are central to understanding the place of the ADF within the executive government today. Seventeenth-century England saw the reign of Charles I, the English Civil War of 1642 to 1651, the following period of rule by the Cromwells and the brief and troubled reign of James II. The Glorious Revolution in which Parliament gave the crown to William and Mary on terms finally quieted much of this upheaval.[17] The spectre of that bloody period in English history hides behind much of the current constitutional relationship between executive, Parliament and judiciary in Britain and Australia, and it has a particular presence in the relationship of each of those

---

13   *State v Singirok* [2004] N2501; *State v Singirok* [2004] PGNC 253; *In the Matter of an Application by Paul Tupuru* [2005] PGNC 162.
14   *State v Enuma* [1997] PGNC 171.
15   *State v Dege* [2002] PGMCJ 1.
16   *State v Enuma* [1997] PGNC 171, 173.
17   *Re Tracey; Ex parte Ryan* (1989) 166 CLR 518, 554–8 ('*Re Tracey*'); Charles Clode, *The Administration of Justice under Military and Martial Law: As Applicable to the Army, Navy, Marines and Auxiliary Forces* (John Murray, 2nd ed, 1874) 1–20; S B Chrimes, *English Constitutional History* (Oxford University Press, 4th ed, 1967) 100–20.

branches of government to the ADF. The 1989 High Court of Australia case of *Re Tracey; Ex parte Ryan* ('*Re Tracey*')[18] places much emphasis on the discipline legislation applying to the ADF having its provenance in the *Bill of Rights 1688* (Imp)[19] and the *Mutiny Act 1689* (Imp).[20] Importantly, military discipline law could not displace the application of civilian law because the *Petition of Right 1628* (Eng),[21] established that civilian law applies to military personnel as much as it applies to civilians. As Brennan and Toohey JJ put it in *Re Tracey*:

> True it is that, by the time of federation, the scope of naval and military law and of the special jurisdictions to enforce that law were governed by statute but the provisions of those Acts, especially the *Army Act* [the successor to the *Mutiny Act*] reflected the resolution of major constitutional controversies.[22]

1 The *Petition of Right 1628*

The *Petition of Right 1628* (Eng) was the first significant enduring constitutional development of the 17th century. Charles I in 1625, the first year of his reign, had issued a Commission to the Lord Marshal and Sergeant-Major of the Army, along with 23 other 'Commissioners', to punish 'soldiers and other dissolute persons … for robberies, felonies, mutinies, or other outrages or misdemeanours which, by Martial Law, ought to be punished by death'. The Commission authorised 'by summary course, as used in Armies in time of War' to put them to death 'for an example of terror to others, and to keep the rest in due awe and obedience'.[23] It also required the erection of gallows or gibbets for the execution of offenders in open view. It excluded most of the jurisdiction of the common-law courts.[24]

---

18 *Re Tracey* (1989) 166 CLR 518, 556–62.
19 1 Wm & M, sess 2 c 2 s6.
20 Ibid c 5.
21 3 Car 1 cl I.
22 *Re Tracey* (1989) 166 CLR 518, 562.
23 See Clode, *The Administration of Justice under Military and Martial Law*, above n 17, 4–5.
24 Ibid. Brennan and Toohey JJ placed great weight upon Clode as an authority in this area in *Re Tracey* (1989) 166 CLR 518, 555.

The *Petition of Right* was a parliamentary attempt to reassert the jurisdiction of the common law and provided that

> the aforesaid commissions for proceeding by Martial Law may be revoked and annulled; and that hereafter no commissions of like nature may issue forth to any person or persons whatsoever to be executed as aforesaid.[25]

Any trials and executions had to be by 'the laws and statutes of the land', and without exemption for those subject to martial law by virtue of being soldiers.[26] According to Clode, a subsequent commission from Charles I, in broadly similar terms to that of 1625, was held to be illegal.[27] From that time on, martial law under the authority of royal prerogative has been considered illegal in England, apart from when James II authorised the extension of the *Articles of War* to the civilian population for a brief period during the Duke of Monmouth's rebellion in 1685.[28] Given the constitutional consequences of James II's reign discussed below, this should be taken as an exceptional instance. William III gave a commission for martial law in Ireland[29] and martial law has existed at various times in other parts of the empire.[30] The *Petition of Right* nonetheless established the constitutional principle that martial law was not part of the law of England as applicable to the civilian population, and that it was not a basis for exemption of military personnel from the jurisdiction of the civilian courts.[31]

2 The Glorious Revolution—the *Bill of Rights 1688* and the *Mutiny Act 1689*

There was further bloodshed and constitutional turmoil in England between the enactment of the *Petition of Right* and the next significant legislative development in the control of military forces. This included the civil war between parliamentary and royal forces, the execution of Charles

---

25 Cited in Clode, above n 17, 6.
26 For the parliamentary proceedings on the petition see Henry I, *Coronation Charter*, (1100) in Carl Stephenson and Frederick George Marcham (eds and trans), *Sources of English Constitutional History: A Selection of Documents from AD 600 to the Present* (Harper and Brothers, 1937) 453–4.
27 Clode, above n 17, 6–8, 53.
28 Ibid.
29 Ibid 8.
30 See R W Kostal, *A Jurisprudence of Power: Victorian Empire and the Rule of Law* (Oxford, 2005), referred to in detail in Chapter 3; and also Military Board, *Australian Edition of Manual of Military Law* (CAGP, 1941) 3–5.
31 *Re Tracey* (1989) 166 CLR 518, 558–9; W S Holdsworth, 'Martial Law Historically Considered' (1902) 18 *Law Quarterly Review* 117, 120; see also reference by Gageler J in *M68* [2016] HCA 1 [155]–[157].

I on 30 January 1649, the Cromwellian interregnum, the restoration of Charles II on 29 May 1660, and the brief reign of James II from 1685.[32] James II's conflict with Parliament led eventually to his forceful overthrow and the invitation by Parliament to William and Mary to take the throne in 1688.[33] Against this background, Parliament enacted the *Bill of Rights 1688* primarily to grant the throne to William and Mary upon terms, but also to prohibit the existence of a standing army without parliamentary authority. It made a clear link between abuses of power by the Crown and the maintenance of a standing army, reciting:

> Whereas the late King James the Second, by the assistance of divers evil counsellors, judges, and Ministers employed by him, did endeavour to subvert and extirpate the Protestant religion and the laws and liberties of the kingdom. [among other things]
>
> 5. By raising and keeping a standing army within this kingdom in time of peace without the consent of parliament and quartering soldiers contrary to the law.
>
> 6. By causing several good subjects, being Protestants, to be disarmed at the same time when papists were both armed and employed contrary to the law.

The following year Parliament passed the *Mutiny Act 1689* to authorise the existence of a standing army whilst requiring and enabling the Crown to keep its forces in good discipline, providing:

> whereas it is judged necessary by their majesties and this present parliament that during this time of danger several of the forces which are now on foot should be continued and others raised for the safety of the kingdom ... and whereas no man may be forejudged of life or limb, or subjected to any kind of punishment by martial law, or in any other manner than by the judgment of his peers and according to the known and established laws of this realm ... it being requisite for retaining such forces as are or shall be raised during this exigence of affairs in their duty [that] an exact discipline be observed, and that soldiers who shall mutiny or stir up sedition or shall desert their majesties' service be brought to a more exemplary and speedy punishment than the usual forms of law will allow.[34]

---

32 Clode, above n 17.
33 *Bill of Rights 1688* (Imp).
34 Recital. The Crown could still issue Articles of War, which were disciplinary orders based upon prerogative power, in addition to, but not contrary to, the *Mutiny Act*, see Holdsworth, 'Martial Law Historically Considered', above n 31, 122.

Initially this was for six-month periods at a time but eventually became an annual authorisation.[35] (The *Army Act 1881* (Imp) eventually replaced the *Mutiny Act* but reenacted many of the provisions of the earlier Act, including the requirement for annual authorisation of a standing army.[36]) It is important to remember that a standing army was a new development in England in the 17th century. Previously armies had been raised for particular campaigns, essentially on a feudal basis. Given the willingness of monarchs and others to resort to military force to overcome political opposition within the country, it is not surprising that Parliament was concerned to have some control over this new and potentially threatening institution.[37] The Crown still controlled the forces but this was subject to parliamentary approval of their existence in standing form, their funding, and the continued submission of those forces to civilian law and courts, as well as a statutory discipline regime for the army.[38] This is not to say that the balance between Crown and parliamentary control over the military forces or the relationship between military and civilian jurisdiction was settled fully at the end of the 17th century.[39] It is perhaps fairer to say that this period established enduring principles which have continued to develop to the present day.

3 The Naval Exception

There is an important exception to note here with respect to naval forces. The historical concern with military forces was that they posed a threat to civilian government because of the physical power at the military's disposal.[40] Even though there had to be an annual Act of Parliament to authorise the continuance of a standing army, there was no similar requirement for the Royal Navy. Its discipline system was statutory from at least 1682, although there were earlier parliamentary ordinances on the subject.[41] Despite the navy being a powerful standing force that enforced the law against civilians, such as foreign smugglers,[42] it apparently did

---

35 *Mutiny Act 1689* (Eng) s 8.
36 *Re Tracey* (1989) 166 CLR 518, 559.
37 Holdsworth, above n 31, 121–2.
38 Clode, above n 17, 18–21. See also *Re Tracey* (1989) 166 CLR 518, 556.
39 See Peter Twist, 'Limits to the Supreme Command, Government and Disposition of the Armed Forces: *Attorney-General for England and Wales v R*' (2002) *New Zealand Armed Forces Law Review* 43.
40 *Re Tracey* (1989) 166 CLR 518, 554–61.
41 Clode, above n 17, 41–2.
42 See H A Smith, *The Law and Custom of the Sea* (Stevens, 3rd ed, 1959) 27.

not pose the same threat to parliamentary government. As Clode put it, '[T]he history of the Naval Code is written in a few sentences, because it has never been made the subject of parliamentary conflict.'[43]

The obvious distinction between the Royal Navy and the British Army is that the Royal Navy has operated primarily offshore with a focus on external security. It was the 'wooden wall' that protected Britain.[44] This distinction is significant for the ADF, with its joint command of the three services,[45] because the historical concerns about the British Army affect the ADF generally in its presence ashore in Australia, while the contrasting lack of historical concern with the Royal Navy influences the ADF generally in its activities outside Australia and at sea.[46] Chapter 6 will return to this point.

4 Significance for Prerogative Power

Parliament's assertion of authority over the Crown's control of military forces through the *Mutiny Act 1689* still left substantial power in the hands of the Crown to employ and regulate military power without resorting to Parliament.[47] Parliament did not seek the actual command of the military forces. As Lord Lawrence stated in *China Navigation Company, Ltd v Attorney-General* ('*China Navigation*'):[48]

> When Parliament has given its consent to the raising and keeping of the army for the year, it leaves the Crown to exercise its prerogative powers as to the manner in which the army is to be raised and kept and in respect to the disposition and use of the army and the administration of its affairs. The manner in which these powers are exercised is constitutionally subject, like the exercise of other prerogatives, to the advice of the Ministers of the Crown, of whom the one particularly responsible for the army was, until recently, the Secretary of State for War.[49]

---

43 Clode, above n 17, 41. See also Charles Clode, *The Military Forces of the Crown: Their Administration and Government* (John Murray, 1869) 179–80.
44 *Re Tracey* (1989) 166 CLR 518, 561.
45 *Defence Act 1903* (Cth) s 9.
46 Cf in this book Chapter 3 on martial law with Chapter 6 on operations beyond the realm.
47 *Attorney-General v De Keyser's Royal Hotel Ltd* [1920] AC 508 ('*De Keyser's Royal Hotel*'); *Burmah Oil Co Ltd v Lord Advocate* [1965] AC 75 ('*Burmah Oil*').
48 [1932] 2 KB 197.
49 Ibid 228.

Some of the most significant residual power of the Crown today in Australia is still found in the prerogatives that relate closely to the ADF, concerning the armed forces, martial law, internal security, the defence of the realm (also known as the war prerogative), and external affairs. Subsequent chapters will address each of these prerogatives in more detail. It is necessary to mention them here to provide some context for the following discussion of current formal constitutional arrangements for the ADF as part of the executive branch of government.

B Control and Disposition of the Forces

It is important at this point to address first the prerogative as to the control and disposition of the forces as the source of the power of command. It is the authority to determine the organisation, structure, placement, arming and equipment of the ADF. Quick and Garran referred to it as follows:

> The command in chief of the naval and military forces of the Commonwealth is, in accordance with constitutional usage, vested in the Governor-General as the Queen's representative. This is one of the oldest and most honoured prerogatives of the Crown … All matters … relating to the disposition and management of the federal forces will be regulated by the Governor-General with the advice of his ministry.[50]

There is a reasonable body of cases to support this proposition. In *China Navigation*[51] in 1932 the House of Lords found for the Crown in rejecting a demand from a British shipping company to place troops on its ships to protect against pirates. The Crown would only do so upon payment for their services, stating:

> In Chitty's *Prerogatives of the Crown* it is said that 'as the constitution of the country has vested in the King the right to make war or peace, it has necessarily and incidentally assigned to him on the same principles the management of the war; together with various prerogatives which may enable His Majesty to carry it on with effect. Thus the King is at the head of his army and navy, is alone entitled to order their movements, to regulate their internal arrangements, and to diminish, or, during war, increase their numbers, as may seem to His Majesty most consistent with political propriety.'[52]

---

50 John Quick and Robert Garran, *Annotated Constitution of the Australian Commonwealth* (Legal Books, first published 1901, reprint 1995) 701–2, quoted in Charles Sampford and Margaret Palmer, 'The Constitutional Power to Make War' (2009) 18(2) *Griffith Law Review* 350, 354.
51 [1932] 2 KB 197.
52 Ibid 207.

The case went on to refer to the preamble to

> The *Statute Law Revision Act*, 1863 (26 & 27 Vict c 125), [which] left unrepealed that part of the preamble of the Act of 1661, which recited that 'within all His Majesty's realms and dominions, the sole supreme government, command, and disposition of the militia and of all forces by sea and land, and of all forts and places of strength, is, and by the laws of England ever was, the undoubted right of His Majesty, and his Royal predecessors, Kings and Queens of England; and that both, or either of the Houses of Parliament cannot, nor ought not to pretend to the same.'[53]

In 1964 in *Chandler v Director of Public Prosecutions*[54] the House of Lords considered *China Navigation* on the issue of protestors entering a Royal Air Force base without authorisation to prevent aircraft taking off or landing. Lord Devlin stated:

> So long as the Crown maintains armed forces for the defence of the realm, it cannot be in its interest that any part of them should be immobilised … It is by virtue of the Prerogative that the Crown is the head of the armed forces and responsible for their operation.[55]

The House of Lords case of *Council of the Civil Service Unions v Minister for the Civil Service* ('*CCSU Case*')[56] and the New Zealand Court of Appeal case of *Curtis v Minister of Defence*,[57] discussed further below, both followed these cases. While there is no Australian case on the point, the reasoning in these cases would seem no less applicable in Australia. The cases reflect the constitutional compromise of the 17th century, in which Parliament asserted control over criminal and disciplinary jurisdiction, as well as the funding of, the armed forces but left their command to the Crown. This is consistent with the view of the theorists that while Parliament should be deliberative, the executive should be able to act with, as Blackstone put it, 'unanimity, strength, and dispatch.'[58] Despite the increasing encroachment of statute to regulate the ADF, arguably the need to be able to respond to *Fortuna* means that it would never be

---

53   *China Navigation* [1932] 2 KB 197, 215; Blackstone cited the same preamble, *Blackstone's Commentaries with Notes of Reference, to the Constitution and Laws, of the Federal Government of the United States; and of the Commonwealth of Virginia* (1803, Hein Online reproduction), 262–3.
54   [1964] AC 763.
55   Ibid 807. See discussion of this case and control and disposition of the forces generally in Peter Rowe, *Defence: The Legal Implications: Military Law and the Laws of War* (Brassey's, 1987) 3–4.
56   [1985] AC 374, 405–406. ('*CCSU Case*').
57   [2002] 2 NZLR 744, 752 ('*Curtis*').
58   *Blackstone's Commentaries with Notes*, above n 53, 250.

wise, or even possible, to reduce every power required for the effective command of the ADF to statutory provisions. This leads to the question of the constitutional structures for command of the ADF.

III The Relationship of the ADF to the Civilian Government

Formal constitutional arrangements cannot prevent militaries from usurping civilian governments. Militaries usually have the physical power at their disposal to enforce their will against a civilian government, whereas the civilian government can usually only rely on the military for physical power. Formal constitutional arrangements also cannot ensure that a military will do exactly what it is told by a civilian government. They cannot prevent cowardice in the face of an external threat or an excess of force in the face of an internal threat. Formal constitutional arrangements can only ever be part of the way in which civilian governments remain in control of military power and protect themselves against it. Political and military culture, leadership, resources, training and a range of other factors are also relevant to achieving the desired relationship between civilian governments and their militaries.[59] As interesting as these other factors might be, it is not for this chapter to consider them. Its aim now is to examine the formal arrangements to see what they reveal about the structure of that relationship. In some cases it is not possible to know with certainty why arrangements are the way they are but it is possible to advance arguments on their current value. Quick and Garran saw them as defining the Commonwealth as the national government: 'The execution and maintenance of the *Constitution*, the execution and maintenance of the Federal laws, and the Command-in-Chief of the naval and military forces, are the foremost attributes of a national government'.[60]

More than this, these arrangements also entrench the principle of military subordination to the civilian government. In doing so, they subject the military to the principle of legality by making it subject to the Parliament and the judiciary. This in turn counters the threat of abuse of power

---

59   See General Sir John Hackett, *The Profession of Arms* (Macmillan 1983) 173–4. For a discussion of the policy aspects of these issues see Andrew Goldsmith and Bob Lowry 'Security Sector Reform' in the Australian Strategic Policy Institute Special Report (2008) March (12), *Australia and the South Pacific: Rising to the Challenge* 29, 25–41.
60   Quick and Garran, above n 50, 700.

and despotism, which Montesquieu saw as the principle purpose for the separation of powers.[61] That these threats have not really materialised in Australia since Federation suggests that the current arrangements serve their purpose and the principle of military subordination to the elected civilian government is of fundamental value to the constitutional order.

A Command and Command-in-Chief of the Australian Defence Force

There is a clear distinction between the command-in-chief held by the Governor-General and the command vested in the Chief of the Defence Force (CDF). This indicates that the ultimate formal source of authority for military power is with the Crown itself, rather than those who exercise military power on its behalf. There is, nonetheless, a close connection between the Governor-General as the commander-in-chief and the CDF, because the Governor-General appoints the military commander. Effectively, the right to exercise military power is granted by the Commonwealth's highest officer.[62] The historical basis of the power of the Crown originally resting on military power is clearly evident in this arrangement.

Section 68 of the Australian *Constitution* provides that: 'The command in chief of the naval and military forces of the Commonwealth is vested in the Governor-General as the Queen's representative'.

Under s 12 of the *Defence Act 1903* (Cth), the Governor-General may appoint the CDF and the Vice-Chief of the Defence Force, and the provision assumes that this occurs. Section 9 of the *Defence Act* then grants the power of command to the CDF over the ADF. Section 8 of the *Defence Act* gives the Defence Minister 'the general control and administration of the Defence Force' and goes on to require that, in exercising their powers, the CDF and the Secretary of the Department of Defence 'must comply with any directions of the Minister'. It is an explicit function of the Chief

---

61 Montesquieu, above n 1, 155, 157.
62 See George Winterton, 'Who is Our Head of State?' (2004) 48(4) *Quadrant* September 60; George Winterton, 'The Evolving Role of the Governor-General' (2004) 48(3) *Quadrant* March 42. Cf, for a view with which this author does not entirely agree on the basis that the Governor-General holds the residue of prerogative power exercisable in the case of necessity as discussed in Chapter 3 and as occurred in Fiji in 2000, see Mitchell Jones, 'The Governor-General as Commander-in-Chief' (2009) 16(2) *Australian Journal of Administrative Law* 82.

of the Defence Force to advise the Minister upon matters relating to the command of the ADF.[63] The *Defence Act* clearly stops short of granting the Minister the power of command.

Command-in-chief is also placed above the level of the elected government. Command-in-chief is not a portfolio that comes and goes in accordance with the priorities of the government of the day. It exists regardless of the policies of the elected government. Command-in-chief is so important that it rests with the leader of the state itself rather than with the leader of the party that forms government. The commander-in-chief is still obliged to act on the advice of the elected government[64] but, if there is uncertainty as to who the leader of the elected government might be, there is no uncertainty as to who the commander-in-chief is.[65]

The grant of command to the CDF is also precise and unambiguous. There is one military commander who appears to have decisive legal charge over the military, and that commander is accountable to the government. The connection between the government and the person charged with wielding military power on its behalf is direct. This indicates that, whilst there is a separation between the civilian government and the ADF, military power is readily available to the civilian government.

B The Relationship to the Elected Civilian Executive

While the ADF is clearly within the executive branch of government there are other important aspects which separate it from, as well as subordinate it to, the elected civilian government.

1 Subject to Ministerial Control but not Command

The importance of discipline to command, discussed further below, may go some way to explaining the distinctly different power of control given to the Minister for Defence. There is an obligation on the CDF to accept

---

63 *Defence Act 1903* (Cth) s 9(2). See Sampford and Palmer, above n 50, 363–5.
64 *FAI Insurances v Winneke* (1982) 151 CLR 342, 365, which is authority for the proposition that the Governor-General ordinarily should act only upon advice; Constitutional Commission, *Advisory Committee on Executive Government: Issues Paper* (Constitutional Commission, 1986) 10; Quick and Garran, above n 50, 406, as cited in Harold Renfree, *The Executive Power of the Commonwealth of Australia* (Legal Books, 1984) 177; Peter Boyce, *The Queen's Other Realms: The Crown and its Legacy in Australia, Canada and New Zealand* (Federation Press, 2008) 124–35.
65 See Hugh Smith, 'A Certain Maritime Incident and Political-Military Relations' (2002) 46(6) *Quadrant* June 38; Sir Ninian Stephen, 'The Governor-General as Commander in Chief' (1983) 14 *Melbourne University Law Review* 563.

the control or direction of the Minister.[66] This assists the principle of responsible government as the military is accountable to the Minister, who is in turn accountable as a member of the elected government and Parliament.[67] Serving members of the ADF cannot be members of Parliament and only members of Parliament can be Ministers.[68] Civilians, other than the Governor-General, also cannot exercise any power of command over members of the ADF.[69] It follows then that Ministers cannot have a power of command over the ADF. The sanction for failing to comply with Ministerial direction or control is not disciplinary. The remedy apparently available to a Minister would be to ask the Prime Minister to advise the Governor-General as Commander-in-Chief to dismiss or not reappoint a CDF that did not follow Ministerial control or direction.[70] A 2015 amendment to the *Defence Act* effectively took this power from the Minister and gave it to the Prime Minister, although it requires that the Prime Minister receive a report from the Minister about the proposed termination.[71] This would appear to have strengthened the position of the CDF in relation to the Minister but the explanatory memorandum to the Bill introducing the amendment does not explain why this has occurred. Even so, in this way the power of command is linked to executive power, but it is also clear that it is a distinct power.

Why have a military not under the command, but under the control of the responsible civilian Minister? The key effect of this arrangement is to separate the military from the civilian government. A military subject to the command of an elected government Minister could be bound to obey commands which draw the military into internal politics or actions found subsequently to be unlawful.[72] A CDF concerned to avoid this could only refuse the Minister's command under risk of prosecution for disobedience. Where a Minister does not have a power of command, a military commander may refuse a Ministerial direction and offer his or her resignation without being subject to disciplinary sanction.

66 *Defence Act 1903* (Cth) s 8.
67 See Clode, above n 17, 57.
68 *Constitution* ss 44, 64.
69 *Defence Force Discipline Act 1982* (Cth) s 27.
70 *Defence Act 1903* (Cth) s 15.
71 *Defence Legislation Amendment (First Principles) Act 2015* (Cth).
72 On the dangers of this in recent Australian history see Smith, above n 65, 39; Rowe, above n 55, 3–5 for the contrasting position in the United Kingdom, where the Secretary of State for Defence acting through the Defence Council exercises command. On the historical context in the British Army see Robert Blake, 'Great Britain: The Crimean War to the First World War' in Michael Howard (ed) *Soldiers and Governments: Nine Studies in Civil–Military Relations* (Eyre & Spottswoode, 1957) 27–31.

2. THE AUSTRALIAN DEFENCE FORCE WITHIN THE EXECUTIVE

The advantage of a control without command relationship between the Minister and the CDF would appear to be to assert civilian control whilst reducing the potential to draw the military into internal politics or potentially unlawful action.[73]

There have been reports at various times of tension between the Minister and the CDF and some uncertainty surrounding the proper nature of the relationship.[74] Interestingly, in the event of a conflict between the Governor-General and the Minister, the CDF's legal obligation is to the Governor-General. Given that the Governor-General has command-in-chief over the ADF and the CDF's commission as an officer obliges him or her to obey the commands of his or her superiors,[75] the CDF would be obliged to obey the command of the Governor-General even if it conflicted with the direction of the Minister.[76] This would be, perhaps, even more the case where the Governor-General issued a general order to the ADF, for example under the call-out provisions of Part IIIAAA of the *Defence Act*.[77] The *Defence Force Discipline Act 1982* (Cth) s 29 makes it an offence for the CDF, or any member of the ADF, to fail to comply with such a general order. Disobedience or failure to comply by the CDF could also be grounds for summary removal from the position of the CDF, not that any grounds would be required according to *Coutts v Commonwealth* (discussed below).[78] Although s 15 of the *Defence Act* now requires that termination be by notice in writing on the recommendation of the Prime Minister, it does not require the provision of reasons and possibly not even the recommendation of the Prime Minister. Even if the convention is that

---

73 It is also worth noting the contrast with arrangements for Ministerial control of police. Ministerial control of the police is more removed, with Ministers only able to give general directions. Operational decisions rest with the police commander in order to ensure the prosecutorial independence of the police force, eg *Australian Federal Police Act 1979* (Cth) s 37.
74 See Mark Thomson, 'Serving Australia: Control and Administration of the Department of Defence' (2011) *Australian Strategic Policy Institute Special Report* June 41, 8–12, 16–18; Deborah Snow and Cynthia Banham, 'Calling Shots in Defence', *Sydney Morning Herald* 28 February – 1 March 2009 7.
75 'Charge and Command you faithfully to discharge your duty as an officer and to observe and execute all such orders and instructions as you may receive from your superior officers', taken from the author's own commission. *Order-in-Council of the Governor-General* 1 November 1991.
76 *Defence Force Discipline Act* s 27 makes it an offence to disobey a lawful command however a lawful command may only be given by a member of the ADF so it would be unlikely to apply to the situation of a command from a civilian Governor-General to the CDF. See discussion in Michael Head, *Calling out the Troops: The Australian Military and Civil Unrest* (Federation Press, 2009) 130–1, quoting Air Vice Marshal Geoffrey Hartnell, *Canberra Papers on Strategy and Defence No 27* (The Australian National University, Canberra 1983) 88.
77 See, eg, *Defence Act 1903* (Cth) s 51A.
78 *Coutts v Commonwealth* (1985) 157 CLR 91.

the Governor-General must act on advice,[79] formally only the Governor-General can appoint or dismiss the CDF. While the CDF would rightly be concerned at any exercise of powers by the Governor-General which were contrary to Ministerial direction, and should then inform the Minister, it would be for the Minister to advise the Governor-General to take a different course. The CDF would still be obliged to follow the Governor-General's command or order over the Minister's direction until such time as the Governor-General gave a new command or order or terminated the appointment of the CDF.

2 The *Tampa* Affair

The *Tampa* Affair in Australia in 2001 raised questions about the extent of executive power and the ADF's proper relationship with government.[80] The *Border Protection (Validation and Enforcement Powers) Act 2001* (Cth) created a 'validation period', defined in s 4, to be the period between 27 August 2001 and the day the *Act* commenced on 27 September 2001. It applies, according to s 5:

> to any action taken during the validation period by the Commonwealth, or by a Commonwealth officer, or any other person, acting on behalf of the Commonwealth, in relation to:
>
> (a) the MV *Tampa*;
>
> (b) the *Aceng*; or
>
> (c) any other vessel carrying persons in respect of whom there were reasonable grounds for believing that their intention was to enter Australia unlawfully; or
>
> (d) any person who was on board a vessel mentioned in paragraph (a), (b) or (c) at any time during the validation period (whether or not the action was taken while the person was on board the vessel).

---

79 See *FAI Insurances v Winneke* (1982) 151 CLR 342, 365, which is authority for the proposition that the Governor-General ordinarily should act only upon advice; Constitutional Commission, *Advisory Committee on Executive Government: Issues Paper* (Constitutional Commission, 1986) 10; Quick and Garran, above n 50, 406, as cited in Renfree, above n 64, 177; Peter Boyce, above n 64, 124–35.

80 Helen Pringle and Elaine Thompson, 'The Tampa Affair and the Role of the Australian Parliament' (2002) 13(2) *Public Law Review (The Tampa Issue)* 128; Smith, above n 65, 38; Michael White, 'Tampa Incident: Some Subsequent Legal Issues' (2004) 78 *Australian Law Journal* 249; Simon Evans, 'The Rule of Law, Constitutionalism and the MV Tampa' (2002) 13(2) *Public Law Review (The Tampa Issue)* 94, 94–6.

2. THE AUSTRALIAN DEFENCE FORCE WITHIN THE EXECUTIVE

Section 6 of the Act states that all action under s 5 during the validation period 'is taken for all purposes to have been lawful when it occurred'. It then goes on to state that no proceedings, civil or criminal, may be instituted or continued in any court in relation to such action against the Commonwealth, a Commonwealth officer or any person who acted on behalf of the Commonwealth[81] although it preserves the jurisdiction of the High Court under s 75 of the *Constitution*.[82]

This legislation was virtually unprecedented in post-Federation Australia and resembled the type of indemnity Act passed after a period of martial law (the subject of Chapter 3).[83] It arose out of the exceptional events of late 2001 involving the ADF's boarding of the MV *Tampa* and the operations to stop unlawful immigration into North-Western Australia by sea.[84] The *Tampa Case*[85] narrowly determined that the actions in relation to the ADF boarding MV *Tampa* and preventing it landing the hundreds of rescued asylum seekers on board were lawful pursuant to the executive power under s 61 of the *Constitution*.[86] Despite this decision, there was considerable argument that these actions were unlawful.[87] Perhaps reflecting this, the second reading speech in the House of Representatives for the *Border Protection (Validation and Enforcement Powers) Act 2001* was on 18 September 2001, seven days after the decision of the Full Court of the Federal Court in the *Tampa Case*.[88]

The *Act* reflects some uncertainty as to the legality of the actions of the ADF during the period in question. The author welcomed the legislation at the time as appropriate to protect the interests of members of the ADF carrying out apparently lawful orders which came through the normal ADF chain of command from the CDF, following the direction of the

---

81 *Border Protection (Validation and Enforcement) Act 2001* s 7.
82 Ibid s 9.
83 Such as the *Martial Law Indemnity Act* 1854 (Vic). Evans was critical of this legislation as contrary to the values of the rule of law, although conceding that this was not a basis of constitutional invalidity, Evans, 'The Rule of Law, Constitutionalism and the MV Tampa', above n 80, 99–101. Pringle and Thompson saw it as an attack on the judiciary and a relative strengthening of the executive within the separation of powers, above n 80, 142. Either view would support the point that the ADF may have been in a situation it should not have been; that is, involved in internal politics.
84 See Warwick Gately and Cameron Moore, 'Protecting Australia's Maritime Borders: The Operational Aspects' in M Tsamenyi and C Rahman (eds), *Protecting Australia's Maritime Borders: The MV Tampa and Beyond* (Centre for Maritime Policy, 2002) 37.
85 *Ruddock v Vadarlis* (2001) 110 FCR 491 ('*Tampa Case*').
86 Ibid 542.
87 See above n 80.
88 *Tampa Case* (2001) 110 FCR 491. To indicate something of the political atmosphere at the time, in Australia, it was also only six days after the terrorist attacks in the United States of 11 September 2001.

Minister for Defence.[89] Still, the existence of the legislation does raise the question of whether the appropriate balance was struck between the ADF acting properly at the direction of the civilian government and acting unlawfully. There was debate at the time as to whether the actions of the ADF gave the government an electoral advantage in the general election of October 2001.[90] This raises the question whether it crossed the line into involvement in internal politics. If the ADF had done so unlawfully, or even with a concern of doing so unlawfully, it also potentially undermined the principle of legality as well as exposing members of the ADF to personal liability. As discussed in Chapter 1, it has been clear since *Entick v Carrington* that 'one should naturally expect that the law to warrant it should be clear in proportion as the power is exorbitant'.[91]

If the matter was uncertain enough as to need an indemnity Act after the event, then arguably the law was not clear enough to warrant the action. It is open then, to query whether the ADF should have been so willing to carry out the directions of the Minister in circumstances of possible illegality that there was a need for the *Border Protection (Validation and Enforcement Powers) Act 2001*.

The *Tampa* Affair is a modern illustration of the potential for uncertainty in defining limits between political power and military power in the Westminster system generally, and the constitutional relationship between the civilian-elected government in Australia and the ADF in particular. It gave a prominence to the exercise of executive power by the ADF only accentuated by subsequent ADF internal security operations in 2002 and 2003, the subject of Chapter 4, and the ADF's wars in Afghanistan from 2001 and Iraq from 2003, which are the subject of Chapter 5. Given the very significant case to which it gave rise, the *Tampa* Affair, more than any other operation, reveals how an ill-defined executive power can challenge the principle of legality.

---

89   Above n 84. This was a highly publicised political decision of the government, rather than a routine operational decision of the ADF, ibid 523–4.
90   See above n 84.
91   (1765) 19 St Tr 1030.

IV The Relationship of the ADF to the Rest of Government

It is not just the ADF's relationship to the elected civilian government that has implications for the limits on its use of the executive power. The ADF's separate relationships with the Parliament, the States and the judiciary are distinct and also impose limits on the use of executive power by the ADF.

A Parliament

1 Exclusion of Serving Military Personnel from Parliament

As 17th-century principles provide a separation between the civilian government and the ADF, equally they govern the relationship between Parliament and the ADF. The tradition of excluding those holding an office of profit under the Crown from the House of Commons dates from the *Act of Settlement 1701*.[92] It developed, presumably, to prevent the Crown influencing the deliberations of Parliament through inducements to individual members. As mentioned above, no full-time member of the ADF can be a member of Parliament as there is a prohibition in s 44 of the *Constitution* on members of the forces wholly employed by the Commonwealth becoming members of Parliament. Reservists may, therefore, sit but not whilst on full-time military service. This virtually prevents members of the ADF from becoming Ministers as s 64 of the *Constitution* states that a Minister may not hold office for more than three months without becoming a member or senator in the Commonwealth Parliament. The overall effect reflects the historical concern to keep the military out of internal politics.[93] Given the history of the 17th century in England in separating military power from political power, it must be one of the most profound limitations on the use of executive power by the ADF, as it powerfully asserts the supremacy of the legislature over the

---

92   *Act of Settlement 1701* (Imp) 12 & 13 Will 3 c 2.
93   Quick and Garran have little to say on the point other than that officers or members of the Imperial Navy or Army are qualified to become members of the Federal Parliament because the disability relates to those paid out of revenues of the Commonwealth, above n 50, 494–4. Harrison Moore does not add anything further. See W Harrison Moore, *The Constitution of the Commonwealth of Australia* (Maxwell, 2nd ed, 1910) 116, 128 and 168. For a contemporary consideration of the issue of military involvement in internal politics in New Zealand see Douglas White QC and Graham Ansell, 'Review of the Performance of the Defence Force in Relation to Expected Standards of Behaviour, and in Particular the Leaking and Inappropriate Use of Information by Defence Force Personnel' (Report to the State Services Commissioner, 20 December 2001).

executive. In particular, it prevents the military from assuming the power of the Parliament, which ensures that government remains in civilian hands and the military remains a servant of the Parliament.

2 Declarations of War

Conversely, as the ADF has no role in Parliament, the Commonwealth Parliament has no role in decisions to deploy the ADF into hostilities. The power to use force outside of Australia derives from the war prerogative or the prerogative to conduct foreign relations (for uses of force less than war such as peacekeeping or enforcement operations), which later chapters will discuss. This was a matter of some controversy with the decision to participate in the Iraq War of 2003.[94] Each chamber of the Parliament debated motions on Australia's involvement. The House of Representatives supported the government's decision and the Senate, where the government did not command a majority, passed a motion to have Australian troops withdrawn.[95] It would appear to be the first time a deployment of Australian forces has not had majority support in both Houses of the Parliament yet, as a matter of law, this made no difference to whether the ADF could participate in the Iraq War.

The Senate subsequently debated the *Defence Amendment (Parliamentary Approval for Australian Involvement in Overseas Conflicts) Bill 2003* but it did not become law. In response to a recommendation from the Prime Ministerial 2020 Summit in 2009 that both Houses of Parliament have the power to approve whether the ADF should deploy to a 'war or warlike situation', the then Labor government stated that it did not support such a change.[96] Far from imposing a limit, this illustrates the absence of restraint upon the government in its operational use of the ADF, at least outside of Australia. The only limits, then, being much as they have been since the Glorious Revolution: that the government is responsible to the Parliament for such actions; that it must rely upon the Parliament to approve the funding of such actions; and that it must answer to the electorate at the end of its term. As discussed above, the Parliament should

---

94   See Sampford and Palmer, above n 50; Geoffrey Lindell, 'Authority for War [Iraq War]' (2003) 16 (May–June) *About the House* 23; Tony Kevin (Rapporteur), *Report of the Australians for War Powers Reform Public Seminar 23 October 2015: Legislating Reform of the War Powers*.
95   Commonwealth, *Parliamentary Debates*, House of Representatives, 18 March 2003, 13170, Senate, 20 March 2003, 9888.
96   Australian Government, *Responding to the 2020 Summit* (Commonwealth of Australia, 2009), 236. Chapter 5 will address the question of the internal legal issues arising from failing to declare war when engaged in armed conflict.

be deliberative and the executive should be able to act with 'unanimity, strength, and dispatch'.[97] This compromise between Parliament and the Crown arguably balances the need to respond to *Fortuna* while preventing such action becoming an abuse of power or despotic. As with the debate over the Iraq War, there will be differing views on whether this balance has been struck but the government remains accountable to the Parliament and the electorate for its actions.

B The States

An occasionally unsettled question is the relationship between the ADF and the power of the States. It is an area where inherited English principles and a federal constitution do not always sit well together. The traditional position since the *Bill of Rights 1688* and the *Mutiny Act 1689* is that the armed forces are subject to the law of the land. The additional application of disciplinary laws to regulate the forces in no way alters the application of all other laws.[98] The difficulty is that in the Australian federal system the ADF is an agency of the Commonwealth Government and the general criminal law is a matter for the States. The *Defence Act 1903* deals with some issues of the application of State laws directly so that, for example, ADF members do not now require a State licence to carry a weapon or drive a vehicle.[99] These provisions prevail over State laws by virtue of s 109 of the *Constitution*.

Can the States regulate other activities of the ADF through the general criminal law? This raises the complex question of intergovernmental immunities, which this book will not address other than to argue that a limited immunity in respect of some of the prerogative and nationhood powers under which the ADF may act is appropriate. In *Pirrie v McFarlane*[100] in 1925, a member of the Royal Australian Air Force was charged under Victorian law with driving a motor vehicle without a licence, although he was acting under the orders of a superior. The High Court applied the traditional English principle, Starke J putting the reason of the majority most succinctly and foreshadowing his judgment in *Shaw Savill & Albion Co Ltd v Commonwealth* stated:[101]

---

97 *Blackstone's Commentaries with Notes*, above n 53, 250.
98 *Re Tracey* (1989) 166 CLR 518, 556–62 (Brennan and Toohey JJ).
99 *Defence Act 1903* (Cth) s 123.
100 (1925) 36 CLR 170.
101 (1940) 66 CLR 344 ('*Shaw Savill & Albion Co Ltd*').

> A soldier or a member of the Air Force does not cease to be a citizen: if he commits an offence against the ordinary criminal law, he can be tried and punished as if he were a civilian. The command of an officer cannot justify a breach of the law.¹⁰²

Isaacs J, in dissent, stated the problem:

> It is on this basis that the English doctrine stands. And so it was in Australia before Federation. But under our *Constitution* an entirely different rule must be observed. Defence is in Commonwealth hands; ordinary citizenship in State hands … *A soldier acting for this purpose is acting not in his capacity of State citizen but as a soldier of the Commonwealth* … In other words, military commands, lawful by Commonwealth law, are not susceptible of denial or abridgment by State law as to citizenship. All the observations of English jurists on this subject have to meet this fundamental distinction [emphasis in original].¹⁰³

This case still stands as the law and the case of *Re Residential Tenancies Tribunal of NSW v Henderson; Ex parte Defence Housing Authority*,¹⁰⁴ in which the High Court found the Defence Housing Authority to be subject to the *Residential Tenancy Act 1987* (NSW), is consistent with it; although these cases concerned driving a motor vehicle and a residential tenancy, matters within the ordinary field of regulation by the States. The point at which State law applies to a member of the ADF, who is acting in accordance with one of the Commonwealth's sole prerogatives such as the defence of the realm, a matter not within the ordinary field of regulation by the States, is less clear.

In the *DHA Case*, Dawson, Toohey and Gaudron JJ gave the opaque test of the States not being able to restrict the capacities of the Commonwealth (which includes its prerogative powers) but being able to regulate the exercise of those capacities where they are exercised 'in the same manner

---

102 Ibid 228.
103 Ibid 205. *Defence Act 1903* s 123 now states that a member of the ADF 'is not bound by any law of a State or Territory … that would require the member to have permission (whether in the form of a licence or otherwise) to do anything in the course of his or her duties as a member of the Defence Force'.
104 (1997) 190 CLR 410 ('*DHA Case*').

as its [the Crown's] subjects'.[105] This would appear to mean that the States cannot legislate to restrict the Commonwealth's prerogative powers with respect to such things as war and defence of the realm, but it can regulate situations where the Commonwealth, through the ADF, is acting like any other citizen, such as driving a car. This will depend heavily upon the factual scenario.

Penhallurick criticises the court's decision in the *DHA Case* as based upon an implication, arguing that constitutional implications can only arise where necessary.[106] A Commonwealth immunity from State law is unnecessary due to the existence of s 109 regarding inconsistency between Commonwealth and State laws. Whilst providing a much clearer rule to apply, this view could require the Commonwealth Parliament to legislate in respect of the prerogative and nationhood powers relevant to the ADF, beyond the extent to which it has already in s 123 of the *Defence Act*. As this book argues, as much as statutory power can provide clarity and, therefore, support the principle of legality, the character of *Fortuna* is such that it is not possible to legislate in advance for every possibility. An uncertain executive power might be a better authority upon which to rely in an unexpected situation than no authority at all. Legislating to immunise all ADF action from the application of State or Territory law risks unintentionally displacing this possibility. On the other hand, legislating to provide more immunity than s 123 already does risks undermining the principle of legality as put by Starke J in *Pirrie v Macfarlane*[107] and *Shaw Savill & Albion Co Ltd*.[108] As opaque as the current test might be in

---

105 Ibid 442. This was a majority view as Brennan CJ agreed with it at 424. Zines was critical of the difficulty of applying this test in Leslie Zines, 'The Nature of the Commonwealth' (1998) 20 *Adelaide Law Review* 83, 92; as was Bradley Selway in 'The Nature of the Commonwealth: A Comment' (1998) 20 *Adelaide Law Review* 95, 99, although he saw the reasoning as 'consistent with a proper understanding of Australian federalism', 99. Dennis Rose expressed a similar view in 'The Nature of the Commonwealth: A Comment' (1998) 20 *Adelaide Law Review* 101, 105. Later Zines usefully distinguished 'prerogatives' unique to the Crown and 'capacities' shared in common with others in Leslie Zines, 'The Inherent Executive Power of the Commonwealth' (2005) 16 *Public Law Review* 279, 279. Gladman also criticises the practical difficulties of this test in Mark Gladman, 'Comment: *Re Residential Tenancies Tribunal of New South Wales and Henderson; Ex Parte Defence Housing Authority* (1997) 190 CLR 410: States' Power to Bind the Commonwealth' (1999) 27 *Federal Law Review* 151, 158–9.
106 Catherine Penhallurick, 'Commonwealth Immunity as a Constitutional Implication' (2001) 29(2) *Federal Law Review* 151, 175–6.
107 (1925) 36 CLR 170, 228.
108 (1940) 66 CLR 344, 355.

the *DHA Case*,[109] it may be the best balance that can be struck between the principle of legality, as effected through State and Territory law, and Commonwealth executive power as a means to respond to *Fortuna*.

Further, Gladman suggests that foreign affairs and national defence should be exclusive powers of the Commonwealth, and therefore immune from State law, by virtue of it being the national government.[110] Taking Blackstone's view of such matters requiring 'unanimity, strength, and dispatch'[111] it would make sense for them to be regulated exclusively by the level of government with responsibility for them, the Commonwealth. It would be consistent with the former colonies in Australia having given over effectively complete control of defence to the Commonwealth through the combined effect of sections 51 (vi),[112] 68,[113] 69,[114] 84,[115] 85,[116] 114[117] and 119[118] of the *Constitution*.[119] It would also be consistent with the States never having had external affairs powers as such. As Barwick CJ put it in the *Seas and Submerged Lands Case*:

> Whilst the power with respect to external affairs is not expressed to be a power exclusively vested in the Commonwealth, it must necessarily of its nature be so as to international relations and affairs. Only the Commonwealth has international status. The colonies never were and the States are not international persons.[120]

This does not resolve the practical question of when an action by the ADF is a matter of foreign affairs or national defence but it does lend weight to the *DHA Case*[121] test being appropriate despite its opacity.

Therefore, with respect to State law as a limitation upon the exercise of executive power by the ADF, the federal character of the *Constitution* provides some limits, although they are not precise. They would appear

---

109 (1997) 190 CLR 410.
110 Gladman, above n 105, 162.
111 *Blackstone's Commentaries with Notes*, above n 53, 250.
112 Power to legislate for defence.
113 Command-in-Chief.
114 Relating to transfer of colonial defence departments to the Commonwealth.
115 Relating to transfer of officers from colonial defence departments to the Commonwealth.
116 Relating to transfer of property from colonial defence departments to the Commonwealth.
117 States not to raise forces without Commonwealth consent.
118 Commonwealth to protect States from invasion and domestic violence.
119 See H V Evatt, *The Royal Prerogative* (Law Book Co, first presented as a doctoral thesis 1924, with commentary by Leslie Zines, 1987) 232–3.
120 (1975) 135 CLR 337, 373.
121 (1997) 190 CLR 410.

to depend upon whether the exercise is of an executive power shared in common with any other citizen, or whether it is an exercise of prerogative power which only the Commonwealth could exercise.[122] Even though much of the general law regulating the conduct of any person in Australia is State law, members of the ADF should only be exempt from its application where they are exercising an executive power of the Commonwealth which only the Commonwealth, and not just any person, could exercise. Even then, as *Shaw Savill & Albion Co Ltd*[123] makes clear and as discussed in Chapter 1, outside of combat with the enemy the armed forces are as much subject to the general law as anyone else.[124] Where the war prerogative is not in issue, the question would have to be, then, whether an ADF action contrary to State law could find authority in the prerogatives with respect to martial law, internal security or external affairs, or the nationhood power with respect to internal security. This is on the view that these powers are capacities of the Commonwealth rather than only the exercise of capacities 'in the same manner as its [the Crown's] subjects'.[125] This helps to limit the exercise of executive power to those situations where necessity justifies it, or the action is external and not subject to State law. This is an expression of the principle of legality which preserves the capacity to respond to *Fortuna*. Subsequent chapters will address this.

C The Judiciary

It turns, then, to consider the relationship of the ADF to the judiciary. There is provision for the courts to exercise judicial review over decisions relating to the ADF made under executive power. There are mechanisms for both the Federal Court and High Court to perform this function. The *Judiciary Act 1903* s 39B provides that:

---

122 If it was a prerogative which a State could share in common with the Commonwealth, such as internal security, then it is probably susceptible to State regulation, in the absence of any prevailing Commonwealth legislation. Lee discusses criteria for the application of State laws in Ricky Lee, 'Applicability of State Laws to Commonwealth Land and Activities' (2002) 6 *University of Western Sydney Law Review* 39, 47.
123 (1940) 66 CLR 344.
124 Ibid 355 (Starke J).
125 *DHA Case* (1997) 190 CLR 410, 442.

[T]he original jurisdiction of the Federal Court of Australia includes jurisdiction with respect to any matter in which a writ of mandamus or prohibition or an injunction is sought against an officer or officers of the Commonwealth.

The *Constitution* s 75(v) also provides that the High Court shall have original jurisdiction in all matters in which a writ of mandamus or prohibition or an injunction is sought against an officer of the Commonwealth.[126] Ordinarily, judicial review of decisions by Commonwealth officials may occur under the *Administrative Decisions (Judicial Review) Act 1977* (Cth) but, by virtue of s 3, it only applies to decisions made under an enactment rather than nonstatutory power such as prerogative power.[127]

Notwithstanding these provisions for judicial review, the courts have traditionally been unwilling to review the exercise of the prerogatives relevant to this book: control and disposition of the forces,[128] martial law,[129] internal emergencies,[130] war[131] and external affairs.[132] The courts have recognised the existence of these prerogatives but have not attempted to define fully the limits of such powers. As will be discussed below, the courts have granted a degree of deference to the Crown in such matters.[133] Traditionally, decisions made under prerogative power were immune from judicial review, notwithstanding that the existence of a claimed prerogative power was always reviewable.[134] The zenith of this approach is arguably the statement of Lord Parker in the 1916 Privy Council prize law case of *The Zamora* that:

---

126 Whilst not deriving from the common law, this jurisdiction is essentially common law as it is mainly (though not exclusively) defined in both provisions by the common-law writs of mandamus or prohibition, or the equitable remedy of injunction, Robin Creyke and John McMillan, *Control of Government Action: Text, Cases & Commentary* (Lexis Nexis Butterworths, 3rd ed, 2012) 41–2, 51–2; Chief Justice Robert French, 'Constitutional Review of Executive Decisions – Australia's US Legacy' Speech to the Chicago Bar Association and the John Marshall Law School (25 and 28 January 2010) published in (2010) 35(1) *University of Western Australia Law Review* 35.
127 *Minister for Arts, Heritage and Environment v Peko-Wallsend Ltd* (1987) 15 FCR 274, 275.
128 *Council of the Civil Service Unions v Minister for the Civil Service* [1985] AC 374, 396, citing with approval *Chandler v Director of Public Prosecutions* [1964] AC 763.
129 *Marais v General Officer Commanding the Lines of Communication* [1902] AC 109 ('*Marais*').
130 *R v Sharkey* (1949) 79 CLR 121.
131 *Shaw Saville & Albion Co Ltd* (1940) 66 CLR 344.
132 *Thorpe v Commonwealth* (No 3) (1997) 144 ALR 677.
133 *Chandler v Director of Public Prosecutions* [1964] AC 763; *Marais* [1902] AC 109. Lee discusses judicial deference in national security matters in H P Lee, '*Salus Populi Suprema Lex Esto*: Constitutional Fidelity in Troubled Times', H P Lee, '*Salus Populi Suprema Lex Esto*: Constitutional Fidelity in Troubled Times' in H P Lee and Peter Gerangelos (eds), *Constitutional Advancement in a Frozen Continent: Essays in Honour of George Winterton* (Federation Press, 2009) 54, 58.
134 *Council of the Civil Service Unions v Minister for the Civil Service* [1985] AC 374, 398 (Lord Fraser).

Those who are responsible for the national security must be the sole judges of what the national security requires. It would be obviously undesirable that such matters should be made the subject of evidence in a court of law or otherwise discussed in public.[135]

This position is arguably no longer likely to be the law. *Al-Jedda v Secretary of State for Defence* ('*Al-Jedda*')[136] went before the Court of Appeal in England in 2010. Chapter 6 will discuss this case in more detail, but the court looked very closely at the detention of a British citizen in Iraq by the British Army. Elias J noted that, 'For centuries the conventional jurisprudence was that the courts could determine the scope of prerogative powers but not the manner of their exercise'.[137]

However, his Honour in that case asserted a greater role for the courts to exercise control over prerogative powers in some cases.[138] This chapter argues that it is becoming less likely that a court will find a matter to be nonjusticiable, preferring instead to hear evidence and argument before either deciding to defer to the executive or granting a remedy against it.[139] This is an argument which this chapter will introduce and which subsequent chapters will address.

1 What is Justiciability?

What is justiciability then? It is an elusive concept closely related to deference.[140] Justiciability turns on a number of issues. These include the suitability of courts to decide on high-level political issues,[141] Act of State doctrine,[142] the absence of a 'matter' in dispute between parties or parties

---

135 [*1916*] 2 AC 77, 107.
136 [2011] 2 WLR 225, 272.
137 Ibid 272.
138 Ibid.
139 See generally Campbell McLachlan, *Foreign Relations Law* (Cambridge University Press, 2014). Chapter 6 will consider this work in more detail.
140 Creyke and McMillan, above n 126, 59–75; Geoffrey Lindell, *The Coalition Wars Against Iraq and Afghanistan in the Courts of the UK, Ireland and the US: Significance for Australia* (Centre for International and Public Law Policy Paper 26, Federation Press, 2005) 3–6, 33–8; Chris Finn, 'The Justiciability of Administrative Decisions: A Redundant Concept?' (2002) 30(2) *Federal Law Review* 239; Noel Cox, '*Black v Chretien*: Suing a Minister of the Crown for Abuse of Power, Misfeasance in Public Office and Negligence' [2002] *Murdoch University Electronic Journal of Law* 26; Lorne Sossin, 'Case Comment: The Rule of Law and the Justiciability of Prerogative Powers: A Comment on *Black v Chretien*' (2002) 47 *McGill Law Journal* 435.
141 *Minister for Arts, Heritage and Environment v Peko-Wallsend Ltd* (1987) 15 FCR 274, 280–1.
142 See Lindell, *The Coalition Wars*, above n 140, 36–7.

with standing[143] and 'polycentricity' (that is, a multifaceted rather than adversarial problem).[144] Put simply, it concerns the suitability of a court to adjudicate on a particular matter.[145]

A good recent example is that of *Curtis v Minister of Defence* ('*Curtis*')[146] concerning judicial review of the decision to disband the Royal New Zealand Air Force Air Combat Force, which involved removing all fighter aircraft from New Zealand service. The New Zealand Court of Appeal held that it was a matter of the control and disposition of the forces and therefore nonjusticiable.[147] Tipping J for the Court struck out the application for judicial review stating that the matter was 'par excellence a non-justiciable question. It is a question which is not susceptible of determination by any legal yardstick'.[148]

His Honour also noted with apparent approval the view of Wilson J in the Supreme Court of Canada in *Operation Dismantle v R*,[149] a case in which judicial review of United States' cruise missile testing in Canada was struck out. Tipping J stated, 'that matters such as those with which the present case is concerned are not justiciable because they involve moral and political considerations which it is not within the province of the Courts to assess.'[150]

Tipping J applied *Chandler v Director of Public Prosecutions*.[151] In that case, Lord Devlin perhaps states the traditional position most clearly as follows:

> A number of matters relating to the safety of the realm and the command of the Royal Forces are now regulated by statute. So far however as this is not the case the powers in that regard are at common law in the prerogative of the Crown acting on the advice of its servants. The powers so left to

---

143 *Habib v Commonwealth* (2010) 183 FCR 62, 79 (Perram J citing Gummow J in *Re Ditfort; Ex parte DCT* (1988) 19 FCR 347, 370–1) 82, 98 (Jagot J cited the same authority to make essentially the same point) ('*Habib*').
144 Finn, above n 140, 242–7.
145 Justice Alan Robertson, 'Commentary on the Boundaries of Judicial Review and Justiciability: Comparing Perspectives from Australian and Canada' (Paper presented at the Australian Institute of Administrative Law (NSW Chapter) Seminar, Sydney, 22 July 2013), 1, and also for a review of recent Australian cases on justiciability.
146 [2002] 2 NZLR 744.
147 Ibid.
148 Ibid 752.
149 [1985] 1 SCR 441, 465.
150 *Curtis* [2002] 2 NZLR 744, 752.
151 [1964] AC 763.

the unfettered control of the Crown include both in time of peace and war all matters related to the disposition and armament of the military, naval and air forces ... In our opinion the manner of the exercise of such prerogative powers cannot be inquired into by the Courts, whether in a civil or a criminal case ... A similar principle underlies the powers of the executive, though pursuant to statute and not the prerogative, to requisition or to do other acts where in its discretion that is considered necessary to the national interest.[152]

These cases reflect two distinct reasons for nonjusticiability in defence matters. The first is the lack of a cause of action and the second is that courts are not well placed to review high-level policy or political decisions in matters of national security. For either reason, this may be because the issues involve questions of allocation of national resources, which are fundamentally political rather than legal in nature. High-level political, or even low-level operational, decisions may also depend upon secret information which cannot be disclosed in court. They may also involve moral or political judgements on the part of a decision-maker, which are entirely matters of discretion. As Dixon J stated in *Shaw Savill & Albion Co Ltd*:

> The Court is not in a position to know or to inquire what measures are necessary for the proper conduct of a warlike operation and must depend upon those upon whom finally rests the responsibility of action.[153]

This is consistent with a theory of executive power requiring 'unanimity, strength, and dispatch'[154] rather than, as French CJ and Gummow J put it in the 2009 High Court of Australia military discipline case of *Lane v Morrison*, the qualities 'of the judicial branch of government for impartiality and nonpartisanship.'[155] For these reasons it is quite appropriate that in such cases the judiciary should defer to the decision of the executive, but, as will be discussed below, it may also be appropriate for a court to hear evidence and argument first rather than just striking out a claim as nonjusticiable. As Hayne and Kiefel JJ stated in *Pape*:

> Reference to notions as protean and imprecise as 'crisis' and 'emergency' (or 'adverse effects of circumstances affecting the national economy') to indicate the boundary of an aspect of executive power carries with

---

152 Ibid 775–6.
153 (1940) 66 CLR 344, 363.
154 *Blackstone's Commentaries with Notes*, above n 53, 250.
155 (2009) 239 CLR 230, 237.

it difficulties and dangers that raise fundamental questions about the relationship between the judicial and other branches of government. … If it is for the Court to decide these matters, questions arise about what evidence the Court could act upon other than the opinions of the Executive, and how those opinions could be tested or supported. Yet, if it is to be for the Executive to decide whether there is some form of 'national emergency' (subject only to some residual power in the Court to decide that the Executive's conclusion is irrational), then the Executive's powers in such matters would be self-defining.[156]

Hearing evidence and argument first rather than just striking out a claim as nonjusticiable is essentially what occurred in the 1985 House of Lords case of *CCSU*,[157] which established in English law that decisions made under prerogative, as opposed to statutory, power may be subject to judicial review.[158] This is a principle which a number of Australian cases have followed.[159] At the same time, the *CCSU Case* also made clear that decisions which dealt with certain subject matter, in that case national security, were not suitable for judicial review. As to what 'national security' might include, the *CCSU Case* gives a number of illustrative, rather than exhaustive, examples as follows:

- 'all matters relating to the disposition and armament of the armed forces'[160]
- 'matters so vital to the survival of the nation as the conduct of relations with foreign states and – what lies at the heart of the present case – the defence of the realm against potential enemies'[161]

---

156 (2009) 238 CLR 1, 122–3.
157 [1985] AC 374.
158 Ibid. This development is discussed generally in positive terms as increasing the accountability of the executive in George Barrie, 'Judicial Review of the Royal Prerogative' (1994) 111 *South African Law Journal* 788; Kate Guilfoyle, 'The Relationship Between the Crown and the Subject: Changes to the Position of the Crown as a Consequence of the Judicial Process' (1998) 17 *Australian Bar Review* 13.
159 Mark Aronson, Bruce Dyer and Matthew Groves in *Judicial Review of Administrative Action* (Lawbook, 4th ed, 2009) 124–34; Creyke and McMillan, above n 126, 59–75. Australian cases which apply or follow the principle in *CCSU Case*, most notably *Minister for Arts, Heritage and Environment v Peko-Wallsend Ltd* (1987) 15 FCR 274. The High Court considered *CCSU Case* with apparent approval in the 2005 case of *Jarratt v Commissioner of Police for New South Wales* (2005) 224 CLR 44, 65, without applying it directly. The earlier 1998 case of *DPP (SA) v B* (1998) 194 CLR 566, 599 also cites *CCSU Case* with approval as part of the development of 'fifty years of administrative law', stating, 'It is important to recognise the expansion of supervisory jurisdiction of the courts marked by *CCSU Case* and *Minister for the Arts, Heritage and Environment v Peko-Wallsend*' (Kirby J).
160 [1985] AC 374, 406 citing *Chandler v Director of Public Prosecutions* [1964] AC 763 (Lord Scarman).
161 Ibid 410 (Lord Diplock).

- '[i]mplicitly actions in or related to combat by reference to *Burmah Oil Co Ltd v Lord Advocate* ('*Burmah Oil*')'[162]
- 'in time of peace as in days of war ... direction of the defence forces ... So are treaties and alliances with other states for mutual defence ...'[163]

These examples touch on most of the prerogatives relevant to this book and have an obvious direct significance for the ADF. Interestingly, this also reflects the way Montesquieu described executive power—the prince 'makes peace or war, sends or receives embassies, establishes the public security, and provides against invasions'.[164]

It is important to note that the Law Lords heard evidence that national security was at issue before deferring to the executive on the question.[165] Despite *Curtis*[166] and *Operation Dismantle v R*,[167] the *CCSU Case* perhaps indicates the trend in judicial review of 'national security' cases, which is to treat them as justiciable before deferring to the executive or finding against it. This is not to argue that *Curtis* and *Operation Dismantle v R* were inappropriately decided at all, but only to state that it should be an exceptional case in which a court should find a claim for judicial review of a 'national security' matter to be nonjusticiable, such as because there is no clear cause of action. It would be more consistent with the principle of legality for a court to treat a matter as justiciable before determining on evidence and argument that it should defer to the executive.

Lindell observes that courts are reluctant to intrude into foreign affairs as well and will at times rely on nonjusticiability to avoid doing so.[168] He observes 'what becomes increasingly difficult to rationalise is how this [reluctance] can be justified given the ever growing scope of judicial review'.[169] Lindell, then, discusses recent English cases where judicial review has started to occur in a limited way in such areas.[170] In Australia, Tamberlin J stated in *Hicks v Ruddock* in 2007:

---

162 Ibid 411 (Lord Diplock).
163 Ibid 421 citing *Chandler v Director of Public Prosecutions* [1964] AC 763 (Lord Roskill).
164 Montesquieu, above n 1, 19.
165 *CCSU Case* [1985] AC 374, 402–403 (Lord Fraser).
166 [2002] 2 NZLR 744.
167 [1985] 1 SCR 441, 465.
168 Lindell, *The Coalition Wars*, above n 140, 33.
169 Ibid.
170 Ibid.

> The modern law in relation to the meaning of 'justiciable' and the extent to which the court will examine executive action in the area of foreign relations and Acts of State is far from settled, black-letter law.[171]

This was a single judge decision.

Perram J went further in *Habib* in stating that 'the effect of this principle is to ensure that whenever a question as to the limits of Commonwealth power arises it is justiciable'.[172] This statement is possibly too broad given the *Shaw Savill & Albion Co Ltd* combat immunity doctrine discussed above. It does however support the view that the rise of judicial review in Australia in general,[173] meaning an increasing requirement for the executive to be accountable for its decisions and therefore more subject to the principle of legality,[174] may well mean that no assumptions can be made as to the extent to which the judiciary may find a decision of the ADF to be nonjusticiable. This is particularly so given the more recent English cases of *Al-Jedda*[175] and the United Kingdom Supreme Court case of *Smith v Ministry of Defence* ('*Smith*') of 2012,[176] discussed in Chapter 5 and, more importantly, the statement of Gageler J in *M68,* quoted above, that:

> The purpose of s 75(v), as Dixon J put it, was 'to make it constitutionally certain that there would be a jurisdiction capable of restraining officers of the Commonwealth from exceeding Federal power'.[177] ... The purpose was to supplement s 75(iii) so as to ensure that any officer of the Commonwealth acted, and acted only, within the scope of the authority conferred on that officer by the *Constitution* or by legislation.[178]

While there may well be areas into which a court should not intrude because it could adversely affect national security, the ability to keep secrets for example being a distinct and essential quality of the executive

---

171 (2007) 156 FCR 574, 600.
172 (2010) 183 FCR 62, 73.
173 See above n 159.
174 *DPP (SA) v B* (1998) 194 CLR 566, 599. Aronson discusses the rise of executive accountability in Mark Aronson, 'Private Bodies, Public Power and Soft Law in the High Court' (2007) 35 *Federal Law Review* 1, 1–4. See also Fiona Wheeler, 'Judicial Review of Prerogative Power in Australia: Issues and Prospects' (1992) 14 *Sydney Law Review* 432, 446–8. On inherent uncertainty in judicial review and the powers of the Crown, see Bradley Selway, 'Of Kings and Officers – The Judicial Development of Public Law' (2005) 33(2) *Federal Law Review* 187.
175 [2011] 2 WLR 225.
176 [2013] UKSC 41.
177 *Bank of New South Wales v The Commonwealth* (1948) 76 CLR 1, 363.
178 *M68* [2016] HCA 1 [126], [145].

in the separation of powers,[179] it is increasingly likely that a court will hear evidence and argument before it decides that it should not intrude further.

The significance of this for the ADF is that it cannot assume judicial review of a traditionally excluded subject will not occur in future. There are still likely to be decisions relating to the ADF, however, which will almost always be unsuitable for judicial review.

Either way, an important point for this book is the history of judicial deference to the executive on matters of national security. This means that there are very few cases which have tested the exercise of prerogative power by military forces, let alone the ADF. Common law may simply not address some powers because they have always been assumed to exist. The courts may clearly impose some limits on the exercise of executive power by the ADF, those limits may be changing though, and it is just not clear what their extent might be in any given case.

2 The Exercise of Powers by the Governor-General in Person: Is 'Direct' Prerogative Power Subject to Judicial Review?

A distinct issue is that of personal exercises of prerogative power by the Sovereign or the Governor-General. The *CCSU Case*[180] did not decide whether a direct exercise of prerogative power was justiciable. The clear suggestion seemed to be that it was not[181] as the Minister was exercising prerogative power in the *CCSU Case*.[182] The nonjusticiable nature of personal decisions of the Sovereign probably derives from the ancient constitutional rule that 'the King can do no wrong'.[183] Although not directly applicable to decisions made under prerogative power, the *Administrative Decisions (Judicial Review) Act 1977* (Cth) precludes review of decisions made by the Governor-General under an enactment.[184] In *R v Toohey; Ex parte Northern Land Council*[185] the court reviewed the exercise of statutory power of the Administrator of the Northern Territory, assuming that office to be vice-regal, although it did not decide on the

---

179 Harrison Moore, above n 93, 292.
180 [1985] AC 374.
181 Ibid 379.
182 Ibid 380.
183 Ibid 379.
184 *Administrative Decisions (Judicial Review) Act 1977* (Cth) s 3.
185 (1981) 151 CLR 170, 186.

question of judicial review of exercises of prerogative power. *Minister for Arts, Heritage and Environment v Peko-Wallsend Ltd*[186] made clear that decisions of the Governor-General in Council should be subject to judicial review, although not in that case.[187]

Whether exercises of prerogative power directly by the Sovereign or the Governor-General are immune from judicial review a priori, or because of their subject matter, is not certain. It is worth noting this issue, however, because a decision relating to the ADF under prerogative power given effect by the Governor-General personally has a different legal character to a decision made within the ADF itself or by the Governor-General in Council.[188]

A potentially important means of maintaining military subordination to the civilian government could be a removal or termination by the Governor-General personally of the CDF, the Vice-Chief of the Defence Force (officers appointed to their positions by the Governor-General under *Defence Act* s 12 discussed above) or other service chief. Termination of the service by the Governor-General personally of such a very senior officer from the ADF would most likely fall under s 15 of the *Defence Act* and the *Defence (Personnel) Regulations 2002* (Cth),[189] and so be an exercise of statutory power. It would not be reviewable by virtue of the *Administrative Decisions (Judicial Review) Act 1977* not applying to decisions of the Governor-General. Such a decision might possibly be reviewable under s 75(v) of the *Constitution* or s 39B of the *Judiciary Act* but, if personal exercises of power by the Governor-General are immune from judicial review a priori, then such a decision could remain unreviewable, particularly given the decisions in *Coutts v Commonwealth*[190] and *Jarratt v Commissioner of Police for New South Wales*[191] discussed below. This could operate as a limit on the exercise of executive power by the ADF through

---

186 (1987) 15 FCR 274.
187 Ibid 278.
188 See *Millar v Bornholt* (2009) 117 FCR 67, 76–7, quoting Sir Ninian Stephen, referring to Sir Victor Windeyer, on this point.
189 Reg 85.
190 (1985) 157 CLR 91.
191 (2005) 224 CLR 44. Another way that the career of a senior officer could be effectively terminated, but as an exercise of prerogative power, could be through compulsory transfer to the reserves. The *Defence (Personnel) Regulations 2002* (Cth) do not address the ending of a very senior officer's career because reg 65, which deals with transfer to the stand-by reserve of such officers *at* the end of their appointment, is silent on compulsory transfer *before* the end of their appointment. A prerogative decision of this nature may also be nonjusticiable if made by the Governor-General personally.

senior officers not having security of tenure, or their appointments not being subject to the scrutiny of the courts. This leads into the question of the relationship of individual members of the ADF to executive power, as opposed to the relationships of the ADF as an institution to the executive power and the other parts of government.

V The Relationship of Members of the ADF to Executive Power

A The Character of Service

With respect to the relationship of individual members of the ADF to the Crown, the obligation of obedience still facilitates the exercise of executive power and the concept of service at the pleasure of the Crown, which limits the scope for its usurpation.[192] While the *Defence (Personnel) Regulations 2002* comprehensively regulate the service of members of the ADF, they do not explicitly extinguish the executive power on the same subject. As mentioned above, there may still be room for some of the earlier principles to operate. Also, even though the *Defence (Personnel) Regulations 2002* do reflect the traditional character of service to a large extent, it is important to refer to the earlier cases to understand that character. As Logan J said of reg 77 of the *Defence Force Regulations*, dealing with redresses of grievance:

> Knowledge of legal history, of the relationship between the Sovereign, the Parliament and the Armed Forces, of the rank structure and chain of command within the Army and of the responsibilities in respect of subordinates assumed by those who hold the Queen's commission in the Defence Force is essential to an appreciation of the nature of the power.[193]

Further, the oath of enlistment prescribed most recently in the *Defence Personnel Regulations* in 2002 states:

> I swear that I will well and truly serve Her Majesty Queen Elizabeth the Second, Her Heirs and Successors according to law … and that I will resist her enemies and faithfully discharge my duty according to law.[194]

---

192 For a modern reappraisal of the relationship in Britain, see Peter Rowe, 'The Soldier as a Citizen in Uniform: A Reappraisal' (2007) 7 *New Zealand Armed Forces Law Review* 1.
193 *Millar v Bornholt* (2009) 117 FCR 67, 72.
194 *Defence (Personnel) Regulations 2002* (Cth) sch 2.

Illustrating the continuity of this relationship, Charles Clode, Solicitor to the War Office in London from 1858 to 1877,[195] had written in 1872:

> Now and for the last 200 years and upwards the substance of the Officer's and Soldier's engagements with the Crown has been the same. The officer's agreement is: 1. As towards his inferiors, to take charge of the Officers and soldiers serving under him, to exercise and well discipline them in arms, and to keep them in good order and discipline (those under him being commanded to obey him as their superior Officer). 2. As towards the Crown and his superiors, to observe and follow such orders and directions as from time to time he shall receive from the Sovereign or any of his superior Officers, according to the rules and discipline of law. The Soldier's agreement (usually confirmed by his oath) is: 1. To defend the Sovereign, his Crown and dignity against all enemies; and 2. To observe and obey all orders of his Majesty and of the Generals and officers set over him.[196]

Clode wrote the following words on the relationship between the Crown and the armed forces in *Military Forces of the Crown: Their Administration and Government* in 1869:

> In the first place, he is bound to obey and to give his personal service to the Crown under the punishments imposed upon him for disobedience by the *Mutiny Act* and *Articles of War*. No other obligation must be put in competition with this; neither parental authority nor religious scruples, nor personal safety, nor pecuniary advantages from other service. All the duties of his life are, according to the theory of Military obedience, absorbed in that one duty of obeying the command of the Officers set over him.[197]

Clode is significant because the High Court of Australia has often referred to him in consistently affirming a view of the relationship between the Crown and members of the armed forces in Australia which is characterised by a long history of obedience of the latter to the former. Callinan J referred to this precise passage in obiter dicta in the relatively recent case of *X v Commonwealth*[198] in 1999. There is some caution as to the use of Clode, Windeyer J stating in *Marks v Commonwealth* in 1964:

---

195 Then, upon administrative reorganisation, Legal Secretary to the War Department from 1877 to 1880, Captain Owen Wheeler, *The War Office: Past and Present* (Methuen, 1914, Taylor and Francis Reprint, 2009) 191–2.
196 Clode, *The Administration of Justice under Military and Martial Law*, above n 17, 73.
197 Clode, *Military Forces of the Crown: Their Administration and Government*, above n 43, 37.
198 *X v Commonwealth* (1999) 200 CLR 177, 233.

His books are a most valuable mine of interesting information, much of it not readily obtainable elsewhere. But it is, I think, a mistake to take all of his statements as if they were, in unqualified terms, authoritative pronouncements of law.[199]

Nonetheless, in relevant military matters, Australian cases have relied heavily on his works and historical material and perceptions generally.

A chronological selection of extracts from the cases would appear to draw strongly upon Clode's view of the relationship between the Crown and the armed forces as being one of obedience. In *Commonwealth v Quince* ('*Quince*'), Williams J stated the following on the power of command, military obedience and the relationship to the Crown:

> *Clode* proceeds to point out … 'Of course in war there is no limit to obedience (which is the first, second, and third duty of a soldier at all times) save a physical impossibility to obey. A subordinate officer must not judge of the danger, propriety, expediency, or consequence of the order he receives: he must obey – nothing can excuse him but a physical impossibility. A forlorn hope is devoted – many gallant men have been devoted. Victories have been obtained by ordering men upon desperate services, with almost a certainty of death or capture.'[200]

His Honour went to say:

> The King remains the titular head of the armed forces of the Crown, and the *Constitution*, s 68, therefore, provides that the command in chief of the Naval and Military Forces of the Commonwealth is vested in the Governor-General as the King's representative. The oath is an oath to serve the King in person according to its tenor. Service in the Air Force, as in the naval or military forces, involves in its most absolute form the right of a member superior in rank to give lawful orders to a member inferior in rank, and the obligation of the member inferior in rank to obey those orders.[201]

---

199 *Marks v Commonwealth* (1964) 111 CLR 549, 577. For another equivocal application of Clode, see Zelman Cowan, 'The Armed Forces of the Crown' (1950) 66 *Law Quarterly Review* 478, 478–9 and 492.
200 (1944) 68 CLR 227, 255.
201 Ibid.

In *Marks v Commonwealth*, Owen J made these observations about the employment relationship between the Crown and members of the armed forces:

> [M]uch of what was said in *Reg v Cuming* (1887) 19 QBD 13 and *Hearson v Churchill* (1892) 2 QB 144 is in point and affords strong support for the quotations from Clode and *Halsbury's Laws of England* which I have set out earlier and which, in my opinion, correctly state the common law … Service is during the pleasure of the Crown, not during the pleasure of the officer.[202]

In 1985, in *Coutts v Commonwealth*,[203] Flight Lieutenant Coutts had failed a medical fitness test which resulted in his transfer to the retired list without his consent. The Governor-General in Council (not the Governor-General alone) approved the termination of his appointment in the permanent service.[204] A majority of the High Court found that the decision to terminate was not reviewable, even though *Coutts v Commonwealth*[205] did not concern defence of the realm at all but a rather routine termination of service in what was really a period of deep peace. While Deane J, with Mason ACJ concurring, saw the termination as statutory and therefore reviewable,[206] Wilson J saw Flight Lieutenant Coutts's termination as squarely within nonjusticiable subject matter: 'In my opinion, the answer to the problem in the present case is dictated by the operation of well-established principles governing the relation to the Crown of members of the armed services'.[207]

Brennan J saw a power to dismiss at pleasure as effectively unreviewable:

> The power to dismiss an officer of the Defence Force, whether it flows from statute or the prerogative, is a power to dismiss at pleasure. That is, the power to dismiss may be exercised at any time and for any reason, or for no reason or for a mistaken reason. In point of law, an officer has no security of appointment.[208]

Dawson J decided for similar reasons.[209]

---

202 (1964) 111 CLR 549, 597.
203 (1985) 157 CLR 91.
204 Ibid 92–3.
205 Ibid.
206 Ibid 110.
207 Ibid 98.
208 Ibid 105.
209 Ibid 117–23.

Coutts has been the subject of academic criticism[210] yet as recent a case as *Jarratt v Commissioner of Police for New South Wales*[211] in 2005 has touched on it and left the principle undisturbed. There, Gleeson CJ made very clear that the relationship of the Crown to the armed forces is still special and outside the rules for other public officials:

> 'The general rule of the common law is that the King may refuse the services of any officer of the Crown and suspend or dismiss him from his office'. It is no longer appropriate to account for the rule in terms of redolent monarchical patronage. The rule has a distinct rationale in its application to the armed forces, but in its application to the public service generally it is difficult to reconcile with modern conceptions of government employment and accountability.[212]

His Honour did not elaborate on what that distinct rationale was but, in the context of a termination decision, it may be that members of the ADF must obey the lawful directions of the government and, if they do not, that they can be removed from service readily. To have it otherwise may undermine the subordination of the military to the civilian government.[213] In *Bromet v Oddie*[214] in 2002, Finn J applied the observations of Dixon J in *Commonwealth v Welsh*, that:

> [I]n considering the meaning and effect of the Air Force Regulations their purpose cannot be neglected, namely to provide rules to govern one of the armed forces of the Crown. The relation to the Crown of members of the armed forces is no new subject; the rules of the common law define it. The regulations are not to be read in disregard of those rules and of the long tradition to which they have contributed.[215]

---

210 See Wheeler, 'Judicial Review of Prerogative Power in Australia', above n 174, 440–1; Mitchell Jones, 'Judicial Review of Administrative Action against Members of the Australian Defence Force: Can a Warrior Win in Court?' (2005) 13(1) *Australian Journal of Administrative Law* 8, 24–6; Finn, above n 140, 254.
211 (2005) 224 CLR 44.
212 Ibid 50, quoting Dixon J in *Fletcher v Nott* (1938) 60 CLR 55, 77, a case which concerned the dismissal of a constable of the New South Wales Police.
213 Jones also provides an extensive review of personnel cases, which generally reveal a significant degree of deference to ADF decisions under command (that is prerogative as opposed to statutory) power, 'Judicial Review of Administrative Action against Members of the Australia Defence Force', above n 210, 24–40. Even though it concerned the dismissal of the Secretary of the Department of Defence, *Barratt v Howard* (2000) 96 FCR 428 does not really assist on this question because it concerned statutory rather than prerogative powers.
214 (2002) 78 ALD 320, 331.
215 (1947) 74 CLR 245, 268.

Logan J referred extensively to these cases and to Clode with approval in *Millar v Bornholt* in 2009.[216]

As discussed above, the *Defence (Personnel) Regulations 2002* modify the common law but do not fundamentally alter the relationship between members of the ADF and the Crown. As Logan J said:

> [O]nce it is appreciated that ... a Service Chief ... may terminate the service of an enlisted member for reasons as ephemeral as that which formed the basis of CPL Millar's termination or that '*the retention of the enlisted member is not in the interest of Australia; or the Defence Force; or the Chief's Service*' (reg 87(1)(g), *Defence (Personnel) Regulations*), the heritage of the common law remains evident.[217]

Where a decision as to the service of a member of the ADF is not directly covered by the regulations then these common-law principles could apply. This could be when the decision is to transfer a very senior officer to the reserve as discussed above or is made by the Governor-General personally, which would be exceptional situations. As a matter of course however, routine decisions made by delegates of the Governor-General or a service chief, as the case may be, are statutory in character. They are also still subject to judicial review, even if not often successfully, on grounds such as the requirement to afford procedural fairness.[218] Even so, Logan J noted in *Millar v Bornholt* that:

> [There should be] a principled restraint on a court conducting judicial review lest the appearance be given that, in respect of the making of value judgements in relation to the Defence Force, command has impermissibly passed from those to whom that task has been consigned by the Governor-General under parliamentary authority to the Judiciary ... Deference is called for in relation to the value judgment [to terminate Corporal Millar's service] made by that military officer.[219]

This deference leaves the ADF as an anomaly in administrative law. The *Report on Australia's Military Justice System* of 2005 indicated that this anomalous position has been under significant scrutiny, at least in the

---

216 *Millar v Bornholt* (2009) 117 FCR 67, 73–6, 85–7.
217 Ibid 87.
218 *Sutton v Commonwealth* [2011] FCA 14 (14 January 2011), *Martincevic v Commonwealth* [2007] 96 ALD 576 and *Millar v Bornholt* (2009) 117 FCR 67; Jones, above n 210, generally.
219 *Millar v Bornholt* (2009) 117 FCR 67, 87–8.

Parliament.²²⁰ It is far from certain whether the High Court will continue to treat the ADF as unique in administrative law terms or subject it to the same degree of scrutiny as any other agency of the executive. As Deane J stated in dissent in *Coutts*:

> The fact that an appointment is during pleasure does not mean that the exercise of a statutory power to terminate it will necessarily be immune from attack even where the power is a truly discretionary one which may be exercised at any time and without reason being assigned.²²¹

Perhaps more tellingly, Major General Sir Victor Windeyer, as Windeyer J of the High Court stated in *Marks v Commonwealth*, 'Duty and Discipline do not march well with Discontent'.²²²

Whether service in the ADF continues to receive judicial deference, these cases illustrate the constitutional relationship of members of the ADF to the Crown which underpins and informs the *Defence (Personnel) Regulations 2002*. Service in the ADF is service of the Crown. There is a clear obligation on the part of members of the ADF to serve the will of the Crown, and the Crown may readily dispense with the services of a member. This is no ordinary employment relationship. History defines this legal relationship to a large extent, and the common law reinforces it. It is unique and in itself provides a limit on the usurpation of executive power by the ADF.

B Discipline and Obedience Connected to Command

This discussion of the character of service in the ADF says much about obedience and for this reason it is important to consider the place of discipline and obedience in the relationship between members of the ADF and the Crown.²²³

---

220 Commonwealth Parliament, Senate Foreign Affairs, Defence and Trade Legislation Committee *Report on Australia's Military Justice System* June 2005. See discussion in Matthew Groves, 'The Civilianisation of Australian Military Law' (2005) 28(2) *University of New South Wales Law Journal* 364.
221 (1985) 157 CLR 91, 114.
222 (1964) 111 CLR 549, 576.
223 On the general requirement for justice, command and obedience in any system of military law see Rodrigo Lorenzo Ponce de Leon, 'The Coming of Age of Military Law and Jurisdiction in the English-Speaking Countries' (2010) 49 *Revue de Droit Militaire et de Droit de La Guerre* 263, 265.

Clode observed in 1874 that:

> The discipline, as incident to the Command, of the Army is vested in the Sovereign. Unity is the very essence of Military Command; and therefore all authority … is derived only from one source, viz, the Crown.[224]

A power of discipline is fundamental to command, that is, to demand obedience under threat of punishment. The duty of obedience is reflected in the following indicative list of offences under the *Defence Force Discipline Act 1982* (Cth):

- s 15F—Offence of failing to carry out orders (with respect to operations against the enemy, which includes pirates and mutineers (s 3));
- s 15G—Imperilling the success of operations (against the enemy);
- s 27—Disobeying a lawful command; and
- s 29—Failing to comply with a general order.

Why is discipline so closely related to command? The reasons appear twofold. Any military force, whether subject to civilian control or not, requires discipline to maintain military effectiveness. In the course of duty, a member of the ADF may have to risk his or her own life or take that of another. Further, a key element of civilian control over the military is that the military has to do what the civilian government tells it to do. As Kirby J put it in 2007 in *White v Director of Military Prosecutions* ('*White*'):

> It is of the nature of naval and military (and now air) forces that they must be subject to elaborate requirements of discipline. This is essential both to ensure the effectiveness of such forces and to provide the proper protection for civilians from service personnel who bear, or have access to, arms.[225]

Therefore to have members of military forces subject to a duty of obedience assists in direct control of military power. As Lord Loughborough said in the 1792 case of *Grant v Gould*:

> [F]or there is nothing so dangerous to the civil establishment of a state, as a licentious and undisciplined army; and every country which has a standing army in it, is guarded and protected by a mutiny act.

---

224 Clode, *The Administration of Justice under Military and Martial Law*, above n 23, 107.
225 (2007) 231 CLR 570, 627. For a discussion of this case see Geoffrey Kennett, 'The *Constitution* and Military Justice after *White v Director of Military Prosecutions*' (2008) 36(2) *Federal Law Review* 231.

> An undisciplined soldiery are apt to be too many for the civil power; but under the command of officers, those officers are answerable to the civil power, that they are kept in good order and discipline.²²⁶

The *Australian Constitution* reflects this relationship between command, discipline and obedience being essential to the constitutional relationship between the armed forces and the government. A connection between command and discipline is clearly drawn in *White* by Gleeson CJ and Callinan J, in addition to the point by Kirby J stated above. Gleeson CJ quoted with apparent approval this contribution of Mr O'Connor's in the *Official Record of the Debates of the Australasian Federal Convention*:²²⁷

> You must have someone Commander-in-Chief, and, according to all notions of military discipline as we are aware of, the Command-in-Chief must have control of questions of discipline, or remit them to properly constituted military courts.²²⁸

Callinan J stated:

> In *R v Bevan; Ex parte Elias and Gordon*²²⁹ Starke J saw that section [s 68] as an instance of the 'special and peculiar' provision contemplated for the management and disciplining of the defence forces and so do I. Another way of putting this is to say that the command and that which goes with it, namely discipline and sanctions of a special kind … are matters of executive power.²³⁰

The reference to Clode by Williams J in *Quince* quoted above on obedience being the first, second and third duty of a soldier also supports this view of command and discipline being essential to the constitutional relationship between the armed forces and the government.²³¹

The issues in *White*,²³² *Re Tracey*²³³ and later *Lane v Morrison*,²³⁴ and other High Court cases relating to the *Defence Force Discipline Act*, related to the extent of the jurisdiction of the ADF to discipline its members under

---

226 (1792) 2 HBL 69, 99–100; 126 ER 434, 450 quoted in *Re Tracey* (1989) 166 CLR 518, 557.
227 Vol 2, 2259.
228 *White* (2007) 231 CLR 570, 583.
229 (1942) 66 CLR 452.
230 *White* (2007) 231 CLR 570, 649.
231 *Quince* (1944) 68 CLR 227, 255.
232 (2007) 231 CLR 570.
233 (1989) 166 CLR 518.
234 (2009) 239 CLR 230. See Henry Burmester, 'The Rise, Fall and Proposed Rebirth of the Australian Military Court' (2011) 39(9) *Federal Law Review* 195; Jason Wall, 'The Validity of Military Courts after *Lane v Morrison*' (2009) 9 *New Zealand Armed Forces Law Review* 130.

this Act, as well as whether this Act is contrary to the requirements for exclusive judicial power under Chapter III of the *Constitution*.[235] The majority judgments in *White* explain the source of authority for military judicial power being in s 51(vi), and outside Chapter III, by reference to legal history.[236] They rely on a number of previous High Court authorities.[237] The essence of this position is that the defence power is a special and distinct power among the other 39 legislative powers provided for in s 51.[238] The system of offences, trials, punishments and appeals provided by the *Defence Force Discipline Act 1982* derives from a longstanding system of statutory control over military discipline dating back to 1688.[239] *Lane v Morrison* strongly reinforced this in striking down the Australian Military Court as unacceptably interposing itself in the relationship between command and discipline.[240] In *Haskins v Commonwealth*, Heydon J recalled the reasons that military discipline laws are necessary: 'In the mournful words of Maitland, it "has been the verdict of long experience, that an army cannot be kept together if its discipline is left to the ordinary common law"'.[241]

---

235 See the discussion on these issues in Groves, above n 220; Andrew Mitchell and Tania Voon, 'Justice at the Sharp End – Improving Australia's Military Justice System' (2005) 28(2) *University of New South Wales Law Journal* 396; Richard Tracey, 'The Constitution and Military Justice' (2005) 28 *University of New South Wales Law Journal* 426; Justice Margaret White, 'The Constitution and Military Justice: *Re Colonel Aird; Ex parte Alpert*' (Paper presented at the Constitutional Law Conference, Sydney, 24 February 2006); John Devereux, 'Discipline Abroad: *Re Colonel Aird; Ex parte Alpert*' (2004) 23 *University of Queensland Law Journal* 485; Ponce de Leon, above n 223, 297–303.
236 *White* (2007) 231 CLR 570, 586, 598.
237 Most notably *Re Tracey* (1989) 166 CLR 518; *Re Aird; Ex parte Alpert* (2004) 220 CLR 308; *R v Bevan; Ex parte Elias and Gordon* (1942) 66 CLR 452; *R v Cox; Ex parte Smith* (1945) 71 CLR 1 among others.
238 *White* (2007) 231 CLR 570, 583, 586, 589.
239 Ibid 592.
240 (2009) 239 CLR 230, 261. Justice Paul Brereton put this as executive power exercised judicially, rather than judicial power exercised outside of Chapter III, in his 'Commentary on Military Justice and Chapter III: The Constitutional Basis of Courts Martial' (Paper presented at the Australian Association of Constitutional Lawyers Seminar, Sydney, 8 May 2013) 5 in direct response, and contrast to, Jonathan Crowe and Suri Ratnapala, 'Military Justice and Chapter III: The Constitutional Basis of Courts Martial' (2012) 40 *Federal Law Review* 161.
241 *Haskins v Commonwealth* (2011) 244 CLR 22, 60, quoting Maitland, *The Constitutional History of England* (1955) 279. On the critical operational need for effective disciplinary law and processes in the Second Australian Imperial Force, and the serious underestimation of this issue at the beginning of the Second World War, see Lieutenant Colonel Lachlan Mead, 'We are more Concerned with the Good Soldier Than the Bad One in War: the Australian Army Legal Department 1939-1942' in Bruce Oswald and Jim Waddell (eds) *Justice in Arms: Military Lawyers in the Australian Army's First Hundred Years* (Big Sky, 2014) 77; and 'Not Exactly Heroic but Still Moderately Useful: Army Legal Work During the Second World War 1939-1945' in Bruce Oswald and Jim Waddell (eds) *Justice in Arms: Military Lawyers in the Australian Army's First Hundred Years* (Big Sky, 2014) 127.

It is also important to recognise that there is an implicit requirement of trust in the duty of obedience. ADF members carrying out apparently lawful orders have to trust that such orders are lawful and will not expose them personally to prosecution or suit. It is not likely or perhaps even possible that an ADF member involved in an operation would be able to assess the nuances of the lawful authority to act under executive power. Were ADF members to be prosecuted or sued for doing what they reasonably believed to be their duty though, it would almost certainly undermine their trust in their superiors and their willingness to obey the command of those superiors. This could, in turn, undermine the constitutional principles of military obedience and military subordination to the civilian government. A Minister or CDF that gave legally questionable directions or orders and was reckless or indifferent to this trust in doing so may well then undermine these principles. This was the potential risk in the Tampa incident discussed above and perhaps partly explains the need for the *Border Protection (Validation and Enforcement Powers) Act 2001*. The *Defence Force Discipline Act* partly addresses this issue in providing, at s 14, that a person is not liable to be convicted of a service offence for an act or omission that was in obedience to a lawful order, or even an unlawful order, which the 'person did not know, and could not reasonably be expected to have known, was unlawful'. This provision cannot immunise an ADF member from prosecution or suit in a civilian court however.[242]

Command and discipline, therefore, provide a constitutional mechanism for ensuring executive power can be effected through the ADF and that the ADF does not usurp executive power, but it does rely to some extent on commands being lawful in order to maintain the obedience of members of the ADF. This reinforces the principle of legality but it can be difficult to fix the boundaries of legality in an area of such inherent uncertainty as ADF operations under executive power. This may be an argument for a broader defence of superior orders which are not manifestly unlawful. These are points to which this book will return in subsequent chapters.

---

242 *Re Tracey* (1989) 166 CLR 518, 556–62.

VI Conclusion

The spectre of the English Civil War still hangs over the relationship between the government and the ADF. There is a deep concern to ensure that the armed forces remain under control, which is twofold: first, is to have an armed force that will follow orders, government or military, to defend against external enemies; second, is to ensure that the armed forces remain under the control of the government and not threaten it. These concerns go to the heart of the existence of an independent state and the existence of constitutional government. As Lord Loughborough stated, it is 'for the peace and safety of the kingdom'.[243]

Not only does the relationship between the government and the ADF go to the very existence of the legal system, it is also uniquely concerned with life and death. A member of the ADF has a duty to kill and risk his or her own life at the command of his or her superiors. There is no other legal relationship like this in our society. It is perhaps not surprising that the courts have seen it as special.

The direct relationship with the Sovereign is cast in terms of command. The command relationship is a personal relationship. It is perhaps emotionally more meaningful to owe obedience and loyalty to a person rather than a concept. As Sir Ninian Stephen put it in his article on 'The Governor-General as Commander-in-Chief', 'it is a close relationship of sentiment'.[244] Command is a personal manifestation of the more conceptual higher-level prerogative power. Statute describes and regulates the relationship but does not ultimately provide the source of the powers or the obligations. It is unlike the corporate authority of the cabinet, the Parliament or an appeal court. It is exercisable by an individual with the power to exercise it and carries with it an implicit obligation to maintain the trust of those who must obey those commands.

What does this say about the limits of the exercise of executive power by the ADF? There are limits inherent in the place of the ADF within the constitutional structures for subordination of the military to the civilian government. These include the distinct nature of command, as well as the relationship between the Minister, Governor-General and the Chief of

---

243 *Grant v Gould* (1792) 2 HBL 69, 99–100; 126 ER 434, 450 quoted in *Re Tracey* (1989) 166 CLR 518, 557.
244 Stephen, above n 65, 571.

the Defence Force which reflects the 17th-century compromise between Parliament and the Crown. Seventeenth-century principles also limit the ability of the ADF to be part of Parliament and subject the ADF to the general law. Within these bounds, however, Parliament and the courts have left considerable authority in the hands of the Crown in the form of prerogative power to defend the realm and to control the forces. Despite the profound importance of the principle of military subordination to the civilian government, the authority remaining with the Crown may still actually extend to displacing civilian authority in certain circumstances. This will be the subject of Chapter 3 on martial law.

3

Martial Law

I Introduction

This chapter will consider martial law in its internal manifestation. Martial law is an elusive phenomenon but, when considered as a distinct prerogative power for maintaining or restoring functional government, it does much to illustrate the potential extent of executive power which the ADF may exercise. Martial law is distinct from merely using force to suppress internal disturbances because it extends to fulfilling some functions of civilian government, even legislative and judicial functions. Australian military forces exercised extensive civilian government functions in northern Australia and the then Australian territories of New Guinea and Papua in the Second World War.[1] Martial law is, therefore, perhaps the most extreme manifestation of executive power as exercised by a military force. As a way of finding the theoretical limits of executive power then, it may even be more useful than analysing war. War need not have much effect on the functions of civilian government at all, as has been the case with ADF warfighting in Afghanistan and Iraq in more recent years. Constitutionally, it is potentially far more significant when a military that is meant to be subordinate to the civilian government assumes some of the functions of that government.

---

1 *National Security (Emergency Control) Regulations 1941* (Cth).

Martial law is a strange legal creature in that references to it date back centuries yet it is still far from settled as to what martial law actually is. The *Petition of Right 1628* (Imp) purported to abolish the practice of martial law in England yet proclamations of martial law continued to occur thereafter in many places where English law applied.[2] The authorities for martial law are limited and Lord Hale described martial law as 'no Law, but something indulged rather than allowed as a Law'.[3] Martial law is distinct from military law in that it describes a set of circumstances rather than a body of law. There is no body of martial law as such. If the imposition of martial law results in the application of military law to civilians, then this is as a means of affording some sort of due process in a way familiar to military officers. It is not because military law applies of its own force by virtue of a state of martial law.[4]

At its highest, martial law permits the military to exercise not only the executive but also some judicial and legislative functions of government. As Sir Charles Napier, once Commander-in-Chief of the British Army in India, said: '[T]he union of Legislative, Judicial and Executive Power in one Person is the essence of Martial Law'.[5]

There are arguments that martial law in fact even authorises what no civilian government could do, including acts such as summarily killing prisoners and slaughtering innocent civilians to terrorise the surviving population into submission.[6] At its lowest, martial law is said not even to exist. It may just be the exercise of the common-law doctrine of necessity. The martial (that is to do with military forces) aspect of martial law only arises because the military may find itself relying on the doctrine but, even so, it is open to military and civilians alike to rely upon the doctrine

---

2   See Charles Clode, *The Military Forces of the Crown: Their Administration and Government* (John Murray, 1869) 179–80.
3   Charles Clode, *The Administration of Justice under Military and Martial Law: As Applicable to the Army, Navy, Marines and Auxiliary Forces* (John Murray, 2nd ed, 1874) 179 quoting Sir Matthew Hale, *The History of the Common Law of England* (E. and R. Nutt and R. Gosling, 1739).
4   Military Board, *Australian Edition of Manual of Military Law* (CAGP, 1941) 5; see discussion of this point in Clode, *The Administration of Justice Under Military and Martial Law*, above n 3, 183–6; W S Holdsworth 'Martial Law Historically Considered' (1902) 18 *Law Quarterly Review* 117, 128; H Erle Richards, 'Martial Law' (1902) 18 *Law Quarterly Review* 133, 133–4; R W Kostal, *A Jurisprudence of Power: Victorian Empire and the Rule of Law* (Oxford, 2005) 331–8.
5   Quoted in Clode, *The Administration of Justice Under Military and Martial Law,* above n 3, 184.
6   W F Finlason, *Treatise on Martial Law as Allowed by the Law of England in Time of Rebellion: With Illustrations Drawn from the Official Documents in the Jamaica Case, and Comments Constitutional and Legal* (Stevens, 1866) cited in Kostal, above n 4, 231–4.

of necessity.[7] Martial law is also relevant to conquered and occupied territories, but this is beyond the realm of discussion here and the subject of a later chapter. Given that there have been occasions when Australian forces have exercised governmental powers over civilians, it is necessary for this book to consider the extent to which the executive power has been or could be the legal basis for the exercise of these powers. Where such powers have relied upon statute this may still illustrate the extent of the executive power where it is not possible to enact legislation in an emergency. This chapter will treat the exercise of governmental powers by military forces over civilians as the exercise of martial law. In the Australian historical examples, however, the term martial law has rarely arisen. The term military control is more common. Neocleous argues that the modern equivalent of martial law is found in emergency and national security legislation.[8] The British experience in Ireland during the First World War and into the 1920s was that the term martial law in itself tended to incite the agitation that martial law powers were meant to suppress. The use of equivalent powers under legislation through the *Defence of the Realm Act 1914* (UK) achieved the same effect but without the politically unacceptable connotations of the term 'martial law'.[9] The development of the extraordinary powers in the *National Security (Emergency Control) Act 1939* (Cth), discussed below, or in Part IIIAAA of the *Defence Act 1903* (Cth) for example, would tend to bear this out for Australia. Even so, martial law as a part of prerogative power or the common law has not disappeared. The term 'martial law' retains pejorative connotations but is useful for this book because there is at least some case law surrounding 'martial law', as opposed to the more euphemistic 'military control'.

It remains possible that there could be circumstances in which the ADF may use martial law powers not provided by statute. This book will argue that the ADF might, in a crisis in which civilian government is unable to function, lawfully assume some civilian executive and legislative functions where it is necessary to do so, usually within a limited area and only for so long as the emergency persists. Prerogative power would authorise this action until restoration of civilian government was possible or until

---

[7] A V Dicey, *Introduction to the Study of the Law of the Constitution* (Macmillan, 10th ed, 1959) 284–6.
[8] Mark Neocleous, 'Whatever Happened to Martial Law? Detainees and the Logic of Emergency' (2007) 143 *Radical Philosophy* 13, 16–18.
[9] Ibid.

legislation authorised the action. Nothing could, however, completely remove the jurisdiction of the courts or permit an enduring change to the *Constitution*. This reflects the limits proposed in Chapter 1.

This chapter will not consider the exercise of disciplinary control by the military over civilians in those situations where civilians have voluntarily subjected themselves to military discipline in order to accompany a force. The *Defence Force Discipline Act 1982* (Cth) now provides for such people as 'defence civilians'.[10] This chapter will also not consider the defence force aid to the civil authority regime of Part IIIAAA of the *Defence Act 1903* (Cth), as this contemplates military power supplementing civilian powers rather than substituting for them.

II What is Martial Law?

There is a considerable body of mainly English legal writing and to a lesser extent case law on what martial law is. It diverges widely. In feudal times the term related to the Court of the Constable and the Marshal which exercised jurisdiction over armies raised through feudal obligation for particular wars.[11] The development of a standing army and the *Mutiny Act 1689* eventually rendered this jurisdiction obsolete, with the last recorded case being in 1737.[12] A number of 19th-century incidents, most notably the Jamaica Rebellion of 1865, later gave rise to a lively debate on what martial law is and what it authorises, and indeed whether it really exists.[13] There are also some useful 20th-century cases arising from British imposition of martial law in South Africa and Ireland. This debate is almost forgotten now and there is scant literature on martial

---

10   *Defence Force Discipline Act 1982* (Cth) s 3.
11   W S Holdsworth, 'Martial Law Historically Considered' (1902) 18 *Law Quarterly Review* 117, 118–19; Clode, *The Administration of Justice under Military and Martial Law*, above n 3, 83; Sir Matthew Hale, *The Prerogatives of the King* (Selden Society, written between 1640 and 1664 but unpublished, D E C Yale (ed) 1976 ed) 123, see *Tabula Quarta – Tempore Belli* and *Pax et Belli Constitutio*, xiv, and generally Chapter XII 'Concerning the Jurisdiction and Office of the Constable and Marshal, Martial Law, *Tempus Belli* and Acquisitions by Right of War'.
12   Holdsworth, 'Martial Law Historically Considered', above n 11.
13   See generally Kostal, above n 4.

law in Australia.[14] The most notable Australian treatment of martial law by H P Lee in *Emergency Powers* in 1984 stated that there had been no recorded instances of martial law since the promulgation of the *Australian Constitution* in 1901.[15] Justice White[16] and Michael Head[17] also state this view. While there may have been virtually no instances of martial law so described—as this chapter will argue—since 1901 there have been significant Australian experiences with martial law in one form or another.

Before turning to the Australian historical examples, it is necessary to outline the debate over martial law in the legal historical literature. Martial law falls into different but at times overlapping categories.

A Conquered and Occupied Territories

The least controversial view of martial law is that it applies to conquered or occupied foreign territory. This is on the basis that, where the previous sovereign authority has been displaced, some sort of law is better than no law. The Duke of Wellington made often-cited comments on this in the House of Lords in 1851:

> Martial law is neither more nor less than the will of the general who commands the army. In fact martial law means no law at all, therefore the general who declares martial law, and commands that it should be carried into execution, is bound to lay down distinctly the rules and regulations and limits according to which his will is to be carried out.[18] Now I have in another country carried out martial law; that is to say, I have governed a large proportion of a country by my own will. But then what did I do? I declared that the country should be governed according to its own national law; and I carried into this my so declared will.[19]

---

14 Interestingly, the debate over liberty and security in the contemporary debate on terrorism reflects many of the same concerns as the controversies over martial law but with less of the imperial context, David Dyzenhaus, *The Constitution of Law: Legality in a Time of Emergency* (Cambridge University Press, 2006) 196–200; Colm O'Cinneide, 'Strapped to the Mast: The Siren Song of Dreadful Necessity, the United Kingdom *Human Rights Act* and the Terrorist Threat' in Miriam Gani and Penelope Matthew (eds) *Fresh Perspectives on the War on Terror* (ANU E Press, 2008) 327, 330–3.
15 H P Lee, *The Emergency Powers of the Commonwealth of Australia* (Law Book Company, 1984) 212.
16 Margaret White, 'The Executive and the Military' (2005) 28(2) *University of New South Wales Law Journal* (Australian Military Law Thematic Edition) 438, 439.
17 Michael Head, *Calling out the Troops: The Australian Military and Civil Unrest* (Federation Press, 2009) 43.
18 Lee, *The Emergency Powers of the Commonwealth of Australia*, above n 15, 213, only cites this first half of the passage.
19 *Hansard*, Third Series, 17 March–10 April, 1851 cited in Neocleous, above n 8, and Holdsworth, 'Martial Law Historically Considered', above n 11, 137.

During the Jamaica controversy of the 1860s, the Duke's statement was cited in support of the use of martial law for internal strife[20] though the less cited latter half of his comments indicated he was referring to his own exercise of powers in foreign territories. United States Attorney-General Cushing (1853–1857) also made the distinction in stating that, 'As exercised in any country by the commander of a foreign army, it is an element of the *jus belli*. It is incidental to the solemn state of war, and appertains to the law of nations'. This was as opposed to 'martial law in one's own country', which was 'a case which the law of nations does not reach'.[21] The distinction is important because, although the exercise of martial law may entail the exercise of many of the same governmental functions whether internally or on foreign territory, the basis for and the scope of the exercise of martial law does differ. The distinction is also important in the Australian context because of the significant Australian exercises of martial law in German New Guinea, Somalia and East Timor which will be the subject of Chapter 6.

B Common Law Doctrine of Necessity

One view sees martial law as simply a manifestation of the common-law doctrine of necessity. This view became most salient as a result of the suppression of the Jamaica Rebellion. In 1865, a number of districts in Jamaica saw an uprising by black plantation workers and other poor against white plantation owners and colonial authorities. Governor Edward Eyre (already famous as the first European to cross the Nullarbor Plain[22]) authorised the suppression of the rebellion with brutal force, summary executions and floggings, as well as courts martial followed by executions.[23] Much of the controversy arising from the Jamaica Rebellion turned on whether martial law authorised the court martial and execution in particular of George Gordon, a black Jamaican landowner and politician.[24] On the narrower view based on the common-law doctrine of necessity, it did not.[25] The Jamaica Committee, created in England in response to the events by a group of reform-minded public

---

20 Kostal, above n 4, 203–4.
21 *Opinions of Attorney-Generals* cited in Lee, above n 15 at n 62, 213–14, and in Holdsworth, 'Martial Law Historically Considered', above n 11, 137.
22 Peter Handford, 'Edward John Eyre and the Conflict of Laws' (2008) 32(3) *Melbourne University Law Review* 822, 828–9.
23 Kostal, above n 4, 12–15.
24 Ibid 14–17.
25 Ibid 278–80.

figures, which included J S Mill,[26] attempted a private prosecution of Governor Eyre. The Committee also attempted the private prosecution of a British Army officer, Brigadier Nelson, and a Royal Navy officer, Lieutenant Brand, who had been members of a court martial which had imposed death penalties.[27] In neither case, *R v Eyre*[28] and *R v Nelson and Brand*,[29] would a grand jury find that the prosecutions should proceed to trial.[30] The charges to the grand juries in each case are therefore valuable treatments of the law of martial law but did not resolve the question of whether martial law was limited to the common-law doctrine of necessity, as neither became binding precedents.[31]

The argument for martial law being only a manifestation of the common-law doctrine of necessity is perhaps best put in the arguments of the counsel for the prosecution in *R v Nelson and Brand*, Mr Fitzjames Stephen.[32] Stephen had initially advised the Jamaica Committee on martial law and Kostal has described his arguments in some detail. There is no later case, such as the case of *Marais*[33] discussed below, which sets out the argument clearly. The limited view is essentially this. The *Petition of Right 1628* abolished martial law in England and, therefore, where English law applies.[34] The Glorious Revolution of 1688 established finally that the Crown is not above the law. The power to take life must be found in law. If the military take life or engage in any other act that

---

26 Handford, above n 22, 836.
27 *Frederick Cockburn's Special Report of the Charge of the Lord Chief Justice of England to the Grand Jury at the Central Criminal Court in the Case of The Queen Against Nelson and Brand* (2nd ed, 1867) ('*Frederick Cockburn's Special Report*'). (This was the report of the case as such and is cited in *Re Tracey; Ex parte Ryan* (1989) 166 CLR 518, 555 ('*Re Tracey*').)
28 Being a charge to a Grand Jury and not a judicial decision as such, W F Finlason, *Report of the Case of The Queen v Edward Eyre on his Prosecution in the Court of Queen's Bench containing the Charge of Mr Justice Blackburn* (Stevens, 1868). See Kostal, above n 4, 395–404. *R v Eyre* (1867–68) LR 3 QB 487 is a report of the earlier decision on whether this matter was triable in England, as distinct from *Phillips v Eyre* (1870) LR 6 QB 1, which was a civil proceeding against Governor Eyre arising out of the same rebellion and supported by the Jamaica Committee.
29 Being a charge to a Grand Jury and not a judicial decision as such, *Frederick Cockburn's Special Report*, above n 27.
30 Finlason, above n 28, 102; *Frederick Cockburn's Special Report*, above n 27, 160; Handford, above n 22, 841–3.
31 Each charge differed on this question, Cockburn LCJ in *R v Nelson and Brand* was equivocal on the issue, *Frederick Cockburn's Special Report*, above n 27, 159, and Blackburn J focused more on Jamaican colonial statutory authority, Finlason, above n 28, 81; Kostal, above n 4, 336–41, 395–404.
32 Kostal, above n 4, 278–80. Cockburn CJ's charge in this case curiously stopped short of endorsing the narrow view. His view was that necessity was in the minds of the officers concerned, i.e. a subjective test rather than an objective test, *Frederick Cockburn's Special Report*, above n 27, 159.
33 [1902] AC 109.
34 See discussion in Clode, *The Military Forces of the Crown*, above n 2, 1–76.

would ordinarily be unlawful in the process of restoring order, it must be shown to be necessary under the common law. If it is not necessary to take life, or any other step purportedly authorised under martial law, then the act is unlawful and punishable as a crime.[35] No appellate court gave an authoritative judgment on Stephen's argument. Cockburn CJ's subsequent charge to the Grand Jury did not support his view fully and the jury did not find that the prosecution should proceed to trial.[36]

Dicey devoted a chapter to martial law in his book, *Introduction to the Study of the Law of the Constitution*, first published in 1885.[37] Although he did not directly refer to the attempted Jamaica prosecutions, he was apparently close to some members of the Jamaica Committee.[38] His view was, of course, not the law and he did not advance this argument in a court. Dicey's work is influential though and courts and writers alike have cited him frequently.[39] He stated that there was no such thing as martial law but did concede that the term was sometimes 'employed as a name for the common-law right of the Crown and its servants to repel force by force in the case of invasion, insurrection, riot or generally of any violent resistance to the law'.[40]

Importantly, every subject, whether uniformed or not, is a servant of the Crown for this purpose and has not only a right but a duty to put down breaches of the peace.[41] There is no distinction between a soldier and a citizen in this regard. Each is authorised and bound to use force, up to and including lethal force, as may be necessary to put down the riot or disturbance.[42] Both soldier and citizen are equally liable to account before a jury for the use of unnecessary force as well as a failure to act.[43] Dicey cites the prosecution of the Mayor of Bristol in *R v Pinney*[44] for failing

---

35   Ibid 278–80; see also the argument of Mr Holborne in the *Case of Ship Money* cited in Holdsworth, 'Martial Law Historically Considered', above n 11, 125, and Cyril Dodd, 'The Case of Marais' (1902) 18 *Law Quarterly Review* 145.
36   *Frederick Cockburn's Special Report*, above n 27, 160; Handford, above n 22, 841–3. Clode rues the lack of a rule of law emerging from this litigation, Clode, *The Military Forces of the Crown*, above n 2, 179.
37   Dicey, above n 7, Chapter VIII.
38   Handford, above n 22, 836.
39   See, eg, *Re Tracey* (1989) 166 CLR 518, 546; Lee, *The Emergency Powers of the Commonwealth of Australia*, above n 15, 215; Military Board, above n 4, 5.
40   Dicey, above n 7, 288.
41   Ibid 289.
42   Ibid.
43   Ibid.
44   (1832) 5 Carrington & Payne 254.

in his duty to suppress the Featherstone riots of 1831 (although he was acquitted).⁴⁵ The significant aspect of Dicey's view is the common-law character of the right and duty to suppress breaches of the peace, noting that he did not see prerogative power as anything more than the residue of powers left in the hands of the Crown.⁴⁶ In this sense martial law was simply another name for existing common-law rights and duties, limited by the doctrine of necessity.

Dicey saw the other form of martial law as being 'the government of a country or a district by military tribunals, which more or less supersede the jurisdiction of the courts'. He stated that this kind of martial law in England is 'utterly unknown to the constitution'.⁴⁷ Dicey did not refer to martial law of conquered or occupied territories outside of England, nor indeed the British Empire outside of England and Ireland. He did discuss *Wolfe Tone's Case*⁴⁸ in which a court martial in Dublin in 1798 sentenced an Irish rebel to death. The Irish Court of King's Bench granted a writ of habeas corpus on the basis that Wolfe Tone was not a military person and therefore not subject to punishment by a court martial. Dicey's point was that even in the midst of a revolutionary crisis martial law was not a part of the common law.⁴⁹

The view of martial law as really being a manifestation of the common-law doctrine of necessity has some appeal in that it firmly asserts the rule of law over the will of a general or the executive more broadly. It is not entirely consistent with all of the authorities however, nor with a significant amount of the practice of martial law. First of all there is the widely cited 1884 case of *Dudley v Stephens*⁵⁰ on necessity which stands as authority for the principle that, in criminal law, necessity is no defence for the taking of life. Any view of martial law that sees it as the common-law doctrine of necessity could not authorise the taking of life. This is a problem for Dicey's view of the duty to repel force with force. It suggests that he is blurring concepts of self-defence and the defence of others, the suppression of riots and the suppression of insurrection. It is also

---

45 Dicey, above n 7, 288–9.
46 Ibid.
47 Ibid 291.
48 (1798) 27 St Tr 614.
49 Dicey, above n 7, 293–4.
50 (1884) 14 QBD 273; see discussion in Simon Bronitt and Dale Stephens, '"Flying Under the Radar" – The Use of Lethal Force Against Hijacked Aircraft: Recent Australian Developments' (2007) 7(2) *Oxford University Commonwealth Law Journal* 265, 267.

important to note that, as discussed in Chapter 1, a view that assimilates the power of the Commonwealth with the powers of a natural person in Australia would not appear to have survived *Williams*.[51] There are more cases which would suggest that martial law relies upon prerogative power; it is limited by necessity but a necessity to restore governmental authority. This is not a doctrine of necessity upon which any citizen can rely. It is also not a basis to suppress a riot with the use of lethal force. Chapter 4 will explore the distinction between the suppression of riot and the suppression of insurrection further.

C Prerogative with Respect to Martial Law

A broader view of martial law is that the body of military law (that is the law applicable normally only to the military) can be asserted over the civilian population because it is necessary to restore a form of government.[52] This is still a view which relies on necessity but sees necessity in different terms because martial law is not another name for the common-law doctrine of necessity but a prerogative of the Crown.

1 During War and Insurrection

Even though martial law within the realm does not necessarily require a state of war, a discussion first of martial law during internal war, as opposed to riots or disturbances, may help to establish its basis as a prerogative of the Crown. On this view, at its highest, only the Crown can wage war.[53] It is lawful to wage war even to suppress an internal rebellion because it threatens the state itself and the Crown's sovereignty over it. It is necessary to restore the functioning of the Crown's government. This is much more than a breach of the peace or riot and it is not for the ordinary subject to exercise common-law powers in response to it.[54] Chitty did not use the term martial law as such but did state:

---

51 *Williams v Commonwealth* (2012) 248 CLR 156 ('*Williams*').
52 This is not to say that military law is the substance of martial law, only that, in a situation of martial law, offences and procedures can be borrowed from military law and applied outside of the military.
53 Joseph Chitty, *A Treatise on the Law of the Prerogatives of the Crown; and the Relative Duties and Rights of the Subject* (Butterworths, 1820) 44–5.
54 See Lee, *The Emergency Powers of the Commonwealth of Australia,* above n 15, 214–17.

The King may lay on a general embargo, and do various acts growing out of sudden emergencies; but in all these cases the emergency is the avowed cause, and the act done is as temporary as the occasion. The King cannot change by his prerogative of war, either the law of nations or the law of the land, by general and unlimited regulations.[55]

There is a surprising degree of consistency in the writers and jurists on the point that the Crown can effectively wage war against an insurrection, so that killing in combat in such situations is lawful. Coke,[56] Hale,[57] Clode,[58] Cockburn LCJ,[59] Blackburn J,[60] Stephen,[61] counsel for the prosecution in *R v Eyre*[62] and *R v Nelson and Brand*,[63] Windeyer,[64] Holdsworth,[65] Finlason,[66] Lendrum[67] and Dicey[68] all maintain, effectively, that the Crown may maintain war against its own subjects where they are in open revolt.[69] By way of example, the Victorian Act XII of 1854 (better identified as the *Martial Law Indemnity Act*) followed the famous Eureka Stockade incident. On 3 December 1854, police and soldiers had attacked a fortification built by miners protesting against government taxes and the way they were collected. Twenty-two miners and four of the troops died in the fighting.[70] With respect to prerogative power, at clause II the *Act* stated:

---

55   Chitty, above n 53, 49.
56   Kostal, above n 4, 249; Clode, *The Military Forces of the Crown*, above n 2, 157–8.
57   Hale, above n 11, 121, 124–32.
58   Clode, *The Administration of Justice under Military and Martial Law*, above n 3, 177–91.
59   Kostal, above n 4, 331.
60   See Handford, above n 22, n 123.
61   Kostal, above n 4, 233.
62   Finlason, *Report of the Case of The Queen v Edward Eyre on his Prosecution in the Court of Queen's Bench Containing the Charge of Mr Justice Blackburn*, above n 28.
63   *Frederic Cockburn's Special Report*, above n 27.
64   Justice Robert Hope, 'Protective Security Review' (Parliamentary Paper 397, Parliament of Australia, 1979), 'Appendix 9: Opinion of Sir Victor Windeyer, KBE, CB, DSO on Certain Questions Concerning the Position of Members of the Defence Force When Called Out to Aid the Civil Power', 280.
65   Holdsworth, 'Martial Law Historically Considered', above n 11, 126–7.
66   Letter from W F Finlason to William Gladstone, 3 February 1868 quoted in Kostal, above n 4, 230.
67   S D Lendrum, 'The "Coorong Massacre": Martial Law and the Aborigines at First Settlement' (1977) 6(1) *Adelaide Law Review* 26, 38–42.
68   Dicey, above n 7, 288.
69   See Neocleous, above n 8, 14; Oren Gross and Fionnuala Ni Aolain, *Law in Times of Crisis: Emergency Powers in Theory and Practice* (Cambridge University Press, 2006) 119–23.
70   See Philip Lynch, 'Juries as Communities of Resistance: Eureka and the Power of the Rabble' (2002) 27(2) *Alternative Law Journal* 83.

> Nothing in this Act contained shall be construed to interfere with Her Majesty's Royal Prerogative or to abridge the right of Her Majesty to do any act warranted by law for the suppression of treason or rebellion.

This provision does not create any prerogative power which did not otherwise exist but it does indicate that the Parliament of Victoria at the time acted as if there was prerogative power to suppress treason and rebellion.[71] There are also references in preambles and recitals in Acts dealing with Ireland from King George III and King William IV to the Crown's 'undoubted prerogative in executing martial law',[72] although, as Cockburn CJ pointed out, a recital does not bring into law anything which was not already part of the law.[73]

The difference in the writing appears to lie, then, in whether this power arises from the common-law doctrine of necessity or from prerogative power. Lee suggests that little turns on this as on both views necessity limits any action.[74] There is only a little authority on this point but what authority there is does seem to suggest that there is a significant difference. On one view, any person could restore the functioning of civilian government, which seems as practically implausible as it does potentially anarchic. On the other view, only the forces of the Crown can restore functioning government, which is practically far more plausible as much as it is more consistent with constitutional order.

It is important to make clear at this point that this book is not arguing that the suppression of insurrection—that is an internal war—is an exercise of the prerogative of martial law. That would be an exercise of the war prerogative. The point is that an insurrection, or invasion, could prevent or destroy the normal functioning of civilian government. As much as it is an exercise of the war prerogative to defeat the enemy, it is an exercise of the prerogative as to martial law for the military to provide a form of government in those circumstances. Despite the title of the *Martial Law Indemnity Act*, this book argues that martial law is not concerned with actions against an enemy, but rather actions to restore or maintain

---

71   As to Acts of Indemnity generally, they are not in themselves the law of martial law, but their common use after periods of martial law does indicate something of the concern of parliaments with respect to the uncertainties of martial law, *Shaw Savill & Albion Co Ltd v Commonwealth* (1940) 66 CLR 344, 357 ('*Shaw Savill & Albion Co Ltd*').
72   Holdsworth, 'Martial Law Historically Considered', above n 11, 126.
73   Ibid 128.
74   Lee, *The Emergency Powers of the Commonwealth of Australia*, above n 15, 216.

government, even if it is the presence of an enemy that creates the necessity of imposing martial law. This leads to a closer examination of the basis for martial law being a prerogative power.

Charles Clode was a legal adviser within the War Office at the time of the Jamaica controversy and indeed advised on the law of martial law in respect of it.[75] His books, the two volume: *The Military Forces of the Crown: Their Administration and Government* of 1869; and *The Administration of Justice under Military and Martial Law* of 1872, in some ways respond directly to the Jamaica events and reflect the official views of the War Office at the time.[76] Notably, as mentioned in Chapter 2, the High Court of Australia has cited Clode's works several times as a persuasive guide to the law.[77] Clode cites with approval the Opinions of Lords Campbell and Cranworth (both former Lords Chancellor) in relation to the Canadian Rebellion of 1837:

> We are of the opinion that the *prerogative* [of executing Martial Law] does not extend beyond the case of persons taken in open resistance, and with whom, by reason of the suspension of the Ordinary Tribunals, it is impossible to deal according to the regular course of Justice. Where the Courts are open, so the Criminals might be delivered to them to be dealt with according to Law, there is not, as we conceive, any right in the Crown to adopt any other course of proceeding [emphasis added].[78]

A more persuasive authority is the Boer War case of *Marais*.[79] In this case the Privy Council gave a decision inconsistent with the common-law doctrine of necessity view of martial law. Mr Marais was in military custody after his arrest and charge for breaching martial law regulations. He had appealed to the Privy Council from a decision of the Supreme Court of the Colony of the Cape of Good Hope. Crucially this meant that the civilian courts were still open and, it was argued, the ordinary rule is that the civil courts should have jurisdiction where the civilian courts are open.[80] The Privy Council held that war could still be raging even if the

---

75 Kostal, above n 4, 475.
76 Clode, *The Military Forces of the Crown*, above 2, 175–8; Clode, *The Administration of Justice Under Military and Martial Law*, above n 3, 179.
77 *Re Tracey* (1989) 166 CLR 518, 555; *X v Commonwealth* (1999) 200 CLR 177, 233; *Marks v Commonwealth* (1964) 111 CLR 549, 577.
78 Clode, *The Administration of Justice Under Military and Martial Law*, above n 3, 187, also citing the *Colonial Governors Instructions* with respect to Martial Law, 183.
79 *Marais v General Officer Commanding the Lines of Communication* [1902] AC 109 ('*Marais*').
80 Ibid 3.

military permitted some courts to remain open for business.[81] The Privy Council took the affidavit evidence of Mr Marais himself as grounds for determining that war was actually raging.[82] Further, where actual war is raging, the actions of the military authorities are nonjusticiable:

> It may often be a question whether a mere riot or disturbance neither so serious nor so extensive as really to amount to a war at all has not been treated with an excessive severity and whether the intervention of the military force was necessary but once let the fact of actual war be established and there is an universal consensus of opinion that the Civil Courts have no jurisdiction to call in question the propriety of the action of the military authorities.[83]

Effectively this must give a broader view of necessity for, if it was open to Mr Marais to have the Supreme Court hear his matter, then it was not strictly necessary for the military to have conduct of his imprisonment and charge. To then hold the matter nonjusticiable would suggest that it saw the matter as one of prerogative power and not the common-law doctrine of necessity. The Privy Council stated 'the truth is, that no doubt has ever existed that where war actually prevails the ordinary Courts have no jurisdiction over the military authorities'.[84]

Starke J expressly approved this statement in *Shaw Savill & Albion Co Ltd*.[85] Notably the advice of the Privy Council closed with the words 'the framers of the *Petition of Right* knew well what they meant when they made a condition of peace the ground of the illegality of unconstitutional procedure'.[86] The Councillors, therefore, directly considered the *Petition of Right* and did not see it as applicable to situations of actual war, even an internal war.

The decision in *Marais* met with some concern at the time in a review by Dodd. Dodd could not see the decision as consistent with the *Petition of Right*. As he points out, the Privy Council did not publish any dissenting opinions, given its constitutional status as an advisory committee for the

---

81 Ibid 5. The US position is apparently more rigid in that if the courts are open then military tribunals cannot operate, see Mark Stavsky, 'The Doctrine of State Necessity in Pakistan' (1983) 16(2) *Cornell International Law Journal* 341, 350–2.
82 *Marais* [1902] AC 109, 114.
83 Ibid 115.
84 Ibid.
85 (1940) 66 CLR 344, 356.
86 *Marais* [1902] AC 109, 5; see also Clode, *The Military Forces of the Crown*, above n 2, 157, on *The Petition of Right* only applying during time of peace.

King rather than being a court. It is not, therefore, possible to know what the contrary views within the Privy Council were in this case.[87] Lee also expresses concern.[88] On the other hand, Holdsworth stated of *Marais* at the time:[89]

> This prerogative is quite different from the power which all citizens have at common law of using the degree of force which is necessary to prevent outrage. That power merely provides the necessary means for quelling a riot. It merely allows an amount of force exactly proportioned to the necessities of the case. It does not allow, as a proclamation of martial law allows, an absolutely freehand in dealing with the enemy.[90]

Subsequent decisions reinforce this view of martial law as a prerogative power. The Privy Council found, not long after in *Tilonko v Attorney-General of Natal* in 1906, that courts martial 'are justified by necessity; by the fact of actual war'.[91] Two Irish cases from the Anglo–Irish War of 1921, *R v Allen*[92] and *R (Garde) v Strickland*[93] were consistent with the Privy Council in that they took affidavit evidence of the existence of a state of war from Sir Nevil Macready, the General Officer Commanding-in-Chief in Ireland. Both cases found that, if the court is satisfied of the existence of a state of war which justifies the application of martial law, then it will not interfere with the actions of the military authorities *durante bello*.[94] Starke J in *Shaw Savill & Albion Co Ltd* cited with approval each of these as well as other Irish cases from the same period on this point.[95] All of Ireland in 1921 was still part of the United Kingdom and a common-law jurisdiction.[96] The Irish courts at this time however did not hold the military to account for the use of unnecessary force, as Dicey might

---

87 Dodd, above n 35, 143–4, 149. Dodd also rejected the idea that the military could not be held liable after the war for acts which went beyond the requirements of necessity. This did not include acts against an alien enemy, 148–9.
88 Lee, *The Emergency Powers of the Commonwealth of Australia*, above n 15, 217–19.
89 [1902] AC 109.
90 Holdsworth, 'Martial Law Historically Considered', above n 11, 129–30. More recently, Lendrum also accepted this distinction, above n 67, 38.
91 [1907] AC 93, 94.
92 [1921] 2 IR 241.
93 [1921] 2 IR 317, 331.
94 *R v Allen* [1921] 2 IR 241, 241; *R (Garde) v Strickland* [1921] 2 IR 317, 331.
95 (1940) 66 CLR 344, 356.
96 The *Irish Free State Constitution Act 1922* (Imp) came into force the following year. In support of the existence of a prerogative for martial law and discussion of the situation in Ireland see H V Evatt, *The Royal Prerogative* (Law Book Co, first presented as a doctoral thesis 1924, with commentary by Leslie Zines, 1987) 90–1.

have had it.[97] This would also suggest that martial law is an expression of prerogative power rather than the common-law doctrine of necessity. This is also consistent with Evatt's view, who considered the similar Irish case of *R v Adjutant General of the Provisional Forces*,[98] that 'the essential nature of Prerogative … is that it confers rights on the Crown which are not and cannot be available to subjects … "Martial Law" is also a theory of necessity'.[99]

The Pakistani case *Reference by His Excellency the Governor-General (under s 213 of the Government of India Act, 1935)*[100] distinguished necessity from state necessity, indicating that some acts justified by necessity can only be an exercise of governmental power rather than a power any citizen can exercise.[101] Harrison Moore, taking *Marais*[102] into consideration, was also of this view in stating:

> It is … undoubtedly true that the tradition of a prerogative to proclaim martial law – to suspend the ordinary law in times of war and rebellion – has passed down to modern times; and … the cases mentioned by the writers referred to … clearly regard that power as a function inherent in the Crown.[103]

The conduct of war appears to be a prerogative power of the Crown and military forces exist primarily to execute this prerogative on the sovereign's behalf.[104] It is arguable, therefore, that the exercise of martial law in the factual circumstances of a war or insurrection is an aspect of prerogative power and not the common-law doctrine of necessity available to any

---

97 See Dicey, above n 7. Lee discusses two cases, *Tilonko v A-G (Natal)* [1907] AC 570 and *Clifford v O'Sullivan* [1921] 2 AC 570 (an Anglo–Irish War case) for the proposition that courts martial are not courts at all but merely tribunals for advising the military commander on matters of summary justice. To summarise his view, this is so that there is some order and regularity in the repression of acts of violence (when there are no courts open to determine such matters). The decisions of courts martial are in fact the decisions of the military commander and not those of courts. They are only justified by the necessities of the war or crisis. In this respect, Lee's view is consistent with this book but not insofar as he was equivocal on whether martial law derived from prerogative power or the common-law doctrine of necessity and appeared more inclined to the latter view, Lee, *The Emergency Powers of the Commonwealth of Australia*, above n 15, 221–3.
98 [1923] 1 IR 5 cited in Evatt, above n 96, 90–1.
99 Ibid 117.
100 PLD 1955 FC (Pak) 435.
101 Ibid 435, 485–6; see Stavksy, above n 81, 368, which discusses other martial law cases. For discussion of the line of martial law cases in Pakistan see also Imtiaz Omar, *Emergency Powers and the Courts in India and Pakistan* (Kluwer Law International 2002) 62–3; and Gross and Aolain, above n 69, 46–54.
102 [1902] AC 109 cited in W Harrison Moore, *Act of State in English Law* (Dutton, 1906, Rothman reprint 1987) 58.
103 Ibid 49–50.
104 See discussion in Gross and Aolain, above n 69, 32–5.

person. This is a preferable view because it is not for any person to exercise the military power of the Crown or to claim to do so on its behalf. Apart from being potentially anarchic, this would be contrary to the theory of executive power requiring unity of purpose. To repeat Blackstone's view as quoted in Chapter 1:

> [T]he executive part of government ... is wisely placed in a single hand by the British constitution for the sake of unanimity, strength, and dispatch. Were it placed in many hands, it would be subject to many wills: many wills, if disunited and drawing different ways, create weakness in a government; and to unite these several wills, and reduce them to one, is a work of more time and delay than the exigencies of state will afford.[105]

2 Outside of War

Leaving war and insurrection to one side, more recently the Fiji Court of Appeal in *Republic of Fiji v Prasad* ('*Prasad*')[106] in 2001 provided a common-law authority for the military to impose martial law on the basis of necessity where there is no functioning civilian government. It suggests that it is the absence of functioning civilian government itself, and not necessarily the circumstances of war, which justify the exercise of the prerogative with respect to martial law. This situation arose from the actions in 2000 of civilians, George Speight and others, taking over the entire Fijian Parliament at gunpoint and most of the government ministers with it. Only the President of Fiji, the Head of State but not the Head of Government, remained outside the Parliament and was able to exercise some constitutional executive authority. The hostage situation lasted many weeks and the elected civilian government simply could not function.[107] The Court described the perhaps unprecedented situation as one in which the imposition of martial law was the only reasonable option in order to avoid anarchy:

> The imperative necessity for prompt action arose out of exceptional circumstances not provided for in the *Constitution*. These circumstances called for immediate action. There was no other course reasonably available to the President at the time the hostage crisis began. Later on,

---

105 *Blackstone's Commentaries with Notes of Reference, to the Constitution and Laws, of the Federal Government of the United States; and of the Commonwealth of Virginia* (1803, Hein Online reproduction) 250.
106 Unreported, Fiji Court of Appeal, Casey J (Presiding), Barker, Kapi, Ward and Handley JJA, 1 March 2001.
107 Ibid 1–4.

as the hostages continued to be confined and anarchy was developing, the Commander quite properly contemplated executive action by way of *martial law* to restore and/or maintain law and order. This was appropriate, so long as the extraordinary and frightening situation lasted. The crisis did not end until all the hostages had been released and some calm restored [emphasis added].[108]

This course of action was open only to the President, through the military commander, as an exercise of executive authority. It was not something any ordinary citizen could have done. The military commander of Fiji, Commodore Bainimarama, exceeded this authority only when he abrogated the constitution and took power from the President:

The doctrine of necessity would have authorised him to have taken all necessary steps, whether authorised by the text of the 1997 *Constitution* or not, to have restored law and order, to have secured the release of the hostages, and then, when the emergency had abated, to have reverted to the *Constitution*. Had the Commander chosen this path, his actions could have been validated by the doctrine of necessity. Instead, he chose a different path, that of constitutional abrogation. The doctrine of necessity does not authorise permanent changes to a written constitution, let alone its complete abrogation.[109]

This is consistent with the point made in Chapter 1 that the doctrine of necessity cannot effect an enduring change to the *Constitution*.

This case of martial law outside of war is a far more profound question than the war cases discussed above. It involved the military actually assuming authority over all of the functions of the civilian government, not just some of them or those within a limited area. Until the point of abrogating the constitution, it was not a coup but rather a military response to truly extraordinary circumstances. Even though *Prasad*[110] considered a number of coup cases, a situation of the military *lawfully* taking over the control of government had virtually no basis in common-law case law or literature.[111] Even so, this case is a clear and recent authority.

---

108 Ibid 16.
109 Ibid 17.
110 Ibid.
111 Although this case was not cited in *Prasad*, the situation bears some resemblance to the 1955 situation of the Governor-General in Pakistan assuming legislative as well as executive powers as the legislature had ceased to function, although this was not a case of martial law due to a military takeover, *Reference by His Excellency the Governor-General (under s 213 of the Government of India Act, 1935)* PLD 1955 FC (Pak) 435.

Commodore Bainimarama's assumption of governmental power and his imposition of martial law also connects to the theoretical discussion in Chapter 1. Montesquieu, Hume, Machiavelli and Blackstone[112] all have seen Locke's need for the executive power to be able to 'do public good without a rule'.[113] It is from this, together with *Prasad*,[114] that it is possible to argue that the prerogative with respect to martial law could extend to situations of the collapse of civilian government, whether within or outside of war. The principles are essentially the same as those for martial law within war in that, without martial law, in such situations there would be no law and no government. The imposition of martial law becomes essential to the continued existence of government and law.[115] The fact that civilian government has ceased to function because of a terrorist act or natural disaster instead of war or insurrection should not necessarily alter when martial law could apply and what its limits might be.

This most extreme example illustrates that the prerogative of martial law could be very powerful and the necessity of the case may arguably authorise the executive through the military, but not just any citizen, to take temporary action well beyond the limits of the written constitution. As the Court stated in *Prasad*:

> The doctrine of necessity enables those in de facto control, such as the military, to respond to and deal with a sudden and stark crisis in circumstances which had not been provided for in the written *Constitution* or where the emergency powers machinery in that *Constitution* was inadequate for the occasion. The extra-constitutional action authorised by that doctrine is essentially of a temporary character and it ceases to apply once the crisis has passed.[116]

---

112 Blackstone did not address martial law directly.
113 John Locke, *Two Treatises of Government* (Mobilereference.com, first published 1689, 2008) (Article 160) 142.
114 Unreported, Fiji Court of Appeal, Casey J (Presiding), Barker, Kapi, Ward and Handley JJA, 1 March 2001.
115 See Nasser Hussain, *The Jurisprudence of Emergency* (University of Michigan Press, 2003) 130.
116 Unreported, Fiji Court of Appeal, Casey J (Presiding), Barker, Kapi, Ward and Handley JJA, 1 March 2001, 16.

Given the broad consideration in *Prasad*[117] of common-law authorities from the Privy Council and around the Commonwealth of Nations, its reasoning is relevant to Australia.[118] The case is also of particular value from a regional common-law perspective as the bench comprised judges from New Zealand, Papua New Guinea, Australia and Tonga.[119]

Notably, the military in Fiji did not seek to interfere with the operation of the courts nor to establish military tribunals or courts martial.[120] This is consistent with the authorities above that martial law does not require rule by courts martial. The main limitation would still appear to be that it is not possible to effect an enduring change to the *Constitution*. All actions must be temporary and necessary. Any remaining constitutional authority, such as the Queen or Governor-General, must remain in place and any military action must be subject to that authority. This is particularly the case for Australia given that s 61 of the *Constitution* vests the executive power of the Commonwealth in the Queen and makes it exercisable by the Governor-General. Given the succession arrangements for the Queen[121] and the Governor-General,[122] or for the monarch to appoint a new Governor-General,[123] it is virtually inconceivable that these offices would cease to function. As proposed in Chapter 1, it is not possible to effect an enduring change to the *Constitution* and therefore remove these constitutional office holders. As much as the ADF might exercise prerogative power in this example, it would clearly do so on behalf of the Crown. As fanciful as this discussion might seem in early 21st-century Australia, it does serve to illustrate the great reservoir of power potentially lying dormant in the prerogative with respect to martial law.[124]

---

117 Ibid.
118 *Reference by His Excellency the Governor-General (under s 213 of the Government of India Act, 1935)* PLD 1955 FC (Pak) 435 is also very relevant here.
119 George Williams, 'Feature – *Republic of Fiji v Prasad*' (2001) 2(1) *Melbourne Journal of International Law* 144, 146. For a critical perspective see Michael Head, 'A Victory for Democracy? An Alternative Assessment of *Fiji v Prasad*' (2001) 2(2) *Melbourne Journal of International Law* 535. As much as Head finds fault with the decision, he does not suggest what other decision the court should have made. This is consistent with his approach generally of providing critique but without arguing for an alternative position.
120 *Prasad* (Unreported, Fiji Court of Appeal, Casey J (Presiding), Barker, Kapi, Ward and Handley JJA, 1 March 2001), 4–5.
121 *Act of Settlement 1701* (Imp).
122 *Letters Patent Relating to the Office of Governor-General of the Commonwealth of Australia*, 21 August 2008.
123 Ibid.
124 Further, Australia's federal structure diffuses power throughout the various capitals of the federation. Should the Commonwealth Government collapse, the Governor-General could appoint a new temporary civilian Commonwealth ministry from among State parliamentarians, *Constitution* s 64.

3. MARTIAL LAW

Despite concerns from Head that such power could lie dormant,[125] the lesson from *Prasad* is that the alternatives would most likely either be anarchy or the assumption of power by unconstitutional means. Neither path is consistent with the rule of law or constitutional government. As Winterton stated, '[O]nce the realm of extra-constitutional power has been entered, there is no logical limit to its ambit'.[126] It is more consistent with the principle of legality that there should be some authority within the law to act in such extreme situations. A return to the normal constitutional order seems more likely when the authority for action derives from within existing constitutional structures.

D Authorised State Terror

An even more extreme view is that martial law is an instrument of state terror. It knows very few bounds and authorises extreme measures of brutality against even innocent civilians in order to terrorise a subject population into submission. As Kostal quoted Finlason, '[T]error is of the very nature of martial law, and deterrent measures – that is measures deterrent by means of terror – are its very essence'.[127]

The limitations are that martial law can only be for the purpose of maintaining or restoring governmental control and cannot be for wanton purposes. The procedure of courts martial must observe some sense of natural justice, although summary executions may also be permissible.[128] The leading proponent of this view was Finlason. He wrote a number of books and letters on the subject of martial law at the time of the Jamaica controversy in the 1860s.[129] It is tempting to dismiss such extreme views as the views of just one author, but Finlason appears to have articulated a widespread belief that this approach was necessary to maintain the

---

125 Head, *Calling out the Troops,* above n 17, 128–37.
126 George Winterton, 'Extra-Constitutional Notions in Australian Constitutional Law' (1986) 16 *Federal Law Review* 223, 239, quoted in H P Lee, '*Salus Populi Suprema Lex Esto:* Constitutional Fidelity in Troubled Times' in H P Lee and Peter Gerangelos (eds), *Constitutional Advancement in a Frozen Continent: Essays in Honour of George Winterton* (Federation Press, 2009) 54.
127 Finlason, *Treatise on Martial Law as Allowed by the Law of England in Time of Rebellion,* quoted in Kostal, above n 4, 232.
128 See Kostal's discussion of Finlason, above n 4, 235–6; see Clode, *The Military Forces of the Crown,* above n 2, 159–62.
129 Kostal, above n 4, 419–20.

Empire.¹³⁰ The use of such an approach in so many parts of the British Empire, such as in the Indian Mutiny of 1857,¹³¹ against Aborigines in Australia,¹³² in General Dyer's ordering of the Amritsar Massacre in 1919,¹³³ the government of the African colonies,¹³⁴ the attempted suppression of the Irish Republic between 1916 and 1922¹³⁵ and in the Jamaica Rebellion itself, and with so little by way of legal consequences for these actions, would suggest that Finlason's view reflects much of the practice of martial law in the British Empire.

Given the inextricable connection between this view of martial law and conceptions of race and empire, and that no court has explicitly supported it, it is possible to dismiss the use of martial law as an instrument of state terror as in any way an arguable view of the law. It abandons legality rather than reinforcing it. It is an exercise of virtually unrestrained power relying upon brutality and fear. It is not possible to reconcile with the firm assertions of restraint in *Entick v Carrington*,¹³⁶ *Shaw Savill & Albion Co Ltd*¹³⁷ nor *A v Hayden*¹³⁸ as discussed in Chapter 1. It is important to recognise this view, however, because of its historical significance and because the term martial law can invoke thoughts of such extreme measures. This may explain why none of the Australian experiences of martial law discussed below use the term martial law.

E What is Martial Law then?

Martial law is, effectively, a consequence of circumstances where the usual functioning of civilian government has practically ceased, even if not altogether or only locally. The first question as to whether martial law can or should apply, then, is one of fact. The military commander can

---

130 Ibid 455–6 citing the British *Manual of Military Law* (1899) and C E Calwell, *Small Wars: Their Principles and Practice* (HMSO, 3rd ed 1899), as well as the sadistic slaughter of Kooka prisoners in the Punjab in 1872, 451–3; see Military Board, above n 4, 197, stating that the laws of war do not apply to 'uncivilised states and tribes'; see also Lendrum, above n 67, 31; G J Cartledge, *The Soldier's Dilemma: When to Use Force in Australia* (AGPS Press, 1992) 155–8.
131 See, eg, Captain Thomas Spankie, 'The Siege of Delhi – 1857' in William Robson, *The Great Sieges of History* (Routledge, Warne & Routledge, 1859) 633, 655–6; Kostal, above n 4, 206.
132 Head, *Calling out the Troops,* above n 17, 43; Lendrum, above n 67, 40–2.
133 See Hussain, above n 115, 99–101.
134 Bernard Porter, *The Lion's Share: A Short History of British Imperialism 1850–1983* (Longman, 2nd ed 1984) 180–1.
135 Neocleous, above n 8, 14–15.
136 (1765) 19 St Tr 1030.
137 (1940) 66 CLR 344.
138 (1984) 156 CLR 532.

exercise a degree of executive, legislative and judicial power over civilians and military alike as long and as much as necessity dictates. Martial law is distinct from military law in that it regulates all subject to it, rather than just the military. It is also a description of a state of affairs rather than being a body of law. The question of whether the courts have to be closed for there to be martial law, with courts martial taking their place, is somewhat misleading.[139] Courts martial may or may not be an aspect of the application of martial law in a given situation. As seen in *Marais'* case, the civilian courts may even remain open while martial law is in place. Martial law can still be in effect without the use of courts martial to try civilians. As Richards commented in 1902 in respect of the *Marais* case:

> The necessity for taking action which infringes on the rights of property or liberty cannot depend on the fact that the courts continue or do not continue to sit: it depends on the necessity created by the presence of an enemy in the country.[140]

Lendrum echoed a similar view.[141] Dodd goes further in saying the military should not be obliged to close the courts to make martial law effective in time of war. Citizens should not be deprived of ordinary justice where the military permits the courts to sit.[142] The courts should be able to accommodate the due prosecution of the war by not exercising all of their functions in respect of the military but still hear ordinary disputes which were not 'injurious to public safety'.[143] The old rule that when the courts are open there is peace and when they are closed there is war developed in a time when warfare was limited in geographical scope. The scale and breadth of machine-age warfare meant that the rule 'seems hardly to appeal to modern ideas'.[144]

---

139 Holdsworth, 'Martial Law Historically Considered', above n 11, 121.
140 Richards, above n 4, 141.
141 Lendrum, above n 67.
142 Dodd, above n 35, 146.
143 Ibid.
144 Ibid. Dodd's main point is still that courts martial may not try civilians when the courts are open, 151.

This is an important issue in the Australian experience of martial law discussed below. Brennan and Toohey JJ in *Re Tracey*[145] went to some length to limit any possibility of courts martial usurping the jurisdiction of the civilian courts.[146] To bring this discussion into the Australian context, there are two aspects then that require further analysis: when martial law can apply and to what extent it can apply. An examination of Australian history may yield the clearest indications as to the Australian law of martial law.

III Martial Law in Australia

In considering the need for lawful authority for executive action, as discussed in Chapter 1, it is open to suggest that the scope of Commonwealth legislative power with respect to defence is a guide to the scope of executive power on defence also. *Williams*[147] makes clear that Commonwealth executive power does not extend as far as Commonwealth legislative power, and certainly does not go beyond it.[148] *Williams* does leave room for prerogative power to operate;[149] so, if a prerogative to exercise martial law exists in Australian law, then, arguably, the Commonwealth may exercise it in cases of necessity. In doing so though, it could not go beyond the limits of its legislative power. The executive could not change the *Constitution* in such a situation, particularly by removing the jurisdiction of the courts, even if necessity might demand temporary and limited displacement of State or judicial power where such powers could not operate. This will be discussed below. What necessity requires is very difficult to define. Therefore, the limits of the Commonwealth's legislative power with respect to defence is really the only guide to the limits of the exercise of the prerogative with respect to martial law. This calls for an examination of situations where the military forces of the Commonwealth have exercised civilian governmental functions.

Historically there have been two sets of circumstances since Federation when Australia has applied martial law. The first, as mentioned, is where Australian forces have taken over territories under foreign jurisdiction, the subject of Chapter 6. The second is when parts of Australia, or areas already under its jurisdiction, such as Papua and New Guinea, have

---

145 (1989) 166 CLR 518.
146 Ibid 554–63.
147 (2012) 248 CLR 156.
148 Chapter 1 nn 111–19.
149 Chapter 1 nn 133–8.

been under military control. The Commonwealth Government imposed military control, as it was termed, in the territories of New Guinea and Papua, as well as the Northern Territory and the northern parts of Western Australia and Queensland in February 1942 after the effective collapse of civilian administration in these places in the face of the first Japanese military attacks (see Map 1).[150]

Map 1. Area of the Territories of New Guinea and Papua under Military Control pursuant to the *National Security (External Territories) Regulations 1942*
Source: Created by Professor Stuart Kaye. © Cameron Moore

Nauru, then an Australian territory, went immediately from Australian civilian control to Japanese military occupation in August 1942.[151] Upon the surrender of Japanese forces to Australian forces in September 1945,[152] there appears to have been military control of the island until it came under Australian, British and New Zealand trusteeship in 1947.[153]

---

150 Discussed below.
151 Jack Haden, 'Nauru: A Middle Ground During World War II' in Pacific Islands Development Program, East-West Center for Pacific Island Studies, University of Hawai'i at Mānoa, *Pacific Islands Report* (2011) 3.
152 Ibid 4.
153 See *Nauru Act 1965* (Cth) Preamble.

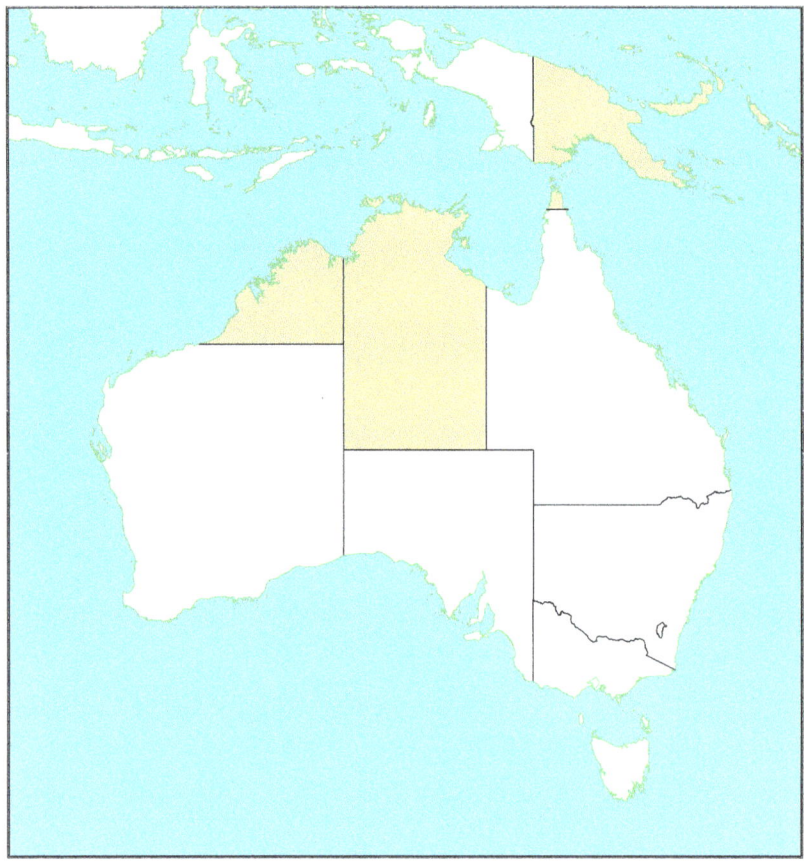

Map 2. Area of Australia under Military Control pursuant to the *National Security (Emergency Control) Regulations 1941*
Source: Created by Professor Stuart Kaye. © Cameron Moore

A Statutory vs Prerogative Power

Importantly, the legal authority for military control in northern Australia, Papua and New Guinea derived from the *National Security (Emergency Control) Regulations 1941* and the *National Security (External Territories) Regulations 1942* respectively. The *National Security (Emergency Control) Act 1939* (Cth), repealed in 1946, authorised both sets of regulations.[154] Whilst this makes the legal basis statutory rather than prerogative power, the legislation indicates some useful points about when and why

---

154 *National Security Act 1946* (Cth) s 2.

martial law may be imposed and the extent of the authority potentially available to military authorities should prerogative power be the basis instead. Perhaps more important is the point that there was a preference for statutory over prerogative authority in these cases. Was it necessary? There are a number of obvious advantages in providing for such power under statute, including the uncertainty surrounding martial law in the authorities and among the leading writers discussed above, as well as the greater clarity and authority that legislation can have. In the case of the States, particularly, as opposed to the Territories, it possibly may also have been advantageous to rely directly on the power to legislate for defence in s 51(vi) of the *Constitution*. The Commonwealth would then have been able to argue that the Commonwealth legislation prevailed over State legislation by virtue of s 109 of the *Constitution*. Moreover, as this book argues, statutory power preserves the supremacy of the legislature over the executive.

Must martial law rely upon statute though? If Parliament does have the time to act, then it would seem that martial law should rely upon statute because it is less plausible to argue that necessity would justify reliance upon prerogative power. This is more consistent with the compromise between Parliament and the Crown of 1688 and the relationship between statute and prerogative discussed in Chapter 1. Perhaps more importantly, it reinforces the principle of military subordination to the civilian government by clearly stating the extent to which military commanders could assume civilian government functions. The need for military control of certain areas was clearly anticipated in the *National Security (Emergency Control) Act* in 1939. The *National Security (Emergency Control) Regulations 1941* and the *National Security (External Territories) Regulations 1942*, through gazette notices, merely specified where and when military control was to have effect. When civilian administration did become ineffective in the places under question, it was a relatively straightforward matter of statutorily imposing military control via gazette notice. This provided greater clarity to the powers in question, which is more consistent with the principle of legality as well as reducing the risk to military personnel of incurring personal liability through exceeding uncertain powers. From this example, it would seem then that martial law should only apply by force of prerogative power in a place under Australian jurisdiction where the civilian administration unexpectedly becomes ineffective, and Parliament does not have time to enact suitable legislation. This would only be as an alternative to there being no functioning government at all, with its associated risk of anarchy. This chapter will address such a situation in Darwin in February 1942 below.

B The Extent of the Power with Respect to Martial Law in Australia

1 The *National Security (Emergency Control) Regulations 1941*

The *National Security (Emergency Control) Regulations 1941* are remarkably brief. The relevant operative provisions are worth reproducing:

> 5(1) The ... officer ... having the operational command of the Military Forces serving in that part [of Australia to which these Regulations apply] may do, or may cause or direct to be done, or may prohibit the doing of, any act or thing, as he thinks necessary for the purpose of meeting any emergency arising in that part or area out of the war or for the purpose of providing for the defence of that part or area.
>
> (2) Without affecting the generality of the last preceding sub-regulation, the ... officer ... may make orders in relation to any of the purposes mentioned in that sub-regulation.
>
> 6. A person to whom an order or direction under these Regulations applies shall not contravene or fail to comply with the order or direction.
>
> 7. The Courts which, immediately prior to the commencement of these Regulations, had jurisdiction in any part of Australia to which these Regulations apply or in any area thereof may, subject to the provisions or any order made under these Regulations, continue to exercise their civil and criminal jurisdiction and to try and punish persons in respect of any offence committed in that part or area.

These regulations applied, at various times, to the Territory of Papua, the Territory of New Guinea, Queensland north of the latitude of 12° South, and Western Australia north of the latitude of 20° South and the entire Northern Territory.[155] Notably, the Minister for the Army administered the regulations and there was no sense in which the Navy or Air Force

---

155 Commonwealth, *Manual of National Security Legislation* 1943, 274.

would exercise these powers.[156] The current joint command arrangements of the ADF would suggest that this particular provision is, therefore, confined to its historical circumstances.

2 Limitations

The powers were clearly extraordinarily broad, combining executive power with what amounted to a legislative power, but with two limitations other than the obvious geographical application. The first is that, under reg 5, the powers had to be exercised for the purpose of meeting any emergency or providing for the defence of the area. This could still be very broad but left some room open for argument that a particular measure was not for such a purpose. For example, a matter of personal conscience such as religious affiliation would probably have been outside the scope of the power noting s 116 of the *Constitution*.[157]

The second limitation relates to the courts. Unlike the formulation of martial law as Dicey put it, '[T]he government of a country or a district by military tribunals, which more or less supersede the jurisdiction of the courts',[158] military control did not mean subjecting the general population to the jurisdiction of courts martial. Section 7 of the *National Security Act 1939* itself made clear that regulations made under it could not authorise provision for the trial by court martial of any person not already subject to naval, military or air force discipline.[159] This is consistent with it being beyond Commonwealth legislative power to infringe Chapter III of the *Constitution*. It is not clear what should happen if the courts in a particular area could not operate due to the military situation. It is also not clear what the consequences were of making reg 7 subject to the provisions

---

156 *National Security (Emergency Control) Regulations 1941* reg 2.
157 Although the High Court did find that some regulation of a religious organisation under the *National Security (Subversive Associations) Regulations* would not be contrary to s 116 insofar as it involved subversive activity, while at the same time invalidating other parts of such regulations as contrary to s 116 insofar as they sought to regulate the advocacy of religious doctrine, in *Adelaide Company of Jehovah's Witnesses v Commonwealth* (1943) 67 CLR 116, 144 (Latham CJ), 156–7 (McTiernan J), 150 (Rich J, who found the regulations beyond the defence power in s 51 (vi) however), 154–5 (Starke J, who found the regulations beyond the power under the *National Security Act 1939* (Cth)), 160 (Williams J, who found the regulations beyond the defence power in s 51 (vi)).
158 Dicey, above n 7, 291.
159 This section also effectively prohibited the imposition of compulsory military or industrial service by way of the regulations as well. This may have reflected the controversy surrounding conscription at the time, with Prime Minister Curtin facing strong dissent within his own Australian Labor Party over whether conscripts should be liable for overseas service or whether there should be conscription at all. See Peter Dennis, Jeffrey Grey, Ewan Morris and Robin Prior, *The Oxford Companion to Australian Military History* (Oxford University Press, 2nd ed, 2008) 156–7.

of any order made under the regulations. Presumably, the local military commander could not remove the jurisdiction of the courts but may have been able to regulate where and when the courts exercised that jurisdiction in a particular area.

If these limitations applied during Australia's most extreme threat in 1942, then presumably they could only be exceeded where a threat exceeded that which existed in 1942. This may require the seat of government itself, together with the administration of the courts, to have been overrun before the law in Australia would recognise courts martial as an acceptable temporary substitute for the civilian courts, or to accept more than limited geographical application of martial law.

3 Papua and New Guinea in the Second World War

The most extensive exercise of martial law powers in the Second World War was by the Army's Australian New Guinea Administrative Unit, which operated in both Papua and New Guinea between 1942 and 1946, when the final handover to civil administration occurred. According to the Commonwealth's *Commission of Inquiry into the Circumstances Relating to the Suspension of Civil Administration of the Territory of Papua in February 1942* by J V Barry KC (the '*Barry Report*'):

> The Commandant [gave] his direction that the Administrator and the members of the Councils and the Judge should leave the territory … On 15th February, 1942, the Administrator and members of the Councils left by flying boat for Australia. The Judge had left the previous day. On 15th February the Commandant issued an order under which he assumed all governmental powers.[160]

The Report found that Major General Morris gave this order lawfully under the *National Security (Emergency Control) Regulations 1941*, which applied to the territories from 12 February 1942.[161] The Territory of Papua issued its own gazette notice indicating the cessation of civilian administration.[162]

---

160 John V Barry, KC and Department of External Territories, *Report of the Commission of Inquiry into the Circumstances Relating to the Suspension of Civil Administration of the Territory of Papua in February, 1942* (Australia: s.n., 1945) ('*Barry Report*'), 24.
161 Ibid 47, 48. Also, Commonwealth, *Manual of National Security Legislation*, above n 155, 274.
162 *Barry Report*, above n 160, 47, 48.

The effect on the exercise of judicial power in the territory was profound, as put by Alan Powell in his history of the Australian New Guinea Administrative Unit (ANGAU):

> The District Officers also bore a greater judicial responsibility than in pre-war days. Under *National Security (External Territories) Regulations* [1942], Major General Morris suspended the judiciary systems of both Territories in February 1942 and, under his authority as senior officer of the military forces in New Guinea, transferred the jurisdiction of the Supreme Courts to District Officers with lesser judicial/magisterial powers to ADOs [Assistant District Officers] and magisterial rights to approved POs [Patrol Officers].[163]

The *National Security (External Territories) Regulations* were not gazetted until April 1942 so this was more likely an example of the military commander regulating the operation of the courts under reg 7 of the *National Security (Emergency Control) Regulations 1941*.

As to transferring the jurisdiction of the two Supreme Courts to the various officers mentioned, the *National Security (Emergency Control) Regulations 1941* did not provide for this. It may have been possible under the *National Security (External Territories) Regulations 1942* insofar as those regulations suspended all of the civil administration in Papua and New Guinea, including the judges.[164] These regulations also gave the External Territories Minister all powers exercisable under any law of either territory, other than the civil (as opposed to criminal) jurisdiction of the two territory Supreme Courts.[165] The Minister acted through the General Officer Commanding.[166] Either Major General Morris' order was unlawful in respect of his powers to transfer the jurisdiction of the Supreme Courts, or, as seems more likely, he might actually have given the various district and patrol officers criminal, as opposed to civil, jurisdiction in accordance with the powers which the regulations granted to the General Officer Commanding.

This criminal jurisdiction was not petty. In responding to one incident of intertribal violence, Major W H H Thompson convicted 43 men for murder and 19 men for rape and handed down sentences of five

---

163 Alan Powell, *The Third Force: ANGAU's New Guinea War, 1942–1946* (Oxford University Press, 2003) 107.
164 *National Security (External Territories) Regulations 1942* regs 4–8.
165 Ibid regs 21, 22.
166 Powell, above n 163, 107.

years each.[167] It is important to note that 'native courts' effectively operated separately from the rest of the judicial system. The combining of executive and judicial power in travelling Army District and Patrol officers who held court in villages to resolve disputes, reminiscent of English justice in the time of William I, continued the previous practice of the civilian administration. Often, the officers were the same people, now with Army rank and uniforms.[168] Whatever these peculiarities of the Territories though, Army officers exercised judicial power.[169]

ANGAU's administrative role was also very extensive. It ran postal services, native education, plantations and agricultural services, district stores, a marine section, hospitals and wider health care as well as radio communications. There was extensive labour recruitment, much of it involuntary. It did as much as, if not more than, the previous civil administrations in terms of governing the Territories.[170] ANGAU's displacement of civil government functions was total.

4 The Limits of Prerogative Power?

It is very important to note that the regulations applied to areas of States as well as Commonwealth Territories. The legislative power of the Commonwealth, in this case, purported to expand to the extent of displacing State government executive and legislative functions and regulating, if not displacing, State judicial functions. There does not appear to have been any challenge to this legislation in the High Court so there may have been a degree of acceptance that Commonwealth legislative power did extend this far when the defence of the nation was at stake. Importantly, in the 1945 case quoted at the beginning of this chapter, *Gratwick v Johnson*,[171] the High Court did uphold a challenge to the *National Security (Land Transport) Regulations* as contrary to s 92 of the *Constitution* requiring freedom of intercourse among the States. There were also challenges to wartime regulations as infringing Chapter III of the *Constitution*. For example, *Silk Bros Pty Ltd v State Electricity Commission of Victoria* concerned the purported vesting of Commonwealth judicial

---

167 Ibid 111.
168 Ibid 116.
169 At the time, it was thought that Chapter III of the *Constitution*, requiring the separation of judicial power, did not apply to the territories, or at least the Territory of Papua, *R v Bernasconi* (1915) 19 CLR 629. For a discussion of cases which have moved away from this view, see Leslie Zines, 'The Nature of the Commonwealth' (1998) 20 *Adelaide Law Review* 83, 83–8.
170 Powell, above n 163, 111–13.
171 (1945) 70 CLR 1.

power in a Fair Rent Board composed of State officials under the *National Security (Landlord and Tenant) Regulations 1941*.[172] The High Court upheld the challenge to the regulations, made under the power to legislate for defence under s 51(vi), as attempting to confer judicial power contrary to Chapter III.[173] These cases not only reflect that there were challenges to the validity of extensive wartime regulatory powers but they also indicate that the High Court would not readily displace express constitutional limitations upon the defence power of the Commonwealth.

What does this mean for prerogative power within areas under Australian jurisdiction? On the basis that the Commonwealth's executive power includes a prerogative to apply martial law when necessity demands it, then, using wartime legislation enacted under the defence power as a guide, if Parliament is unable to act in time, the prerogative would appear to extend to the imposition of very broad powers of military control.

This appears to be what occurred in Darwin in the days after the first Japanese raid on 19 February 1942. Justice Lowe gave a secret interim *Royal Commission Report on the Air Raids on Darwin* to the Commonwealth Cabinet on 9 March 1942.[174] He stated that civil order and administration completely collapsed immediately after the raid, with widespread panic and looting. The military commandant, therefore, took complete charge of Darwin from 21 February.[175] Even by the afternoon of 19 February some police believed that they were under military control through martial law.[176] The Town Major (so described) then governed the town, as well as organising the evacuation of women (and presumably children) and the accommodation of the remaining men in camps.[177]

---

172 (1943) 67 CLR 1, 9, 10, 17 (Latham CJ, with whom the other justices agreed).
173 Wheeler argues that, despite High Court justices performing significant nonjudicial roles in wartime, even by the standards of the 1940s, judicial independence was widely considered to be a valued constitutional principle, in Fiona Wheeler, 'Parachuting In: War and Extra-Judicial Activity by High Court Judges' (2010) 38(3) *Federal Law Review* 485, 496–500.
174 Commonwealth, Air Raids on Darwin, *Interim Report* (1942). Newman Rosenthal discusses Justice Lowe's experience of the Commission and the fraught circumstances in which it occurred, in *Sir Charles Lowe: A Biographical Memoir* (Robertson and Mullens, 1968), 102–17. Notably, Justice Lowe also conducted a Royal Commission into the 'Brisbane Line' controversy, mentioned in Chapter 5, as well as two other national security-related Royal Commissions into the Canberra air disaster of 1940 and the Communist Party in Victoria in 1949, which Rosenthal discusses on pages 118, 96 and 127 respectively.
175 Ibid 9.
176 Ibid 9.
177 Ibid 10.

Military control under *National Security (Emergency Control) Regulations 1941* did not take effect until gazetted on 28 February 1942.[178] The hand of *Fortuna* seems to be apparent here.

This formalisation of military control, the lack of adverse comment in Justice Lowe's report or in Cabinet, or any related litigation all point to necessity being seen as justifying the military's assertion of martial law in this case. It is consistent with the view of Latham CJ on the maxim *salus populi suprema lex* in *Gratwick v Johnson* in 1945, as quoted at the beginning of this chapter.[179] It is worth noting that the *Barry Report* stated that the basis for the exercise of martial law, so described, in Papua could only have been statutory in that case, although it acknowledges the possibility of circumstances 'sufficient to justify the exercise of the prerogative'.[180] The assertion of martial law in Darwin was an alternative to anarchy and so upheld lawful authority. It was not a usurpation of civilian authority because, in a local sense, there was none. The very temporary duration of the period before the *National Security (Emergency Control) Regulations* came into force did not offend the relationship between Parliament and the Crown. This assertion of martial law upheld constitutionalism because, if the military had done nothing instead, there would have been no constitutional authority at all.

The main limits in that situation in Darwin, or any future situation like it, would arguably be that the exercise of martial law powers must relate to the purpose of meeting any emergency or providing for the defence of the area, and they must be geographically confined to the area where civilian government has ceased to be effective. It would also appear that as long as there is the possibility of the courts being able to exercise their jurisdiction, the military cannot displace the judicial power, although it may regulate its exercise such as determining where and when courts could sit. Were the situation truly dire and there was no prospect of the courts being able to exercise jurisdiction, then possibly military tribunals may temporarily take their place but only to preserve matters, such as through remand or injunction proceedings, where necessity required it until the courts could proceed to provide a final determination. This could only be until the functioning of judicial power was restored. This is not a case of

---

178 Commonwealth, *Manual of National Security Legislation*, above n 155, 274.
179 (1945) 70 CLR 1, 11–12.
180 *Barry Report*, 47.

the ADF breaching the *Constitution* but rather taking limited measures justified by necessity in response to an aspect of the *Constitution*, in this case judicial power, ceasing to operate. It would also not be possible to effect an enduring change to the *Constitution* through the prerogative for martial law.[181]

IV Conclusion

At the time of writing this chapter, there is only the most remote possibility that martial law would become applicable in Australia. The only conceivable scenarios would be an actual invasion or the collapse of civilian government. While much of the case law and literature concerns martial law during insurrection or war, this book argues that, noting *Prasad*, the ADF could also exercise the prerogative with respect to martial law where civilian government has collapsed for other reasons. Prerogative power would appear to extend to the conduct of a broad range of governmental functions where Parliament could not act in time, and where justified by necessity. Such functions may include maintaining law and order, issuing local decrees and regulating the function of the courts. At its most extreme, martial law could possibly extend to assuming control of all civilian government functions. There would seem to be an extremely high threshold to overcome though before the ADF could assume judicial functions itself in places under Australian jurisdiction. The emergency legislation applicable in northern Australia and the Territories of New Guinea and Papua is instructive in this regard. It permitted extensive military control of civilian life although it did not authorise the conduct of courts martial in the place of civilian courts (noting that 'native courts' in New Guinea and Papua were not courts martial even if Army officers exercised judicial power through them). If an extreme emergency made it necessary, this legislation would be a guide to the extent to which the

---

181 As to the requirements of necessity, it may be that some of the debate about proportionality is relevant to assessing whether action is necessary. It is worth noting that proportionality is not seen as a doctrine of constitutional law in Australia and it usually only relates to legislative action, see Dan Meagher, 'The Common Law Principle of Legality in the Age of Rights' (2011) 35 *Melbourne University Law Review* 449; Christopher Michaelsen, 'Reforming Australia's National Security Laws: The Case for a Proportionality-based Approach' (2010) 29(1) *University of Tasmania Law Review* 31. Nonetheless, it may be that necessity could be informed by the test of whether measures are 'appropriate and adapted' to the purpose, Justice Susan Kiefel, 'Proportionality: A Rule of Reason' (2012) 23 *Public Law Review* 85, 91, quoting Deane J in *Commonwealth v Tasmania* (1983) 158 CLR 1 260, 88 ('*Tasmanian Dam Case*').

ADF could perform civilian government functions until the Parliament could pass appropriate legislation, or until it could restore normal civilian government. Where martial law is an alternative to no law at all, then it upholds the values of constitutional government.

4
Internal Security

I Introduction

Section 119 of the *Constitution* states:

> Protection of States from invasion and violence
>
> The Commonwealth shall protect every State against invasion and, on the application of the Executive Government of the State, against domestic violence.

Clearly the *Constitution* contemplates some internal security role for the Commonwealth. Even if s 119 does not mention Commonwealth military or naval forces, having the obligation to protect against invasion in the same sentence as that for domestic violence strongly suggests the use of such forces for internal security.[1] Having a Commonwealth Government of limited powers, and a federal division of responsibility which leaves primary responsibility for internal security to the States, makes finding authority for ADF internal security action less than straightforward. English common-law principles do not apply neatly within Australia's federal structure. Dixon J made clear in *R v Sharkey* that:

> Section 119 of the *Constitution* provides that the Commonwealth shall protect every State against invasion and, on the application of the Executive Government of the State, against domestic violence. The reference to invasion explains the words 'and of the several States'

---

1   Stephenson shares this view in Peta Stephenson, 'Fertile Ground for Federalism: Internal Security, the States and s 119 of the *Constitution*' (2015) 43 *Federal Law Review* 289, 295.

in s 51 (vi), the defence power. But what is important is the fact that, except on the application of the Executive Government of the State, it is not within the province of the Commonwealth to protect the State against domestic violence. The comments made by Quick & Garran in the *Constitution of the Australian Commonwealth* bring out clearly the distinction between matters affecting internal order and matters, which though in one aspect affecting internal order, concern the functions or operations of the Federal Government: 'The maintenance of order in a State is primarily the concern of the State, for which the police powers of the State are ordinarily adequate. But even if the State is unable to cope with domestic violence, the Federal Government has no right to intervene, for the protection of the State or its citizens, unless called upon by the State Executive.'[2]

This federal division of responsibility will be central to much of this discussion.

This book distinguishes internal security from martial law because it is possible for the ADF to act for internal security purposes without assuming civilian government functions, although a situation of martial law may also require the ADF to conduct internal security operations. The term 'internal security' for this book encompasses any operational deployment of the ADF to use force for law enforcement purposes for civil disturbance or major event security. It will also use the term 'public order' where it relates more closely to the references under discussion.

Internal security is a concern which attracts much attention from commentators because the prospect of troops on the street is a chilling one.[3] Internal security has also been a practical and theoretical legal issue

---

2   (1949) 79 CLR 121, 150. Zines appears to support Dixon J's statement in Leslie Zines, 'The Inherent Executive Power of the Commonwealth' (2005) 16 *Public Law Review* 279, 279.
3   Michael Head is the leading critic in Australia of the use of the ADF for internal security, see 'The Military Call-out Legislation – Some Legal and Constitutional Questions' (2001) 29(2) *Federal Law Review* 273; 'Calling out the Troops – Disturbing Trends and Unanswered Questions' (2005) 28 *University of New South Wales Law Journal* 479; 'Australia's Expanded Military Call-out Powers: Causes for Concern' (2006) 3(2) *University of New England Law Journal* 125 (including a criticism of this author's views on 146–7) and *Calling out the Troops: The Australian Military and Civil Unrest* (Federation Press, 2009). See also Arne Willy Dahl, 'Military Assistance to the Police in Situations Requiring the Use of Armed Force' (Keynote Address at the New Zealand Armed Forces Law Conference, Trentham Army Camp, Upper Hutt, New Zealand, 9 February 2007); Simon Bronitt, 'Balancing Security and Liberty: Critical Perspectives on Terrorism Law Reform' in Miriam Gani and Penelope Matthew (eds), *Fresh Perspectives on the War on Terror* (ANU E Press, 2008) 81. On the history of the British experience, Colm O'Cinneide, 'Strapped to the Mast: The Siren Song of Dreadful Necessity, the United Kingdom *Human Rights Act* and the Terrorist Threat' in Miriam Gani and Penelope Matthew (eds) *Fresh Perspectives on*

since before Federation.[4] The fears of a standing army in 17th-century England seem to have seeped into a modern Australian political culture which almost supposes a constitutional bar to using the ADF for internal security, even with the presence of s 119.[5] For example, Mason CJ, Wilson and Dawson JJ in *Re Tracey; Ex parte Ryan* stated that '[i]t is not the ordinary function of the armed services to "execute and maintain the laws of the Commonwealth"'.[6] Despite requests, the Commonwealth has not actually relied upon s 119 to protect a State.[7] There is also a line of thinking in obiter dicta and extracurial judicial writing which sees the Commonwealth as having an inherent right of self-protection because the Commonwealth has occasionally used the ADF internally to protect Commonwealth interests.[8] The Bowral call-out to protect visiting Commonwealth Heads of Government in 1978 is the most prominent example of this.[9]

The *Defence Act 1903* (Cth) now provides a statutory footing for most potential internal security actions by the ADF.[10] There are still some possible actions which fall outside the statutory framework however. What then are the limits of any residual executive power for internal security? Can the ADF break the law in order to restore it? The limits for internal security would appear to be very similar to those for internal martial law but the difference is that there have been prominent instances of the ADF conducting internal security operations without statutory authority.

---

the War on Terror (ANU E Press, 2008) 327, 330–3. For a general discussion of internal security powers in the United Kingdom and New Zealand see Kiron Reid and Clive Walker, 'Military Aid in Civil Emergencies. Lessons from New Zealand' (1998) 27 *Anglo-American Law Review* 133.

4   Justice Robert Hope, 'Protective Security Review' (Parliamentary Paper 397, Parliament of Australia, 1979), app 16 'The History of Military Involvement in Civilian Security in Britain and Australia'.

5   See Head, *Calling out the Troops: The Australian Military and Civil Unrest*, above n 3, 10–11; A R Blackshield, 'The Siege of Bowral – the Legal Issues' [1978] 4(9) March *Pacific Defence Reporter* 6, 9; Simon Bronitt and Dale Stephens, '"Flying Under the Radar" – The Use of Lethal Force Against Hijacked Aircraft: Recent Australian Developments' (2007) 7(2) *Oxford University Commonwealth Law Journal* 265; Richard Fox and Jodie Lydecker, 'The Militarisation of Australia's Federal Criminal Justice System' (2008) 32(5) *Criminal Law Journal* 287, 291–2, although this author does not agree with the contention made that 'it is clear' that the federal executive is *not* required to wait for a request from a state executive to intervene to suppress domestic violence under s 119.

6   (1989) 166 CLR 518, 540 ('*Re Tracey*'). See Head, *Calling out the Troops: The Australian Military and Civil Unrest*, above n 3, 150–3.

7   Elizabeth Ward, 'Call out the Troops: An Examination of the Legal Basis for Australian Defence Force Involvement in Non-Defence Matters–Update of a Background Paper issued 5 September 1991' (1997) *Commonwealth Parliament Bills Digest*, Appendix A.

8   Discussed below at Part IV.
9   Discussed below at Part IV A.
10 Part IIIAAA.

Interestingly there are three key incidents and they are all relatively recent. The first is the 1978 Bowral call-out mentioned above. The other two are the use of fighter jets to provide security for the Commonwealth Heads of Government Meeting in 2002 and the visit of the President of the United States in 2003.[11] The prerogative for control and disposition of the forces would have been sufficient authority for the ADF at least to be present in each of these instances. The question is whether the ADF could have then used force just upon the authority of executive power and not relying upon statute. A further question is whether this executive authority relied upon incidental executive power, which would be power available to any citizen, a prerogative power or the nationhood power. The source of such executive power could have important implications for its limits.

This chapter will first consider the prerogative for the control and disposition of the forces. It will then address the effect of Part IIIAAA of the *Defence Act* on the availability of executive power for internal security. It will then turn to the implications of the source of the executive power, whether ordinary citizens' powers, prerogative or nationhood power, for the use of the ADF under such power. It will then analyse the three uses of the ADF under executive power for internal security. It will also consider how the *Tampa* incident fits into this analysis. It will argue that there is scope for the ADF to conduct internal security operations under executive power but it does not extend to the use of lethal force. This executive power authority will also only extend beyond the powers available to any ordinary person in the clearest cases of necessity.

II Control and Disposition of the Forces

The prerogative for the control and disposition of the forces is important in relation to internal security because it is the authority for the Crown to place its forces where it chooses, whether on bases or in public places. Whilst some Australian case law and comment has focused upon aspects of this prerogative in respect of the employment relationship between the Crown and members of the ADF,[12] it is more significant in respect of internal security for giving the executive government the authority to

---

11 Discussed below at Part IV.
12 *Commonwealth v Quince* (1944) 68 CLR 227 ('*Quince*'); *Marks v Commonwealth* (1964) 111 CLR 549; *Coutts v Commonwealth* (1985) 157 CLR 91.

place, organise and equip its forces.[13] Whilst there is no Australian case law directly on point, there is little reason to think that the reasoning of the cases on control and disposition of the forces discussed in Chapter 2, such as *China Navigation Company Ltd v Attorney-General*[14] and *Chandler v Director of Public Prosecutions*,[15] would not be relevant to an assessment of the prerogative as to disposition of the ADF. This is important because 'call-out', explained further below, is not required to be able to move forces about. The prerogative for control and disposition of the forces means that the ADF has freedom of movement anyway.[16] Call-out just places forces at the disposal of the civil authority to use force. As will be discussed below, it is for the purpose of 'Aid to Civilian Authorities' as the title of the *Defence Legislation Amendment (Aid to Civilian Authorities) Act 2006* (Cth) indicates. Forces are not confined to their bases the rest of the time. For example, call-out as such is not required to allow the ADF to give noncoercive assistance in natural disasters or even for strikebreaking, although the extent to which this is lawful after *Pape v Commissioner of Taxation* and *Williams v Commonwealth* is another question.[17] Importantly, it is this prerogative which would also authorise the arms and equipment that the ADF uses. It could authorise the provision of riot-control equipment, or live small-arms rounds or armoured vehicles.[18]

---

13   See Peter Rowe, *Defence: The Legal Implications: Military Law and the Laws of War* (Brassey's, 1987) 3–4.
14   [1932] 2 KB 197.
15   [1964] AC 763.
16   There is no particular legal authority which states that military units require freedom of entry to be able to enter a city or other local government area. Freedom of entry appears just to be a ceremonial survival from feudal times as the author has not located any legal authority which relates to it.
17   (2009) 238 CLR 1 ('*Pape*') and (2012) 248 CLR 156 ('*Williams*'). Notably, of the English context, Geoffrey Marshall in *Constitutional Conventions: The Rules and Forms of Political Accountability* (Clarendon Press, 1984) stated that 'the deployment and use of the armed forces is a prerogative of the Crown and there seems to be no reason why the Crown should need express authority to order troops to do what it is lawful for anyone to do (to fight fires, for example)', 163–8. Such action in Australia might rely upon a prerogative with respect to emergencies generally, or the nationhood power, as discussed in Chapter 1. Post *Williams* however such action might actually require statutory authority. This point does not particularly relate to the ADF as it does not involve the use of military force, even if it involves the use of military resources, so it will remain unexplored.
18   *Defence Act 1903* (Cth) s 123 states that members of the ADF do not require permission under a State or Territory law to carry a firearm or do anything else in the course of their duties. This section does not provide the actual authority for the carriage of the weapon or the conduct of the duty though, which would be authorised by the prerogative under discussion.

Taking to the street, air or sea and looking ready to use force could obviously create a perception of threat or political intimidation so it must be done with such concerns in mind.[19] Part 3 of the *Defence Force Regulations* apply 'if the Defence Force is called out under any lawful authority other than Part IIIAAA of the Act'.[20] Importantly, reg 11C(2)(a) states that, in utilising the Defence Force in such a call-out, the Chief of the Defence Force, 'must not stop or restrict any protest, dissent, assembly or industrial action, except where there is a reasonable likelihood of the death of, or serious injury to, persons or serious damage to property'.

The *Defence Act 1903* Part IIIAAA Defence Force Aid to the Civil Authority provisions discussed below prohibit actions of this type under s 51G as well. In as recent a case as *Haskins v Commonwealth*[21] in 2011, Heydon J recalled the potential for military forces to threaten internal security themselves, citing Maitland:[22]

> [l]ow though the reputation of Cromwell is among those who love human liberty, he made a great negative contribution to that cause after his forces ensured the victory of the House of Commons over King Charles I. During the Commonwealth:
>
> 'England came under the domination of the army, parliament itself becoming the despised slave of the force that it had created. At the Restoration the very name of a standing army had become hateful to the classes which were to be the ruling classes.'[23]

Whilst moving forces from one place to another would be authorised by the prerogative for control and disposition of the forces, patrolling streets without a call-out might look like a usurpation of civil authority which the prerogative would not authorise. The important point here is that whilst there may be a point at which moving forces about could look like an unauthorised call-out, of itself, placing forces in various places does not require a call-out.[24] It is important to make this point before discussing the concept of call-out further.

---

19   Fox and Lydecker, above n 5, 301–2; Head *Calling out the Troops: The Australian Military and Civil Unrest*, above n 3, 46.
20   Reg 11A.
21   (2011) 244 CLR 22.
22   F W Maitland, *The Constitutional History of England* (Cambridge University Press, 1955) 326.
23   *Haskins v Commonwealth* (2011) 244 CLR 22, 60.
24   Fox and Lydecker, above n 5, 302, state that having troops on standby is not the same as calling out the ADF.

III Part IIIAAA

A History

Use of the ADF for internal security under executive power excited significant comment after the 'Siege of Bowral' in 1978.[25] In the *Protective Security Review* which followed, Justice Hope recommended that ADF internal security operations should be on a statutory basis because of the uncertainty of relying upon common-law powers.[26] Interest in the issue diminished, however, and it was 20 years before this recommendation had effect when, with the prospect of the Sydney Olympics, Parliament passed amendments to the *Defence Act* concerning Defence Force Aid to the Civil Authority.[27] It was not long before events demonstrated the limitations of the new Part IIIAAA of the Act concerning Defence Force Aid to the Civil Authority. The often-cited attacks of 11 September 2001 in the United States substantially increased the perception of the threat of terrorism.[28] The use of civil airliners to attack large buildings was also completely outside of the traditional hijacking, sieges, kidnapping, assassination, bombing or chemical or biological attack contemplated in Part IIIAAA of the *Defence Act*. The 2000 amendments simply did not contemplate attacks from the air or sea or the need to use force in the air or maritime environment.[29] The inconceivable became manifest, *Fortuna* presented itself.

Part IIIAAA of the *Defence Act* could not authorise the subsequent combat air patrols over the Commonwealth Heads of Government Regional Meeting in Coolum in 2002 and the visit of the President of the United

---

25 Term taken from Blackshield, above n 5, 6. For a history of this and earlier strikebreaking incidents involving the ADF, see Head, *Calling out the Troops: The Australian Military and Civil Unrest*, above n 3, 37–60.
26 Hope, above n 4, 175, app 18.
27 Bills Digest No 13, 2000–1, Defence Legislation Amendment (Aid to Civilian Authorities) Bill 2000. See discussion in Fox and Lydecker, above n 5, 292–3.
28 See Senator Robert Hill, Defence Minister, 'Defence Minister, Senator Robert Hill, Outlines the Contribution of the Australian Defence Force towards Security for the Forthcoming CHOGM meeting' (Press Release, 22 Feb 2002).
29 The author recalls being asked specifically at the time of the drafting of the legislation whether it needed an air or maritime aspect and, after consideration, replying 'no'. For a critique of Part IIIAAA, see Bronitt and Stephens, above n 5; and also Bronitt, above n 3; Head, 'The Military Call-out Legislation – Some Legal and Constitutional Questions'; Head, 'Calling out the Troops – Disturbing Trends and Unanswered Questions'; Head, 'Australia's Expanded Military Call-out Powers: Causes for Concern', Head, *Calling out the Troops: The Australian Military and Civil Unrest*, 100–22, above n 3.

CROWN AND SWORD

States in 2003.³⁰ It also could not provide any additional authority for warships to use force for the augmented security patrols around Australian offshore oil and gas platforms which commenced in 2005.³¹

The approach of the 2006 Melbourne Commonwealth Games and the creation of Border Protection Command (then Joint Offshore Protection Command) in 2005 provided impetus to amend the legislation.³² In early 2006, Parliament added substantial new powers to Part IIIAAA to provide for the use of force in the air and at sea as well as enhanced powers in the land environment.³³ The ADF relied upon these powers, although without using force, to provide combat air patrols for both the Commonwealth Games in 2006 and the Asia-Pacific Economic Community Leaders' Forum in Sydney in 2007.³⁴ The latter event did see a Royal Australian Air Force fighter jet intercept a light aircraft which had strayed into a restricted zone over Sydney, although without doing more than warn the light aircraft off.³⁵

B Key Provisions and Limits

Since 2006, Part IIIAAA of the *Defence Act* has provided, inter alia, for the use of lethal force by the ADF to destroy certain aircraft in the air and ships at sea,³⁶ as well as to defend property designated as critical infrastructure,³⁷ even without a direct threat to life.³⁸ It also provides cordon and search powers, both at sea³⁹ and ashore,⁴⁰ around the sites of incidents, including around moving ships on the high seas.⁴¹ It has

---

30   Department of Defence, *Submission to Senate Legal and Constitutional Committee, Inquiry into Defence Legislation Amendment (Aid to Civilian Authorities) Bill* (2005) 3.
31   Ibid 4.
32   Ibid 3–4.
33   *Defence Legislation Amendment (Aid to Civilian Authorities) Act 2006* (Cth). Notably, the German Constitutional Court struck down comparable German legislation in 2006 as contrary to the fundamental right to life, Bundesverfassungsgericht (BVerfG – Federal Constitutional Court) 59 *Neue Juristische Wochenschrift* (NJW) 751 (2006), discussed in Oliver Lepsius, 'Human Dignity and the Downing of Aircraft: The German Federal Constitutional Court Strikes Down a Prominent Anti-terrorism Provision in the New Air-transport Security Act' (2006) 7(9) *German Law Journal* 761.
34   Department of Defence, *Operation DELUGE* (9 May 2007).
35   See Tom Allard, Alexandra Smith, Jordan Baker and David Braithwaite, 'Cessna Pilot Flew into Dogfight with RAAF', *Sydney Morning Herald*, (online), 10 September 2007.
36   *Defence Act*, s 51SE.
37   Ibid s 51IB.
38   Ibid s 51CB.
39   Ibid ss 51SF–51SK, 51SL, 51SM.
40   Ibid ss 51K–51R.
41   Ibid s 51SF.

4. INTERNAL SECURITY

provision for a certain degree of protection from liability for ADF members acting under orders.[42] The powers are at least as extensive as any found in the common-law world.

Without addressing the detail of the legislation, the key limitations are, essentially:

- that domestic (as opposed to external) violence must be occurring or is likely to occur,
- any authorised action must be to protect Commonwealth interests,
- that, where relevant, any State or self-governing Territory is not, or is unlikely to be, able to protect the Commonwealth interest, and
- that the ADF should be utilised.[43]

The last requirement implies that a military level of capability is required to respond to the threat. The Act requires that the Prime Minister, Attorney-General and Defence Minister be satisfied of these requirements before the Governor-General can make an order calling out the ADF.[44]

There are variations on these requirements. In the offshore area, there is only a requirement that the authorising ministers be satisfied that there be a threat to Commonwealth interests and that the ADF should be utilised to respond to it before the Governor-General can issue a call-out order.[45] There is also provision for an anticipatory call-out with respect to air threats[46] or to respond to a request from a State or self-governing Territory to protect it from domestic violence.[47] The Prime Minister alone or the two other authorising ministers together, or one of them together with the Deputy Prime Minister, Treasurer or Foreign Affairs Minister, can, without an order from the Governor-General, make an expedited call-out order.[48] Such an order can last for only five days.[49]

---

42   Ibid s 51WB.
43   Ibid s 51A.
44   Ibid s 51A.
45   Ibid s 51AA.
46   Ibid s 51AB.
47   Ibid ss 51B, 51C.
48   Ibid s 51CA.
49   Ibid s 51CA(7)(b).

C Statutory Interpretation

Section 51Y of the *Defence Act* is careful to preserve any power the ADF may otherwise have outside the statutory provisions. It states, in unusual language for a statute: 'This Part [Part IIIAAA] does not affect any utilisation of the Defence Force that would be permitted or required, or any powers that the Defence Force would have, if this Part were disregarded'. This section would appear to preserve prerogative powers with respect to control and disposition of the forces (most importantly the movement of the forces), war, external operations other than war and even martial law.[50]

On the face of it, s 51Y would permit the exercise of internal security powers under the authority of executive power as well. Part 3 of the *Defence Force Regulations* also clearly contemplates this and provides limited regulation of the responsibilities of the Chief of the Defence Force and interaction with State and Territory authorities in a call-out *other than* under Part IIIAAA. As discussed in Chapter 1, however, necessity should be a limit upon the use of executive power within the realm. *Defence Force Regulation* 11B actually requires that the Chief of the Defence Force only utilise the ADF 'in a way that is reasonable and necessary' in such situations. As discussed, there are compelling reasons for preferring statutory power to authorise the use of lethal force over executive power, not least being the supremacy of the Parliament over the executive. If Part IIIAAA provides a comprehensive set of internal security powers, it would be very difficult to argue that it is necessary to rely upon executive power to do what the legislation provides for, as long as the legislation is operating as it should. This is not to say that Part IIIAAA extinguishes executive power on the same topic, it just makes it mostly unnecessary, and therefore unjustifiable, to resort to executive power.

It comes then to consider when it might be necessary to resort to executive power to authorise internal security operations by the ADF. The conceivable situations, except two, are only remotely likely but it is worth restating that the first iteration of Part IIIAAA in 2000 did not contemplate the threats which presented on 11 September 2001, only the year after it came into force. The need to resort to executive power to respond to contingencies, or *Fortuna*, is consistent with the theory of executive power discussed in Chapter 1.

---

50 See Head, *Calling out the Troops: The Australian Military and Civil Unrest*, above n 3, 122–6.

4. INTERNAL SECURITY

As to unforeseen threats, there are few scenarios which the legislation could not cover. It is very broad in its scope and appears deliberately drafted to address the widest range of possibilities. The terms 'domestic violence'[51] and 'threat' 'to Commonwealth interests'[52] would cover nearly all potential reasons for the ADF to use force outside of war. Even so, should an unforeseen threat to internal security emerge which the legislation did not address then, where necessity demanded, this chapter argues that the ADF could rely upon executive power to authorise internal security operations.

It is slightly more possible to imagine the statutory framework being inoperable due to the inability of key officials to act, such as the Prime Minister, other authorising ministers or the Governor-General. In these situations, executive power may be available. Such a scenario could be one of martial law because the elected government had ceased to function, such as occurred in Fiji in 2000.[53] The other possibility is where civilian government continues but the Prime Minister, Attorney-General and Defence Minister, as well as the Deputy Prime Minister, Treasurer and Foreign Minister could not act, perhaps due to a bomb blast where they were all together. In the martial law situation, the ADF would need to exercise internal security powers on its own authority. In the latter situation, the Governor-General might assume such powers herself or himself, or quickly swear in a new government from other ministers. In either case, the procedural requirements for authorising the use of the ADF in accordance with Part IIIAAA could not operate (unless the newly sworn ministers could act in accordance with the legislation). In such a case, necessity should permit reliance upon executive power to authorise ADF internal security operations.

As to foreseeable threats, at the other extreme, an internal security situation might actually be beneath the statutory threshold for the application of Part IIIAAA. There could be situations where there is no general level of domestic violence or threat to Commonwealth interests that would warrant the exercise of Part IIIAAA, but they could require the use of force nonetheless. Examples might include small-scale protests at ADF

---

51 Eg *Defence Act* s 51A.
52 Eg ibid s 51AA.
53 *Republic of Fiji Islands v Prasad* (Unreported, Fiji Court of Appeal, Casey J (Presiding), Barker, Kapi, Ward and Handley JJA, 1 March 2001) ('*Prasad*').

bases[54] or around ADF personnel that turned violent. The ADF in this case would need to be acting to prevent an effect on itself. Where this is the case, the powers of ordinary citizens might provide an authority to act. This will be discussed below.

There is a further foreseeable scenario which lies outside the scope of Part IIIAAA as the legislative scheme does not apply beyond the Australian offshore area. For the purposes of Part IIIAAA, s 51(1) defines the Australian offshore area to extend no further than the seas and airspace over the continental shelf. Section 51(1) provides for areas prescribed by the regulations but no such regulations exist. The effect of this is that, should a threat arise in relation to an Australian-flagged vessel beyond the Australian offshore area, there would be no power available under Part IIIAAA to deal with it. Any action would have to rely upon executive power. Such a situation might arguably be an external rather than an internal security operation. Given that Australian-flagged vessels are subject to Australian criminal law by virtue of s 6 of the *Crimes at Sea Act 2000* (Cth), and not any other national law when such vessels are in international waters, the concerns over the use of the ADF for internal security operations discussed in the introduction to this chapter would also be applicable. It is worth considering, then, the extent to which the powers of ordinary citizens or prerogative power might authorise security actions in relation to Australian-flagged vessels outside the Australian offshore area.

Quite apart from threats, there is also the possibility of a High Court challenge to Part IIIAAA powers which resulted in the invalidity of some or all of that part. Should the ADF have been relying upon powers which were subsequently found to have been invalid at the time, then the court may look to see whether executive power could have authorised the same action. It is not possible to speculate in any more detail but such a situation would not be unlike that in the *Tampa Case*[55] where the *Migration Act 1958* (Cth) did not apply to a situation where it might have been expected to. As discussed in Chapter 1, executive power supplied the authority instead. For this reason, s 51Y of the *Defence Act* may potentially be very significant in the case of any invalidity in Part IIIAAA.

---

54   See the discussion of the protest at the Nurunngar Base in South Australia in 1989. Members of the 2nd Cavalry Regiment were hastily dispatched to assist South Australian Police protect the base, although they were not reportedly required to use any force. The operation relied upon ordinary statutory and common-law powers of arrest and self-defence. Ward, above n 7 (no page numbers).
55   *Ruddock v Vadarlis* (2001) 110 FCR 491 ('*Tampa Case*').

IV Three Sources of Authority and their Limitations

A Ordinary Powers of Members of the ADF

Chapter 3 rejected Dicey's view that the Crown had no prerogative with respect to martial law. This was partly because Dicey saw the Crown as having only the same common-law power and obligation as any other subject to quell a riot or similar disturbance.[56] Dicey's view on martial law is hard to maintain in the face of the cases discussed in that chapter. His views on the shared powers of Crown and subject though with respect to riots and similar disturbances—that is, internal security as opposed to martial law—are a different matter. The ordinary Australian citizen today does have some limited power to respond to a violent situation and this is a power upon which the Commonwealth, through members of the ADF, might also rely.

In each jurisdiction, there is common-law or statutory power for any person to make an arrest for an indictable offence, as well as various common-law and statutory defences of self-defence or defence of another, preventing a crime, necessity, and also of sudden and extraordinary emergency.[57] Members of the ADF, whether acting in their personal capacity or in the course of their duty, are also always citizens.[58] These powers and defences are also available to them. In this sense, the Commonwealth could require members of the ADF, in the course of their duty, to defend themselves and others or make an arrest by virtue of the same authority that any citizen could do these things.[59] This could be an exercise of the prerogative with respect to control and disposition of the forces as expressed through

---

56 A V Dicey, *Introduction to the Study of the Law of the Constitution* (Macmillan, 10th ed, 1959) 284–6.
57 Eg Arrest or Preventing Crime: *Crimes Act 1900* (ACT) s 349ZC; *Criminal Code Act 2002* (ACT) s 41; *Crimes Act 1914* (Cth) s 3Z; *Criminal Code Act* (NT) ss 27(e), 33 of Schedule 1; *Criminal Code Act 1899* (Qld) ss 25, 266; *Criminal Code Act 1924* (Tas) s 39; *Criminal Code 1913* (WA) ss 25, 243. Self-Defence, Necessity or Sudden and Extraordinary Emergency: *Zecevic v DPP (Vic)* (1987) 162 CLR 645, 660; *R v Loughnan* [1981] VR 443, 448; *Criminal Code Act 2002* (ACT) s 42; *Criminal Code Act 1995* (Cth) ss 10.3 & 10.4; *Crimes Act 1900* (NSW) ss 418–22 (noting that New South Wales has codified the law of self-defence); *Criminal Code Act* (NT) s 28(f); *Criminal Code Act 1899* (Qld) ss 31(1)(c), 271(1), 272, 273; *Criminal Code Act 1924* (Tas), s 46; *Crimes Act 1958* (Vic) ss 9AB–9AF; *Criminal Code 1913* (WA) ss 31(3), 248, 249, 250; see Broniit, above n 3, 53.
58 *Re Tracey* (1989) 166 CLR 518, 547 (Mason CJ, Wilson and Dawson JJ).
59 See Royal Australian Air Force, *Operations Law for RAAF Commanders* (Australian Air Publication 1003, 2004) 45.

command power, or as part of its express power under s 61 to execute and maintain the laws of the Commonwealth. This is consistent with the statement of French CJ in *Williams* that:

> [T]he executive power of the Commonwealth extends to the doing of all things which are necessary or reasonably incidental to the execution and maintenance of a valid law of the Commonwealth once that law has taken effect. That field of action does not require express statutory authority, nor is it necessary to find an implied power deriving from the statute. The necessary power can be found in the words 'execution and maintenance … of the laws of the Commonwealth' appearing in s 61 of the *Constitution*. The field of non-statutory executive action also extends to the administration of departments of State under s 64 of the *Constitution* and those activities which may properly be characterised as deriving from the character and status of the Commonwealth as a national government.[60]

It is not for this chapter to go into the detail of the powers of arrest and self-defence and related powers as it is a complex area of the law on its own, particularly given the subtle differences between the various Australian jurisdictions, and it has been well traversed elsewhere.[61] The main point is that such powers and defences are available to ordinary citizens, and therefore to members of the ADF. The question then is the extent to which the Commonwealth can require members of the ADF to exercise their own powers as ordinary citizens on behalf of the Commonwealth.

Of course, when well-armed, equipped, uniformed and organised members of the ADF exercise any of the powers of an ordinary citizen it is not the same as any ordinary citizen exercising these powers. As discussed in Chapter 1, Winterton saw a fundamental difference between government

---

60   *Williams* (2012) 248 CLR 156, 191; See also limited discussion of 'ordinary and well recognised functions of government', 234 (Gummow and Bell JJ), s 61 grants a power to spend where authorised by statute or the *Constitution*, 249, recognised power of Commonwealth to inquire which is held in common with every other citizen, 206 (Hayne J), Commonwealth may exercise the capacities of a juristic person 'in the ordinary course of administering a recognised part of the Commonwealth government', 342 (Crennan J), 'an activity not authorised by the *Constitution* could not fall within the power of the Executive', 373–4 (Kiefel J). Other than the reference to French CJ, these references are indirect at best in support of this point but they indicate views which are at least not inconsistent with it. Gabrielle Appleby and Stephen McDonald, 'Looking at the Executive Power Through the High Court's New Spectacles' (2013) 35(2) *Sydney Law Review* 253, 261, note this as a source of executive power as well but do not cite an authority for it.

61   See Rob McLaughlin, 'The Use of Lethal Force by Military Forces on Law Enforcement Operations – Is There a "Lawful Authority"?' (2009) 37(3) *Federal Law Review* 441, 459, 467; G J Cartledge, *The Soldier's Dilemma: When to Use Force in Australia* (AGPS Press, 1992) 155–8; and general Australian criminal law texts such as Simon Bronitt and Bernadette McSherry, *Principles of Criminal Law* (Thomson Lawbook Co, 3rd ed, 2010).

doing what any citizen could do and a citizen doing the same things.[62] *Williams* would indicate that such actions may not be Commonwealth actions per se as the Commonwealth does not have the same powers as that of a natural person. Hayne J in *Williams* touched on this, without resolving the matter fully, in referring to *Clough v Leahy* and the power of an official to seek information and ask questions:

> Griffith CJ recognised that a State, as a polity, acts through individuals and accepted that an officer of the State executive was not somehow prevented, when 'acting for the Crown', from undertaking action that 'every man is free to do', being 'any act that does not unlawfully interfere with the liberty or reputation of his neighbour or interfere with the course of justice'.[63]

His Honour did not take this to mean that a polity generally, or the Commonwealth in particular, therefore had the same capacities as a natural person.[64] While only an observation by one judge in the case, it would suggest however that officials acting in the course of their duty may rely upon their own powers as a natural person in the course of that duty. This is consistent with *Pirrie v McFarlane*,[65] as discussed in Chapter 2. Further, as discussed in more detail below, the individual ADF member would be the subject of any prosecution for an excess use of power, not the Commonwealth. However, as discussed in Chapters 1 and 2, the Commonwealth might be the subject of civil action for exceeding its power with respect to the control and disposition of the forces or to execute and maintain the laws of the Commonwealth, or as vicariously liable for the actions of its officials. As Gageler J stated in *M68*:

> The inclusion of s 75(iii) had the consequence of exposing the Commonwealth from its inception to common law liability, in contract and in tort, for its own actions and for actions of officers and agents of the Executive Government acting within the scope of their de facto authority.[66]

---

62   He saw this as an exercise of prerogative power, George Winterton, *Parliament, the Executive and the Governor-General* (Melbourne University Press, 1983) 112.
63   *Williams* (2012) 248 CLR 156, 257–8 quoting *Clough v Leahy* (1904) 2 CLR 139, 155, 167, 157; Appleby and Macdonald, above n 60, 262, 275, note that *Williams* did not really consider this area of executive power.
64   *Williams* (2012) 248 CLR 156.
65   (1925) 36 CLR 170, although that case did not concern the use of force.
66   *Plaintiff M68 v Minister for Immigration and Border Protection* [2016] HCA 1 [125] ('*M68*'), citing *James v The Commonwealth* (1939) 62 CLR 339, 359–60; cf *Little v The Commonwealth* (1947) 75 CLR 94, 114.

The consequence of this is that the Commonwealth could only require members of the ADF to effect arrests and defend others where it relates to another Commonwealth power.[67] This is a limitation on the use of the powers of members of the ADF which they possess by virtue of also being citizens. For example, it would appear to relate to the execution and maintenance of a law of the Commonwealth to protect foreign dignitaries visiting events such as CHOGM (Commonwealth Heads of Government Meeting) and APEC. In particular it is an offence under the *Crimes (Internationally Protected Persons) Act 1976* (Cth) to attack such a person.[68] It follows that, even without specific statutory authority such as Part IIIAAA, a member of the ADF could act to defend such a person and arrest the assailant, much as any other citizen has the power to do.[69]

Alternatively, ADF members operating under quite low-level authority, such as unit or detachment command might, where necessary, use the powers of an ordinary citizen to protect themselves, their mission, their equipment or their base or, indeed, members of the local community where disorder might affect the local ADF presence as part of the prerogative with respect to control and disposition of the forces.[70] It might be difficult to argue that such action was an exercise of a power of the Commonwealth if the disturbance really had no effect on the local ADF presence at all.

The main difference is that the ADF member is likely to be much more capable of such action than any ordinary citizen. On the other hand, it would not very likely be an exercise of Commonwealth executive power to require ADF members to exercise these powers to maintain order in the streets around their own homes. As discussed, this would be a matter for the relevant State or Territory police, or the ADF member in their personal capacity. This is an important limitation arising from the federal structure of the *Constitution*, as proposed at the end of Chapter 1. This would be consistent with the careful distinction in Part IIIAAA between calling out

---

67   *Williams* (2012) 248 CLR 156.
68   *Crimes (Internationally Protected Persons) Act 1976* (Cth) ss 3A, 8.
69   This is consistent with Renfree's view, Harold Renfree, *The Executive Power of the Commonwealth of Australia* (Legal Books, 1984) 457–61.
70   See also *Defence Act* s 72P relating to the offence of unauthorised entry to Defence premises, which is very widely defined in s 71A to include virtually any place occupied by the ADF, or *Crimes Act 1914* (Cth) s 30K relating to the offence of obstructing or hindering Commonwealth government services.

the ADF to protect Commonwealth interests as opposed to responding to requests from States and self-governing Territories to protect against domestic violence, reflecting the fundamental limitation of federalism.[71]

1 Liability of ADF Members

As mentioned above and consistent with the principle of legality such as found in *A v Hayden*[72] as discussed in Chapter 1, members of the ADF who exercise powers of arrest or defence of others are personally liable to criminal prosecution for any excess of force which occurs. This is a key limitation. As much as such action might be an exercise of Commonwealth power, without additional specific statutory power such as Part IIIAAA, members of the ADF carrying out the Commonwealth's requirement to maintain the law have no more power than any ordinary citizen in doing so. Apart from in Queensland,[73] Western Australia,[74] Tasmania,[75] and for certain war crimes,[76] obeying orders is no defence to criminal charges. It may be that this defence should be more broadly available where such orders are not manifestly unlawful. As quoted in the introduction to this book, Starke J neatly stated the position with regard to liability for following orders in *Shaw Savill & Albion Co Ltd*:

> If any person commits … a wrongful act or one not justifiable, he cannot escape liability for the offence, he cannot prevent himself being sued, merely because he acted in obedience to the order of the Executive Government or any officer of State.[77]

Further, without special statutory powers, a member of the ADF stands in the same position as an ordinary citizen with regard to enforcing the law. In his much-quoted *Charge to the Bristol Grand Jury on a Special Commission,* 1832, Lord Tindal CJ said:

> The law acknowledges no distinction in this respect between the soldier and the private individual. The soldier is still a citizen, lying under the same authority to preserve the peace of the King as any other subject.[78]

---

71 *Defence Act* ss 51A, 51B, 51C.
72 (1984) 156 CLR 532.
73 *Criminal Code 1899* (Qld) s 31.
74 *Criminal Code 1913* (WA) s 31.
75 *Criminal Code Act 1924* (Tas) s 38, only in regard to riots.
76 *Criminal Code Act 1995* s 268.116(3).
77 *Shaw Savill & Albion Co Ltd v Commonwealth* (1940) 66 CLR 353 344, ('*Shaw Savill & Albion Co Ltd*').
78 5 C & P 254, 261 quoted in H P Lee, *The Emergency Powers of the Commonwealth of Australia* (Law Book Company, 1984) 229.

Re Tracey made clear that the position in Australia is the same.[79] It would also not be possible to argue that a matter was nonjusticiable within the terms of *Council of the Civil Service Unions v Minister for the Civil Service*, discussed in Chapter 2.[80]

2 Necessity

Another important consequence of the exercise of the powers of an ordinary citizen by a member of the ADF is that the threshold of necessity might be easier to satisfy, insofar only as it relates to the liability of ADF members. Necessity is usually an element of the exercise of the power of arrest or the right of self-defence. For example, s 266 of the *Criminal Code Act 1899* (Qld) states:

> It is lawful for a person to use such force as is reasonably necessary in order to prevent the commission of an offence which is such that the offender may be arrested without a warrant.[81]

As far as the ADF member is concerned, as opposed to the Commonwealth, the standard of necessity required for any exercise of the power of an ordinary citizen is only the same as any citizen would have to satisfy in conducting the same actions. It is a matter for the Commonwealth, rather than the ADF member, as to whether there is a general level of domestic violence that has to occur, as with Part IIIAAA, or unforeseen or extraordinary circumstances as might be required to rely upon prerogative or nationhood power (discussed below).

3 A Duty to Suppress?

A notable point made by Dicey is that there is a positive duty upon members of the armed forces to help restore order in situations of riot and disturbance and the like.[82] This is because this is an obligation which any subject has. Dicey cites *R v Pinney*[83] from 1832 as authority for this but this was a case about a magistrate, not any ordinary subject.[84] The common-law rights and duties in that case were for a justice of the peace to put down a riot and for the King's subjects to assist the justice in

---

79 (1989) 166 CLR 518, 547 (Mason CJ, Wilson and Dawson JJ).
80 [1985] AC 374.
81 *Criminal Code Act 1899* (Qld) s 266.
82 Reid and Walker, above n 3, 134–5, note doubts on this point.
83 (1832) 3 B & AD 349.
84 Dicey, above n 56, 284–6.

doing so. It did not see the obligations of ordinary subjects as anything like those of a justice.[85] Marshall suggests that the emerging convention in the United Kingdom has been not to permit troops to suppress public disorder without ministerial approval, in spite of the common-law duty.[86] This common-law duty must now be at least questionable. Rowe certainly rejects such a view with respect to soldiers or citizens.[87] To begin with, the power to quell a riot is effectively a power of government even if, absent statute, it rests upon a common-law basis. Describing this as the duty of any citizen or subject seems to have disguised the fact that since the Bristol riots in 1832, the subject of *R v Pinney*[88] and Lord Tindal LCJ's *Charge to the Bristol Grand Jury on a Special Commission*,[89] there is no record of a prosecution of a military member for failing in this duty.[90] Suppressing riots and dealing with emergencies has primarily been a governmental function. A court faced with this question may well decide that the development of police forces since then has relieved the ordinary subject of this duty.

If this is the case, it seems unlikely that a member of the ADF would have an obligation, independent of his or her chain of command, to act to assist to put down a riot. If maintaining internal security is actually a governmental function, it should be done at the direction of government. In the case of the ADF, this would mean through the chain of command and not by individual members. In *R v Clegg*, the 1995 appeal case of a British soldier found to have used excessive force in self-defence whilst on patrol in Northern Ireland, Lord Lloyd quoted Lord Diplock's more recent perspective on the issue in *Attorney-General for Northern Ireland's Reference*:[91]

> There is little authority in English law concerning the rights and duties of a member of the armed forces of the Crown when acting in aid of the civil power; and what little authority there is relates almost entirely to the duties of soldiers when troops are called upon to assist in controlling

---

85 *R v Pinney* (1832) 3 B & AD 349, 354.
86 Marshall, above n 17, 163–8.
87 Rowe, above n 13, 45–7.
88 Dicey, above n 56, 284–6.
89 5 C & P 254.
90 Rowe, above n 13, 45; Cartledge, above n 61, 158, discusses the court martial of Lieutenant Colonel Brereton and Captain Warrington for failure in their duty in respect of the riots, stating 'Brereton committed suicide before the completion of his court martial and Warrington was cashiered'. Reported in Charles Clode, *The Military Forces of the Crown: Their Administration and Government* (John Murray, 1869) 179–80.
91 [1977] AC 105, 136–7.

> a riotous assembly. Where used for such temporary purposes it may not be inaccurate to describe the legal rights and duties of a soldier as being no more than those of an ordinary citizen in uniform. But such a description is in my view misleading in the circumstances in which the army is currently employed in aid of the civil power in Northern Ireland … In theory it may be the duty of every citizen when an arrestable offence is about to be committed in his presence to take whatever reasonable measures are available to him to prevent the commission of the crime; but the duty is one of imperfect obligation and does not place him under any obligation to do anything by which he would expose himself to risk of personal injury, nor is he under any duty to search for criminals or seek out crime. In contrast to this a soldier who is employed in aid of the civil power in Northern Ireland is under a duty, enforceable under military law, to search for criminals if so ordered by his superior officer and to risk his own life should this be necessary in preventing terrorist acts. For the performance of this duty he is armed with a firearm, a self-loading rifle, from which a bullet, if it hits the human body, is almost certain to cause serious injury if not death.[92]

The point here is that the soldier's duty arose from his superior orders and not independently from the common law.

Further, if internal security is a government function, then, in accordance with the division of responsibility of powers in the federation discussed above, public order rests with the States. It is not for the Commonwealth, or members of the ADF as a local initiative, to interfere with State responsibilities. With respect to 'domestic violence' in particular, s 119 of the *Constitution* makes clear that *Commonwealth* action to protect a State against domestic violence should occur at the request of the executive government of the State.[93] This obligation would then rest with the Commonwealth, not members of the ADF having the obligation to suppress a riot as any other citizen may have. It would appear that ADF members, as Commonwealth officials in State jurisdictions, could not have the same positive duty to suppress riots as members of the armed forces might have in English common law which Dicey asserts. The situation might be different in the Commonwealth's Territories, whether

---

92   [1995] 1 AC 482, 497. As a result of new evidence, Clegg was subsequently retried and acquitted of murder in 1999. He was found guilty of a lesser charge of unlawful wounding, for which he was also acquitted on appeal in 2000. These trial cases were not reported in the law reports. Nicholas Watt, 'Paratrooper Lee Clegg cleared of last charge over death of teenagers' *Guardian* (online), 1 February 2000, cited in Head, *Calling out the Troops: The Australian Military and Civil Unrest*, above n 3, 169.
93   See generally Stephenson, above n 1.

4. INTERNAL SECURITY

self-governing or not, but the effect of s 119 in respect of the States would appear to preclude an obligation upon individual members of the ADF to maintain internal security.

B Prerogative Power

Chitty's observation in relation to the King's war prerogative, quoted more fully in Chapter 3, that the 'King may … do various acts growing out of sudden emergencies' appears relevant to internal security as well.[94] Blackstone, albeit in relation to justice generally, stated that the King was the 'general conservator of the peace of the Kingdom'.[95] Should Part IIIAAA be inoperable in an internal security situation, as discussed above, or the legislation repealed for some reason, prerogative power to maintain internal security could be relevant. A key point is that the courts will treat the repression of riots and other internal disturbances as justiciable as they do not amount to the conduct of war, even if an exercise of prerogative power.[96]

Although a case concerned with the war prerogative, in 1964 in *Burmah Oil*[97] Viscount Radcliffe made useful observations on the flexible nature of the prerogative, which echo those made by Chitty, including its possible applications to public safety emergencies such as riots:

> [T]he prerogatives of the Crown have been many and various, and it would not be possible to embrace them under a single description … Others were as much duties as rights and were vested in the Sovereign as the leader of the people and the chief executive instrument for protecting the public safety. No one seems to doubt that a prerogative of this latter kind was exercisable by the Crown in circumstances of sudden and extreme

---

94 Joseph Chitty, *A Treatise on the Law of the Prerogatives of the Crown; and the Relative Duties and Rights of the Subject* (Butterworths, 1820) 49.
95 *Blackstone's Commentaries with Notes of Reference, to the Constitution and Laws, of the Federal Government of the United States; and of the Commonwealth of Virginia* (1803, Hein Online reproduction) 265. Sir Matthew Hale appears not to have distinguished the King's war prerogative, including the power to suppress rebellion, from any separate prerogative with respect to internal security, Sir Matthew Hale, *The Prerogatives of the King* (Selden Society, written between 1640 and 1664 but unpublished, D E C Yale (ed) (1976 ed) 123, see *Tabula Quarta – Tempore Belli* and *Pax et Belli Constitutio*, xiv, and generally Chapter XII 'Concerning the Jurisdiction and Office of the Constable and Marshal, Martial Law, *Tempus Belli* and Acquisitions by Right of War'.
96 *Marais v General Officer Commanding the Lines of Communication* [1902] AC 109 115 ('*Marais*'). This is perhaps because any proceedings have been criminal proceedings against an official, such as *R v Pinney* (1832) 3 B & AD 349 and the *Charge to the Bristol Grand Jury on a Special Commission* 5 C & P 254, rather than an application for judicial review.
97 *Burmah Oil Co Ltd v Lord Advocate* [1965] AC 75 ('*Burmah Oil*').

emergency which put that safety in peril. There is no need to say that the imminence or outbreak of war was the only circumstance in which that prerogative could be invoked. Riot, pestilence and conflagration might well be other circumstances; but without much more recorded history of unchallenged exercises of such a prerogative.[98]

With respect to English common law, Rowe sees the use of military force to put down riots as a prerogative power governed by the common-law doctrine of necessity.[99] Renfree sees that prerogative as being available to the Commonwealth as well.[100] There is no Australian authority on this point but there is the 1989 English case of *R v Secretary of State for the Home Department, Ex parte Northumbria Police Authority* ('*Northumbria Police Case*'), which identifies a prerogative with respect to keeping the peace or maintaining public order. Nourse LJ said:

> The wider prerogative must have extended as much to unlawful acts within the realm as to the menaces of a foreign power. There is no historical or other basis for denying to the war prerogative a sister prerogative of keeping the peace within the realm. I have already expressed the view that the scarcity of references in the books to the prerogative of keeping the peace within the realm does not disprove that it exists. Rather it may point to an unspoken assumption that it does. That assumption is, I think, made in the judgment of Lord Campbell CJ in *Harrison* v *Bush* (1855) 5 E & B 344, 353 ... Of special importance for their demonstration of the Crown's part in keeping the peace are these words of Lord Blackburn in *Coomber v Berkshire Justices*, 9 App Cas Q 61, 67, which may have been based on *Blackstone's Commentaries* (1830), vol 1, p 343:
>
> 'The sheriff also was bound to raise the hue and cry, and call out the posse comitatus of the county whenever it was necessary for any police purposes; in so doing he was acting for the Crown, but the burthen fell on the inhabitants of the county.'
>
> I am of the opinion that a prerogative of keeping the peace within the realm existed in mediaeval times, probably since the Conquest and, particular statutory provision apart, that it has not been surrendered by the Crown in the process of giving its express or implied assent to the modern system of keeping the peace through the agency of independent police forces.[101]

---

98 Ibid 114–15.
99 Rowe, above n 13, 44–7.
100 Renfree, above n 69, 466–7.
101 [1989] 1 QB 26, 58–9.

This case only concerned the provision of riot equipment to the police by the Home Secretary without statutory authority. It did identify that the armed forces could exercise the prerogative,[102] but in doing so did not describe any specific actions beyond that which any ordinary citizen could take. It might extend to putting troops on the street with the apparent intention of using force but there is virtually no authority that justifies the use of lethal force beyond the requirements of self-defence.

McLaughlin notes that *Attorney-General for Northern Ireland's Reference*[103] and some earlier cases may appear to grant some limited authority to shoot fleeing suspects without an immediate associated threat to life.[104] These cases are not consistent with more recent authorities though, and may be explicable by the political context of the Northern Ireland troubles. *Attorney-General for Northern Ireland's Reference*[105] is not even really consistent within itself.[106] McLaughlin is emphatic that there is no broader power for military forces in Australia or the United Kingdom to use lethal force in internal security operations beyond that required for self-defence.[107] Particularly as *Attorney-General for Northern Ireland's Reference*[108] referred to statutory powers, there is no authority for the prerogative power with respect to public order alone to authorise the use of lethal force. There is not even authority for any direct interference with the liberties of members of the public beyond that which any ordinary citizen could lawfully exercise.

1 Necessity

Consistent with the theoretical discussion in Chapter 1, necessity may possibly authorise nonlethal actions under prerogative power which no ordinary citizen could perform. In a situation like the Bowral example discussed below, this may possibly include the cordon and search of areas, maintaining vehicle checkpoints and so on.[109] This is different to the use

---

102 Ibid 51. Zines criticised this case as too wide and having too little basis in authority, hoping that it would not be followed in Australia. In Zines, 'The Inherent Executive Power of the Commonwealth', above n 2, 287.
103 [1977] AC 105.
104 McLaughlin, above n 61, 459, 467.
105 [1977] AC 105.
106 McLaughlin, above n 61, 459, 467.
107 Ibid 467–9. Head also discusses this issue, Head, *Calling out the Troops: The Australian Military and Civil Unrest*, above n 3, 165–77.
108 [1977] AC 105.
109 Cartledge, above n 61, 131, 136.

of the powers of an ordinary citizen because it goes beyond actions which any ordinary citizen could perform. Necessity in the case of prerogative power to restore internal security would have to be a state necessity in the sense discussed in the previous chapter on martial law.[110] In the absence of any authority this is a most uncertain area of the law.[111] The necessity would have to be very clear if members of the ADF were to be able to avoid personal criminal or civil liability for what would otherwise be unlawful acts. Lord Pearce usefully distinguished the stricter requirements of necessity in case of riot as opposed to war in *Burmah Oil*:

> It may well be that, so far as riot and rebellion within the realm are concerned, 'the power of the Crown, like the power of any other magistrate and, indeed, of every citizen, is derived from and measured by the necessity of the case.' See Professor Holdsworth's *History of English Law*, vol. 10, pp 708–9 ... But the right of the Crown to take extreme measures or declare martial law against its own subjects differs from its rights when there is a state of war against enemy subjects and is more jealously regarded by the law. And no authority has been cited to show that the Crown prerogative in war has been regarded as having the same limitations as its rights in dealing with riot and rebellion.[112]

This is perhaps why there have been indemnity acts[113] in the past where internal security actions have been legally questionable and, therefore, perhaps why there is a dearth of authority on the subject.

2 Federal Division of Responsibility

While necessity still must justify and limit the use of prerogative power in the Australian context perhaps, more significantly, the scope of the ADF to take internal security action is also limited by the scope of Commonwealth executive power. As mentioned above, general public order is a matter for the States, not the Commonwealth.[114] The 2002 *Inter-Governmental Agreement on Australia's National Counter-Terrorism Arrangements* recognised this as it provided for the States to refer quite

---

110 See Mark Stavsky, 'The Doctrine of State Necessity in Pakistan' (1983) 16(2) *Cornell International Law Journal* 341, 350–2.
111 As to the uncertainty of necessity as a common-law defence see *R v Loughnan* [1981] VR 443.
112 *Burmah Oil* [1965] AC 75, 144.
113 *Martial Law Indemnity Act* 1854 (Vic).
114 *R v Sharkey* (1949) 79 CLR 121, 150. See also Head, *Calling out the Troops: The Australian Military and Civil Unrest*, above n 3, 67; Blackshield, above n 5, 6. See generally H V Evatt, *The Royal Prerogative* (Law Book Co, first presented as a doctoral thesis 1924, with commentary by Leslie Zines, 1987) 226–38.

specific powers to criminalise terrorist acts to the Commonwealth[115] while retaining primary jurisdiction for operational responses to terrorism.[116] As a result, the Commonwealth's responsibility for internal security is less for general public order matters, such as riots, than it is for the security of such matters as foreign dignitaries, including around major events, the conduct of federal elections, the postal service, the execution of court processes, and the air and maritime domains.[117]

These are not matters which the authorities for the prerogative with respect to public order really touch upon. They will be discussed within the context of nationhood power below. Renfree saw them as aspects of the 'King's peace in relation to the Commonwealth', and therefore probably matters of prerogative power.[118] As stated in Chapter 1, Twomey[119] argues that there is a prerogative power of self-protection relying upon *Burmah Oil*[120] and so there is no need for a nationhood power source of authority. She does not cite a pinpoint reference in the case however and it is difficult to see how it could be authority for a federal government to intervene in a State to protect its own functions. If there can have been no new prerogatives since 1689, when there was no contemplation of a federal Commonwealth of Australia, it is difficult to see how prerogative power could authorise Commonwealth intervention in a State to protect Commonwealth functions. For this reason it is arguably preferable to refer to the text of s 61 itself, a nationhood power approach, for the source of authority. Where the Commonwealth could be concerned with general public order, it would be in the Territories[121] and in situations so serious as to be beyond the capacity of the States to cope and leading to a request for Commonwealth assistance.[122]

---

115 This occurred under s 51(xxxvii) of the *Constitution*, see, eg, *Terrorism (Commonwealth Powers) Act 2003* (NSW), sch 1 of which actually provided the relevant draft amendments to the Commonwealth *Criminal Code Act 1995*.
116 *Inter-Governmental Agreement on Australia's National Counter-Terrorism Arrangements* 2002 (24 October 2002) paragraph 2.4 <www.dpc.wa.gov.au/ossec/CounterTerrorismArrangements/ProtectingCriticalInfrastructure/Documents/2002IGAonCounter-TerrorismArrangments.pdf>. See Stephenson, above n 1, 309–12.
117 *Inter-Governmental Agreement on Australia's National Counter-Terrorism Arrangements*, para 2.4 (e). See also Head, *Calling out the Troops: The Australian Military and Civil Unrest*, above n 3, 77–97.
118 Renfree, above n 69, 460–1.
119 Anne Twomey, 'Pushing the Boundaries of Executive Power – *Pape*, the Prerogative and Nationhood Powers' (2010) 34(1) *Melbourne University Law Review* 314, 332–4.
120 [1965] AC 75.
121 On call-out on the Gazelle Peninsula, Papua New Guinea (then an Australian territory), where troops did not actually deploy, see Ward, above n 7 (no page numbers).
122 See Michael Eburn, 'Responding to Catastrophic Natural Disasters and the Need for Commonwealth Legislation' (2011) 10(3) *Canberra Law Review* 81, 87–91.

If the division of responsibilities between the States and the Commonwealth leaves general public order to the States, can the Commonwealth exercise prerogative power to maintain public order on behalf of the States? As discussed in the introduction to this chapter, s 119 of the *Constitution* provides that the Commonwealth shall protect the States from domestic violence. The condition is that this be on the application of the executive government of the State. This appears to be a quid pro quo for the States transferring their military capability to the Commonwealth under ss 69 and 114 of the *Constitution*.[123] Given that at the time of drafting the *Constitution*, nationhood power was not a concept known to constitutional law,[124] it is likely that the effect of these provisions was meant to be that the Commonwealth would exercise prerogative power to maintain public order in the States. Section 119 recognises that the States had jurisdiction over public order, and therefore had the relevant prerogative power, but that the Commonwealth had the military capability to enforce it. It would appear, then, that when the Commonwealth intervenes in a State to protect against domestic violence, at the application of the executive government of the State, it can rely upon the authority of prerogative to do so.[125] This would be no different in a Territory, except that there would be no constitutional requirement for the Commonwealth to receive a request from the executive government of the Territory concerned.[126]

C Nationhood Power

Chapter 1 discussed that there may be a basis to use the ADF under nationhood power where there is no prerogative available. This is likely only to be in circumstances where the English character of the prerogative cannot operate within Australia's distinct constitutional arrangements. This makes the actual experience in Australia of the use of the ADF for internal security, which this chapter will discuss below, at least as significant as the predominantly English common-law authorities on restoring public order. As the prerogative to restore order resides primarily with the States, the Commonwealth therefore might only act unilaterally when it is doing so to protect its own functions. Such unilateral action would most likely be an exercise of nationhood power because, as discussed above, there

---

123 See Evatt, above n 114, 232–3.
124 See Twomey, above n 119, 327–43.
125 See Renfree, above n 69, 467–9. This is consistent with Stephenson's view that s 119 is not the source of the power but merely regulates it, above n 1, 292.
126 See Renfree, above n 69, 484–6.

are no authorities which would support prerogative power as the basis to protect Commonwealth government functions.[127] It is a distinct issue in the debate which followed the Bowral call-out as to whether it was actually some of form of nationhood power which provided the source of executive power in that situation.[128]

As discussed in Chapter 1, in an extreme case, nationhood power justified by necessity may even extend to restoring State government functions without a request from the State concerned, where the State was no longer capable of making the request. If a State government effectively collapsed, it would most likely be 'peculiarly within the capacity and resources of the Commonwealth Government' to restore its functioning.[129] This view relies upon the text of s 61 as well as the theory that executive power must be able to respond to contingency, *Fortuna*. As prerogative power in the Australian setting could not extend that far, the only power that could be available is nationhood power. Experience in Australia has not tested the limits to this point but it has provided some significant exercises of using the ADF which illustrate the potential scope of nationhood power.

V The Three ADF Internal Security Operations under Executive Power

A Bowral 1978

Justice Hope in his *Protective Security Review* of 1979 provided a detailed description of the events which became known as the 'Bowral call-out', the essence of which is as follows.[130] On 13 February 1978, a bomb exploded outside the Hilton Hotel in Sydney, killing two people, fatally wounding another and injuring a further eight people.[131] A number of visiting heads of government were staying at the Hilton Hotel for the Commonwealth Heads of Government Regional Meeting (CHOGRM).[132] The meeting

---

127 See also discussion in Joe McNamara, 'The Commonwealth Response to Cyclone Tracy: Implications for Future Disasters' (2012) 27(2) *The Australian Journal of Emergency Management* 37.
128 See Lee, *The Emergency Powers of the Commonwealth of Australia*, above n 78, 207 and Blackshield, above n 5, 7, discussed further below.
129 *Pape* (2009) 238 CLR 1, 63.
130 Hope, above n 4.
131 Ibid 258; Lee, *The Emergency Powers of the Commonwealth of Australia*, above n 78, 195.
132 Hope, above n 4, 257.

was due to visit Bowral the next day for two days.[133] Prime Minister Fraser and Premier Wran of New South Wales met to discuss the appropriate response.[134] The New South Wales Police Commander stated that he did not have adequate resources to guarantee the security of the visitors between Sydney and Bowral. A meeting of the Federal Cabinet the same day decided to call out the ADF to provide security between Sydney and Bowral.[135] With the concurrence of Premier Wran, there was no formal request from the Government of New South Wales for protection. The call-out would essentially be to protect the interests of the Commonwealth, that is the security of the visiting heads of government.[136] At a meeting of the Executive Council later the same day, the Governor-General signed an order-in-council calling out the ADF.[137] It stated, in part:

> Whereas I am satisfied, by reason of terrorist activities and related violence that have occurred in the State of New South Wales, that it is necessary
>
> a. for the purpose of safeguarding the national and international interests of the Commonwealth of Australia;
> b. for giving effect to the obligations of the Commonwealth of Australia in relation to the protection of internationally protected persons.[138]

There was no specific statutory basis for this call-out, other than the indirect reference to the *Crimes (Internationally Protected Persons) Act 1976* (Cth), and the ADF relied upon no specific statutory powers. Also on 13 February 1978, the Minister for Foreign Affairs signed a Requisition of the Civil Authority requiring Brigadier Butler, the officer commanding the forces involved, to order his forces out. The Minister for Foreign Affairs signed a requisition ordering those forces in on 16 February 1978. The Governor-General revoked the call-out order at an Executive Council meeting on 20 February, when the last of the visitors had left Australia.[139]

Approximately 1,900 armed Army and Royal Australian Air Force (RAAF) personnel secured the route between Sydney and Bowral with equipment including helicopters, armoured personnel carriers and mine

---

133 Ibid 258.
134 Ibid.
135 Ibid 257–62.
136 Ibid 258–9.
137 Ibid 257–62.
138 Ibid 321.
139 Ibid 258–9, 262, see also 'Appendix 15: Documents Relating to the Call Out of the Defence Force During the Commonwealth Heads of Government Regional Meeting, Sydney, February 1978', 320–3.

detectors. The arrangements were to have the New South Wales police interact directly with the civil community and for the ADF to maintain a low profile, conducting searches for explosives and surveillance of the area generally.[140] Even so, the ADF had Rules of Engagement authorising the use of lethal force as a last resort, with the emphasis on minimum force.[141]

In essence a very large ADF presence secured the CHOGRM travel route for three days, with authority to use lethal force. The legal basis for this action was executive power. The only explicit powers available to the ADF would have been those available to an ordinary citizen relating to arrest, self-defence and necessity. There was a good deal of consideration after the event of the legal basis of the Bowral call-out. The opinions of Justice Hope in his *Protective Security Review* and former High Court Justice Sir Victor Windeyer in his extracurial legal opinion annexed to that Review[142] are worth examination.

1 Protecting Commonwealth Interests and Nationhood Power

The opinions of Justice Hope and Sir Victor Windeyer in the *Protective Security Review* are the most thorough consideration of the legal basis of the 1978 operation. Sir Victor did not cite authority for the proposition that the Commonwealth has the inherent power 'to employ members of its Defence Force "for the protection of its servants or property or the safeguarding of its interests"',[143] other than the constitutional commentary of Quick and Garran referring to the United States case *Re Debs* of 1895.[144] Sir Victor saw such power as an incident of nationhood:

> The power of the Commonwealth Government to use the armed Forces at its command to prevent or suppress disorder that might subvert its lawful authority arises fundamentally, I think, because the *Constitution*

---

140 Ibid 260–1. See also Malcom Fraser and Margaret Simons, *Malcolm Fraser: The Political Memoirs: Commemorative Edition* (Melbourne University Press, 2015) 135, citing this author's views on the Bowral call-out as published in Cameron Moore, '"To Execute and Maintain the Laws of the Commonwealth" The ADF and Internal Security – Some Old Issues with New Relevance' (2005) 28(2) *University of New South Wales Law Journal* 523.
141 Hope, above n 4, 263.
142 Hope, above n 4, 'Appendix 9: Opinion of Sir Victor Windeyer, KBE, CB, DSO on Certain Questions Concerning the Position of Members of the Defence Force When Called Out to Aid the Civil Power', 277.
143 Hope, above n 4, 279, quoting from the *Australian Military Regulations*, although explicitly stating that these regulations do not create the power, but assume it. See also Ward, above n 7, for a view of Sir Victor's opinion.
144 158 US 564 (1895).

created a sovereign body politic with the attributes that are inherent in such a body. The Commonwealth of Australia is not only a federation of States. It is a nation.[145]

Referring to section 61, Sir Victor said that:

> [T]he ultimate authority for the calling out of the Defence Force ... was thus the power and the duty of the Commonwealth to protect the national interest and to uphold the laws of the Commonwealth. Being by order of the Governor-General, acting with the advice of the Executive Council, it was of unquestionable validity.[146]

Justice Hope agreed with Sir Victor and elaborated further on this point. He relied upon the obiter dicta of Dixon J in the *Communist Party Case*, quoting the following passage (excluding that in square brackets):

> [In point of constitutional theory the power to legislate for the protection of an existing form of government ought not to be based on a conception, if otherwise adequate, adequate only to assist those holding power to resist or suppress obstruction or opposition or attempts to displace them or the form of government they defend. As appears from *Burns v Ransley* (1949) 79 CLR, at p 116 and *R v Sharkey* (1949) 79 CLR, at pp 148, 149, I take the view that the power to legislate against subversive conduct has] a source in principle that is deeper or wider than a series of combinations of the words of s 51 (xxxix) with those of other constitutional powers. I prefer the view adopted in the United States, which is stated in *Black's American Constitutional Law* (1910), 2nd ed, s 153, p 210, as follows: '... it is within the necessary power of the federal government to protect its own existence and the unhindered play of its legitimate activities. And to this end, it may provide for the punishment of treason the suppression of insurrection or rebellion and for the putting down of all individual or concerted attempts to obstruct or interfere with the discharge of the proper business of government'.[147]

Justice Hope also referred to the obiter dicta of Dixon J in *R v Sharkey*, including this statement quoted from Quick and Garran, the first part of which appeared in the introduction to this chapter:

---

145 Hope, above n 4, 'Appendix 9: Opinion of Sir Victor Windeyer, KBE, CB, DSO on Certain Questions Concerning the Position of Members of the Defence Force When Called Out to Aid the Civil Power', 279.
146 Ibid 280. It is important to note that Sir Victor was not asked to give an opinion on the constitutional validity of the call-out, but rather on the powers and obligations of a member of the Defence Force when called out, and whether there should be changes to the law relating to them.
147 *Australian Communist Party v Commonwealth* (1951) 83 CLR 1 ('*Australian Communist Party*'); Hope, above n 4, 28.

If, however, domestic violence within a State is of such a character as to interfere with the operations of the Federal Government, or with rights and privileges of federal citizenship, the Federal Government may clearly, without a summons from the State, interfere to restore order. Thus if a riot in a State interfered with the carriage of the federal mails, or with interstate commerce, or with the right of an elector to record his vote at federal elections, the Federal Government could use all force at its disposal, not to protect the State, but to protect itself. Were it otherwise, the Federal Government would be dependent on the Governments of the States for the effective exercise of its powers.[148]

Justice Hope suggested that a relevant Commonwealth statute would indicate a Commonwealth interest, but that there could be Commonwealth interests worthy of protection by the ADF even without a relevant statute. He gave the example of protecting a visiting United States nuclear submarine.[149]

It is important to note however that Dixon J, in the *Communist Party Case*[150] and *R v Sharkey*[151] discusses only the legislative power of the Commonwealth operating with the executive power to intervene to protect its interests. He did not discuss executive power as the sole source of authority in this context. To rely on this authority, one has to presume that the executive power can authorise action on the basis of the words in s 61, which state 'extends to the execution and maintenance of this Constitution, and of the laws of the Commonwealth'.[152]

A number of those who wrote on the Bowral call-out at the time have not disputed that executive power authorised the operation. Lee wrote that '[i]t is also possible to justify such intervention by invoking a doctrine of inherent power, in this instance, inherent executive power of self-protection.'[153] Blackshield stated:

---

148 (1949) 79 CLR 121, 150.
149 Hope, above n 4, 152, although ordinary citizens' powers to defend others or defend property might be sufficient to do this.
150 (1951) 83 CLR 1.
151 (1949) 79 CLR 121.
152 Justice Hope stated that 'Generally speaking, where the Commonwealth has power to legislate, it also has executive power' above n 4, 32. *Williams* (2012) 248 CLR 156, clearly makes this view of the law no longer tenable on such a bare formulation.
153 Lee, *The Emergency Powers of the Commonwealth of Australia*, above n 78, 207.

> The object of calling out the troops was not to protect the people of New South Wales against 'domestic violence', but to protect eleven visiting heads of state against possible threats to their safety ... The Commonwealth, in calling out the troops, was thus protecting an inherent interest of its own ... just as the 1971 [*Public Order (Protection of Persons and Property) Act*] legislation was clearly valid as an exercise of Commonwealth legislative power over external affairs (*Constitution* s 51 vi) [sic: should be s 51(xxix)], so the CHOGRM call-out was valid as an exercise of the corresponding executive power ... the Commonwealth's executive power ... includes an amorphous and unexplored bundle of attributes of sovereignty, inherent in the fact of nationhood and of international personality.[154]

As discussed in Chapter 1, there has been some significant case law on nationhood power since 1978. Even so, the views expressed above are consistent with a view of nationhood as the source of power, even if more recent jurisprudence has refined the source and characteristics of that power.[155] However, while a number of authorities support the 'incident of nationhood' as a source of power, the High Court's more recent cases concern such things as financial crises[156] or the Bicentennial celebration.[157] These cases do not specifically address the use of force by the ADF for internal security.[158] The High Court judgment that most directly addressed the use of force under nationhood power was that of Isaacs J in *R v Kidman*.[159] His Honour described the existence of necessary executive powers for the Commonwealth's inherent right of self-protection, stating that 'a man obstructing any Commonwealth officer in the performance of his duty may be thrust aside with all the force necessary to enable the officer to perform his duty'.[160] The only source of executive authority for the Bowral call-out could have been nationhood power as there is no readily identifiable prerogative power to protect visiting dignitaries, and, as Premier Wran and Prime Minister Fraser decided, the security of CHOGRM was a Commonwealth responsibility.

---

154 Blackshield, above n 5, 7; Cartledge, above n 61, 131.
155 Particularly *Williams* (2012) 248 CLR 156 and *Pape* (2009) 238 CLR 1.
156 *Pape* (2009) 238 CLR 1.
157 *Davis v Commonwealth* (1988) 166 CLR 79.
158 See discussion on coercive aspects of the executive power in Graeme Hill, 'Will the High Court 'Wakim' Chapter II of the Constitution?' (2003) 31(3) *Federal Law Review* 445, 458–9.
159 (1915) 20 CLR 425.
160 Ibid 440–1. In the *Communist Party Case* (1951) 83 CLR 1, 188, 259, Fullagar J quoted Isaacs J with approval on this point, but in respect of a Commonwealth power to legislate for its own protection.

B CHOGM 2002 and POTUS 2003

The Government clearly stated in each case of the use of the ADF—to protect the Commonwealth Heads of Government Meeting (CHOGM) in 2002 and to protect the President of the United States in 2003—that such actions were to fulfil Australia's obligations to protect visiting heads of state and government.[161] There was no public review of these actions akin to the Hope *Protective Security Review*, and there are few relevant documents in the public domain. Based on the public statements however, the 2002 and 2003 operations relied upon the same legal basis as that for the Bowral call-out, even if the procedural aspects may have differed.

As discussed, the potential threat from the air to the 2002 CHOGM at Coolum took the use of the ADF for internal security outside the provisions of Part IIIAAA. The Defence Minister announced that the RAAF would use force against civilian aircraft perceived to be a threat to CHOGM.[162] Conceivably, this could have involved the shooting down of civilian aircraft by fighter jets in order to prevent a suicidal crash into the meeting place. There was no clear statement as to the legal basis of this operation at the time although it was made clear subsequently in the 2005 Department of Defence *Submission to Senate Legal and Constitutional Committee Inquiry into Defence Legislation Amendment (Aid to Civilian Authorities) Bill*.[163] In 2003 the ADF conducted a similar operation over Canberra to protect the visiting President of the United States. As stated by the official Defence Spokesperson, Brigadier Hannan:

> [O]n this occasion we'll also be providing a number of F/A-18 fighter aircraft that will provide protection in the very unlikely event of a threat emerging from the air. This isn't the first time we've done this, the public will be familiar with the arrangements that were put in place for CHOGM last year and these arrangements will be similar.[164]

---

161 See Robert Hill, above n 28; Department of Defence, *Submission to Senate Legal and Constitutional Committee*, above n 30.
162 Senator Robert Hill, above n 28.
163 Department of Defence, *Submission to Senate Legal and Constitutional Committee*, above n 30, 10.
164 Brigadier Mike Hannan, 'Defence Support to US President's Visit' (Transcript of Official Interview by Defence Spokesperson, 21 October 2003) <www.defence.gov.au/media/2003/ACF9A5.doc> (site discontinued).

C Implications for Executive Power

None of the three operations in question actually saw the use of force but each of them contemplated it. Even without the use of any force, in the case of the Bowral call-out, the call-out procedure itself ensured that the actions of the ADF in patrolling around Bowral were clearly subordinate to the control of the civilian government. Had the need to use force escalated, it would not have been within the power of ordinary citizens to cordon off public areas and control the movement of people and vehicles in order to protect visiting dignitaries. If this had occurred, and the operation had gone beyond the authority which the powers of ordinary citizens could have provided, it could only have been under the authority of nationhood power as there was no prerogative or statute authorising more forceful action. Given that the bomb blast at the beginning of the meeting was unexpected and the Commonwealth had a responsibility to protect the dignitaries, executive power, whatever its characterisation, arguably was available to authorise necessary action to protect life. It was the only source of power available within the time period. Parliament did not have time to grant relevant statutory power. Necessity is a key limitation and, again, an imprecise one but in this case the action was quite limited in both geographical scope and intensity. If the Bowral call-out had required more than the powers of ordinary citizens, it might have been consistent with a characterisation of executive power as a means to respond to *Fortuna*.

The difficulty is that, as discussed, there is very little authority to do such things under prerogative power, let alone nationhood power. The authorities for nationhood power do not extend explicitly to the conduct of internal security operations by the ADF. The closest authority involving ADF action is the *Tampa Case* which is subject to much criticism, as discussed in Chapters 1 and 2, and can be confined to border protection actions.[165] A reliance on nationhood power for ADF internal security operations is only arguable at best. It should be relied upon, as French CJ put it in *Pape*,[166] 'conservatively' because to rely upon such precarious authority for extreme measures such as putting troops on the street could challenge the principle of legality and enter the realm of extraconstitutional power. As much as nationhood power exists, without more substance it could become a pretext rather than a lawful authority in such a situation.

---

165 (2001) 110 FCR 491. See below n 176 for examples of criticism.
166 (2009) 238 CLR 1, 24.

As Winterton feared, 'once the realm of extra-constitutional power has been entered, there is no logical limit to its ambit'.[167] Such action could also expose ADF personnel to personal liability for carrying out unlawful orders, which they would likely obey because of Australia's long heritage of military subordination to the civilian government.[168]

As with prerogative power, nationhood power alone could not be an authority to use lethal force or force likely to cause serious injury, nor to deprive a person of their liberty. Nationhood power could only authorise such action when ordinary criminal law would permit it.[169] Nationhood power alone might be argued, without the support of the powers available to ordinary citizens, where it justifies the minimum necessary encroachment upon the law. It might authorise interference with freedom of movement such as in the examples mentioned above of blocking roads, maintaining vehicle check points and possibly even trespassing upon property or person by searching vehicles, buildings and people where the threat to life warranted it. It might be little different to prerogative power in that regard but possibly even more fraught with uncertainty.

The combat air patrols in 2002 and 2003, on the other hand, had a different character. They were planned well in advance for a foreseeable threat.[170] The prerogative as to the disposition of the forces would have been sufficient to authorise fighter aircraft to patrol the skies. While clearly it is not for any ordinary person to use a fighter jet to defend another, it would be difficult to argue that necessity could justify anything further than what the ordinary criminal law of defence of others would authorise.

In the air there are no intermediate levels of force available between warning and lethal levels of force, such as cordoning off areas or setting up road blocks, because it is physically impossible. After escalating through levels of warning to an aircraft, possibly including warning shots fired close to it, the only use of force option possible is firing at or into the aircraft with most likely lethal consequences. Any firing at or into an aircraft is highly likely to cause death. If nationhood power alone should

---

167 George Winterton, 'Extra-Constitutional Notions in Australian Constitutional Law' (1986) 16 *Federal Law Review* 223, 238, quoted in H P Lee, '*Salus Populi Suprema Lex Esto:* Constitutional Fidelity in Troubled Times' in H P Lee and Peter Gerangelos (eds), *Constitutional Advancement in a Frozen Continent: Essays in Honour of George Winterton* (Federation Press, 2009), 54.
168 *Re Tracey* (1989) 166 CLR 518, 538, 546 (Mason, CJ, Wilson and Dawson JJ); also *CPCF v Minister for Immigration and Border Protection* [2015] HCA 1 (French CJ) ('*CPCF*').
169 See Blackshield, above n 5, 10.
170 Hannan, above n 164.

not extend to the use of lethal force, then it seems that only when it operates together with the law of the defence of others could it authorise the use of any force in the air. If the requirements of the defence of others are not met then it is difficult to see how any other use of force against an aircraft could be lawful.[171] Bronitt and Stephens would appear to share this view.[172] For this reason no additional executive power, beyond simply having aircraft in the air, should have been available because it could not authorise any action in the air other than the use of lethal force. In respect of the combat air patrols in 2002 and 2003 then, ADF members could only have used the powers they have as ordinary citizens, such as the law of defence of others.

Nationhood power was also important insofar as it might justify Commonwealth intervention outside of s 119 but even then, State police forces have virtually no capacity to respond to a threat from the air. Air patrols over a State hardly seem to be an intrusion in that State contrary to s 119, so a resort to a nationhood power argument to justify this seems unlikely to be necessary.

VI *Tampa*?

Where does the use of the ADF to board the MV *Tampa* in 2001 under the authority of executive power fit into all of this? Although this book has discussed the profound implications of the *Tampa Case*[173] for nationhood power, executive power more generally and the incident as a whole for the relationship between the ADF and the elected civilian government, it has not yet discussed the implications of the *Tampa* incident for the limits on the use of the ADF under executive power. Was it internal security or was it an external security operation? Within the taxonomy of this book it could possibly be both. Chapter 6 will discuss external security operations other than war. It will analyse such operations as being external to Australia and relying upon prerogative power, where there is no intention to prosecute offences within Australian courts. Conceivably the *Tampa* operation could have met this description but it also occurred within Australia's territorial sea off Christmas Island,[174] a place within Commonwealth

---

171 Except in an armed conflict.
172 Bronitt and Stephens, above n 5, 267–9.
173 (2001) 110 FCR 491.
174 Ibid 491.

4. INTERNAL SECURITY

jurisdiction but constitutionally external to the States and Territories.[175] The significance of this is that the implications of the *Tampa* incident for the use of the ADF under executive power are essentially unique to the circumstances of border protection.

In the *Tampa Case*, French J, referring to an ancient prerogative to expel aliens, saw the executive power as 'measured by reference to Australia's status as a sovereign nation'.[176] This is not the same as a prerogative with respect to emergencies or internal security, or external affairs. Noting the discussion in Chapter 1 about whether this decision should have relied on prerogative power or nationhood power, either way, the power in question relates to preventing the entry of aliens. Section 7A of the *Migration Act* since 2001 has explicitly preserved only a very specific field for executive power in this regard:

> The existence of statutory powers under this Act does not prevent the exercise of any executive power of the Commonwealth to protect Australia's borders, including, where necessary, by ejecting persons who have crossed those borders.

Insofar then as the *Tampa Case*[177] provides authority for the ADF to use executive power, it is limited to protecting Australia's borders. It does not provide a more expansive authority with respect to internal security more generally, notwithstanding the implications of the case for so many aspects of the relationship between the ADF and executive power. Importantly, this

---

175 *NSW v Commonwealth* (1975) 135 CLR 337 ('*Seas and Submerged Lands Case*').
176 (2001) 110 FCR 491, 542. There was a thematic edition of the *Public Law Review*, being (2002) 13(2) *Public Law Review* 85 titled *The Tampa Issue* with the following articles: John McMillan, 'Comments on the Justiciability of the Government's Tampa Actions', 89; Simon Evans, 'The Rule of Law, Constitutionalism and the MV Tampa' 94; Kim Rubenstein, 'Citizenship, Sovereignty and Migration: Australia's Exclusive Approach to Membership of the Community', 102; Graham Thom, 'Human Rights, Refugees and the MV Tampa Crisis', 110; Donald Rothwell, 'The Law of the Sea and the MV Tampa Incident: Reconciling Maritime Principles with Coastal State Sovereignty', 118; and Helen Pringle and Elaine Thompson, 'The Tampa Affair and the Role of the Australian Parliament', 128. See also Hugh Smith, 'A Certain Maritime Incident and Political-Military relations' (2002) 46(6) *Quadrant* 38; Sir Ninian Stephen, 'The Governor-General as Commander in Chief' (1983) 14 *Melbourne University Law Review* 563; Michael White, 'Tampa Incident: Some Subsequent Legal Issues' (2004) 78 *Australian Law Journal* 249; and Stuart Kaye, 'Tampering with Border Protection: The Legal and Policy Implications of the Voyage of the MV Tampa' in Martin Tsamenyi and Chris Rahman (eds), *Protecting Australia's Maritime Borders: The MV Tampa and Beyond* (Centre for Maritime Policy, 2002) 59. Virtually all of these articles were critical, directly or indirectly, of at least some aspects of the government's handling of this incident.
177 (2001) 110 FCR 491.

provision also does not create any 'executive power of the Commonwealth to protect Australia's borders', it merely ensures the Act does not prevent the exercise of any such executive power which may exist.

Given the judgments in *CPCF* and *M68* discussed in Chapter 1, it is difficult now to argue that there is any executive power to protect Australia's borders. Only Keane J supported it in *CPCF*[178] but even French CJ did not take the opportunity to develop his earlier position on the issue.[179] Conversely, Hayne and Bell JJ stated clearly that there was no executive power 'to prevent the persons concerned entering Australian territory without a visa'.[180] After lengthy consideration, Kiefel rejected the proposition[181] and in *M68* Gordon J also rejected the idea.[182] The more arguable view therefore is that any power to protect Australia's borders from nonviolent threats must be found in statute, not executive power.

VII Conclusion

The *Tampa Case*[183] does not assist much in an analysis of the use of executive power for internal security by the ADF. Part IIIAAA seems almost to cover the field with respect to ADF internal security powers now, but there are conceivable situations where this legislation might not apply and there may have to be a resort to executive power. An analysis of *Pape*[184] and *Williams*[185] and Australia's constitutional structure, some English common-law authorities, as well as ADF experience, indicates that there are three main potential sources of this executive power—'executing or maintaining a law of the Commonwealth' or the exercise of a prerogative or nationhood power. Supporting the exercise of each of these sources of power is the aspect of executive power which the ADF members share in common with any citizen. The main limitation for the ADF in using this power, in addition to the limitations which would apply to any citizen doing such things as effecting an arrest or defending themselves, is that its use must be relate to 'executing or maintaining a law of the Commonwealth' or the exercise of a prerogative or nationhood

---

178 [2015] HCA 1 [476]–[495].
179 Ibid [40]–[42].
180 Ibid [137]–[151].
181 Ibid [258]–[293].
182 [2016] HCA 1 [372].
183 (2001) 110 FCR 491.
184 (2009) 238 CLR 1.
185 (2012) 248 CLR 156.

power. Given that such power is the most ordinary, in that any ordinary citizen may exercise it, it is ironic that it has been essential to the three nonstatutory ADF security operations around Bowral in 1978, over CHOGM in 2002 and to protect the visit of the President of the United States in 2003.

As to prerogative power, Australia's federal division of responsibilities means that the prerogative for maintaining public order, a central aspect of internal security, lies with the States. The ADF could only possibly rely upon this prerogative in maintaining public order in the Territories, or when there is a request from the executive government of a State. This creates a greater significance for nationhood power. There is a strong view in some cases, the Hope *Protective Security Review* and among some scholars that the Commonwealth has an inherent right to protect itself and its functions. In the absence of an identifiable prerogative for this purpose it may well be that nationhood power could be the source of executive authority for the ADF to protect the Commonwealth and its functions, such as by protecting visiting dignitaries or in restoring a collapsed State government. Any action relying upon prerogative or nationhood power alone that went beyond the power available to any ordinary citizen would have to be justified by state necessity. Any such power is fraught with uncertainty however.

Internal security by the ADF, in practice, has really relied upon the powers available to an ordinary citizen or upon Part IIIAAA of the *Defence Act*. Nationhood power may have justified Commonwealth action within States in the three incidents as not being contrary to s 119. There has been no constitutional challenge by a State though, and there has been no use of force such as to cause death or injury, or any significant damage to property. As a result, there has been no real judicial testing of ADF powers with respect to internal security. Taking French CJ's warning to approach executive power 'conservatively' then,[186] the use of force in ADF internal security operations should be no more than any citizen could exercise and must relate to maintaining a law of the Commonwealth or supporting the exercise of a prerogative or nationhood power. This is the limit of federalism as proposed in Chapter 1. Prerogative power, in the case of a request under s 119 or in a Territory, or nationhood power, to protect a Commonwealth interest, arguably, could only authorise more, nonlethal, force in the clearest cases of necessity.

---

186 *Pape* (2009) 238 CLR 1, 24.

5

War

I Introduction

War is potentially the most destructive exercise of executive power by the ADF. As this chapter will discuss, it can involve deliberate killing, injuring, damaging of property and detention. It might also include seizing enemy shipping in port at the outbreak of hostilities, interning enemy alien civilians, breaching traffic regulations in order to move military equipment, destroying property in order to deny it to an advancing enemy or in order to construct defences, and requisitioning property for military purposes. Ironically, perhaps, whilst possibly the best-recognised prerogative, its substance is one of the least considered in both case law and literature. The war prerogative seems mainly just to have operated and been accepted. The decision to go to war is nonjusticiable and government decisions concerning the conduct of hostilities have been mostly free from judicial scrutiny. There is ample regulation of the conduct of hostilities in international law and this finds expression in statutory form in the *Criminal Code Act 1995* (Cth) and the *Geneva Conventions Act 1957* (Cth). This statutory law is still silent however on where the authority lies for a member of the ADF to target and kill someone—or do anything else—in the execution of war; on the face of the statutes, this is murder. There is not a single case that positively asserts prerogative power as the authority for such action. There is a combat immunity from liability doctrine in *Shaw Savill & Albion Co Ltd v Commonwealth* (1940) 66

CLR 344 ('*Shaw Savill & Albion Co Ltd*') but this is as far as the case law goes. War then sits as a strangely powerful prerogative without positive authority to explain its substance.

War seems to have remained a matter for prerogative power because of its dynamic and often unpredictable nature. Even if the commencement of war is well foreseeable, the course of events once it has commenced often is not. In Australia, consistently with the English constitutional compromise of the 17th century, Parliament has stayed out of the conduct of military operations. It has approved the funding of war and regulated administrative and economic matters in support of national war efforts.[1] Parliament has proscribed certain conduct during military operations but it has essentially left it to the executive to decide when and how to use the ADF.[2] Notably, war does not in itself justify, or even necessarily require, military interference with any of the constitutional limitations described in Chapters 1 and 2 such as subordination to the civilian government, the separation of powers or the federal system.[3] Where this occurred it would be more a question of martial law.

This chapter will argue then that the limits of the war prerogative are primarily a question of statutory interpretation together with an assessment of necessity in a particular case. The proximity of the action in question in relation to engagement with the enemy is central to this assessment of necessity. The clearest point appears to be that the acquisition of property, including its destruction, must be on just terms by virtue of the express constitutional limit on the power of the Commonwealth Parliament. This relates to the limits of statutory power and the express provisions of the *Constitution* proposed in Chapter 1.

---

1   See Geoffrey Lindell, 'Authority for War [Iraq War]' (2003) 16 (May–June) *About the House*, 23, 23–4.
2   *Criminal Code Act 1995* (Cth) Div 268; Deirdre McKeown and Ray Jordan, 'Parliamentary Involvement in Declaring War and Deploying Forces Overseas' (Background Note, Parliamentary Library, Commonwealth, 2010) gives a detailed summary of parliamentary records in regard to Australia's warlike operations since 1914.
3   War might affect interpretations which shift the balance of power towards central government as Brian Galligan discusses in respect of the Second World War in *The Politics of the High Court: A Study of the Judicial Branch of Government in Australia* (University of Queensland Press, 1987) 126–30.

II Sources

A Writers

A number of writers have considered the war prerogative. Hale devoted a chapter to the subject in his *Prerogatives of the King*, stating that 'the necessities of a time of war make those things legal which otherwise were not in time of peace'.[4] As far as the traditional theorists are concerned, war was perhaps the main reason that they often cast executive power as requiring flexibility, strength and unity of purpose, as these are the qualities most likely to bring success to a sovereign in war.[5] Montesquieu identifies the conduct of war and foreign relations together as the central and primary concerns of executive power:

> In each state there are three sorts of powers: legislative power, executive power over the things depending on the right of nations, and executive power over the things depending on civil right. By the second, [the prince or the magistrate] he makes peace or war, sends or receives embassies, establishes security, and prevents invasions …[6]

Blackstone stated:

> Upon the same principle the king has also the sole prerogative of making war and peace. For it is held by all the writers on the law of nature and nations, that the right of making war, which by nature subsisted in every individual, is given up by all private persons that enter into society, and is vested in the sovereign power: and this right is given up, not only by individuals, but even by the entire body of people, that are under the dominion of a sovereign.[7]

---

[4] Sir Matthew Hale, *The Prerogatives of the King* (Selden Society, written between 1640 and 1664 but unpublished, D E C Yale (ed) 1976 ed) 123, see *Tabula Quarta – Tempore Belli* and *Pax et Belli Constitutio*, xiv, and generally Chapter XII 'Concerning the Jurisdiction and Office of the Constable and Marshal, Martial Law, *Tempus Belli* and Acquisitions by Right of War'.

[5] See, eg, Charles de Secondat, Baron de Montesquieu, *The Spirit of the Laws* (Anne Cohler, Basia Miller and Harold Stone trans and eds, Cambridge University Press, 1989) Book 11, Ch 6, 156–7 [trans of *De L'Esprit de Lois* (first published 1748)], 161; *Blackstone's Commentaries with Notes of Reference, to the Constitution and Laws, of the Federal Government of the United States; and of the Commonwealth of Virginia* (1803, Hein Online reproduction) 250.

[6] Montesquieu, above n 5, 156–7.

[7] *Blackstone's Commentaries with Notes*, above n 5, 257.

Clode stated that, 'The Defence of the Realm the Constitution has wisely intrusted [sic] to the Crown.'[8] Dicey did not identify a war prerogative but only a common-law right shared between 'the Crown and its servants to repel force by force in case of invasion ...', as discussed in Chapter 3.[9] In 1920, E F Churchill saw the wide powers allowed to the Crown under the *Defence of the Realm Consolidation Act 1914* (UK) as consistent with the 17th-century constitutional settlement, stating:

> Thus, though Parliament had, by 1689, circumscribed the prerogative of the Crown to legislate, to tax and to maintain a special *droit administratif,* it was unwilling to weaken the discretionary power of the Crown in matters pertaining to the defence of the realm.[10]

Zines, Evatt and Renfree are the most notable of a very few Australian authors who have considered the war prerogative.[11] Pertinently, while Evatt stated in 1924 that the war prerogative 'is recognised on all sides', he also commented that '[m]any extravagant claims were made by the Executive during the late War without there being necessity for the Courts to deal finally with the validity thereof'.[12]

---

8   Charles Clode, *The Administration of Justice under Military and Martial Law: As Applicable to the Army, Navy, Marines and Auxiliary Forces* (John Murray, 2nd ed, 1874) 1–20; Oren Gross and Fionnuala Ni Aolain, *Law in Times of Crisis: Emergency Powers in Theory and Practice* (Cambridge University Press, 2006) 82–4.
9   A V Dicey, *Introduction to the Study of the Law of the Constitution* (Macmillan, 10th ed, 1959) 288.
10 E F Churchill, 'The Dispensing Power and the Defence of the Realm' (1921) 37(October) *Law Quarterly Review* 412, 440.
11 Leslie Zines, 'The Inherent Executive Power of the Commonwealth' (2005) 16 *Public Law Review* 279, 287, recognising powers to intern enemy aliens, requisition ships, destroy property to deny it to an enemy and erect fortifications to repel an invasion; Harold Renfree, *The Executive Power of the Commonwealth of Australia* (Legal Books, 1984) 461–2; H P Lee, *The Emergency Powers of the Commonwealth of Australia* (Law Book Company, 1984) 37–57; G J Cartledge, *The Soldier's Dilemma: When to Use Force in Australia* (AGPS Press, 1992), 131; Charles Sampford and Margaret Palmer, 'The Constitutional Power to Make War' (2009) 18(2) *Griffith Law Review* 350, 355–7; Lindell, 'Authority for War', above n 1; Geoffrey Lindell, *The Coalition Wars Against Iraq and Afghanistan in the Courts of the UK, Ireland and the US – Significance for Australia* (Centre for International and Public Law Policy Paper 26 2005), 3–6, 33–8. With respect to the comparable Canadian position, see The Office of the Judge Advocate General, Canadian Forces, 'The Crown Prerogative' <www.forces.gc.ca/en/about-reports-pubs-military-law-strategic-legal-paper/crown-prerogative-guide.page>; Phillippe Lagassé, 'Parliamentary and Judicial Ambivalence toward Executive Prerogative Powers in Canada' (2012) 55(2) *Canadian Public Administration* 157, 162–3.
12 H V Evatt, *The Royal Prerogative* (Law Book Co, first presented as a doctoral thesis 1924, with commentary by Leslie Zines, 1987) 248. Evatt did not identify the extravagant claims.

B Cases

Sir Edward Coke's Report of the *Case of the King's Prerogative in Saltpetre* is one of the earliest case law references on the King's prerogative to defend the realm,[13] which Starke J cited in *Shaw Savill & Albion Co Ltd*.[14] Despite the inherent significance of the war prerogative, it is not one that has often arisen for consideration in Australia. Most of the defence cases in Australia have concerned the legislative power of the Commonwealth.[15]

The High Court has considered the war prerogative only infrequently.[16] There are some First World War cases which touched upon it. The references to it in *Farey v Burvett*,[17] a case concerned with the prices of flour and bread, were essentially obiter dicta. *Zachariassen v Commonwealth* concerned the Comptroller of Customs not permitting a Russian ship to sail from Melbourne in 1916 unless it carried wheat to the United Kingdom, instead of sailing for Chile to collect nitrate as intended by its owner.[18] As part of its defence, the Commonwealth argued that the war prerogative authorised this action and the High Court stated that the Commonwealth could argue this justification at trial.[19] Both Gavan Duffy J in the High Court and the Privy Council, affirming the High Court's decision, stated that the Commonwealth itself was not exercising the war prerogative but was doing so on behalf, and under the authority, of the King.[20] *Joseph v Colonial Treasurer (NSW)* was concerned with the procurement of wheat but confirmed that the Commonwealth,[21] as opposed to the States, is able to exercise aspects of the war prerogative on behalf of the King.[22] This chapter will address the question of when the prerogative became exercisable by the Commonwealth itself instead of on behalf of the King.

---

13 (1606) 12 Co Rep 12, 14.
14 (1940) 66 CLR 344, 354.
15 See, eg, *Andrews v Howell* (1941) 65 CLR 255; *Stenhouse v Coleman* (1944) 69 CLR 457; *R v Foster* (1949) 79 CLR 43; *Australian Communist Party v Commonwealth* (1951) 83 CLR 1 ('*Communist Party Case*'); *Re Tracey; Ex parte Ryan* (1989) 166 CLR 518 ('*Re Tracey*'); *Thomas v Mowbray* (2007) 233 CLR 207. See discussion in Lee, *The Emergency Powers*, above n 11, 9–37.
16 The Commonwealth did come into existence during the Boer War in South Africa 1899–1902 but it was a war of quite limited scope from an Australian perspective and the High Court did not come into existence until after it ended, *Judiciary Act 1903* (Cth).
17 (1916) 21 CLR 433, 440, 452, 465, 466.
18 (1917) 24 CLR 166, 167–71.
19 Ibid 184–5, 187–8.
20 Ibid 187; *Commonwealth v Zachariassen and Blom* (1920) 27 CLR 552, 557 (Viscount Finlay, for their Lordships).
21 (1918) 25 CLR 32.
22 Ibid 46–7 (Isaacs, Powers, Rich JJ).

Two Second World War cases, *Federal Commissioner of Taxation v Official Liquidator of E O Farley Ltd (In Liq)*,[23] a case concerning the priority of the Crown as a creditor, and *Carter v Egg & Egg Pulp Marketing Board (Vic)*,[24] a challenge to a market control scheme, affirmed the existence of the war prerogative but did not elaborate much on the scope of the power other than to note that it is available to the Commonwealth and can be extensive. Much more recently, Crennan J also recognised the war prerogative in *Williams v Commonwealth* referring to:

> the exercise of prerogative powers accorded to the Crown at common law (now reposed in the Commonwealth Executive alone[25]), such as the power to enter a treaty or wage war.[26]

Kiefel J acknowledged the existence of such a power in *CPCF v Minister for Immigration and Border Protection*,[27] as did Keane J.[28] Gageler also acknowledges the existence of this power in *Plaintiff M68 v Minister for Immigration and Border Protection* ('*M68*').[29]

1 *Shaw Savill & Albion Co Ltd*

Fortunately, the 1940 High Court case of *Shaw Savill & Albion Co Ltd* goes some way to drawing limits around the extent of the war prerogative.[30] It makes a strong, though not precise, distinction between when the war prerogative prevails over the ordinary law and when the ordinary law applies to the armed forces, even in war. Dixon J was expansive in his description of the combat immunity doctrine. He stated that:

> It could hardly be maintained that during an actual engagement with the enemy or a pursuit of any of his ships the navigating officer of a King's ship of war was under a common-law duty of care to avoid harm to such non-combatant ships as might appear in the theatre of operations. It cannot be enough to say that the conflict or pursuit is a circumstance affecting the reasonableness of the officer's conduct as a discharge of the duty of care, though the duty itself persists. To adopt such a view would mean that whether the combat be by sea, land or air our men go into action

---

23 (1940) 63 CLR 278, 320.
24 (1942) 66 CLR 557, 572.
25 *Barton v Commonwealth* (1974) 131 CLR 477, 498.
26 (2012) 248 CLR 156, 342 ('*Williams*').
27 [2015] HCA 1 [260] ('*CPCF*').
28 Ibid [484].
29 [2016] HCA 1 [164].
30 (1940) 66 CLR 344.

accompanied by the law of civil negligence, warning them to be mindful of the person and property of civilians. It would mean that the Courts could be called upon to say whether the soldier on the field of battle or the sailor fighting on his ship might reasonably have been more careful to avoid causing civil loss or damage. No-one can imagine a court undertaking the trial of such an issue, either during or after a war. To concede that any civil liability can rest upon a member of the armed forces for supposedly negligent acts or omissions in the course of an actual engagement with the enemy is opposed alike to reason and to policy. But the principle cannot be limited to the presence of the enemy or to occasions when contact with the enemy has been established. Warfare perhaps never did admit of such a distinction, but now it would be quite absurd. The development of the speed of ships and the range of guns were enough to show it to be an impracticable refinement, but it has been put out of question by the bomber, the submarine and the floating mine. The principle must extend to all active operations against the enemy. It must cover attack and resistance, advance and retreat, pursuit and avoidance, reconnaissance and engagement. But a real distinction does exist between actual operations against the enemy and other activities of the combatant services in time of war. For instance, a warship proceeding to her anchorage or manoeuvring among other ships in a harbour, or acting as a patrol or even as a convoy must be navigated with due regard to the safety of other shipping and no reason is apparent for treating her officers as under no civil duty of care, remembering always that the standard of care is that which is reasonable in the circumstances … It may not be easy under conditions of modern warfare to say in a given case upon which side of the line it falls.[31]

Dixon J's test does not require direct contact with the enemy, as 20th-century technology permitted engagement with the enemy from a distance. His test does though require 'active' or 'actual operations against the enemy', which excludes doing things when not engaged with the enemy which any ordinary person would have to do, such as 'navigating with due regard'. His Honour stated that the course, speed and darkened state of HMAS *Adelaide* were nonjusticiable matters because:

> The Court is not in a position to know or to inquire what measures are necessary for the proper conduct of a warlike operation and must depend upon those upon whom finally rests the responsibility of action.[32]

---

31 Ibid 361–2.
32 Ibid 363.

It should be a matter for the trial court however, as to whether the warship was engaged in active operations against the enemy, and therefore had no liability to the MV *Coptic* in respect of improper navigation.[33] Rich ACJ, McTiernan and Williams JJ also saw such matters covered by combat immunity as nonjusticiable at any time.[34] Starke J stated that such matters could become justiciable after the war.[35]

The Court unanimously allowed the matter to proceed to trial.[36] While this elaboration of the combat immunity doctrine does not provide precise content to the war prerogative, it does mark a strong distinction between acts of war and other operations occurring during the course of war. The Court will treat acts of war as nonjusticiable and yet, even in war, apply the law to any other actions of the armed forces as it would to anyone else. The defendants in the 'Commando Court Martial' in 2011 successfully relied upon *Shaw Savill & Albion Co Ltd* in interlocutory proceedings before the Chief Judge Advocate.[37] Although they had inadvertently killed noncombatant children in the course of defending themselves from small arms fire, they did not owe a duty of care to others on the battlefield during actual combat operations.[38] This is not a case authority in itself but nonetheless provides a persuasive contemporary application of the *Shaw Savill & Albion Co Ltd* combat immunity doctrine.[39]

2 *Smith v Ministry of Defence*[40]

The 2013 United Kingdom Supreme Court case of *Smith v Ministry of Defence*[41] carefully considered the combat immunity doctrine in *Shaw Savill & Albion Co Ltd*.[42] Notably, it did not doubt the existence of the

---

33 Ibid 364.
34 Ibid 344.
35 Ibid 356–7.
36 Ibid 344. *Thomas v Mowbray* (2007) 233 CLR 207 considered this case in 2007, at 489, but it was concerned primarily with the Commonwealth's legislative power for the purpose of defence, although it did usefully state that the defence of the realm could include defence from internal threats, at 503.
37 (1940) 66 CLR 344.
38 Transcript of Proceedings, *Sergeant J and Lance-Corporal D*, Australian Defence Force General Court Martial Pre-trial Directions Hearing, Brigadier Westwood, Chief Judge Advocate, 20 May 2011, 1–3, 36. On the controversy as to whether the DMP should have prosecuted these charges, see Justice Paul Brereton, 'The Director of Military Prosecutions, the Afghanistan Charges and the Rule of Law' (2011) 85 *Australian Law Journal* 91.
39 (1940) 66 CLR 344. Gageler J also acknowledged the existence of the combat immunity doctrine in *CPCF* [2015] HCA 1 [368].
40 *Smith v Ministry of Defence* [2013] UKSC 41 ('*Smith*').
41 [2013] UKSC 41.
42 (1940) 66 CLR 344.

combat immunity doctrine in the common law or distinguish it as an Australian, as opposed to English, doctrine.[43] The case involved claims relating to deaths of British soldiers in Iraq occurring when a British tank fired upon another British tank in error, as well as two separate incidents where lightly armoured 'Snatch' Land Rover vehicles failed to protect their occupants from the blasts of improvised explosive devices.[44] The claims did not seek to question decisions made in the course of actual combat operations, or the high-level political decisions to commit troops to Iraq and the manner in which they were equipped generally. Rather the claims focused on the failure to provide specific protective equipment to the tanks and land rovers which might have prevented the deaths and also the decision to commit those vehicles to the particular operations in question without that equipment.[45] These are quite different factual scenarios to the collision between HMAS *Adelaide* and the MV *Coptic* as in that case the harm did not result directly from enemy action or in the course of actual combat. *Smith* therefore deals with matters much closer to combat operations and also with the deaths of the Crown's own troops, not civilians or the enemy.[46]

The majority and dissenting judgments reveal an interesting and important divergence in the application of both the combat immunity doctrine and the concept of nonjusticiability. The majority position was that the claims were justiciable as they related to decisions made in the gap between the nonjusticiable tactical decisions made in actual combat operations and the high-level political decisions relating to commitment to war and equipment procurement.[47] Even so, Lord Hope, on behalf of the majority, emphasised that, at trial, the evidence might indicate that combat immunity should apply to the decisions in question. In this case, the trial court should favour its application where appropriate. Lord Hope stated:

> [I]t is of paramount importance that the work that the armed services do in the national interest should not be impeded by having to prepare for or conduct active operations against the enemy under the threat of litigation if things should go wrong. The court must be especially careful, in their

---

43   *Smith* [2013] UKSC 41 [84]–[93].
44   Ibid [1]–[8].
45   Ibid [9]–[12].
46   Ibid.
47   Ibid [99] (Lord Hope).

case, to have regard to the public interest, to the unpredictable nature of armed conflict and to the inevitable risks that it gives rise to when it is striking the balance as to what is fair, just and reasonable.[48]

It was not for the Supreme Court to make decisions on the application of combat immunity however without having heard the evidence; noting that the trial judge found against the Commonwealth in respect of the collision between HMAS *Adelaide* and the MV *Coptic*.[49] Lord Hope saw his position as consistent with *Shaw Savill & Albion Co Ltd*.[50]

By way of contrast, Lord Mance, in dissent, stated that the matters should simply be nonjusticiable because to put the claims to trial would inevitably result in questioning the decisions of operational commanders in actual operations against the enemy.[51] If the purpose of the combat immunity doctrine was to avoid, in his words, 'judicialising warfare' then the claims should be nonjusticiable.[52] Lord Mance also saw his position as consistent with *Shaw Savill & Albion Co Ltd*.[53] His view would appear to be that the threat of litigation would impede decisive operational action and inappropriately impose the judicial branch into the sphere of the executive. This view reflects the theory that it would be inconsistent with the qualities of flexibility, strength and unity of purpose, favoured by writers such as Blackstone and Montesquieu, which are desirable in the executive.[54] Lord Carnwath agreed with Lord Mance except that he viewed the Snatch Land Rover claims as occurring after combat operations in Iraq had ceased and being during a period of peacekeeping.[55] The combat immunity doctrine, therefore, did not apply to the Snatch Land Rover claims.

Smith illustrates the difficulties in applying Dixon J's test for combat immunity and discerning on which side of the line any particular action might fall,[56] which his Honour himself said would not be easy.[57] If the aim of the combat immunity doctrine is not to 'judicialise warfare' then Lord Mance's position is the most prudent. Lord Hope's view prevailed,

---

48 Ibid [100].
49 Ibid [93], [95]–[96].
50 Ibid [93]–[94]; (1940) 66 CLR 344.
51 *Smith* [2013] UKSC 41 [125].
52 Ibid [150].
53 Ibid; (1940) 66 CLR 344.
54 Montesquieu, above n 5, 161; *Blackstone's Commentaries with Notes*, above n 5, 250.
55 *Smith* [2013] UKSC 41 [187].
56 Ibid.
57 *Shaw Savill & Albion Co Ltd* (1940) 66 CLR 344, 361–2.

however, so it appears that, at least in English law, combat immunity does not necessarily mean that a matter is nonjusticiable and it will be a matter of evidence and argument at trial as to whether combat immunity applies. Tugenhadt and Croft argue that this case unacceptably narrows the doctrine because it will make military 'leaders focus on the duty of care rather than adaptability and mission success'.[58] A United Kingdom House of Commons Defence Committee stated in its 2013 report titled *UK Armed Forces Personnel and the Legal Framework for Future Operations* that:

> We are concerned about the failure of the previously well understood and accepted principle of combat immunity, most recently evidenced in the Supreme Court majority judgment in June 2013 allowing families and military personnel to bring negligence cases against the MoD [Ministry of Defence] for injury or death. This seems to us to risk the judicialisation of war and to be incompatible with the accepted contract entered into by Service personnel and the nature of soldiering. It also challenges the doctrine of the best application of proportionate response with the unintended consequence that it might lead to far bloodier engagements on the battlefield as commanders may take fewer risks with their own troops and make more use of close air support or remotely actioned weapons, resulting in greater violence against the opposition with potentially greater numbers of civilian casualties. More legal certainty might result in less destructive conflicts.[59]

Despite this, in future it might be difficult to argue that the courts should never put a matter to trial before determining that combat immunity applies. The statutory regime in div 268 of the *Criminal Code Act 1995* proscribing conduct contrary to the law of armed conflict, discussed below, necessarily means that courts may now look into the operational decisions of commanders. *Shaw Savill & Albion Co Ltd* itself indicates that,[60] even in 1940, the High Court of Australia was prepared to send aspects of a matter back to the trial court to determine whether it was operational

---

58   Thomas Tugenhadt and Laura Croft, *The Fog of Law: An Introduction to the Legal Erosion of British Fighting Power* (Policy Exchange, 2013) 31–2. As much as this author shares the concerns in this report of the judicialisation of warfare, because this book argues that combat immunity should mean immunity from liability and not *necessarily* immunity from suit, and also because the nature of warfare does not lend itself to being able to prescribe in advance in legislation what should be immune and not, this book does not necessarily support the proposal to legislate for combat immunity at 56–7.
59   United Kingdom, House of Commons Defence Committee, *UK Armed Forces Personnel and the Legal Framework for Future Operations* Paper No HC 931, Session 2013–2014 (2013) 47.
60   (1940) 66 CLR 344.

or not and, therefore, covered by combat immunity. This supports the principle of legality, but it remains to be seen if it undermines combat effectiveness or leads to bloodier conflicts.

III When Does the War Prerogative Apply?

When does the war prerogative apply? This issue has been confused somewhat since the practice of declaring war and making peace fell into disuse after the end of the Second World War.[61] The Governor-General made the first and last declarations of war on behalf of Australia in 1941 against Japan,[62] Finland, Hungary and Romania,[63] and in 1942 against Bulgaria[64] and Thailand.[65] Previously the King had issued declarations of war on behalf of the Empire in 1914[66] and 1939.[67] This is discussed further below. A declaration served the very useful purpose in domestic law of clearly enlivening the war prerogative. It was one of the few ways in which the executive could change legal rights and obligations within the realm merely by declaration and without the authority of an Act of Parliament, a court order or a private law instrument such as a contract.[68] Upon the declaration, within certain rules, enemy aliens and shipping within the realm became liable to seizure[69] and enemy combatants to lethal attack or capture.[70] There were potentially legal effects upon Australian subjects as well, such as making it more difficult to have dealings with enemy aliens without committing an offence.[71]

---

61   See Sampford and Palmer, above n 11, especially 366–9; see also McKeown and Jordan, above n 2.
62   Commonwealth, *Gazette*, No 252, 9 December 1941, 2727 cited in McKeown and Jordan, above n 2, 31; See Commonwealth, *Parliamentary Debates*, House of Representatives, 16 December 1941, (Dr H V Evatt) quoted in Sampford and Palmer, 358–9.
63   Commonwealth, *Gazette*, No 251, 8 December 1941, 1849, cited in McKeown and Jordan, above n 2, 31.
64   Commonwealth, *Gazette*, No 14, 14 January 1942, 79, cited in McKeown and Jordan, above n 2, 31.
65   Commonwealth *Gazette*, No 198, 20 July 1942, 1733, cited in McKeown and Jordan, above n 2, 31.
66   Commonwealth *Gazette*, No 50, 3 August 1914, 1335, cited in McKeown and Jordan, above n 2, 31.
67   Commonwealth *Gazette*, No 63, 3 September 1939, 1849, cited in McKeown and Jordan, above n 2, 31.
68   See L Oppenheim, *International Law: A Treatise: Vol II: War and Neutrality* (Longmans, 2nd ed, 1912), 128–43.
69   Department of Defence, *Commonwealth War Book*, 1956 vii, ch III, 12, ch IX, 10.
70   Oppenheim, above n 68, 63.
71   On trading with the enemy and the prerogative power of the Crown to approve such trading by licence, see *Donohue v Schroeder and Kabutz* (1916) 22 CLR 362. (This case is only one page in length.) See Evatt, above n 12, 179.

5. WAR

The formerly secret *Commonwealth War Book* of 1956[72] is illustrative of the types of measures contemplated in the height of the Cold War; and with the Second World War in relatively recent memory. It was the plan for the coordination and initiation of all government action on the actual or imminent outbreak of war.[73] This is significant given that the Cold War period was the last time government probably considered taking such measures within Australia. Under this plan, many measures required statutory authorisation but, for example, the requisition of merchant shipping under 200 tons could be by prerogative power alone,[74] preventing the departure of certain aliens could be done by deliberately delaying the exercise of existing statutory powers[75] and the seizure of enemy-flagged merchant ships was to be authorised by order-in-council[76] (although subject to condemnation as prize by a State or Territory Supreme Court sitting as a prize court).[77] The exercise of *Droit de Prince*, the right to delay temporarily the departure of nonenemy shipping at the outbreak of war so as to prevent the spread of news of naval or military operations, was also to be by authority of prerogative power alone.[78]

Were Australia to go to war in the second decade of the 21st century, it is not clear at what point these measures would operate. It was not a practical issue with respect to armed conflict with Iraq in 1991[79] or 2003,[80] or Afghanistan in 2001.[81] If Australia became involved in war

---

72   Department of Defence, *Commonwealth War Book*, 1956.
73   Ibid vii.
74   Ibid ch III, 12, ch IX, 10. See Eric Dean, 'New Zealand Requisition of Ships in Time of War or Other Like Emergency' (1987) 4 *Maritime Law Association of Australia and New Zealand Journal* 21.
75   Department of Defence, *Commonwealth War Book*, above n 72, ch VII, 2.
76   Ibid ch VIII, 2–3. Interestingly this was to be done by Customs Officers acting with the support of naval or military parties. On the prerogative power to seize enemy shipping, exercisable by Customs or military personnel, see *Blom v Commonwealth* (1917) 24 CLR 189. (Another one-page case. The Privy Council heard it on appeal together with *Zachariassen v Commonwealth*, discussed above, affirming both decisions of the High Court, (1920) 27 CLR 552.)
77   Department of Defence, *Commonwealth War Book*, above n 72, ch VIII, 13. On days of grace for enemy ships to depart, see *The Turul* [1919] AC 515, a Privy Council case on appeal from the Supreme Court of NSW sitting as a prize court. The Hungarian ship in this case could not be confiscated because the Governor-General's proclamation regarding days of grace was not sufficiently clear.
78   Department of Defence, *Commonwealth War Book*, above n 72, ch IX, 10.
79   See Commonwealth, *Parliamentary Debates*, House of Representatives, 4 December 1990, 4319–25 (Bob Hawke) reproduced in the 'The First Gulf War' in Rod Kemp and Marion Stanton (eds), *Speaking for Australia: Parliamentary Speeches that Shaped Our Nation* (Allen and Unwin, 2004) 253.
80   See Commonwealth, *Parliamentary Debates*, House of Representatives, 18 March 2003, 13170, Senate, 20 March 2003, 9888, 12505–512 reproduced in the 'The Second Gulf War' in Kemp and Stanton, above n 79, 299.
81   Not debated in Parliament at the outbreak of hostilities, see McKeown and Jordan, above n 3, 20, 33.

with North Korea, for example, it is not clear at what point North Korean diplomats, shipping and aliens would acquire enemy status. It might be at the point that the executive government, most likely the Prime Minister, announced its commitment to military action. This could be the de facto declaration of war even if the term 'declaration of war' itself did not appear in the announcement. If military action was depending upon North Korea complying with an ultimatum, the war prerogative might only be enlivened at the point at which the ADF actually commenced combat operations against North Korean targets.[82] Clarity on this issue might emerge only in the event of a challenge through the courts by an affected North Korean in Australia.[83] Even then, if there was no action against North Korean persons or interests in Australia, the matter might not arise at all.[84]

Sanctions under United Nations Security Council Resolutions governed much of Australia's relationship with Iraq in 1991 and 2003,[85] Afghanistan in 2001,[86] and still govern much of Australia's current relationship with North Korea.[87] These resolutions had effect in Australian law through regulations made under the *Charter of the United Nations Act 1945* (Cth). Such regulations meant, or would mean, in most cases, that there was or would be no further need for actions under the war prerogative to move against enemy persons and interests in Australia at the outbreak of hostilities as this had, or would already have, occurred.

Notwithstanding the existence of relevant regulations under the *Charter of the United Nations Act,* Australian reliance upon a United Nations Security Council Resolution as an international law authority to engage in armed conflict, as occurred with North Korea in 1950[88] and Iraq in 1991,[89] is probably not directly relevant to whether the war prerogative is enlivened

---

82   The traditional pre-UN Charter position did have the benefit of greater clarity. See Oppenheim, above n 68, 61.
83   Such as occurred in *The Turul* [1919] AC 515, discussed at n 77.
84   See Sampford and Palmer, above n 11, 370–84.
85   *Charter of the United Nations (Sanctions – Iraq) Regulations 2006*. See Simon Chesterman, Thomas Franck and David Malone, *Law and Practice of the United Nations: Documents and Commentary* (Oxford University Press, 2008) 52–63; Lord Alexander of Weedon, 'Iraq, the Pax Americana and the Law', (Justice Tom Sargant Memorial Annual Lecture, London, 14 October 2003).
86   *Charter of the United Nations (Sanctions – Afghanistan) Regulations 2001*. (Made in June 2001, before the 11 September attacks.)
87   *Charter of the United Nations (Sanctions – Democratic People's Republic of Korea) Regulations 2008*.
88   Security Council (SC), Res 84, UN SCOR, 476th mtg, UN Doc S/1588 (7 July 1950).
89   SC Res 678, UN SCOR, 2963rd mtg, UN Doc S/RES/678 (29 November 1990).

or not. As *Bradley v Commonwealth* made clear,[90] the *Charter of the United Nations* is not automatically part of Australian law. The war prerogative existed prior to the *Charter* in any event and does not depend upon the authority of the *Charter* to operate. There is also no particular authority which requires a declaration of war from the Crown for the war prerogative to operate. As *Shaw Savill & Albion Co Ltd* clearly states 'such matters are not justiciable'.[91] For example, the *Communist Party Case*[92] noted the existence of hostilities in Korea in 1950 but did not question the lack of a declaration of war.[93] International law may very usefully inform a court as to whether an armed conflict is in existence or not, but the question of whether the war prerogative applies is fundamentally one for national, not international, law. Indeed, s 4 of the *Defence Act* still provides for proclamations of war, although it defines war narrowly to mean an attack or apprehended attack on Australia. Australian law, therefore, does not prevent a return to the use of declarations of war, or at least a state of hostilities, particularly if such declarations were made only in circumstances consistent with the right to use force in international law.[94]

As Sampford and Palmer point out, the absence of some form of legal order from the Governor-General does cast doubt upon whether it is possible to state that the actions against Iraq in 1991 and 2003, and Afghanistan in 2001 properly relied upon the war prerogative.[95] They regret that this reduced the level of scrutiny which the Governor-General might have been able to provide over such decisions.[96] This is an important point. Further, a legal order invoking the war prerogative, however described, could serve to eliminate much doubt as to the applicability of the war prerogative discussed below.[97]

---

90 (1973) 128 CLR 557, 583, Barwick CJ and Gibbs J rejected Security Council resolutions which had not been given legislative recognition in Australia as justification for executive action within Australia that would otherwise have been unlawful.
91 (1940) 66 CLR 344, 356 (Starke J); See discussion of English and Irish cases on this point in Lindell, *The Coalition Wars*, above n 11, 7–13, 29–30.
92 (1951) 83 CLR 1.
93 *Communist Party Case* (1951) 83 CLR 1, 196.
94 See Sampford and Palmer, above n 11, 367.
95 Ibid 370–84.
96 Ibid 378–81.
97 See Tony Kevin (Rapporteur) *Report of the Australians for War Powers Reform Public Seminar 23 October 2015: Legislating Reform of the War Powers*.

The need to be able to identify the enemy is central to much of the exercise of the war prerogative. As will be discussed below, the war prerogative provides authority to take hostile action against the enemy and the enemy's interests, and the presence of the enemy also permits interference with the rights of Australian citizens. Determining who the enemy is in the case of an interstate conflict, such as with Iraq, is relatively clear. When the enemy is not a recognised state with armed forces, such as with the Taliban in Afghanistan or the Viet Cong in Vietnam, the matter is less straightforward. The problem is that, if it is difficult to determine who the enemy is, it is difficult then to distinguish whether a deliberate killing is a lawful exercise of the war prerogative or murder.[98] This goes to the heart of the principle of legality. There is no case authority on this point, which suggests that it has not been a matter of dispute in a court in any of the ADF counter insurgency operations in Malaya, Borneo, Vietnam, Afghanistan or Iraq. The courts may now derive some guidance from Division 268 of the *Criminal Code Act 1995*, particularly references such as in s 268.35 to 'individual civilians not taking a direct part in hostilities' or the references in the *Geneva Conventions Act* to *Additional Protocol I* to the *Geneva Conventions* ('*Additional Protocol I*'),[99] which addresses irregular combatants.[100] This legislation incorporates much of the international law of armed conflict into Australian law. Such international law, whether customary or conventional, as well as the extensive associated scholarly debate, would be relevant to statutory interpretation in any cases of ambiguity in the legislation.[101]

A War vs Defence of the Realm

The terms 'defence of the realm' and 'the war prerogative' appear to be used interchangeably in the authorities because in English law it seems that the prerogative to declare war and make peace is indistinguishable from the power to defend the realm. Dicey makes no distinction and

---

[98] See Rob McLaughlin, 'Legal-policy Considerations and Conflict Characterisation at the Threshold between Law Enforcement and Non-international Armed Conflict' (2012) 13(1) *Melbourne Journal of International Law* 94, 112, 121.
[99] *Geneva Conventions Act 1957* (Cth) s 5, sch 1.
[100] *Protocol Additional to the Geneva Conventions of 12 August 1949 and Relating to the Protection of Victims of International Armed Conflicts*, (opened for signature 8 June 1977) 1125 UNTS 3 (entered into force 7 December 1978) art 44 ('*Additional Protocol I*').
[101] See below n 180. So too would recent English cases arising from the conflicts in Iraq and Afghanistan, discussed below in this chapter and in Chapter 6.

5. WAR

Blackstone only talks of the prerogative to make war,[102] not to defend the realm.[103] Imperial arrangements, perhaps, made a distinction useful from the time of federation in 1901 to 1941, when Australia effectively declared war independently of the United Kingdom against Japan, but *Farey v Burvett*[104] and Evatt[105] still made no distinction. In 1941, the Curtin Government took the view that it was consistent with the status of the dominions as a result of the *Balfour Declaration*[106] from the Imperial Conference of 1926 for Australia to make its own declarations of war.[107] It arranged for the King to make a special Royal Instrument assigning the Governor-General the power to declare war against Japan,[108] and separately with Finland, Romania, and Hungary,[109] as well as Bulgaria[110] and Thailand.[111] The Governor-General then made the appropriate proclamations.[112] Zines observes that it is arguable that, as a result of the Imperial Conference of 1926 seeing the dominions as being able to exercise international personality, the power to make war had, therefore, already became part of the 'executive power of the Commonwealth' and exercisable by the Governor-General within the terms of s 61 of the *Constitution*.[113] The alternative view is that such powers required an express grant from the King to the Governor-General, in accordance with s 2 of the *Constitution*, which provides for the powers of the Governor-General.[114] The retrospective application of the *Statute of Westminster Adoption Act*

---

102 Dicey, above n 9.
103 *Blackstone's Commentaries with Notes*, above n 5, 43–50.
104 (1916) 21 CLR 433.
105 Evatt, above n 12, see, eg, 178–83.
106 Inter-imperial Relations Committee, 'Report, Proceedings and Memoranda' (E IR/26 Series) *Imperial Conference* 1926.
107 McKeown and Jordan, above n 2, 4.
108 Commonwealth, *Gazette*, No 104, 7 April 1942, 859, cited in McKeown and Jordan, above n 2, 31; Commonwealth, *Parliamentary Debates*, House of Representatives, 16 December 1941, (Dr H V Evatt) quoted in Sampford and Palmer, above n 11, 358–9.
109 Commonwealth, *Gazette*, No 14, n 64, 31.
110 Ibid.
111 Commonwealth, *Gazette*, No 198, above n 65, 31.
112 See above nn 61–7.
113 Leslie Zines, 'The Growth of Australian Nationhood and its Effect on the Powers of the Commonwealth' in Leslie Zines (ed) *Commentaries on the Australian Constitution: A Tribute to Geoffrey Sawer* (Butterworths, 1977) 30–5. Zines notes that Evatt, as Attorney-General, expressly declined to give an opinion on this point, 31.
114 Ibid.

1942 (Cth) to the outbreak of war with Germany on 3 September 1939[115] appeared to settle, finally, that the Governor-General could exercise the war prerogative in full.[116]

The Commonwealth had, nonetheless, previously exercised aspects of the war prerogative in the conduct of war, even if other aspects of the power resided with the King.[117] As Isaacs J put it in *Farey v Burvett*:

> These provisions [ss 2, 51(vi), 61, 114, 119] carry with them the royal war prerogative, and all that the common law of England includes in that prerogative so far as it is applicable to Australia. The creation of a state of war and the establishment of peace necessarily reside in the Sovereign himself as the head of the Empire, but apart from that, the prerogative powers of the Crown are exercisable locally. The full extent of the prerogative it is not necessary now to define, but it is certainly great in relation to the national emergency which calls for its exercise, as may be seen by reference to *Chitty on the Prerogatives of the Crown* (49, 50).[118]

There does not seem to have been an issue arising which has required such a distinction since 1941 however, so this book will treat the power to declare war and make peace, and the power to conduct war, or defend the realm, as deriving from the same prerogative.

B A Duty to Defend the Realm?

A curious point which this chapter must deal with is the question of whether there is a duty upon the Crown to defend the realm due to the mandatory language of s 119 of the *Constitution* requiring the

---

115 (Cth), s 3.
116 If the passing of the war prerogative to the Commonwealth occurred in full as a result of Australia acquiring international personality in 1926 following the *Balfour Declaration*, then this might arguably have a bearing on whether the prerogative is exercisable by the cabinet as is effectively the current practice, or must be exercised by the Governor-General in accordance with the Royal Instrument. The express nature of the Royal Instrument, which grants the power to the Governor-General rather than the cabinet, suggests that the latter view is stronger because the *Balfour Declaration* was a statement from an imperial conference rather than a legal document. For a discussion of who should exercise the prerogative see Sampford and Palmer, above n 11.
117 Renfree, above n 11, 462. For an interesting analysis of the connection between the court martial in HMAS *Australia* in 1942 and the *Statute of Westminster Adoption Act 1942* (Cth), as well as the attitude of the Curtin Government to British control see Chris Clark, 'The Statute of Westminster and the Murder in HMAS *Australia*, 1942' (2009) 179 *Australian Defence Force Journal* 18.
118 (1916) 21 CLR 433, 452–2; See Evatt, above n 12, 178–83, 226–38.

Commonwealth to protect every State against invasion. The 1932 Privy Council case of *China Navigation* is the leading case on the duty of the Crown.[119] It states the general principle this way,

> The argument begins with the very general statement in *Calvin's Case* (1): 'For as the subject oweth to the King his true and faithful ligeance and obedience, so the Sovereign is to govern and protect his subjects,' which in turn is founded on a passage in Glanville as to the relation between the landlord and his tenant by homage. Henry II would, I think, have been surprised to hear that if his tenant went to China the King was bound to follow and protect him.[120]

The case goes on to elaborate upon the nature of the duty to defend the realm as follows:

> [T]he manner in which the King should perform this alleged duty is entirely in his discretion; that it is for the King to say whether any case for its exercise has arisen and in whose favour it ought to be exercised, and that the King could not be compelled by any process of law to perform it; it is 'a duty of what is called imperfect obligation. Supposing that the King were to neglect that duty, I know of no legal means—that is, no process of law—common law or statute law—by which the Crown could be forced to perform that duty, but there is that duty of imperfect obligation on the part of the Royal authority': per Brett LJ in *Attorney-General* v *Tomline*.[121]

In addition to the common-law position in *China Navigation*,[122] the Commonwealth has assumed an obligation to defend the several states from invasion by virtue of s 119 of the *Constitution*, as a quid pro quo for the colonies transferring their military and naval forces to the Commonwealth and giving up their right to raise such forces without the approval of the Commonwealth.[123] Given the reasoning in *China Navigation*,[124] and the Commonwealth's constitutional obligation, any

---

119 *China Navigation Company Ltd v Attorney-General* [1932] 2 KB 197 ('*China Navigation*').
120 Ibid 211.
121 Ibid 223. The single judge decision in *Hicks v Ruddock* (2007) 156 FCR 574, 594 cites *China Navigation* and notes that an imperfect obligation can still have legal consequences, but this decision went to whether the duty to afford diplomatic, rather than military, protection was justiciable. This is also quite a different question as to whether such a duty is enforceable, which, in the case of Mr Hicks, ultimately it was not.
122 [1932] 2 KB 197.
123 *Joseph v Colonial Treasurer* (1918) 25 CLR 32, 46–7.
124 [1932] 2 KB 197.

legal obligation to exercise the war prerogative is at best an imperfect one. It may create a legal basis upon which the Commonwealth may act but not a clear measure upon which it may be held to account.[125]

For example, what if the Brisbane Line did really exist and it was the policy of the government in 1942 to let the Imperial Japanese Forces occupy those parts of Australia north and west of a line stretching from Brisbane to Adelaide before offering serious resistance?[126] Assuming a subsequent Australian and allied victory permitted this, could the Queensland government, for example, have brought an action in the High Court to the effect that the Commonwealth had breached its constitutional duty to exercise the prerogative power to defend the entire nation? What would the remedy be—a declaration or compensation for damages? Could the High Court even find the allocation of scarce defence resources in the face of an invasion to be justiciable? Success in such an action seems unlikely given these questions over holding the Commonwealth to a legal duty to exercise the prerogative to defend the realm. Such a duty might be more a political duty, the consequences for the breach of which lie in the political realm, such as a motion of no confidence in the Parliament. *China Navigation* usefully quotes Blackstone on this being a political duty, not a legal one:

> According to Blackstone, Comm i, 251: 'In the exertion therefore of those prerogatives, which the law has given him, the King is irresistible and absolute, according to the forms of the constitution. And yet, if the consequence of that exertion be manifestly to the grievance or dishonour of the kingdom, the Parliament will call his advisers to a just and severe account.'[127]

---

125 See discussion on this point in Peter Gerangelos, 'The Executive Power of the Commonwealth of Australia: Section 61 of the *Commonwealth Constitution*, "nationhood" and the Future of the Prerogative' (2012) 12(1) *Oxford University Commonwealth Law Journal*, 97, 101.
126 Commonwealth, *Parliamentary Debates*, House of Representatives, 22 June 1943, 56–64 (Eddie Ward) reproduced in the 'The Brisbane Line' in Kemp and Stanton, above n 79, 101; Newman Rosenthal, *Sir Charles Lowe: A Biographical Memoir* (Robertson and Mullens, 1968) 118–26 on the Lowe Royal Commission into the claims of Eddie Ward of the existence of the Brisbane Line policy. According to Rosenthal, the only basis for the claim was a military appreciation presented by General Sir Iven Mackay, Commander-in-Chief, to the Advisory War Council of the Curtin Government in February 1942 on where the next line of defence should be were the Japanese to force Allied forces out of northern Australia. Justice Lowe thought this to be entirely appropriate planning even though the Council rejected the plan. The Menzies government was no longer even in power when Japan entered the war despite Ward's allegation that it was a plan of that government, 119–20, 126. In establishing the Royal Commission into the claims, Prime Minister Curtin clashed openly with Ward on this issue on the floor of Parliament, 121–2.
127 [1932] 2 KB 197, 242.

The duty of the Commonwealth under s 119 might best be argued in a legal sense where a State or private person claimed that the Commonwealth was acting unlawfully or ultra vires in a purported exercise of the prerogative as to war and defence of the realm. The Commonwealth's defence may be that it is exercising its constitutional duty under s 119. Examples might be the deployment of troops or construction of defences, which this chapter considers below.

IV The War Prerogative and Statute

As to the substance of the war prerogative, there is no reference in an Australian statute to its existence. Recently, Australia has engaged in armed conflict in Afghanistan against insurgents, not the armed forces of the state of Afghanistan.[128] Public information makes clear that this involved seeking out and attacking the enemy[129] as well as detaining people against their will.[130] This means deliberately seeking to cause death and destruction of property without fulfilling the requirements of the law of self-defence or detaining someone without necessarily fulfilling the requirements of an arrest. This could possibly amount to murder,[131] manslaughter,[132] criminal damage[133] or forcible confinement[134] under the Australian Capital Territory *Crimes Act 1900*, which applies to operations in Afghanistan through the effect of the *Defence Force Discipline Act 1982* (Cth).[135] While the Director

---

128 Stephen Smith, Minister for Defence, 'Afghanistan – Detainee Management' (Ministerial Statement and Paper, 16 May 2013).
129 Department of Defence, *Inquiry Officer's Report into the Death of Lance Corporal Jared William MacKinney* (6 January 2011) <www.defence.gov.au/publications/coi/reports/IOI%20Report%20into%20death%20of%20LCPL%20MacKinney%20in%20AFG%20on%2024%20Aug%2010%20scanned%20for%20release.pdf>.
130 Stephen Smith, above n 128.
131 *Crimes Act 1900* (ACT) s 12.
132 Ibid s 15.
133 Ibid s 116.
134 Ibid s 34.
135 *Defence Force Discipline Act 1982* (Cth) Section 61 (3) states:
   A person who is a defence member or a defence civilian is guilty of an offence if:
   (a) the person engages in conduct outside the Jervis Bay Territory (whether or not in a public place); and
   (b) engaging in that conduct would be a Territory offence, if it took place in the Jervis Bay Territory (whether or not in a public place).
Section 4A *Jervis Bay Territory Acceptance Act* 1915 (Cth) applies the law as it applies in the Australian Capital Territory (ACT). This provision came into force through the *ACT Self-Government (Consequential Provisions) Act 1988* (Cth) as the Jervis Bay Territory was part of the ACT until ACT self-government. It appears to have been expedient simply to continue the law of the jurisdiction in force as ACT law.

of Military Prosecutions has the discretion as to whether to prosecute under this Act,[136] as mentioned above, the 2011 manslaughter prosecution of two commandos in relation to the accidental death of Afghan children clearly demonstrates that this discretion may be exercised in favour of prosecution.[137]

The *Crimes at Sea Act 2000* (Cth) also applies to actions occurring on or 'in the course of activities controlled from' Australian ships,[138] including ADF ships,[139] at sea anywhere in the world.[140] This Act imports the criminal law of various States and Territories so that it applies at sea.[141] In the case of activities beyond the area adjacent to Australia, it applies the law of the Jervis Bay Territory, which is the law of the Australian Capital Territory (ACT).[142] Therefore, in the Middle East, for example—the location of much of the ADF's exercise of war powers in recent decades—the substantive criminal law of the ACT also applies to ADF actions at sea in addition to its application through the *Defence Force Discipline Act*. A key difference is that it is the Commonwealth Attorney-General rather than the Director of Military Prosecutions who must consent to any prosecution under the *Crimes at Sea Act 2000* of an offence alleged to have occurred beyond the area adjacent to Australia.[143] Again, the existence of this discretion is not a reason to assume there would be no prosecutions of ADF members under this Act.

The important point here is that the substantive criminal law of the ACT applies to members of the ADF at war anywhere in the world as if they were in Canberra.[144] This confronts the principle of legality as stated by Starke J in *Shaw Savill & Albion Co Ltd*:

> The King cannot change by his prerogative of war, either the law of nations or the law of the land, by general and unlimited regulations. Indeed, the law has been clear, I think, since the judgment of Lord Camden in

---

136 *Defence Force Discipline Act* s 103.
137 Transcript of Proceedings, *Sergeant J and Lance-Corporal D* (Australian Defence Force General Court Martial Pre-trial Directions Hearing, Brigadier Westwood, Chief Judge Advocate, 20 May 2011), 1–3, 36.
138 *Crimes at Sea Act* s 6.
139 Ibid s 4.
140 Ibid s 6.
141 Ibid s 2 sch 1 'The Co-operative Scheme'.
142 Ibid s 6.
143 Ibid ss 6, 7.
144 The *Crimes (Aviation) Act 1991* (Cth) does not operate in the same way as it does not provide for matters 'in the course of activities controlled from' Australian aircraft. It would, therefore, seem to have little potential application to actions by ADF aircraft during war.

Entick v *Carrington*,[145] that a public officer cannot defend himself by alleging generally that he has acted from necessity in the public interest and for the defence of the realm, whether he has or has not the express or implied command of the Crown.[146]

The challenge, then, is to determine how exercises of the war prerogative can be consistent with the principle of legality.

The only statutory defence available to a charge relating to deliberate killing, destruction and detention in war would appear to be that of lawful authority under s 43 of the *Criminal Code 2002* (ACT), which operates with respect to all offences against Australian Capital Territory laws. The deliberate nature of such actions, at the level of national policy, would work against other possibly relevant defences, such as duress, sudden and extraordinary emergency or self-defence, being applicable. Section 43 requires that the actions be authorised under a law and provides as follows:

Lawful authority

A person is not criminally responsible for an offence if the conduct required for the offence is justified or excused under a law.

Conceivably, acts of war should be justified or excused under the law relating to the war prerogative.[147] However, the Dictionary to the *Criminal Code 2002* (ACT) defines 'law' to mean an Act or subordinate law. The war prerogative is not in any Act or subordinate law. The question remains then, how is deliberate killing, destruction and detention in war not contrary to the applicable legislation?

The answer to this question, arguably, lies in statutory interpretation. It seems highly unlikely that Parliament would have intended to prevent deliberate killing, destruction and detention under the war prerogative. As a matter of statutory construction, it is a presumption that Parliament would not limit the prerogative powers of the Crown without express words.[148] It should be possible to presume that so important a prerogative as the war prerogative is available in the absence of any contrary indication

---

145 *Entick* v *Carrington* (1765) 19 St Tr 1030.
146 *Shaw Savill & Albion Co Ltd* (1940) 66 CLR 344, 355.
147 See Robert McLaughlin and Bruce Oswald, '"Wilful Killing" During Armed Conflict: Is There a Defence of Proportionality in Australia?' (2007) 18 *Criminal Law Forum* 1, 26–8.
148 *Barton v Commonwealth* (1974) 131 CLR 477, 508; *Tampa Case* (2001) 110 FCR 491, 540. See D C Pearce and R S Geddes, *Statutory Interpretation in Australia* (Lexis Nexis Butterworths, 7th ed, 2011) 181.

by Parliament.[149] This might be the appropriate place for the argument of French J in the *Tampa Case* for a power 'so central to its sovereignty that it is not to be supposed that the Government of the nation would lack under the power conferred upon it directly by the *Constitution*'.[150] This would mean that the preferable interpretation of relevant provisions of the *Defence Force Discipline Act* or the *Crimes at Sea Act 2000*, which apparently proscribe the conduct of warfare through deliberate killing, destruction and detention, is that they do not actually proscribe such actions when it occurs in the conduct of warfare. As such, these provisions do not expressly relate to the conduct of warfare, and they should not be interpreted to apply to the conduct of warfare. This is not a case of 'covering the field' as Parliament has not purported to provide the same powers as might be available under the war prerogative.

More significantly, perhaps, the *Defence Force Discipline Act* has a number of specific provisions which address conduct in relation to the enemy,[151] including, for example, an offence of failing to use utmost exertions to carry out operations against the enemy.[152] The Act defines the enemy as:

> [A] body politic or an armed force engaged in operations of war against Australia or an allied force and includes any force (including mutineers and pirates) engaged in armed hostilities against the Defence Force or an allied force.[153]

This is significant because it allows the Crown to determine who the enemy is by virtue of whom it conducts armed hostilities against. These provisions of the *Defence Force Discipline Act* indicate that Parliament has provided for the conduct of war and has not intended to proscribe deliberate killing, destruction and detention under the war prerogative. This is a view of the law which accords generally with the practice of Parliament, the courts and the Crown with respect to warfare since the English Civil War as discussed in Chapter 2.[154] As Dixon J stated in *Shaw Savill & Albion Co Ltd*, and as quoted above:

---

149 See Sampford and Palmer, above n 11, 359–62.
150 (2001) 110 FCR 491, 543.
151 *Defence Force Discipline Act 1982* (Cth) ss 15–19.
152 Ibid s 15F.
153 Ibid s 3.
154 See Peter Rowe, *Defence: The Legal Implications: Military Law and the Laws of War* (Brassey's, 1987) 3–5; and Office of the Judge Advocate General, above n 11, [2.6.5]–[3.6.2]. It is also a view of the law which would favour an accused member of the ADF, which is another relevant rule of statutory interpretation, *Beckwith v R* (1976) 135 CLR 569, 576.

The uniform tendency of the law has been to concede to the armed forces complete legal freedom of action in the field, that is to say in the course of active operations against the enemy, so that the application of private law by the ordinary courts may end where the active use of arms begins.[155]

Indeed, where Parliament has sought to regulate the powers of the Crown to wage war,[156] in div 268 of the *Criminal Code Act* and the *Geneva Conventions Act*, Parliament has been mostly careful to be consistent with the international law of armed conflict,[157] which permits deliberate killing, destruction and detention.[158] This chapter will discuss some of the specific provisions of div 268 in relation to actions against persons and property below.

An important point worth noting about legislative proscription of conduct in war is that, consistently with Starke J's restatement of the principle of legality in *Shaw Savill & Albion Co Ltd*,[159] ADF members may still commit ordinary crimes or disciplinary offences in places where the ADF is engaged in warfare. Legislation still needs to provide for murder, rape, theft or assault, for example, wherever the ADF is. The war prerogative authorises the conduct of warfare, it does not excuse any criminal act or disciplinary infringement which occurs where warfare is taking place. Attempts to regulate the conduct of armed forces, so as to keep them 'in good order and discipline',[160] are at least as old as the common law.[161] In interpreting disciplinary or criminal statutes so as to allow the war prerogative to operate, it is necessary to distinguish between lawful acts of war and criminal or disciplinary misconduct as well as civil wrongs. Section 11 of the *Defence Force Discipline Act* addresses this issue to some extent in providing that, in assessing the standard of recklessness, a service tribunal:

> shall have regard to the fact that the member was engaged in the relevant activities in the course of the member's *duty* or in accordance with the requirements of the Defence Force, as the case may be [emphasis added].

---

155 (1940) 66 CLR 344, 362.
156 McLaughlin and Oswald, above n 147, 27.
157 Noting the discussion about 268.24 in McLaughlin and Oswald, ibid, 27.
158 Discussed below under heading V.
159 (1940) 66 CLR 344.
160 Charles Clode, *The Military Forces of the Crown: Their Administration and Government* (John Murray, 1869) 73, citing the text of an officer's oath to the Crown upon appointment.
161 Hale attributed a standing law for the army to King Arthur, above n 4, 119–20; UK Ministry of Defence, *Manual of the Law of Armed Conflict* (Oxford University Press, 2004) 6–7; Geoffrey Corn, Victor Hansen, Richard Jackson, Christopher Jenks, Eric Talbot Jensen and James Schoettler, *The Law of Armed Conflict: An Operational Approach* (Wolters Kluwer, 2012) 36–7; Gerry Rubin, 'Why Military Law? Some United Kingdom Perspectives' (2007) 26(2) *University of Queensland Law Journal* 353, 361.

It is worth noting that the *Defence (Personnel) Regulations 2002* requires enlisted personnel to swear an oath to 'resist her [Majesty's] enemies and faithfully discharge my *duty* according to law'.[162] This is consistent with the duty of the Crown to defend the realm and the Commonwealth to defend the several states, even if the duty is one of imperfect obligation, as discussed above.

Similarly, in regard to negligence, s 11 of the *Defence Force Discipline Act* also provides that a service tribunal:

> shall ... have regard to the standard of care that would have been exercised by a reasonable person who:
>
> (a) was a member of the Defence Force with the same training and experience in the Defence Force or other armed force as the member charged; and
>
> (b) was engaged in the relevant activities in the course of the member's duty or in accordance with the requirements of the Defence Force, as the case may be.

The law of armed conflict, as expressed in the Australian law in div 268, also goes some way in regulating this distinction. There is still an important place for the common law however and, even as s 11 of the *Defence Force Discipline Act* quoted above suggests, the customs and usages of warfare or customs of the sea. This chapter will now turn to this explicit regulation of the conduct of war.

V Powers and Limits

As to what the war prerogative authorises, a survey of the cases indicates that while war is the exemplar of the connection between executive power and *Fortuna*, the war prerogative does have limits. Three main areas emerge where the war prerogative authorises actions which would otherwise be unlawful; these are: actions against the person—causing death, injury and indefinite detention; against property—either acquiring or destroying it; and where the war prerogative might authorise action that would otherwise be contrary to ordinary civil regulatory requirements, such as traffic restrictions, pollution controls, building regulations and so on.

---

162 *Defence (Personnel) Regulations 2002* (Cth) sch 2.

A Actions against the Person

1 Causing Death and Injury

The martial law cases provide authority for the courts treating the conduct of military authorities during war as nonjusticiable or that it might be lawful to use military force to suppress an insurrection.[163] There is no case or statute however which explicitly states that it is lawful to target a person deliberately in war with the intention of killing them because that person is an enemy, and not in self-defence or the defence of others. There is much law, whether statutory, common or international law, as well as practice which presumes that such action is lawful. Notably, and perhaps ironically, Murphy J appeared to make this presumption in *A v Hayden*[164] in his strong rejection of any other basis upon which the executive might order someone to kill, as quoted in Chapter 1:

> The Executive power of the Commonwealth must be exercised in accordance with the *Constitution* and the laws of the Commonwealth. The Governor-General, the Federal Executive Council and every officer of the Commonwealth are bound to observe the laws of the land ... I restate these elementary principles because astonishingly one of the plaintiffs asserted through counsel that it followed from the nature of the executive government that it is not beyond the executive power, even in a situation other than war, to order one of its citizens to kill another person. Such a proposition is inconsistent with the rule of law. It is subversive of the *Constitution* and the laws. It is, in other countries, the justification for death squads.[165]

It is from this that it is possible to construct an argument for it to be lawful to kill deliberately in war. There is slightly more authority for detention in war being lawful.

English law has recognised the custom and usages of war since feudal times.[166] Hale recognised, 'the proper jurisdiction of the constable and marshal ... [but] in these proceedings the customs and laws of war ought to direct their judgment ...'[167] Although articles and ordinances of war

---

163 Eg *Marais v General Officer Commanding the Lines of Communication* [1902] AC 109; *R v Allen* [1921] 2 IR 241; *R (Garde) v Strickland* [1921] 2 IR 317.
164 (1984) 156 CLR 532.
165 Ibid, 562.
166 See H Erle Richards, 'Martial Law' (1902) 18 *Law Quarterly Review* 133.
167 Hale, above n 4, 119–20, but also generally Chapter XII 'Concerning the Jurisdiction and Office of the Constable and Marshal, Martial Law, *Tempus Belli* and Acquisitions by Right of War'.

were originally prerogative instruments,[168] and the Court of the Constable and Marshal a prerogative rather than a common-law court,[169] it might, nonetheless, be arguable on this basis that the common law has recognised that it is lawful to kill deliberately as part of the conduct of warfare. The references to custom and usages of war are scanty and indirect however, and do not usually explicitly authorise deliberate killing.[170]

As stated above, the international law of armed conflict is effectively now incorporated into Australian law by div 268 of the *Criminal Code Act 1995*. This means that any offences relating to the law of armed conflict must now be found in this Act or other statute law. The Full Court of the Federal Court in *Nulyarimma v Thompson*[171] notably found that the effect of the Act was to abolish any offence not found in the Code or other statute law.[172] The international law crime of genocide against Aboriginal people in Australia, therefore, was not cognisable in the courts.[173] Although, even if there can be no common or international law offences, it is still relevant to refer to common law or international law in arguing that specific acts of killing in war are lawful, as well as in interpreting div 268.[174]

This is important because the international law of armed conflict permits the deliberate killing not only of combatants but also innocent noncombatants where their deaths are incidental to the targeting of a military objective.[175] In understanding the extent of the war prerogative then it is essential to read div 268 to identify what it does not state as much as for what it does. This is on the basis that Parliament has proscribed specific conduct in war, essentially that which the international law of armed conflict prohibits, but has remained silent on what the war prerogative authorises. Much of what the war prerogative authorises then is by necessary implication from what div 268 does not proscribe.[176]

---

168 See, eg, 'The Laws and Ordinances of War' Letters Patent given to Sir Thomas Howard, General of all His Majesty's Forces, 1639 in Clode, *The Military Forces of the Crown,* above n 160, 166–71.
169 Hale above n 4, 119–20, but also generally Chapter XII 'Concerning the Jurisdiction and Office of the Constable and Marshal, Martial Law, *Tempus Belli* and Acquisitions by Right of War'.
170 'The Laws and Ordinances of War' above n 168, 166–71; Military Board, *Australian Edition of Manual of Military Law* (CGP, 1941) 194; Oppenheim, above n 68, citing British War Office, *Land Warfare: An Exposition of the Laws and Usages of War on Land for the Guidance of Officers of His Majesty's Army* (1912), 78–82; UK Ministry of Defence, above n 162, 7.
171 (1999) 96 FCR 153.
172 Ibid 172.
173 Ibid 161. See discussion in Lindell, *The Coalition Wars*, above n 11, 29–30.
174 *Jumbunna Coal Mine NL v Victorian Coal Miners' Association* (1908) 6 CLR 309, 363.
175 *Additional Protocol I,* arts 43, 44, 51.
176 On statutory interpretation, the international law of armed conflict and div 268, and s 268.24 in particular, see McLaughlin and Oswald, above n 147, generally and at 31–3.

For this reason it is worth quoting in full and analysing some particular provisions of the *Criminal Code Act*:

268.35 War crime—attacking civilians

A person (the *perpetrator*) commits an offence if:

(a) the perpetrator directs an attack; and

(b) the object of the attack is a civilian population as such or individual civilians not taking direct part in hostilities; and

(c) the perpetrator's conduct takes place in the context of, and is associated with, an international armed conflict.

Penalty: Imprisonment for life.

It is implicit in this provision that it is not an offence in an international armed conflict to attack military personnel or even civilians who are taking a direct part in hostilities.[177] If the ADF's operation against the insurgency in Afghanistan was part of an international armed conflict, then this provision would suggest that deliberately killing insurgents— that is civilians taking a direct part in hostilities—is not an offence. If the war in Afghanistan was actually a noninternational armed conflict, then s 268.70 makes similar provision for civilians not taking an active part in hostilities.[178] The Act does not define either type of conflict[179] so it would be a matter of interpretation for which there would be much international

---

177 See Nils Melzer, *Interpretive Guidance on the Notion of Direct Participation in Hostilities Under International Humanitarian Law* (International Committee of the Red Cross, 2009).

178 **268.70 War crime—murder**

(1) A person (the *perpetrator*) commits an offence if:

(a) the perpetrator causes the death of one or more persons; and

(b) the person or persons are not taking an active part in the hostilities; and

(c) the perpetrator knows of, or is reckless as to, the factual circumstances establishing that the person or persons are not taking an active part in the hostilities; and

(d) the perpetrator's conduct takes place in the context of, and is associated with, an armed conflict that is not an international armed conflict.

Penalty: Imprisonment for life.

(2) To avoid doubt, a reference in subsection (1) to a person or persons who are not taking an active part in the hostilities includes a reference to:

(a) a person or persons who are *hors de combat*; or

(b) civilians, medical personnel or religious personnel who are not taking an active part in the hostilities.

See also s 268.77.

179 Other than to include a military occupation in the definition of an international armed conflict, Dictionary to the *Criminal Code Act 1995*.

law and scholarly commentary to assist.[180] Arguably, a certificate from the Minister for Foreign Affairs under s 268.124 could be conclusive proof that the *Geneva Conventions* and *Additional Protocol I* applied in relation to a question arising in proceedings under the Act.[181] This really goes to whether an armed conflict is in existence or not, not necessarily whether a conflict is an international or a noninternational armed conflict, so the international law and commentary could still be relevant to a court's interpretation of the offence provisions.[182]

As to attacking civilian objects, the *Criminal Code Act 1995* provides:

268.36 War crime—attacking civilian objects

A person (the *perpetrator*) commits an offence if:

(a) the perpetrator directs an attack; and

(b) the object of the attack is not a military objective; and

(c) the perpetrator's conduct takes place in the context of, and is associated with, an international armed conflict.

Penalty: Imprisonment for 15 years.

Similarly this provision would indicate that it is not an offence to attack military objectives in an international armed conflict, which directly relates to the provision below:[183]

268.38 War crime—excessive incidental death, injury or damage

(1) A person (the *perpetrator*) commits an offence if:

(a) the perpetrator launches an attack; and

(b) the perpetrator knows that the attack will cause incidental death or injury to civilians; and

---

180 *Prosecutor v Tadic* 105 ILR 419, 488 quoted in A P V Rogers, *Law on the Battlefield* (Manchester University Press, 2nd ed, 2004) 218–19 and discussion 215–25; UK Ministry of Defence, above n 166, 27–35, 383–8; Corn et al, above n 166, 65–104; Gloria Gaggioli, *Report of the Expert Meeting of the Use of Force in Armed Conflicts: Interplay Between the Conduct of Hostilities and Law Enforcement Paradigms* (International Committee of the Red Cross, 2013); International Committee of the Red Cross, *Report of the 31st International Conference of the Red Cross and Red Crescent on International Humanitarian Law and the Challenges of Contemporary Armed Conflicts*, 2011.
181 *Geneva Red Cross Conventions,* (opened for signature 12 August 1949), 75 UNTS 31, 85, 135, 287 (entered into force 21 October 1950), schs 1 to 4 of the *Geneva Conventions Act 1957* (Cth).
182 See discussion in McLaughlin and Oswald, above n 147, 25. See the extensive discussion of the law relating to noninternational armed conflicts in *Serdar Mohammed v Secretary of State for Defence* [2015] EWCA Civ 843 [167]–[176].
183 The equivalent provision for a noninternational armed conflict is s 268.77.

(c) the perpetrator knows that the death or injury will be of such an extent as to be excessive in relation to the concrete and direct military advantage anticipated; and

(d) the perpetrator's conduct takes place in the context of, and is associated with, an international armed conflict.

Penalty: Imprisonment for life.

Examining this provision indicates that it is not an offence in an international armed conflict to cause incidental death or injury to civilians provided that it would not be excessive in relation to the concrete and direct military advantage anticipated. Obviously, the military advantage test is very subjective but it is the subject of considerable international jurisprudence and scholarly commentary, which would be directly relevant to interpreting this provision.[184] This provision does not apply to a noninternational armed conflict and, therefore, arguably, the stricter offence of causing death to persons not taking an active part in hostilities in s 268.70, quoted in footnote 179, could apply in such situations.[185]

2 Detention

The international law of armed conflict permits the indefinite detention of combatants as prisoners of war until the end of hostilities.[186] It is also not dependent upon a combatant having committed an offence.[187] It is not contrary to the international law of armed conflict to be a combatant and detention as a prisoner of war is not a punishment.[188] In fact, prisoner-of-war status attracts some significant rights and protections under the international law of armed conflict.[189] There is no explicit authority in Australian law for the taking of prisoners of war. Indeed, there is a strong presumption against indefinite detention without charge, let alone

---

184 See the commentary on art 8(2)(b)(iv) of the *Rome Statute of the International Criminal Court*, (opened for signature on 17 July 1998) 2187 UNTS 90 (entered into force 1 July 2002), which this section implements into Australian law, in Kriangsak Kittichaisaree, *International Criminal Law* (Oxford University Press, 2001) 162–4; Jean-Marie Henckaerts and Louise Doswald-Beck, *Customary International Humanitarian Law Volume II: Practice* (Cambridge University Press, 2005) cite the International Criminal Tribunal for Yugoslavia's *Martic Case* (Review of the Indictment, 8 March 1996) and the *Kupreskic Case* (Judgment, 14 January 2000), 322, but see more broadly 297–335. See generally eg, Corn et al, above n 166, 175–81, 187–9.
185 McLaughlin and Oswald's analysis, above n 147, of s 268.24, relating to wilful killing in international armed conflict, is also relevant to s 268.70.
186 *Third Geneva Convention on Prisoners of War*, art 118.
187 Ibid art 4.
188 Ibid arts 87, 99; see UK Ministry of Defence, above n 166, 141.
189 *Third Geneva Convention on Prisoners of War*; See, eg, UK Ministry of Defence, above n 166, 158–84.

conviction.[190] Although in *M68* Gageler J cited *Chu Kheng Lim v Minister for Immigration, Local Government and Ethnic Affairs* in acknowledging a 'prerogative to detain such as that which might arise in relation to enemy aliens in time of war' and quoted from that case in noting the status of aliens within Australia and the exception for enemy aliens:

> Under the common law of Australia and subject to qualification in the case of an enemy alien in time of war, an alien who is within this country, whether lawfully or unlawfully, is not an outlaw.[191]

There is also some statutory recognition that it is lawful to take prisoners of war and it is from this that it is possible to infer that the authority to do so lies in the war prerogative.

Section 7 of the *Defence Force Discipline Act* applies that Act to prisoners of war, subject to and as defined by reference to the *Geneva Conventions Act* and the *Third Geneva Convention,* which deals with prisoners of war. The *Geneva Conventions Act* makes provision for the trial of prisoners of war and civilian internees for offences they may have committed, but not for being enemy combatants or aliens.[192] It also allows for State and Territory Supreme Courts to hear applications to determine whether a person is entitled to prisoner of war status.[193] Further, the *Geneva Conventions Act* has the four *Geneva Conventions*, as well as *Additional Protocol I* and *Additional Protocol III*, as schedules to the Act, although without directly incorporating them into Commonwealth law. Both the *Defence Force Discipline Act* and the *Geneva Conventions Act* assume however that the authority to take prisoners of war lies elsewhere.[194] Similarly, s 268.99 of the *Criminal Code Act 1995* proscribes unjustifiable delay in the repatriation of prisoners of war and other detainees but without identifying the domestic legal authority to take such prisoners and detainees to begin with, other than to refer to the *Third* and *Fourth Geneva Conventions*. The only authority that could then authorise taking prisoners of war is the war prerogative.

---

190 *Al Kateb v Godwin* (2004) 219 CLR 562, 616–17; *CPCF* [2015] HCA 1 [45] (French CJ), [96] (Hayne and Bell JJ), [196], [218] (Crennan J), [380] (Gageler J); [453] (Keane J).
191 [2016] HCA 1 [149] quoting *Chu Kheng Lim v Minister for Immigration, Local Government and Ethnic Affairs* (1992) 176 CLR 1, 19 (Brennan, Deane and Dawson JJ (with whom Mason CJ agreed)).
192 *Geneva Conventions Act*, ss 11, 12.
193 *Geneva Conventions Act*, s 10A.
194 This was also the case with the *National Security (Prisoners of War) Regulations 1943* (Cth). *The Australian Digest* (Lawbook, 2nd ed, 1968) Vol 2, which deals extensively with 'Defence and War', does not mention any prisoner-of-war cases. This suggests that taking of prisoners of war was not a matter of legal controversy.

These references also mention civilian internees within the meaning of the *Fourth Geneva Convention* and *Additional Protocol I*. Article 42 of the *Fourth Geneva Convention* permits the internment of civilians 'if the security of the Detaining Power makes it absolutely necessary'.[195] With respect to international armed conflict, on the basis that the statutory provisions cited above also mention civilian internees, without there being a statutory authority to intern them, presumably the war prerogative also provides the power to intern civilians in war. The international law of armed conflict also informs when the ADF may intern or detain such civilians and also when they must be released,[196] as well as the treatment of such people whilst interned or detained.[197]

There may also be other situations of civilian internment or detention in noninternational armed conflict where the Geneva law mentioned does not assist. The Court of Appeal for England and Wales recently considered this issue in the 2015 case of *Serdar Mohammed v Secretary of State for Defence* ('*Serdar Mohammed*') and found that the international law of armed conflict, whether conventional or customary, does not authorise detention in noninternational armed conflicts:

> We have concluded that in its present stage of development it is not possible to find authority under international humanitarian law [also known as the law of armed conflict] to detain in an internationalised non-international armed conflict by implication from the relevant treaty provisions, Common Article 3 and APII. As to customary international law, despite the interplay of treaty-based sources of international humanitarian law and customary international law sources, the possibility that the requirements for the emergence of a customary rule of international humanitarian law, and the position of the ICRC [International Committee of the Red Cross], we do not consider that it is possible to base authority to detain in a non-international armed conflict on customary international law.[198]

---

195 See discussion in Jelena Pejic 'Procedural Principles and Safeguards for Internment/Administrative Detention in Armed Conflict and Other Situations of Violence' (2005) 87(858) *International Review of the Red Cross* 375.
196 See s 268.33—unlawful confinement. The section refers to the *Geneva Conventions* and *Additional Protocol I*.
197 *Fourth Geneva Convention* generally and *Additional Protocol I*, arts 45, 75.
198 [2015] EWCA Civ 843 [167]–[176] (The Lord Chief Justice of England and Wales, Lloyd-Jones, Beatson LJJ) (parentheses added). The appeal in this case was decided after 28 March 2016, the date which this book reflects the law up until, but before publication. In *Al-Waheed v Ministry of Defence; Serdar Mohammed v Ministry of Defence* [2017] UKSC 2 ('*Al-Waheed*') (being two appeals heard together) Lord Sumption, with whom Lady Hale agreed, provided the leading judgment for the majority and confirmed this point [13]–[17].

The Court stated that it was not possible to make an argument from the absence of prohibition in this case, although it was interesting that it looked to international law in making this point and did not address the war prerogative at all.[199] Chapter 6 will return to this issue. The Court took the position then that such authority as there is to detain in a noninternational armed conflict must derive from the law of the nation in which the armed conflict is taking place. In this case, Afghan law permitted detention by foreign military forces assisting the Afghan government for 96 hours before a detainee had to be released or handed over to the Afghan criminal justice system.[200] This was not the position argued for by the Secretary of State in the proceedings,[201] nor the position of the International Committee of the Red Cross generally,[202] but stands as the most persuasive common-law authority on the question. Apart from being a clear statement on the issue, the quote from this case is also worth reproducing to illustrate the use by a common-law court, as suggested above, of the relevant international law.

There are also concerns with the exercise of prerogative power to detain civilians in time of war within Australia, whether during international or noninternational armed conflict. Despite the war prerogative traditionally extending to control of enemy aliens within the realm,[203] during the

---

199 *Serdar Mohammed* [2015] EWCA Civ 843 [195]–[198].
200 Ibid [129]–[137]. *Al-Waheed* [2017] UKSC 2 then determined that authority to detain 'for imperative reasons of security' could be found in the relevant authorising United Nations Security Council Resolutions, [30], [48] but this point related to the obligations of the United Kingdom under the European *Convention for the Protection of Human Rights and Fundamental Freedoms* (opened for signature 4 November 1950), ETS 005 (entered into force 3 September 1953), implemented through the *Human Rights Act 1998* (UK), and so, while important, is less directly applicable to Australia. Australia's international human rights obligations are nonetheless relevant to detention in situations of noninternational armed conflict. In the Human Rights Committee, *Replies to the List of Issues (CCPR/C/AUS/Q/5) to be Taken Up in Connection with the Consideration of the Fifth Periodic Report of the Government of Australia (CCP/C/AUS/5)* UN Doc CCPR/C/AUS/Q/5/Add.1 (21 January 2009), the Australian Government stated, 'Australia assures the Committee that in all cases it respects the fundamental rights and freedoms provided for under the Covenant, and to the extent that Australia is in a position to afford them during military or civilian operations occurring outside Australia, it will as a matter of policy endeavour to implement reasonable and appropriate measures in the circumstances', 5.Whilst this is a policy statement it nonetheless illustrates that such obligations should at least be taken into account.
201 *Serdar Mohammed* [2015] EWCA Civ 843 [207], [222].
202 Ibid [218], [237]–[240].
203 As noted by Gageler J in *M68* [2016] HCA 1 [149] citing *Chu Kheng Lim v Minister for Immigration, Local Government and Ethnic Affairs* (1992) 176 CLR 1, 19 (Brennan, Deane and Dawson JJ (with whom Mason CJ agreed)); Zines, 'The Inherent Executive Power of the Commonwealth', above n 11, 287, citing *R v Bottrill; Ex parte Kuechenmeister* [1947] KB 41; House of Commons Public Administration Select Committee, United Kingdom, *Taming the Prerogative: Strengthening Ministerial Accountability to Parliament: Fourth Report* (2004) 4.

Second World War, the *National Security (Aliens Control) Regulations 1940–1943* (Cth) created a comprehensive statutory scheme for dealing with enemy aliens. Although now repealed, the previous existence of these regulations indicates that neither Parliament nor the Executive were willing to leave interference with the rights and liberties of civilian enemy aliens in Australia to prerogative power alone. It also suggests that it might not be possible to argue that it was necessary to rely upon prerogative power alone when control of enemy aliens has previously been the subject of a comprehensive statute. It might be necessary, and therefore justifiable, to rely upon prerogative power to control enemy aliens in an extreme situation when war might have erupted unexpectedly and enemy aliens posed a direct and serious threat. Given that in Australia's only existential crisis of 1942 the matter was the subject of legislation, it might be more difficult to argue that it was necessary to rely upon prerogative power – that is, unless the situation was more dire than that in 1942.

It is difficult to discern between law and good policy in this regard. A statutory regime supports the supremacy of Parliament. It also supports the principle of legality in that members of the public in Australia, even if enemy aliens, should not be deprived of their liberty on the basis that, as previously cited, 'the law to warrant it should be clear in proportion as the power is exorbitant'.[204] Even so, as this aspect of the prerogative has authority supporting it,[205] it is no longer the subject of a comprehensive statute and is the subject of an international law regime, at least in respect of international armed conflict, preferring reliance upon statute might be more a matter of good policy rather than law.

B Actions against Property

In *Shaw Savill & Albion Co Ltd*, Dixon J stated:

> There is no authority dealing with civil liability for negligence on the part of the King's forces when in action, but the law has always recognized that rights of property and of person must give way to the necessities of the defence of the realm.[206]

---

204 *Entick v Carrington* (1765) 19 St Tr 1030.
205 See generally above n 203.
206 (1940) 66 CLR 344, 362.

War has traditionally involved extensive interference with property rights.[207] This has occurred, as will be discussed, through acquisition of property for defence purposes or through damage and destruction in the course of battle, to deny its use to the enemy or as a result of accidents. This raises questions of the extent to which the war prerogative can authorise this interference with property. Similar questions of statutory interpretation arise, as with actions against the person, as to whether the war prerogative displaces the application of general criminal law offences that would, prima facie, apply to deliberate acquisition, damage and destruction of property. Fortunately, in the case of property, there is a body of relevant case law which indicates that such action can be a lawful exercise of the war prerogative in the face of the enemy. There is still some uncertainty over how proximate the enemy must be. There has also been uncertainty over whether such action must be compensated on just terms, which now appears to be resolved in favour of compensation. As to negligent action, *Shaw Savill & Albion Co Ltd* has provided the 'combat immunity doctrine'.[208]

1 Damage and Destruction

The 1964 House of Lords case *Burmah Oil*[209] involved the destruction of oil refineries in Burma in order to deny them to the advancing Japanese Army in 1942.[210] As with the case of *De Keyser's Royal Hotel*[211] discussed below, the right of the Crown to take private property in *Burmah Oil* was not in dispute.[212] The question was whether compensation should be payable, the claim being effectively a common-law claim, with the majority deciding that it should be.[213] *Burmah Oil* does not attempt to provide an exhaustive analysis of the war prerogative but it did do much to state when and to what extent the Crown can interfere with private property rights in exercising it.[214] The majority of the Lords in this case

---

207 See Richards, above n 166, cited with approval in *Shaw Savill & Albion Co Ltd* (1940) 66 CLR 344, 362.
208 (1940) 66 CLR 344.
209 *Burmah Oil Co Ltd v Lord Advocate* [1965] AC 75 ('*Burmah Oil*'). See discussion in Campbell McLachlan, *Foreign Relations Law* (Cambridge University Press, 2014) 266–7, supporting the position that compensation should have been payable.
210 *Burmah Oil* [1965] AC 75, 75.
211 *Attorney-General v De Keyser's Royal Hotel Ltd* [1920] AC 508 ('*De Keyser's Royal Hotel*').
212 [1965] AC 75, 143.
213 Ibid 97. The action was commenced in Scotland but appears to be the equivalent of a common-law claim as no statutory basis for the claim was pleaded.
214 Ibid.

placed much emphasis on the scholarship of civil lawyers and De Vattel in particular. De Vattel distinguished between acts preparatory to battle and acts occurring in the heat of the battle itself. Battle damage was not compensable whereas preparatory acts were.[215] The point on compensation is, perhaps, not as important as the point that, in both categories, extensive interference and even destruction of private property is lawful insofar as it is necessary for the conduct of military operations.[216] (This is not unlike the military advantage test known to the law of armed conflict.[217]) This case also moved away from the doctrine of necessity as applicable to any person and saw it more as an exercise of the war prerogative being limited only by necessity. In an age of total warfare, only the Crown can decide to do such acts as destroy oil refineries to deprive the enemy of fuel.[218]

The minority acknowledged De Vattel but placed more emphasis on United States Supreme Court cases with similar facts, which saw little distinction between preparatory acts and battle damage.[219] (The majority also addressed these United States cases but generally saw them as decided on different principles.[220]) Viscount Radcliffe, in the minority, cited Field J in *United States v Pacific Railroad*:[221]

> Whatever would embarrass or impede the advance of the enemy, as the breaking up of roads, or the burning of bridges, or would cripple or defeat him, as destroying his means of subsistence, were lawfully ordered by the commanding general. Indeed it was his imperative duty to direct their destruction. The necessities of the war called for and justified this. The safety of the State in such cases overrides all considerations of private loss – *Salus populi* is then, in truth, *suprema lex*.[222]

---

215 Ibid 130, 141 citing De Vattel, *Droit des Gens* (1798) Book III, c XV. Zines, 'The Inherent Executive Power of the Commonwealth', above n 11, 287, saw both categories of damage as compensable but only cites Stanley De Smith and Rodney Brazier, *Constitutional and Administrative Law* (Penguin, 7th ed, 1994).
216 *Burmah Oil* [1965] AC 75, 141, 144, 148, 159–60, 162.
217 *Additional Protocol I*, art 52.
218 *Burmah Oil* [1965] AC 75, 99. In another case decided after 28 March 2016, the date which this book reflects the law up until, but before publication, *Rahmatullah (No 2) v Ministry of Defence* [2017] UKSC 1, (a separate aspect of the appeal from the *Serdar Mohammed* case, relating specifically to Act of State doctrine), Lady Hale, with whom the majority agreed, stated that 'destruction, of property, for example in the course of battle, was indeed a government act.' [36].
219 *Burmah Oil* [1965] AC 75, 127–30.
220 Ibid 159–61.
221 120 US 227 (1887).
222 *Burmah Oil* [1965] AC 75, 133.

Interestingly Viscount Radcliffe also helpfully refers to John Locke's *True End of Civil Government*,[223] specifically Chapter 14 'Of Prerogative', and states:

> The essence of a prerogative power, if one is to follow Locke's thought, is ... to act for the public good, where there is no law, or even to dispense with or override the law where the ultimate preservation of society is in question.[224]

Given this broad view of the war prerogative, it is perhaps not surprising then that Viscount Radcliffe was unwilling to see such destruction of private property as compensable.[225] Compensation aside, the telling point from both the majority and minority is the very broad view given to the power to interfere with private property in the course of operations in war. Importantly the case also draws out that necessity becomes easier to argue the closer the action is to the face of the enemy. Although *Burmah Oil*[226] does not refer to *Shaw Savill & Albion Co*, the majority's emphasis on De Vattel's distinction between acts done in battle and acts done preparatory to battle may be significant given the distinction in *Shaw Savill & Albion Co Ltd* between actual operations against the enemy and other operations.[227] The general rule appears to be that the closer an action is to the face of the enemy, the more it is likely to be a lawful exercise of the war prerogative.[228] It is consistent with the doctrine of combat immunity in *Shaw Savill & Albion Co Ltd* that destruction occurring outside of actual operations against the enemy should be compensable. It is more important however that prerogative power to destroy property where necessary is available, even if it is not in battle but rather to deny that property to the enemy. It is perhaps appropriate that there is a requirement to compensate for destruction outside of battle so that a military commander may be more careful in determining whether it is necessary to cause such destruction.

---

223 John Locke, 'An Essay Concerning the True, Original, Extent and End of Civil Government (1690)' in Sir Ernest Barker (ed) *Social Contract: Essays by Locke, Hume and Rousseau* (Oxford University Press, 1946) 137.
224 *Burmah Oil* [1965] AC 75, 118.
225 Ibid 134–5.
226 [1965] AC 75.
227 (1940) 66 CLR 344.
228 See Renfree, above n 11, 463–5.

2 Acquisition

The 1920 House of Lords case of *De Keyser's Royal Hotel* is significant in drawing a distinction between prerogative acts in the face of an emergency and those for which more time is available.[229] In this case, the Royal Flying Corps requisitioned a hotel in London to be its administrative headquarters during the First World War.[230] The proprietor of the hotel protested but relinquished possession to the Army.[231] The question was whether the prerogative or the *Defence of the Realm Consolidation Act 1914* (UK) authorised the occupation of the hotel and whether compensation was payable.[232] The Law Lords found for the proprietor of the hotel[233] and entered into an interesting analysis of the relationship between prerogative and statute. Essentially, there was no dispute that the taking of the hotel was lawful, whether under prerogative or statute.[234] Given that there was a statute in place which provided for compensation in such an event, however, it should be preferred to reliance upon the prerogative power alone.[235] This is consistent with the argument of this book that statutory power should be preferred to prerogative power covering the same field, except in extraordinary situations of necessity. It was not clear, ultimately, as to whether compensation would have been payable had the taking been under the prerogative alone, hence the House of Lords had to reconsider this question in *Burmah Oil*[236] as discussed above.[237] Insofar as the war prerogative is concerned, Lord Sumner made the following observation:

> Of course, with the progress of the art of war, the scope both of emergencies and of acts to be justified by emergency extends, and the prerogative adjusts itself to new discoveries, as was resolved in the *Saltpetre Case*; but there is a difference between things belonging to that category of urgency, in which the law arms Crown and subject alike with the right of intervening and sets public safety above private right, and things which, however important, cannot belong to that category, but, in fact, are simply committed to the general administration of the Crown.[238]

---

229 [1920] AC 508.
230 Ibid 509.
231 Ibid 523.
232 Ibid 523.
233 Ibid 581.
234 Ibid 523.
235 Ibid 529.
236 [1965] AC 75.
237 *Tampa Case* (2001) 110 FCR 491 referred extensively to this discussion, as discussed in Chapter 1.
238 *De Keyser's Royal Hotel* [1920] AC 508, 565.

This indicates that the necessity of responding with urgency to an emergency in war can authorise acts against property which would otherwise be unlawful. The courts will be careful to draw a distinction however between what is necessary and what is merely important. This is consistent with the reasoning of *Shaw Savill & Albion Co Ltd*, as both Starke J and Dixon J referred approvingly to *De Keyser's Royal Hotel*.[239]

Australia's written *Constitution* creates a significant difference from the English perspective on this issue due to the existence of s 51 (xxxi), which provides:

> The Parliament shall, subject to this Constitution, have power to make laws for the peace, order, and good government of the Commonwealth with respect to:
>
> the *acquisition of property* on just terms from any State or person for any purpose in respect of which the Parliament has power to make laws [emphasis added].[240]

Compensation is not necessarily a direct concern of the ADF in combat operations. It would more likely be the Department of Defence that would address such questions. It is worth exploring the issue mainly as a limit on the power to acquire property. That is to say, that it must at least be an indirect operational concern of the ADF whether any acquisition of property should be on just terms.

In 1943 in *Johnston, Fear & Kingham & The Offset Printing Company Pty Ltd v Commonwealth*[241] the Commonwealth had taken possession of an offset printing press under the *National Security (Supply of Goods) Regulations 1939–1942* (Cth). The owners argued that the acquisition was not on just terms in accordance with s 51 (xxxi).[242] The case therefore essentially turned on the invalidity of Commonwealth legislation to acquire property on anything other than just terms. As to the acquisition of property under prerogative or executive power, Latham CJ made the following obiter dicta comment:

---

239 (1940) 66 CLR 344, 354, 363.
240 See Renfree, above n 11, 463–5, and the list of compulsory acquisition cases in connection with defence which he cites at n 85.
241 (1943) 67 CLR 314 ('*Johnston, Fear & Kingham*').
242 Ibid 315.

5. WAR

> It may be that the prerogative of the Crown authorizes the seizure and use of property in the course of war-like operations without any compensation to the owner. The Commonwealth *Constitution* does not contain any such provision as that which is to be found in the fifth amendment of the American *Constitution* – 'Nor shall private property be taken for public use without just compensation.' This is an absolute prohibition of any taking of private property for public use without just compensation, whether or not a statute purports to authorize such a taking. The Commonwealth *Constitution* contains no such provision. The only reference to the subject is contained in a positive grant of legislative power. The limitation upon the legislative power of the Commonwealth Parliament does not necessarily involve any corresponding limitation with respect to the executive power of the Commonwealth.[243]

This comment is significant for a number of reasons. It is the first direct comment in the jurisprudence of the High Court upon the power of the Commonwealth to seize property in the course of warlike operations. It clearly indicates that prerogative power might authorise such action. The comment is also significant because it distinguishes between legislative authority to acquire property, which is subject to the just terms requirements of s 51 (xxxi), and executive authority to seize property in warlike operations, which may not be compensable at all (noting that this case preceded *Burmah Oil*);[244] although the idea that the executive power might extend beyond limits of the Commonwealth's legislative power would not appear to have survived *Williams*,[245] as discussed in Chapter 1. The executive power cannot extend beyond the legislative power so any acquisition of property by prerogative power,[246] outside of damage and destruction directly in battle, would be subject to the limitation upon the power of the Commonwealth Parliament to acquire property on anything other than just terms.[247] It is not even open to make an exception on the grounds of necessity as compensation is essentially a post hoc consideration. It is difficult to contemplate a situation where it would be necessary not to afford just terms compensation for the acquisition

---

243 *Johnston, Fear and Kingham* (1943) 67 CLR 314, 318–19.
244 [1965] AC 75.
245 (2012) 248 CLR 156.
246 Chapter 1 nn 111–19.
247 Noting that just terms does not mean just compensation but rather what is fair, including what is in the interests 'of the public or of the Commonwealth', and not arbitrary, *Grace Bros Pty Ltd v Commonwealth* (1946) 72 CLR 269, 290–1. Keifel J cited this part of Dixon J's judgment with approval in *JT International SA v Cth* (2012) 86 ALJR 1297, 1368, which concerned legislation to enforce plain packaging of tobacco products, which the High Court decided was not an acquisition of property within the terms of s 51 (xxxi) of the *Constitution*.

of property. That said, damage, destruction or even temporary occupation of property in battle are arguably not subject to this limitation as they are justified by the necessity of combat and subject to the combat immunity doctrine in *Shaw Savill & Albion Co Ltd*.[248]

Although Latham CJ did not mention *De Keyser's Royal Hotel*,[249] it is interesting to note how it informed other judgments in *Johnston, Fear & Kingham*.[250] Starke J referred to it, among other cases, in stating that 'Actual war operations and military necessity require further consideration, and so does the requisitioning of property for war purposes …'[251] Conversely, McTiernan J quoted Lord Atkinson's statement in that case that '[n]either the public safety nor the defence of the realm requires that the Crown should be relieved of a legal liability to pay for the property it takes from one of its subjects'.[252]

Less than a year later, the High Court gave its judgment in *Minister of State for the Army v Dalziel*.[253] Mr Dalziel owned land in Sydney which the Minister took indefinite possession of under the *National Security (General) Regulations 1939–1943* (Cth). The Court found that the regulation in question did not provide for acquisition on just terms and was therefore invalid.[254] Latham CJ dissented and drew on *De Keyser's Royal Hotel*[255] to make a distinction between temporary taking of possession—that is, requisition—of property due to the exigencies of war and permanent acquisition, which requires a transfer of title.[256] The strength of the majority judgments in *Minister of State for the Army v Dalziel* that any deliberate

---

[248] (1940) 66 CLR 344. This position might find some more recent support in the High Court case of *JT International SA v Cth* (2012) 86 ALJR 1297, where Hayne and Bell JJ at 1335, with whom the majority agreed, stated that where the Commonwealth acquires no interest of a proprietary nature, there can be no acquisition of property within the terms of s 51 (xxxi) of the *Constitution*. Arguably, destruction, damage and temporary occupation in battle also create no proprietary interest for the Commonwealth and so are not compensable on just terms. As stated above, the main question for this book is whether there is a power for the ADF to damage, destroy or acquire property. The question of whether such action subsequently requires the payment of compensation is of only indirect importance. To pursue the longstanding scholarly debate on acquisition on just terms would therefore place undue emphasis on a point which, although important in constitutional scholarship, is tangential to this book.
[249] [1920] AC 508.
[250] (1943) 67 CLR 314.
[251] Ibid 325.
[252] Ibid 329, quoting *De Keyser's Royal Hotel* [1920] AC 542.
[253] (1944) 68 CLR 261.
[254] *National Security (General) Regulations 1939–1943* (Cth) reg 60H.
[255] [1920] AC 542.
[256] *Minister of State for the Army v Dalziel* (1944) 68 CLR 261, 280–2.

acquisition of property by the Commonwealth under statute,²⁵⁷ whether temporary or permanent, must attract just terms compensation seems to have rendered the rest of Latham CJ's dissenting view on this point of no further value. The strengthening of his position from *Johnston, Fear & Kingham* on the prerogative power to acquire property,²⁵⁸ however, is significant given the reasoning in *Burmah Oil* above.²⁵⁹ His Honour stated that 'Taking possession of land belonging to another person may be authorized by the royal prerogative or under a valid statute (or regulation)'.²⁶⁰ None of the other justices addressed this point so that, although stated in dissent, it provides a useful indication that the prerogative does extend this far. Given *Shaw Savill & Albion Co Ltd*,²⁶¹ presumably this could only be temporarily in the course of actual operations against the enemy. An example would be the destruction of a wharf or airfield or the acquisition of a hotel to become a hospital where the threat from the enemy was sufficient to justify such action as necessary. However, the deliberate destruction of the hotel or a municipal water supply, for example, might not be justified as necessary. Neither would contribute directly to enemy war-fighting capacity nor would they likely be classified as military objectives in accordance with s 268.36 of the *Criminal Code Act 1995*, discussed above, if they fell into enemy possession.

C Breach of Regulatory Requirements

The final area where the ADF may need to act contrary to statute in war relates to State and Territory regulatory requirements. It is likely that ADF operations in Australia during war would prima facie be subject to a range of regulatory requirements. As mentioned in Chapter 2, the *Defence Act* provides as follows:

123 Immunity from certain State and Territory laws

(1) A member of the Defence Force is not bound by any law of a State or Territory:

(a) that would require the member to have permission (whether in the form of a licence or otherwise) to use or to have in his or her possession, or would require the member to register, a vehicle, vessel, animal, firearm or other thing belonging to the Commonwealth; or

---

257 Ibid.
258 (1943) 67 CLR 314.
259 [1965] AC 75.
260 *Minister of State for the Army v Dalziel* (1944) 68 CLR 261, 270.
261 (1940) 66 CLR 344.

(b) that would require the member to have permission (whether in the form of a licence or otherwise) to do anything in the course of his or her duties as a member of the Defence Force.

This section would address many State and Territory regulatory requirements involving licences, registrations or permits but, arguably, would not extend to cover activities for which it might not be possible to obtain permission under State or Territory law because they would simply be prohibited.[262] For example, ADF combat operations in or near Australia could be expected to result in a range of regulatory breaches of any number of laws relating, for example, to roads and traffic, the environment or building regulation. This could happen through the manoeuvring of tanks on roads, the construction of fortifications, aircraft noise over built up areas, the transport of explosives or operations inconsistent with protection of terrestrial or marine nature reserves.

At this point it is worth returning to the application of State laws discussed in Chapter 2, as well as Commonwealth regulatory control, and putting the combat immunity doctrine in *Shaw Savill & Albion Co Ltd*[263] together with the principles of legality and State regulation of Commonwealth executive power stated in the *DHA Case*.[264] The *DHA Case*[265] did not refer to *Shaw Savill & Albion Co Ltd*[266] but it did address the principle of legality and the cases related to it. Brennan CJ, although in a single judgment, perhaps expressed the position of the majority most clearly:

> But if the proscribed act is done or the proscribed omission is made by the servant or agent without statutory authority, there is no prerogative power in the Crown in right of the Commonwealth to dispense the servant or agent from liability under the State criminal law. In *A v Hayden* I sought to explain the relevant principle:

> The incapacity of the executive government to dispense its servants from obedience to laws made by Parliament is the cornerstone of a parliamentary democracy ... By the *Bill of Rights* the power to dispense from any statute was abolished. Whatever vestige of the dispensing power then remained, it is no more. The principle, as expressed in the *Act of Settlement*, is that all officers and ministers ought to serve the Crown according to the laws ...

---

262 Eg *Marine Pollution Act 1987* (NSW) s 8 'Prohibition of discharge of oil or oily mixtures into State waters'.
263 (1940) 66 CLR 344.
264 *Re Residential Tenancies Tribunal of NSW v Henderson; Ex parte Defence Housing Authority* (1997) 190 CLR 410 ('*DHA Case*').
265 Ibid.
266 (1940) 66 CLR 344.

> It follows that, absent Commonwealth statutory authority, the Crown in right of the Commonwealth cannot authorise its servants or agents to perform their functions in contravention of the criminal laws of a State and cannot confer immunity upon them if, in performing those functions, they contravene those laws. For that reason, *Pirrie v McFarlane* was, in my respectful opinion, rightly decided.[267]

The joint judgment of Dawson, Toohey and Gaudron JJ stated this rule:

> If in regulating activities engaged in by the Crown and its subjects alike a State statute extends as a matter of construction to the Crown in right of the Commonwealth, then that Crown is bound by the statute in the same way as the subject is bound, subject always to any inconsistency with a valid Commonwealth law.[268]

This is consistent with the reasoning in *Shaw Savill & Albion Co Ltd*[269] that when the armed forces in war are not actually engaged with the enemy, noting that it is possible to engage the enemy from a distance, then those forces should obey laws of general application, including State and Territory laws. This is not to say that State laws could restrict the war prerogative of the Commonwealth, because the exercise of the war prerogative is not an activity in which the subject can engage 'alike' with the Commonwealth.[270] As Dawson, Toohey and Gaudron JJ, in the majority, stated:

> The States ... do not have specific legislative powers which might be construed as authorising them to restrict or modify the executive capacities of the Commonwealth. No implication limiting an otherwise given power is needed; the character of the Commonwealth as a body politic, armed with executive capacities by the *Constitution*, by its very nature places those capacities outside the legislative power of ... a State ... [p]rerogative [is] part of the definition of Commonwealth executive power going, as it does, to the rights or privileges of the Crown in right of the Commonwealth.[271]

From this it is possible to argue that so central a prerogative as the war prerogative is a Commonwealth capacity for which it is beyond the power of the States to legislate. A broad rule would appear to be that the closer an

---

267 (1997) 190 CLR 410, 427–8; see also Brennan and Toohey JJ in *Re Tracey* (1989) 166 CLR 518, 576.
268 *DHA Case* (1997) 190 CLR 410, 447.
269 (1940) 66 CLR 344.
270 *DHA Case* (1997) 190 CLR 410, 447.
271 Ibid 440–1.

action is to engagement in actual operations against the enemy, the more likely it is to be lawful, even if prima facie contrary to laws of general application.

This is clearly far from being an easy rule to apply. As Dixon J noted in *Shaw Savill & Albion Co Ltd*, as quoted above, 'It may not be easy under conditions of modern warfare to say in a given case upon which side of the line it falls'.[272] The contrasting judgments in *Pirrie v McFarlane* illustrate this inherent tension in the relationship between the ADF, as a Commonwealth entity, and the States.[273] Starke J said of members of the forces that 'if he commits an offence against the ordinary criminal law, he can be tried and punished as if he were a civilian'.[274] Then again, Isaacs J in dissent stated that 'military commands, lawful by Commonwealth law, are not susceptible of denial or abridgment by State law'.[275] That both statements appear equally applicable to the application of State law to ADF operations in war only serves to underscore the difficulty of discerning the lawfulness of any particular ADF action. Actions in combat against the enemy should be free of the application of State law. Actions closely related to combat against the enemy, such as manoeuvring forces and equipment or the construction of defences where it is to face an imminent threat from the enemy should also be free from the application of State law. State law could apply to other routine ADF activities within State jurisdiction however, which any citizen could undertake during wartime.

VI Conclusion

The war prerogative is a curious element of the executive power of the Commonwealth in that it is so well recognised in theory and practice, yet there is so little authority with which to give it substance. Much of this would appear to be due to the nonjusticiable character of most acts of war and the traditional deference of Parliament to the executive on the conduct of military operations. What case authority there is addresses the margins of when the war prerogative may or may not apply, and not so much what the war prerogative may or may not authorise. Fortunately,

---

272 (1940) 66 CLR 344, 362.
273 (1925) 36 CLR 170.
274 Ibid 228.
275 Ibid 205.

there is sufficient case authority arising from the Second World War in *Shaw Savill & Albion Co Ltd*[276] and *Burmah Oil*[277] to identify that the war prerogative will authorise combat operations against a possibly distant enemy using much of the technology of modern warfare, such as aircraft, submarines and long range ordnance. From this recognition in these cases it is possible to read the applicable statutes with a view to what they do not say about the war prerogative as much as for what they do say.

The High Court's repeated affirmation of the principle of legality in relation to defence matters in *Shaw Savill & Albion Co Ltd*[278] and the *DHA Case*[279] (in addition to *A v Hayden*[280] discussed in Chapter 1) means that it is not possible simply to understate the relevance of this legislation. With regard to legislation of general application, such as the criminal law of the Australian Capital Territory, which applies to ADF operations through the *Defence Force Discipline Act* and the *Crimes at Sea Act 2000*, statutory interpretation can, arguably, address the principle of legality. It seems very unlikely that the Parliament would have proscribed the deliberate causing of death, destruction and detention under the war prerogative without express words. To the contrary, even though not authorising such deliberate action, there are a number of provisions of the *Defence Force Discipline Act* which presume that such action lawfully occurs. This is also the case with the legislation which Parliament has explicitly applied to the conduct of warfare; that is, div 268 of the *Criminal Code Act* and the *Geneva Conventions Act*. It appears mostly to be drafted carefully to avoid proscribing the deliberate causing of death, destruction and detention permitted by the international law of armed conflict. Where an act is of questionable necessity, such as interning civilian enemy aliens in Australia, the prerogative may not be enough and statutory authority may be required.

Shaw Savill & Albion Co Ltd,[281] and the United Kingdom Supreme Court decision in *Smith*,[282] made clear that actions under the war prerogative will be protected only by the combat immunity doctrine when they involve actual operations against the enemy. Otherwise the armed forces

---

276 (1940) 66 CLR 344.
277 [1965] AC 75.
278 (1940) 66 CLR 344.
279 (1997) 190 CLR 410.
280 (1984) 156 CLR 532.
281 (1940) 66 CLR 344.
282 [2013] UKSC 41.

must comply with the general law as much as any other citizen must. It will not necessarily be clear as to which side of this distinction any particular ADF action in war will fall. The closer the action is to being actual operations against the enemy, the more likely it is to be justified as a necessary exercise of the war prerogative. The test of necessity in the case of war becomes, then, an assessment of whether an action was in the course of actual operations against the enemy. As *Smith* indicates,[283] this is far from being an easy test to apply, which is consistent with the inherent uncertainty of the concept of *Fortuna*. The principles of both legality and the supremacy of Parliament would, however, likely lead to the application of combat immunity being done conservatively.

---

283 Ibid.

6

External Security

I Introduction

> [The federative (external affairs) power] is much less capable to be directed by antecedent, standing, positive laws than the executive, and so must necessarily be left to the prudence and wisdom of those whose hands it is left in, to be managed for the public good.'[1]

External security operations other than war have been the most extensive ADF operations in recent decades and, despite the extensive coercive powers exercised, there is even less positive legal authority to support them than there is for war. The main distinction between such operations and war is that they do not involve combat against an enemy, the war prerogative is not applicable and there is no doctrine of combat immunity. The use of force is that required for self-defence and mission accomplishment, essentially a law enforcement approach.[2] For the most part, external security operations other than war have occurred under the international law authority of United Nations Security Council resolutions and include the naval presence in the Middle East since 1990, the 1993 Somalia operation and operations in East Timor since 1999.

---

1 John Locke, 'An Essay Concerning the True, Original, Extent and End of Civil Government (1690)' in Sir Ernest Barker (ed) *Social Contract: Essays by Locke, Hume and Rousseau* (Oxford University Press, 1946) 124.
2 See Bruce Oswald, 'The Law of Military Occupation: Answering the Challenges of Detention During Contemporary Peace Operations?' (2007) 8(2) *Melbourne Journal of International Law* 311, 314–15; Rob McLaughlin, 'The Use of Lethal Force by Military Forces on Law Enforcement Operations – Is there a "Lawful Authority"?' (2009) 37(3) *Federal Law Review* 441, 442–6.

(There have been numerous other operations under the authority of the United Nations or other international agreements which this book does not consider because of their essentially noncoercive nature.[3]) There have also been operations of a coercive nature under other international agreements such as the *France–Australia Maritime Co-operation Agreement* in respect of the Southern Ocean,[4] as well as piracy operations off Somalia since 2009.[5] This chapter will not address the Solomon Islands mission in any detail because the use of force in that case relied upon Solomon Islands statutory authority.[6]

Act of State doctrine would most likely be the principal plea in response to claims against the Crown arising from exercises of the external affairs prerogative, such as to enforce United Nations Security Council Resolutions. Harrison Moore's 1906 book *Act of State in English Law* defined Act of State against aliens in this way:

> To make an act of State which will oust the jurisdiction of the Court the act must be made clearly the act of the Crown, the actor being made the representative of the Crown's authority, and this requires some real and unmistakable assumption of responsibility by the Crown. Subject to this condition being satisfied, it would appear that the nature of the act is immaterial; that the essential feature of this immunity is the authority

---

3   The prerogative as to the control and disposition of the forces would be enough to authorise this, *Attorney-General v Nissan* [1970] AC 179, 195 ('*Nissan*'). As to the spectrum of noncoercive and coercive operations under United Nations authority, see B C Boss, *Law and Peace: A Legal Framework for United Nations Peacekeeping* (PhD thesis, University of Sydney, 2006) 25–65.
4   *Treaty Between the Government of Australia and the Government of the French Republic on Cooperation in the Maritime Areas Adjacent to the French Southern and Antarctic Territories (TAAF), Heard Island and the McDonald Islands*, signed 24 November 2003, [2005] ATS 6 (entered into force 1 February 2005).
5   Department of Defence, 'Operation Slipper' (2012) <www.defence.gov.au/Operations/OpManitou/>.
6   The *Facilitation of International Assistance Act 2003* (Solomon Islands) enacts the *Agreement between Solomon Islands, Australia, New Zealand, Fiji, Papua New Guinea, Samoa and Tonga Concerning the Operations and Status of the Police and Armed Forces and Other Personnel Deployed to Solomon Islands to Assist in the Restoration of Law and Order and Security*, (opened for signature 24 July 2003) [2003] ATS 17 (entry into force 24 July 2003) ('*Regional Assistance Mission to Solomon Islands Agreement*') art 6(4) grants to members of the participating armed forces 'the powers, authorities and privileges of the Solomon Islands Police Force'. This could attract the defence of lawful authority under s 43 of the *Criminal Code Act 2002* (ACT), because the Solomon Islands legislation meets the definition of a law under the Dictionary to the *Criminal Code 2002* (ACT). The legislation is also an Act of State of Solomon Islands in its own jurisdiction and cannot be questioned in an Australian court, based upon *Petrotimor Companhia de Petroleos SARL v Commonwealth* (2003) 126 FCR 354, 368–9, in which the Federal Court lacked jurisdiction to determine the exercise of a power by a foreign government within its territory, in that case the Portuguese Government in respect of its then colony in East Timor. (Please note that Solomon Islands is the official name, not *the* Solomon Islands, *Constitution of Solomon Islands 1978*.)

6. EXTERNAL SECURITY

> from which it emanates; and that the Crown can throw its shield over every act done against aliens so as to protect the actor in all proceedings, civil or criminal.[7]

Dicey had a similar view, stating that

> an act done by an English military or naval officer in a foreign country to a foreigner, previously authorised or subsequently ratified by the Crown, is an act of state, but does not constitute any breach of law for which an action can be brought against the officer in an English court.[8]

This chapter will discuss Act of State doctrine at length as an immunity doctrine to protect ADF actions under the foreign affairs prerogative, which would be a companion to the combat immunity doctrine for ADF operations in war as discussed in Chapter 5. Much uncertainty attends Act of State doctrine however, including, as for combat immunity, whether it renders matters nonjusticiable, or justiciable but providing a defence.

The Royal Australian Navy (RAN) has been stopping and boarding vessels in the Gulf, Arabian and Red Seas intermittently since 1990 to enforce United Nations Security Council Resolutions.[9] Such operations are a type of naval constabulary operation. Naval constabulary operations are coercive operations for a national or international law enforcement purpose.[10] They are quite distinct from the conduct of naval warfare. In the international law of the sea, the right of a State to enforce United Nations Security Council Resolutions, or national laws, balances against the rights afforded to states by the *Law of the Sea Convention*[11] to have their vessels exercise innocent passage[12] in territorial seas and freedom

---

7   W Harrison Moore, *Act of State in English Law* (Dutton, 1906, Rothman reprint 1987) 93–4.
8   A V Dicey, *Introduction to the Study of the Law of the Constitution* (Macmillan, 10th ed, 1959) 306 n 3.
9   SC Res 1790, UN SCOR, 5808th mtg, UN Doc S/Res/1790 (18 December 2007); SC Res 665, UN SCOR, 2938th mtg, S/Res/665 (25 August 1990); Commonwealth, *Parliamentary Debates*, House of Representatives, 4 December 1990, 4319–25 (Bob Hawke), reproduced in the 'The First Gulf War' in Rod Kemp and Marion Stanton (eds), *Speaking for Australia: Parliamentary Speeches that Shaped Our Nation* (Allen and Unwin, 2004) 253; Sea Power Centre of Australia, *Database of Royal Australian Navy Operations, 1990–2005 – Working Paper No 18* (Seapower Centre Australia, 2005) xiv and generally; Department of Defence, 'Operation Slipper'.
10   Royal Australian Navy, *Australia's Maritime Doctrine: RAN Doctrine 1 2000* (Defence Publishing Service, 2000) 65–9.
11   For the majority of States which are party to it, *Law of the Sea Convention*, (opened for signature 10 December 1982) 1833 UNTS 3 (entered into force 16 November 1994), arts 19, 110 ('*Law of the Sea Convention*').
12   Innocent passage is a limited right of surface navigation for foreign ships in the territorial sea, which extends up to 12 nautical miles from the coast, *Law of the Sea Convention*, arts 3, 17.

of navigation[13] in international waters.[14] While Australia has extensive national legislation for enforcing its coastal State rights,[15] until the *Maritime Powers Act 2013* the Parliament had been virtually silent on enforcement of United Nations Security Council Resolutions and like international instruments at sea. Such operations could only have relied upon executive power for their authority. Such Australian authorities as exist that might support this[16] do not address the modern international law of the *Charter of the United Nations* and international enforcement operations that are not war.[17] This leaves a question as to what authority there really is in Australian law to enforce international law instruments like United Nations Security Council Resolutions at sea.

The other key type of external security operation is the exercise of martial law in occupied foreign territory. Whilst closely related to martial law exercised internally, martial law in foreign territories usually arises for different reasons and does not have the same limitations. Australian military forces have exercised civilian government functions, mainly restoring or maintaining law and order in German New Guinea between 1914 and 1921, in Somalia in 1993 and in East Timor in 1999 and 2000.[18] Even though the exercise of martial law outside the realm relates closely to the war prerogative, it is functionally quite different to the conduct of war. A more accurate description might be that it is the conduct of external affairs.

Before considering these historical examples, this chapter will first consider the work of writers and the relevant authorities on the prerogative with respect to external affairs. It will then turn to an analysis of the possible sources of and limitations upon the power for the ADF to conduct external security operations. ADF external security operations are subject to contrary statutes and local law. In the face of contrary statutes, it is

---

13 Freedom of navigation is the freedom to navigate in, under and over international waters subject mainly only to the requirement to give due regard to other users. In the international law of the sea, there is a limited list of grounds upon which a State may interfere with freedom of navigation upon the high seas, such as for piracy, slavery and being without nationality, *Law of the Sea Convention*, arts 87, 90, 110.
14 See, eg, *Law of the Sea Convention*, arts 19, 110.
15 See, eg, *Maritime Powers Act 2013* (Cth); *Fisheries Management Act 1991* (Cth); *Customs Act 1901* (Cth); *Migration Act 1958* (Cth).
16 Discussed below at section 3 of part II this chapter.
17 For an early appreciation of this issue see Robert Wilson, *International and Contemporary Commonwealth Issues* (Duke University Press, 1971) 182–91.
18 All discussed below in Part III.

possible to argue that ADF external security operations are lawful through statutory interpretation; essentially the same argument as Chapter 5 made with respect to the war prerogative. As there is no Australian authority for a coercive use of the external affairs prerogative however, this chapter will argue that external operations other than war may really only be arguable as lawful by reference to English case law on Act of State doctrine and the prerogative power for external affairs. Such arguments still may not be sufficient, given the approach of *Williams* to the text and structure of the *Constitution* and the need to find authority for executive action, as well as the principle of legality more generally, as discussed in Chapter 1.

II The Authority for and Theory of External Security

A Prerogative Power

1 Legal History

Some part of the explanation for the authority to use the ADF for external operations must lie in the fact that the 17th-century compromise did not purport to limit the Crown's prerogatives beyond the realm. Prerogative power provided much of the authority for the development of the British Empire in the 17th to 19th centuries,[19] including acquisition of territory and the establishment and operation of Crown Charter Companies such as the British East India Company.[20] It was also the authority to govern many colonies,[21] as in the early years of the settlement in New South Wales.[22] It may make sense, therefore, to see external operations as a continuation of this form of power. Notably, Brennan J in *Mabo v Queensland No 2* ('*Mabo*') saw the Crown's assertion of sovereignty over

---

19 Sir Matthew Hale, *The Prerogatives of the King* (Selden Society, written between 1640 and 1664 but unpublished, D E C Yale (ed) 1976 ed) 42–4.
20 Harrison Moore, *Act of State in English Law*, above n 7, 103–7, discusses a number of cases in which the British East India Company had immunity for its sovereign acts of state as a Crown Charter Company, as opposed to its commercial activities as a trading company.
21 See Jerry Dupont, *The Common Law Abroad: Constitutional and Legal Legacy of the British Empire* (Rothman, 2001) xiii–xix. Campbell McLachlan, *Foreign Relations Law* (Cambridge University Press, 2014) critically appraises this historical development, 14–16, 276–85.
22 An order-in-council of 6 December 1786 designated New South Wales as a penal colony, Dupont, *The Common Law Abroad*, 318, but there was no legislative basis for government in the colony until the Act *4 Geo IV 1823* (the *New South Wales Act 1823* (Imp)).

parts of Australia as nonjusticiable.[23] A different historical example of the exercise of the external or foreign affairs prerogative is the unsettled and now almost certainly obsolete concept of pacific blockade. Pacific blockade was a naval blockade imposed in circumstances outside of war in order to assert diplomatic pressure.[24] Such coercive naval operations were then for the purpose of achieving a foreign affairs objective rather than being the conduct of war. Therefore, historically, the exercise of the Crown's prerogative in respect of external affairs generally has been extensive.

2 Writers

As to the writers traditionally quoted on prerogative power, Hale only addressed the extent of the King's power outside the realm of England in terms of colonies and other possessions, stating that 'the English laws were gradually introduced by the king without the concurrence of an act of parliament'.[25] This indicates that before 1689 the Crown's power beyond the realm was not subject to the law of England, except where English settlers brought the common law with them.[26] Nothing in the constitutional settlement of 1689 did anything directly to limit the Crown's power beyond the realm, other than to make it subject to any applicable Act of Parliament. Dicey stated that 'the conduct of negotiations with foreign powers and the like, are exempt from the direct control or supervision of parliament'.[27] Blackstone stated that '[w]hat is done by the royal authority, with regard to foreign powers, is the act of the whole nation',[28] for which the only accountability was to Parliament rather than the courts. He devoted ten pages to the extent of prerogative power in respect of foreign affairs.[29] Chitty devoted a chapter to colonies and another to foreign matters and stated that 'the constitution … with regard to foreign affairs … has invested his Majesty with the supreme exclusive

---

23   *Mabo v Queensland (No 2)* (1992) 175 CLR 1, 31–2, ('*Mabo*').
24   See discussion of 'Forcible Measures Short of War' in C J Colombos, *International Law of the Sea* (McKay, 6th ed, 1967), 464–74; Smith viewed pacific blockade as obsolete in 1959, H A Smith, *The Law and Custom of the Sea* (Stevens, 3rd ed, 1959) 144.
25   Hale, above n 19, 43.
26   Ibid 44.
27   Dicey, above n 8, 464.
28   *Blackstone's Commentaries with Notes of Reference, to the Constitution and Laws, of the Federal Government of the United States; and of the Commonwealth of Virginia* (1803, Hein Online reproduction) 260.
29   Ibid 251–60.

power of managing them …'[30] H A Smith wrote that the conduct of foreign affairs relied mainly upon prerogative power because 'the Courts regard foreign policy as being for the most part a matter with which they have no jurisdiction to interfere'.[31] Clode made observations on the Army beyond the realm, rather than just foreign affairs, in stating that:

> No doubt when the Army is beyond the Realm of England and the *Mutiny Act* has not been made specially applicable, then Martial Law – as it existed prior to the *Petition of Right* – prevails. In *Barwis v Keppel*,[32] the Court held that when the Army is out of the National Dominions, the Crown acts by virtue of its Prerogative and not under the *Mutiny Act* and the *Articles of War*.[33]

Consistent with the legal history, English writers traditionally have recognised then a broad prerogative with respect to external affairs generally.

As to earlier writers on the Australian law on external affairs, Evatt states that '[t]he peculiar rights of the King in relation to foreign affairs are fully recognised by the authorities', although he does not cite those authorities but rather quotes Dicey on this point.[34] Evatt's discussion gives examples of sending ambassadors, the making of treaties and making war and peace.[35] His main concern however, writing in 1924, was with the extent to which the dominions exercised the external affairs prerogative independently of the imperial government rather than the substance of that prerogative.[36] Renfree says little on the topic of executive power with respect to external affairs although he does quote *R v Burgess; Ex parte Henry* in which Latham CJ stated that '[u]nder s 61 of the *Constitution*, the Executive government of the Commonwealth can deal administratively with the external affairs of the Commonwealth …'[37] Evatt and Renfree

---

30   Joseph Chitty, *A Treatise on the Law of the Prerogatives of the Crown; and the Relative Duties and Rights of the Subject* (Butterworths, 1820) 40.
31   H A Smith, 'The Nature of Our Constitutional Law' (1920) 36 *Law Quarterly Review* 140, 146.
32   (1766) 95 ER 831; 2 Wilson, KB 314.
33   Charles Clode, *The Military Forces of the Crown: Their Administration and Government* (John Murray, 1869) 176.
34   H V Evatt, *The Royal Prerogative* (Law Book Co, first presented as a doctoral thesis 1924, with commentary by Leslie Zines, 1987) 142.
35   Ibid 143.
36   Ibid 142–69.
37   (1936) 55 CLR 608, 644, quoted in Harold Renfree, *The Executive Power of the Commonwealth of Australia* (Legal Books, 1984) 457.

do not really add much to the English writers, therefore, other than to recognise that Commonwealth executive power extends to external affairs to some extent.

As to Act of State and the use of the external affairs prerogative coercively, in addition to Moore and Dicey, quoted above, Holdsworth addressed the issue directly in his 1941 article 'The History of Acts of State in English Law'.[38] He considered various aspects of Act of State doctrine, including that relevant to this chapter, stating 'acts done outside the jurisdiction of the English courts and previously authorized or subsequently ratified by the Crown, which have damaged an alien, are acts of state'.[39]

Holdsworth identifies the authority for such acts as the Crown's prerogative in relation to foreign affairs. He cites the 1807 case of *The Rolla*[40] as the earliest example of this principle, in which an American ship breached a British pacific blockade of Monte Video. In response to an argument that the British naval commander did not have authority to impose the blockade, the court found that the British government had legitimated the blockade action insofar as it affected subjects of other countries.[41] Holdsworth also cites *Buron v Denman*,[42] discussed below, to make the point that Acts of State may occur outside of war, stating the traditional view that:

> The Crown, by virtue of its prerogative over foreign affairs, has a free hand, subject only to the risk of provoking war, in its dealings with aliens outside the jurisdiction of the English courts; and that therefore its acts done in the course of those dealings are acts of state.[43]

Lindell directly addresses the issue but in the context of war rather than external security operations. He makes clear that the traditional position is that matters of external affairs are traditionally nonjusticiable, although he notes, as discussed above, that the traditional deference of the courts in this area may be diminishing.[44] He states:

---

38   W S Holdsworth, 'The History of Acts of State in English Law' (1941) 41(8) *Columbia Law Review* 1313.
39   Ibid 1320.
40   (1807) 165 ER 963, 6 C Robinson 364.
41   Holdsworth, 'The History of Acts of State in English Law', above n 38, 1248.
42   (1848) 2 Ex 167; 154 All ER 450.
43   Holdsworth, 'The History of Acts of State in English Law', above n 38, 1321.
44   Geoffrey Lindell, *The Coalition Wars Against Iraq and Afghanistan in the Courts of the UK, Ireland and the US – Significance for Australia* (Centre for International and Public Law Policy Paper 26, Federation Press 2005), 3–6, 33–8.

[Act of State doctrine] relates to the immunity from legal liability for the exercise of prerogative powers in relation to foreign affairs ... The scope of the doctrine and the resulting immunity were uncertain even before the House of Lords established in 1985 that prerogative powers were not immune from judicial review ... and it is even more uncertain now. But I have suggested before that to the extent that any such immunity still exists, it would operate in Australia as part of the 'executive power of the Commonwealth' under s 61 of the *Australian Constitution*.[45]

It is not clear if Lindell is hinting at nationhood power being the more appropriate aspect of executive power when it comes to external affairs. It would be consistent with French J's view of executive power as 'measured by reference to Australia's status as a sovereign nation', rather than through prerogative power.[46] For the reasons put in Chapter 1 however, prerogative power in the context of the use of coercive powers by the ADF is arguably more consistent with the principle of legality.

It is worth noting at this point that, between Harrison Moore, Dicey, Holdsworth and Lindell, Act of State can appear to be a term synonymous with a coercive exercise of the external affairs prerogative (that is, a power in itself), a doctrine of immunity to protect such exercises of prerogative power from liability or an aspect of the nonjusticiability doctrine, which means that a court should not hear a matter. Act of State doctrine can even appear to be all three of these things together in this writing. As Cane states:

> It would be helpful if the term 'Act of State' were used in only one sense. In the preceding discussion, I have followed the suggestion of Lord Reid in using the term to refer only to a certain class of non-justiciable acts, namely those done in the course of foreign affairs.[47]

More recently, McLachlan limited a plea of Act of State to exclude the jurisdiction of the courts to two situations only. The first is where the matter is one of interstate relations, which can only be resolved on 'the plane of

---

45   Ibid 37. Horan also notes that Black CJ and French J rejected an argument on costs that the boarding of the MV *Tampa* was a nonjusticiable Act of State in *Ruddock v Vadarlis (No 2)* (2001) 115 FCR 229, 242 ('*Tampa Case*') in Chris Horan, 'Judicial Review of Non-statutory Executive Powers' (2003) 31(3) *Federal Law Review* 551, 557. See Chief Justice Robert French, 'Constitutional Review of Executive Decisions – Australia's US Legacy' (Speech to the Chicago Bar Association and the John Marshall Law School, 25 and 28 January 2010) (2010) 35(1) *University of Western Australia Law Review* 35.
46   *Tampa Case* (2001) 110 FCR 491, 542.
47   Peter Cane, 'Prerogative Acts, Acts of State and Justiciability' (1980) 29(4) *International and Comparative Law Quarterly* 680, 700.

international law'.⁴⁸ This is consistent with the authorities discussed below and a preferable approach to matters which are not suitable for domestic adjudication. The second is the combat immunity doctrine discussed in Chapter 5.⁴⁹ As much as this book argues that Act of State doctrine should be a companion doctrine to that of combat immunity, given the legal and operational distinction between having an enemy and not having an enemy, there is too much potential for confusion to make the doctrines synonymous.

In this sense, the writers reflect the ambiguity of the authorities and it comes then to place this discussion in the context of those authorities.

3 Authorities

The legal authority of the executive to engage in external security operations which use force and yet are not war has not been questioned in an Australian court.⁵⁰ The High Court case of *Thorpe v Commonwealth* is authority for the conduct of foreign affairs being nonjusticiable, but was a single judge decision which did not concern coercive action.⁵¹ Kirby J referred to the single judgment of Gummow J in the Federal Court in *Re Ditfort; Ex parte DCT*,⁵² which dealt at length with nonjusticiability of external affairs, although Gummow J did leave open the possibility of some matters of external affairs potentially being justiciable by virtue of s 75(v) of the *Constitution*.⁵³ Notably, *Thorpe v Commonwealth*⁵⁴ did not distinguish between claims in tort or other claims in deciding that the conduct of foreign relations is nonjusticiable.⁵⁵ This would be consistent with McLachlan's view, discussed above, of some matters being nonjusticiable as they are matters of interstate relations which can only be resolved on the plane of international law.

---

48   McLachlan, above n 21, 289–91.
49   Ibid 291–3.
50   The *Tampa Case* essentially concerned a national naval constabulary operation which relied more on a power to exclude aliens than the prerogative to conduct foreign affairs. *Tampa Case* (2001) 110 FCR 491, 542.
51   *Thorpe v Commonwealth (No 3)* (1997) 144 ALR 677, 681, citing *R v Burgess; Ex parte Henry* (1936) 55 CLR 608, n 60. See discussion in Horan, above n 45, 561 on this case concerning policy and not having immediate legal consequences and, therefore, not actually giving rise to a 'matter' over which the court could exercise jurisdiction.
52   (1988) 19 FCR 347.
53   Ibid 367–72.
54   (1997) 144 ALR 677.
55   For a discussion of the distinction see Cane, above n 47.

(a) The Relationship between International Law and Australian Law

Is a United Nations Security Council resolution enough to authorise coercive action outside Australia, such as interference with freedom of navigation in international waters or occupation of foreign territory and, if so, how? There is actually no Australian authority directly on this point. In *Bradley v Commonwealth*[56] the Commonwealth Government had sought to cut mail and telephone services to the Rhodesia Information Office in Sydney. Barwick CJ and Gibbs J rejected the view that Security Council resolutions which had not been given legislative recognition in Australia justified such executive action within Australia which would otherwise have been unlawful.[57] The case did not address the issue of the authority of United Nations Security Council Resolutions outside of Australia, however.

International law essentially involves obligations between nation states. Australia's international treaty obligations, therefore, are not a direct part of Australian law unless incorporated into legislation.[58] Unless required to do so by Australian law then, an ADF commander is also not personally legally bound nor empowered to observe Australia's international legal obligations. Parliament can legislate contrary to Australia's international legal obligations as well, provided that it does so with words which clearly express this intention.[59] There is no explicit general requirement in Australian law for operations authorised under prerogative power to conform to Australia's international legal obligations either.[60]

Act of State doctrine relates to the conduct of external affairs so, while international law cannot directly authorise or limit an ADF external security operation, it might inform the substance of the external affairs

---

56 (1973) 128 CLR 557.
57 *Bradley v Commonwealth* (1973) 128 CLR 557, 583. The Cole Inquiry in 2005 also heard argument that United Nations Security Council Resolutions are not part of Australian law, 'Joint Opinion of James Renwick and Christopher Ward on the Status of United Nations Resolutions and Sanctions in Australian Domestic Law of 9 December 2005', Commonwealth of Australia, *Inquiry into Certain Australian Companies in Relation to the UN Oil for Food Programme* (2006) Appendix 1.
58 *Chow Hung Ching v R* (1948) 77 CLR 449, 471; *Bradley v Commonwealth* (1973) 128 CLR 557, 583; see Chief Justice Robert French, 'Oil and Water? International and Domestic Law in Australia' published in Mary Hiscock and William van Caenegem (eds), *The Internationalisation of Law: Legislating, Decision-making, Practice and Education* (Edward Elgar, 2010) 211.
59 *Horta v Commonwealth* (1994) 181 CLR 183, 195–6.
60 See discussion by Geoffrey Lindell in 'Judicial Review of International Affairs' in Brian Opeskin and Donald Rothwell (eds), *International Law and Australian Federalism* (Melbourne University Press, 1997) 160 and also McLachlan, above n 21, 124–5.

prerogative and the extent to which Act of State doctrine might protect actions under it. This chapter will, therefore, consider the way in which international law might for this purpose be a 'source'[61] or 'a legitimate and important influence on the common law, especially when international law declares the existence of universal human rights'.[62] This is because international law enforcement instruments authorising Australia's action in a particular operation, such as United Nations Security Council Resolutions, are the clearest indicator of what the foreign policy purpose of an ADF mission is.

(b) Act of State Doctrine

It comes now to consider the authorities on Act of State doctrine.[63] There are a number of aspects to the doctrine,[64] such as concerning the acts of foreign sovereigns within their own jurisdiction,[65] but this chapter is primarily concerned with prerogative acts against aliens beyond the realm. It is important because, much as with the war prerogative, it is where international law meets prerogative power. The most cited case of *Buron v Denman*[66] is on point because it concerned a Royal Navy torching of a Spanish-owned slaving business in West Africa and the liberation of its slaves. This was not an act of war. The British government ratified this action as an Act of State and so no action could be maintained against the Royal Navy captain, meaning that the matter was nonjusticiable.[67]

---

61 *Chow Hung Ching v R* (1948) 77 CLR 449, 477, Dixon J citing J L Brierly in (1935) 51 *Law Quarterly Review* 31, cited by I A Shearer, 'The Relationship Between International Law and Domestic Law' in Opeskin and Rothwell (eds), *International Law and Australian Federalism* (Melbourne University Press, 1997) 49.
62 *Mabo* (1992) 175 CLR 1, 55.
63 See Lindell, 'Judicial Review of International Affairs', above n 60, 190–1.
64 See generally Harrison Moore, *Act of State in English Law*, above n 7.
65 *Petrotimor Companhia de Petroleos SARL v Commonwealth* (2003) 126 FCR 354. For a failure on the part of the Commonwealth to have a matter dismissed as concerning nonjusticiable Acts of State of foreign governments see *Habib v Commonwealth* (2010) 183 FCR 62 ('*Habib*'). This is also the aspect of the doctrine with which *Plaintiff M68 v Minister for Immigration and Border Protection* [2016] HCA 1 ('*M68*') was concerned, being the validity of the laws of Nauru and which none of the judgments would address, although the case did not use the term 'Act of State' except in the headnote.
66 (1848) 2 Ex 167; 154 All ER 450. See Moore, *Act of State in English Law*, above n 7, 94; For some discussion of Commander Denman's anti-slaving campaign see Humphrey Fisher, 'Book Review: Johnson Asiegbu, *Slavery and the Politics of Liberation 1787–1861: A Study of Liberated African Emigration and British Anti-Slavery Policy*' (1971) 34(1) *Bulletin of the School of Oriental and African Studies, University of London* 188, 188–90. For a critique of this case, Act of State doctrine and the United States position, particularly in its occupation of Cuba, see Howard Thayer Kingsbury, 'The "Act of State" Doctrine' (1910) 4(2) *American Journal of International Law* 359, particularly 361–2.
67 (1848) 154 Ex 167; All ER 450, 459. See discussion in Lindell, 'Judicial Review of International Affairs', above n 60, 90–1 as well as Lindell, *The Coalition Wars*, above n 44, 33–7 and in McLachlan, above n 21, 281–5, who strongly doubts the contemporary value of this case.

The 2007 case of *Hicks v Ruddock*[68] indicated that Act of State doctrine in Australia today is not so certain, although it was a single judge decision on an application for summary judgment.[69] It concerned Mr Hick's internment without trial by the United States in the notorious Guantanamo Bay Naval Base in Cuba after having been captured in Afghanistan. The United States' view was that he was fighting for the Taliban, the military organisation with whom United States and Australian forces were fighting there.[70] Mr Hicks sought an order of habeas corpus and judicial review of the Commonwealth's decision not to request his release.[71] The Commonwealth argued that the actions of the United States were Acts of State, being sovereign acts of a foreign government,[72] a different aspect of Act of State doctrine than this chapter considers. The Commonwealth also argued that the matter was nonjusticiable as it concerned foreign relations.[73] Tamberlin J did not accept the Commonwealth's arguments in support of its application for summary judgment, stating:

> The modern law in relation to the meaning of 'justiciable' and the extent to which the court will examine executive action in the area of foreign relations and Acts of State is far from settled, black-letter law … There are no bright lines which foreclose, at this pleading stage, the arguments sought to be advanced in the present case.[74]

This case was an interlocutory matter and primarily concerned the Acts of State of a foreign government outside of Australia, rather than the Acts of State of Australia outside of Australia. Nonetheless, it did see the area of foreign relations as potentially justiciable and Act of State doctrine as unsettled generally, not just in respect of the aspect of the doctrine before the court.[75]

---

68 (2007) 156 FCR 574; see Marley Zelinka, '*Hicks v Ruddock* versus *The United States v Hicks*' (2007) 29(3) *Sydney Law Review* 527.
69 *Hicks v Ruddock* (2007) 156 FCR 574, 576.
70 Ibid 577.
71 Ibid 576.
72 Ibid 576.
73 Ibid 576.
74 Ibid 600.
75 McMillan notes the lack of success in arguing Act of State in the *Tampa Case* (2001) 110 FCR 491 in John McMillan, 'Comments on the Justiciability of the Government's Tampa Actions' (2002) 13(2) *Public Law Review* 85, 90 (titled *The Tampa Issue*).

The 2004 case of *Ali v Commonwealth* had also earlier questioned whether Act of State doctrine was a part of Australian law.[76] It concerned an interlocutory step in the Supreme Court of Victoria in a claim for false imprisonment in Nauru by agents of the Commonwealth. It is the only case known to the author which concerns coercive action by the Commonwealth pursuant to its prerogative to conduct foreign relations.[77] Bongiorno J declined to accept immediately that Act of State doctrine provided immunity from suit:

> *Buron v Denman*[78] has been accepted as correct by English courts … although not for the proposition contended for in this case. There is, therefore, no authority directly binding upon this Court which would compel its being applied in this case with respect to the act of state doctrine with which it is concerned. Mr Burnside QC's submissions on behalf of the plaintiffs have focused on a number of matters which he contends lead to the conclusion that it does not represent the common law of this country at this time. He submitted that at the time it was decided notions of Crown immunity from suit were, as yet, unaffected by later statutory reforms so that redress in respect of actions which would have constituted torts if committed by a private citizen went unredressed when committed by the Crown. More importantly he referred to the different constitutional position of the Crown in Australia in 2004 compared to that of the Crown in England almost 160 years earlier by reference to the joint judgment of Gummow and Kirby JJ in *The Commonwealth v Mewett*[79] in which their Honours said at 545:
>
> 'What then was the consequence of the introduction of Ch III of the Constitution? The establishment of the judicial power of the Commonwealth as an essential element in the federal system meant that doctrines of executive immunity from curial process which had been developed in England could not be carried immediately into the federal system. Chapter III required adjudication upon "matters" of a nature unknown in England. It also required that in Australia the common law be informed by the structure of and institutions established by the *Constitution*. This, by covering cl 5 thereof, was made binding on the courts, judges and people of every State and of every part of the Commonwealth "notwithstanding anything in the laws of any State".'[80]

---

76 *Ali v Commonwealth* [2004] VSC 6 (Unreported, Bongiorno J, 23 January 2004).
77 As opposed to *M68* [2016] HCA 1, which concerned executive power to expel aliens.
78 (1848) 2 Ex 167.
79 (1997) 191 CLR 471.
80 *Ali v Commonwealth* [2004] VSC 6 (Unreported, Bongiorno J, 23 January 2004).

6. EXTERNAL SECURITY

If Act of State doctrine did apply, it could render a Commonwealth action immune from liability but the court would need to hear evidence and argument to determine if that was the case, hence making it justiciable. For reasons unknown to the author, there is no record of *Ali v Commonwealth* proceeding further.[81]

Turning to the 2010 case of *Habib v Commonwealth* ('*Habib*') discussed in Chapter 1, while Black CJ stated that 'it was not in contention that [Act of State doctrine] forms part of the common law of Australia', he did say that its scope is in dispute.[82] *Habib* was also concerned with the justiciability of acts of state of foreign governments, and the extent of the complicity of Commonwealth officers in alleged acts of torture. Torture is an offence against Australian law for which any public official anywhere in the world is liable to prosecution in an Australian court without any particular connection to Australia.[83] Jagot J said that it reflected Parliament's 'extreme revulsion' for torture.[84] Given the necessary implication of the purpose of the statute, there is no scope to argue that acts of torture could ever be justified as lawful exercises of the foreign affairs prerogative. As Jagot J stated, '[A]ct of state doctrine yields to any contrary Parliamentary intention'.[85] In approving of *Habib* generally, in the 2014 case of *Belhaj v Straw* the Court of Appeal of England and Wales (Civil Division), described *Habib* as a case having 'facts which bear a striking resemblance to those in the present case' and stated that 'we should add that we find the judgment of Jagot J compelling'.[86]

In dealing with the extreme and clearly unlawful act of torture the case does not therefore really clarify the extent to which Act of State doctrine could apply to coercive, yet lawful, exercises of executive power by the Commonwealth outside of Australia pursuant to the foreign affairs prerogative. Perram J, however, was forceful in stating:

---

81 Ibid.
82 (2010) 183 FCR 62, 66. Perram J made similar comments, 77.
83 *Criminal Code Act 1995* s 274.2, other sections on torture are referred to below.
84 *Habib* (2010) 183 FCR 62, 96 citing *Jones v Saudi Arabia* [2007] 1 AC 270, [15].
85 Ibid 98.
86 [2014] EWCA Civ 1394 [96]–[102]. The UK Supreme Court dismissed the government's appeal in this in *Belhaj v Straw; Rahmatullah (No 1) v Ministry of Defence* [2017] UKSC 3 (the appeals being heard together). Again, this case arose before publication but after the date which this book reflects the law until, being 28 March 2016.

To the extent that act of state doctrine would confer immunity from suit on the Commonwealth it is inconsistent with the constitutional orthodoxy of this country and its application is to be rejected in a fashion as complete as it is emphatic.[87]

It is quite likely that this statement does reflect the law with respect to immunity from suit but not necessarily with respect to immunity from liability. It might also not extend to matters more of a policy nature which do not directly impact upon individuals and which do not give rise to a 'matter', such entering into a treaty as in *Thorpe v Commonwealth* discussed above.[88]

The Australian cases indicate a divergence between Australian and English law on this point. The United Kingdom does not have a written or federal constitution nor does it have an equivalent of Chapter III concerning judicial power. Nonetheless, it is significant that even without these constitutional elements, the United Kingdom Attorney-General was also unsuccessful in a plea of Act of State in *Nissan*[89] before the House of Lords in 1970 in relation to the British Army's acquisition of a hotel in Cyprus, which was owned by the British subject who brought the action.[90] Lord Morris stated the conceptual difficulty with Act of State doctrine:

> I do not view with favour a rule which can give immunity if wrongful acts are done abroad but no immunity if such acts are done in this country and even if done to a resident foreigner. The general principle has been that if a wrong is of such a character that it would have been actionable if committed in England and if the act is not justifiable by the law of the place where it was committed then an action may be founded in this country.[91]

Lindell also refers to the 2004 case of *Bici v Ministry of Defence* ('*Bici*')[92] in which the United Kingdom did not rely on the doctrine in relation to negligent shooting of Kosovan civilians by British forces operating under a United Nations Security Council Resolution.[93] Notably Elias J was the sole judge in this matter and later gave judgment in *Al-Jedda v Secretary of State for Defence* ('*Al-Jedda*'),[94] discussed below.

---

87   Ibid 74.
88   (1997) 144 ALR 677, 681.
89   [1970] AC 179; see Lindell, 'Judicial Review of International Affairs', above n 60, 191.
90   *Attorney-General v Nissan* [1970] AC 179, 179 ('*Nissan*').
91   Ibid 195; see R J Whitington, 'Case Comment: Act of State – *Attorney-General v Nissan*' (1970) 3 *Adelaide Law Review* 522.
92   *Bici v Ministry of Defence* [2004] EWHC 786.
93   Lindell, *The Coalition Wars*, above n 44, 37.
94   [2011] 2 WLR 225.

6. EXTERNAL SECURITY

The 2000 United Kingdom Court of Appeal case of *R v Secretary of State; Ex parte Thring* ('*Thring*'), concerning Royal Air Force enforcement of a no-fly zone over Iraq in the 1990s, did give clear support to Act of State doctrine in English law.[95] The judgment cited *Buron v Denman*[96] and the *CCSU Case*[97] in deciding that the matter was nonjusticiable.[98] It should be treated with some caution however as the plaintiff was a British taxpayer who objected to taxes being spent on an operation that he argued violated the law of armed conflict. The lack of a clear cause of action meant that the case was likely to have been decided differently than if it was brought by a person who had suffered loss or damage directly as a result of the bombing.

There is a distinction however between *Bici*[99] and *Nissan*[100] on one hand and *Thring*[101] on the other. *Bici*[102] concerned negligent acts and *Nissan*[103] concerned incidental acts, whereas *Thring*[104] concerned deliberate acts directly pursuant to Britain's foreign policy. As this chapter will discuss, this indicates that Act of State doctrine could operate to protect actions for the purpose of achieving the foreign policy objective—that is, the mission— whether justiciable or not, and not negligent actions or incidental acts insufficiently connected to the mission, which should be justiciable. This is consistent with Cane's view, who argued in his analysis of *Nissan* that Acts of State are exercises of prerogative power in relation to foreign affairs.[105] An Act of State is both a defence to a claim in tort and a doctrine of nonjusticiability when seen as a lawful exercise of this prerogative.[106] Where an act does not have the character of an exercise of the foreign affairs prerogative, then it should not attract Act of State immunity and should be justiciable.[107] Lord Wilberforce illustrated the problem in *Nissan* in a way that points to the potential significance of the relevant

---

95 *R v Secretary of State; Ex parte Thring*, Court of Appeal (Civil Division) (Unreported, Pill, Clarke, Bennett LJJ, 20 July 2000) per Pill LJ ('*Thring*').
96 (1848) 2 Ex 167.
97 *Council of the Civil Service Unions v Minister for the Civil Service* [1985] AC 374, 405–406.
98 *Thring*, Court of Appeal (Civil Division) (Unreported, Pill, Clarke, Bennett LJJ, 20 July 2000) Pill LJ, 4, Bennett J, 6.
99 [2004] EWHC 786.
100 [1970] AC 179.
101 Court of Appeal (Civil Division) (Unreported, Pill, Clarke, Bennett LJJ, 20 July 2000).
102 [2004] EWHC 786.
103 [1970] AC 179.
104 Court of Appeal (Civil Division) (Unreported, Pill, Clarke, Bennett LJJ, 20 July 2000).
105 [1970] AC 179.
106 Cane, above n 47, 681–2.
107 Ibid 694–700.

international law instrument,[108] in this case the agreement between the British and Cypriot governments, as informing the application of Act of State doctrine:

> Between these acts and the pleaded agreement with the government of Cyprus the link is altogether too tenuous, indeed it is not even sketched out; if accepted as sufficient to attract the description of act of state it would cover with immunity an endless and indefinite series of acts, judged by the officers in command of the troops to be necessary, or desirable, in their interest. That I find entirely unacceptable.[109]

Importantly, obiter dicta in *Al-Jedda* took up this point.[110] Mr Al-Jedda was a dual British and Iraqi national. The issue of his internment by British forces in Iraq from 2004 for security reasons, without charge or conviction, was the subject of a number of actions and appeals. The 2007 case in the House of Lords turned on the application of the *Human Rights Act 1998* (UK).[111] It considered the extent to which the United Kingdom's obligations under *United Nations Security Council Resolution 1546* in relation to Iraq displaced obligations under that Act up until the commencement of the *Constitution of Iraq* in May 2006.[112] A 2011 case in the European Court of Human Rights turned on international human rights law questions and found that Mr Al-Jedda's ongoing internment was a breach of his right to liberty as it could not be indefinite.[113]

The case which this chapter will consider went before the Court of Appeal in England in 2010 and concerned Mr Al-Jedda's internment after the commencement of the *Constitution of Iraq* in May 2006.[114] As a result of the operation of the *Private International Law (Miscellaneous Provisions) Act 1995* (UK), Iraqi law applied to Mr Al-Jedda's internment, and the court found that Iraqi law authorised that internment.[115] The statute

---

108 [1970] AC 179.
109 Ibid 210; see discussion in Peter Rowe, *Defence: The Legal Implications: Military Law and the Laws of War* (Brassey's, 1987) 4.
110 [2011] 2 WLR 225.
111 *R (On the Application of Al-Jedda) v Secretary of State for Defence* [2008] 1 AC 332.
112 See Bruce Oswald CSC, 'Detention of Civilians on Military Operations: Reasons for and Challenges to Developing a Special Law of Detention' (2008) 32(2) *Melbourne University Law Review* 524, 537.
113 *Al-Jedda v United Kingdom* (2011) 53 EHRR 23.
114 There were also other proceedings involving the UK Home Secretary taking away Mr Al-Jedda's British citizenship, *Al-Jedda v Secretary of State for the Home Department* [2012] EWCA Civ 358.
115 *Al-Jedda* [2011] 2 WLR 225.

law in question is not directly relevant to this chapter but two of the judgments gave notable obiter dicta consideration to Act of State doctrine, prerogative power and the international law issues.

Arden LJ did not see the occupation of Iraq post the invasion of 2003 as an extension of the war prerogative but, due to a relevant United Nations Security Council resolution, as an Act of State pursuant to the international obligations of the United Kingdom:

> Firstly, in my judgment, *Al-Jedda (No 1)* established that the United Kingdom was entitled and bound under its obligations under article 103 of the UN Charter to intern persons where this was necessary for the internal security of Iraq. Internment for this purpose would clearly qualify as an act of state. My conclusion that act of state is a defence here does not go wider than this. It applies, in my judgment, because of the overriding force of UNSCR 1546. If courts hold states liable in damages when they comply with resolutions of the UN designed to secure international peace and security, the likelihood is that states will be less ready to assist the UN achieve its role in this regard, and this would be detrimental to the long-term interests of the states.[116]

In this judgment, Act of State was a defence rather than a doctrine of nonjusticiability. Further, Act of State immunity could apply even to actions against a British national:

> Secondly, the fact that Mr Al-Jedda is a British national is not, in my judgment, a bar to the raising of the defence of act of state in respect of acts done abroad as part of a general policy of internment carried out under the authority of the UN for imperative reasons of security.[117]

Arden LJ also distinguished *Nissan* in this way:

> [T]he *Nissan* case [1970] AC 179 is in my judgment clearly distinguishable. It was no part of the peacekeeping function of the troops to take property without paying for it. In the present case, internment was part of the role which the British contingent of the MNF [multi-national force] were specifically required to carry out. The acceptance and carrying out of those obligations was an exercise of sovereign power. It is inevitable that a detainee would suffer the loss of his liberty while he was detained.[118]

---

116 Ibid 253.
117 Ibid 254.
118 Ibid.

Dyson JSC declined to address the Act of State issue. Elias LJ did agree that the internment of Mr Al-Jedda was an Act of State for the reasons which Arden LJ gave but did not agree with Arden LJ on the point of Act of State doctrine creating immunity even with respect to British nationals abroad.[119] The Act of State argument on behalf of the Crown therefore failed but Elias LJ gave a considered suggestion on the issue of whether the Crown could exercise prerogative powers against its own subjects abroad:

> An alternative approach, more in line with current concepts of the relationship between the courts and the Crown, may be to recognise that whilst the state in pursuance of its treaty obligations may have the power to detain as an exercise of prerogative power, none the less the court can question the way in which that power is exercised as it can any other exercise of prerogative power, at least where, as here, the act is in principle amenable to the court's jurisdiction. I see no reason in principle why the courts ought not to be able to review an act of the executive interfering with personal liberty in order to test whether its actions have been lawful by the appropriate application of traditional judicial review principles. The court could, for example, satisfy itself that detention is proportionate to the risks at stake, and ensure at least elementary principles of fairness in the detention process.[120]

Elias J, therefore, saw the action as justiciable, although the court may still find it a lawful exercise of prerogative power.

The judgments of Arden and Elias LJJ together actually appeared to offer a way forward for the law of both England and Australia on Act of State doctrine and prerogative power. However, Rowe was of the view that Act of State doctrine is unlikely to authorise the detention of foreign nationals in foreign territory. He only cited Elias J on detaining a British national[121] and *Nissan*[122] to support this view however, and his paper was also primarily concerned with international law but nonetheless showed some prescience in respect of the later decision in *Serdar Mohammed*.[123]

---

119 Ibid 274.
120 Ibid.
121 Peter Rowe, 'Is there a Right to Detain Civilians by Foreign Armed Forces during a Non-international Armed Conflict?' (2012) 61 *International and Comparative Law Quarterly* 697, 707–8 at n 62 citing *Al-Jedda v Secretary of State for Defence* [2010] EWCA Civ 758, Elias LJ, [213] (which is the same case as [2011] 2 WLR 225 cited in the Introduction at n 22).
122 Rowe, ibid, n 61 citing *Nissan* [1970] AC 179, Lord Reid at 213.
123 *Serdar Mohammed v Secretary of State for Defence* [2015] EWCA Civ 843 [217] ('*Serdar Mohammed*').

6. EXTERNAL SECURITY

As mentioned in Chapter 1, *Serdar Mohammed* was a 2015 decision of the England and Wales Court of Appeal (Civil Division) concerning the detention of Mr Mohammed by the British Army in Afghanistan in 2010.[124] The case also joined other claims relating to detention by the British Army in Afghanistan and Iraq.[125] As in *Al-Jedda*, it turned primarily on the application of the *Human Rights Act 1998* (UK) in respect of public law claims but also considered Act of State doctrine in respect of private law claims in tort for false imprisonment.[126] As opposed to the obiter dicta of *Al-Jedda*, the judgment in *Serdar Mohammed* gave extensive consideration to Act of State doctrine after hearing full argument.[127] For this reason it is worthy of full consideration as a recent and persuasive common-law authority.

The issue most relevant to this discussion was whether the Secretary of State could justify detention of Mr Mohammed beyond 96 hours by the defence of Act of State, given that there was no authority in Afghan, international or English law for the detention.[128] The Court determined that 'Crown' or 'domestic' Act of State, as opposed to the Act of State of a foreign government, had two aspects.[129] The first aspect concerned justiciability; that is to say whether the matter is suitable for a decision by the court. The second aspect of Act of State was a defence to a claim in tort. As to the first aspect, the Court determined that 'there is no requirement here to adjudicate on questions of policy in the absence of "judicial and manageable standards" suitable for application by the courts' and it would 'not be required to rule on the legality or otherwise of high level policy decisions such as whether to participate in the multi-national force.'[130] Instead,

> [o]n the contrary, the court is well equipped to deal with such issues, albeit arising under the law of a foreign state. As the [trial] judge observed, determining whether an individual has been unlawfully deprived of his liberty is quintessentially a matter for a court[131]

---

124 [2015] EWCA Civ 843 [1]–[5].
125 Ibid [11]–[27].
126 Ibid [8]–[10].
127 Ibid [299]–[376].
128 Ibid [300]–[301].
129 Ibid [310]–[311].
130 Ibid [323].
131 Ibid.

and that justiciability 'must be determined by the court on the basis of the subject matter in dispute'.[132] The Court therefore rejected an argument that the nonjusticiability aspect of Act of State doctrine barred the private law claim in tort of Mr Mohammed.[133] In so doing, the Court also stated that 'the observations in *Al-Jedda* on the applicability of the act of state principle cannot be justified on grounds of non-justiciability'.[134] This position is consistent with the argument made in Chapter 5 of this book, and also in relation to *Habib* above, with respect to nonjusticiability. The remaining issue then is Act of State as a defence to a claim in tort.

As a matter of principle, the Court saw that there are important public policy reasons for maintaining the defence of Act of State, even if only on a very limited basis, stating:

> Notwithstanding the fact that the subject matter may be justiciable, there will be circumstances in which it will be essential that our courts should have a residual power to bar claims founded on foreign law on grounds of public policy. Thus, for example, if *Buron v Denman* fell for decision today, the claim for compensation for loss of the claimant's slaves and damage to his slaving activities would unhesitatingly be rejected, if on no other ground, on the basis that property rights in slaves arising in foreign law should not be recognised and that to afford such a remedy in such circumstances would be offensive to the public policy of this country. However, we would expect that, in circumstances in which the claim is justiciable, such a bar on grounds of act of state would be infrequently applied, and the absence of decided cases supports this view.[135]

The Court preferred a more nuanced rule, asking instead:

> [W]hether, in the particular circumstances of each case, there are compelling considerations of public policy which would require the court to deny a claim in tort founded on an act of the Executive performed abroad.[136]

This is a more realistic rule which favours the principle of legality and eschews arbitrariness, while still retaining scope for a court to recognise that some coercive acts in external security operations may actually uphold the international rule of law. It is worth noting that the Court acknowledged that Act of State could be a defence to a criminal act as well.[137]

---

132 Ibid [324].
133 Ibid [330].
134 Ibid [331].
135 Ibid [349].
136 Ibid [359].
137 Ibid [311], [337].

In applying this rule to Mr Mohammed's claim, the Court considered that the British detention policy was outside and contrary to that set by the International Security Assistance Force, under authority granted by the relevant United Nations Security Council Resolutions.[138] The British policy was also contrary to Afghan law and, despite the purpose of the mission being to assist the Afghan Government which retained responsibility for law and order, the Secretary of State did not seek alteration to provisions of the United Kingdom/Afghanistan Memorandum of Understanding nor Afghan law.[139] Further, notably, the Secretary of State did not put proposals for relevant legislation to the United Kingdom Parliament.[140] The Court could 'therefore see no compelling considerations of public policy which prevent reliance on Afghan law as the basis of the claims in tort brought in these proceedings.'[141] In applying this rule to the other claimants detained in Iraq the Court drew a different conclusion in that United Nations Security Council Resolutions applicable to Iraq created an obligation on the United Kingdom to detain or intern 'for imperative reasons of security'.[142] In providing guidance to the tribunal which would subsequently deal with the Iraq claims, noting that this was an appeal on a question of law only, the Court stated:

> The existence of such an obligation would, at the very least, be support for the view that the court is here concerned with policy in the conduct of foreign relations. Moreover, this would, in our view, be a highly relevant consideration, notwithstanding that the relevant obligations in international law have not been given effect in domestic law within the United Kingdom.[143]

The lesson for the ADF appears to be then, should an Australian court apply this precedent, that any coercive action under the external affairs prerogative must be in accordance with the applicable international law authority for the operation, such as a United Nations Security Council Resolution, and should also be in accordance with local law except where compelling considerations of public policy prevent reliance upon that law. Australia's international human rights obligations should

---

138 Ibid [363].
139 Ibid.
140 Ibid.
141 Ibid [364].
142 Ibid [368]. *Al-Waheed v Ministry of Defence; Mohammed v Ministry of Defence* [2017] UKSC 2 moved back from this position only in that the UNSCR gave an authorisation to detain even if it did not create an obligation (Lord Sumption) [20].
143 Ibid [363].

inform these policy considerations. Further, the government may need to seek authority from Parliament for such action. Noting the strong statements against executive detention outside war in *CPCF v Minister for Immigration and Border Protection* and *M68* discussed in Chapter 1, this appears to be a realistic application of Act of State doctrine and one which ADF operations in Somalia and East Timor may have satisfied, although there may be some equivocation in respect of seeking the authority of Parliament.

It is interesting that the Court in *Serdar Mohammed* did not state the basis upon which British forces could have targeted and killed Mr Mohammed, a Taliban commander, although it did acknowledge that it could have been lawful for British forces to do so.[144] It did not state that it was the war prerogative, even though the international law with respect to noninternational armed conflict applied.[145] The Court therefore either did not address this point because it did not need to or because the implicit basis was actually the foreign affairs prerogative, for which the defence of Act of State would be available. Given that the Court itself notes the lack of authority since *Buron v Denman* for such coercive action,[146] as quoted above, it is preferable that the offensive use of lethal force against Mr Mohammed would instead be a matter for the war prerogative and the combat immunity doctrine. This approach would also be consistent with the decision in the 'Commando Court Martial', which applied the combat immunity doctrine to operations in Afghanistan in 2009.[147]

This chapter will return to questions of Act of State doctrine after considering its Australian constitutional setting and Australia's practice on the coercive use of the external affairs prerogative. It might help to draw conclusions on the doctrine after discussing the extent of the ADF's coercive use of the external affairs prerogative in operations.

---

144 Ibid [213], [237], [240], [243], [252].
145 Ibid. *Al-Waheed* [2017] UKSC 2 likewise did not address this point.
146 Ibid [349].
147 Transcript of Proceedings, *Sergeant J and Lance-Corporal D*, Australian Defence Force General Court Martial Pre-trial Directions Hearing, Brigadier Westwood, Chief Judge Advocate, 20 May 2011, 1–3, 36.

6. EXTERNAL SECURITY

B Australian Constitutional Considerations

Before discussing the Australian practice of external security operations, it is worth noting that, in the Australian constitutional context, external security operations being outside the realm arguably do not intrude directly upon the limits imposed by the *Constitution* as discussed in Chapters 1 to 4 of this book. The conduct of military operations beyond the realm does not interfere with civilian government functions within Australia. There is also a presumption that legislation does not apply extraterritorially without express words.[148] At the same time, the power of the Commonwealth Parliament to legislate extraterritorially does not interfere directly with the States[149] and it follows that neither does the extraterritorial application of executive power. The presumption against extraterritorial application of legislation also reflects that external executive action does not intrude upon the sphere of Parliament.

Within the theory of the separation of powers, in determining whether there is scope for the prerogative to operate outside the realm, necessity is less of a factor. Geographic externality is usually enough because there is less direct competition between the executive and legislative branches in the external sphere.[150] If Parliament does legislate for an external matter then

---

148 *Jumbunna Coal Mine NL v Victorian Coal Miner's Association* (1908) 6 CLR 309, 363.
149 *Seas and Submerged Lands Case* (1975) 135 CLR 337, 373.
150 It is notable that externality alone is a sufficient basis for the exercise of Commonwealth legislative power under s 51 (xxix) of the *Constitution, Polyukhovich v R* (1991) 172 CLR 501, 531 (Mason CJ), 599 (Deane J), 632–4 (Dawson J), 713 (McHugh J), 696 (Gaudron J), applied in *Horta v Commonwealth* (1994) 181 CLR 183, 194 (per curiam). In respect of the legislative aspect of the power, Rothwell states that 'The power has extensive application in regard to matters, things, events, or persons physically external to Australia', in Donald Rothwell, 'The High Court and the External Affairs Power: A Consideration of its Inner and Outer Limits' (1993) 15 *Adelaide Law Review* 209, 237. Murray said of *XYZ v Commonwealth* (2006) 227 CLR 532 that 'The *XYZ* case has only confirmed the breadth of the "geographic externality" aspect [of the external affairs power]' in Sarah Murray 'Back to ABC after XYZ: Should We Be Concerned About "International Concern"?' (2007) 35(2) *Federal Law Review* 315, 326. Edson, on the other hand, argues that 'the decision [*XYZ*] cast fresh doubt upon the principle of geographic externality' on the basis that three justices dissented on the extent (Kirby J) or existence (Callinan and Heydon JJ) of the principle, in Elise Edson 'Section 51(xxix) of the Australian *Constitution* and "Matters of International Concern:" Is There Anything to be Concerned About?' (2008) 29(2) *Adelaide Law Review* 269, 313. However, Twomey, despite also raising 'serious questions about its cogency' concludes that '*XYZ* was another re-endorsement of the geographical externality interpretation of s 51(xxix)' in Anne Twomey 'Geographic Externality and Extraterritoriality: *XYZ v Commonwealth*' (2006) 17 *Public Law Review* 253, 263. If externality is a sufficient basis for the exercise of the legislative power with respect to external affairs under s 51 (xxix) it is relevant in considering the extent of the prerogative with respect to external affairs which, to be consistent with *Williams v Commonwealth* (2012) 248 CLR 156 ('*Williams*'), cannot be assumed to be as extensive as the legislative power and therefore cannot be more extensive.

the executive is bound,[151] subject to the requirement for express words with respect both to extraterritoriality and limiting prerogative power.[152] Where there is no applicable legislation there need be no determination as to the necessity for responding to a particular issue in order for there to be room for the executive to exercise prerogative power. The main legal constraint on external exercises of power, therefore, is whatever statutory law applies extraterritorially, such as the *Defence Force Discipline Act 1982* (Cth), the *Criminal Code Act 1995* (Cth) and the *Crimes at Sea Act 2000* (Cth). The ADF also remains subject to the jurisdiction of Australian courts as discussed in Chapter 2. This is not to argue that if there is a prerogative with respect to foreign or external affairs that, therefore, the Commonwealth executive may do anything outside of Australia any person could do or which the Commonwealth might legislate upon. To be consistent with the principle of legality, and particularly *Williams*,[153] it is still necessary to argue that the prerogative authorises the action in question. This is the task of the remainder of this chapter. The judgments in *CPCF*[154] and *M68* only emphasise this concern. As Gageler J stated in *M68*:

> The Executive Government and any officer or agent of the Executive Government acting in the ostensible exercise of his or her de facto authority is always amenable to habeas corpus under s 75(iii) of the Constitution.[155] Habeas corpus is in addition available as an incident of the exercise of the jurisdiction of the High Court under s 75(v) of the Constitution in any matter in which mandamus, prohibition or an injunction is bona fide claimed against any officer of the Commonwealth.[156] That inherent constitutional incapacity of the Executive Government of the Commonwealth to authorise or enforce a deprivation of liberty is a limitation on the depth of the *non-prerogative* non-statutory executive power of the Commonwealth conferred by s 61 of the Constitution [emphasis added].[157]

With this theoretical background, it comes now to analyse the practice of ADF external security operations.

---

151 *R v Burgess; Ex parte Henry* (1936) 55 CLR 608, 657–9; *Habib* (2010) 183 FCR 62, 98 (Jagot J).
152 *Barton v Commonwealth* (1974) 131 CLR 477, 508; *Tampa Case* (2001) 110 FCR 491, 540. See D C Pearce and R S Geddes, *Statutory Interpretation in Australia* (Lexis Nexis Butterworths, 7th ed, 2011) 174–7, 181.
153 (2012) 248 CLR 156.
154 *CPCF v Minister for Immigration and Border Protection* [2015] HCA 1 ('*CPCF*'), [45] (French CJ), [96] (Hayne and Bell JJ), [196], [218] (Crennan J), [380] (Gageler J); [453] (Keane J).
155 *R v Davey; Ex parte Freer* (1936) 56 CLR 381, 384–5; *Chu Kheng Lim v Minister for Immigration, Local Government and Ethnic Affairs* (1992) 176 CLR 1, 20.
156 *Re Refugee Review Tribunal; Ex parte Aala* (2000) 204 CLR 82, 90–1.
157 *M68* [2016] HCA 1 [161]–[162].

III External Security Operations

A Naval Constabulary Operations

1 International Enforcement Instruments and Legislation

The RAN has conducted operations in the Middle East intermittently since 1990 to enforce *United Nations Security Council Resolution* 665 and *United Nations Security Council Resolution* 1546, as well as in support of coalition counterterrorism operations.[158] Where Commonwealth legislation has incorporated United Nations Security Council Resolutions, there has been no provision for enforcing them at sea.[159] Section 6 of the *Charter of the United Nations Act 1945* (Cth) grants a power to the Governor-General to make regulations to give effect to United Nations Security Council Resolutions. This section specifically states, however, that it is only 'in so far as those decisions require Australia to apply measures *not* involving the use of armed force [emphasis added]'. None of the various United Nations Security Council Resolutions for which the Governor-General has made regulations have powers for enforcement at sea.[160]

Notably, the *Law of the Sea Convention* also permits enforcement action by all States in international waters for piracy and to a lesser extent slavery.[161] Australia has provided statutory enforcement powers at sea for piracy and there are criminal offences in Australian legislation for slavery.[162] Enforcement powers for both offences are available under the

---

158 SC Res 665, UN SCOR, 2938th mtg, S/Res 665 (25 August 1990); SC Res 1546, UN SCOR, 4987th mtg UN Doc S/Res/1546 (8 June 2004) as currently extended at various times; see also Royal Australian Navy, above n 10, 67. There was also, arguably, some limited maritime enforcement power in East Timor under *United Nations Security Council Resolution* 1264, which does not appear to have been exercised, SC Res 1264, UN SCOR, 4045th mtg UN Doc S/Res/1264 (15 September 1999). This is on the basis that operative para 3 gave authority to 'restore peace and security in East Timor', which presumably extended to its immediate maritime environment, see Felicity Rogers, 'The International Force in East Timor – Legal Aspects of Maritime Operations' (2005) 28(2) *University of New South Wales Law Journal* 566, 578–9.
159 The *Charter of the United Nations Act 1945* (Cth) s 5 implemented aspects of the *Charter of the United Nations*.
160 Eg *Charter of the United Nations (Sanctions – Iraq) Regulations 2006*.
161 *Law of the Sea Convention*, art 110. The Convention also has enforcement provisions for illegal broadcasting but only for ships of states which are particularly connected to the broadcasts, arts 109, 110.
162 *Crimes Act 1914* (Cth) ss 51–6 and also *Maritime Powers Act 2013* (Cth) s 17.

Maritime Powers Act 2013.[163] Further, Australia and France have a mutual obligation to assist each other in enforcement at sea under the *France Australia Maritime Co-operation Agreement*.[164]

Naval constabulary operations can involve a range of coercive activities.[165] These include stopping and diverting commercial vessels and possibly firing at or into them in order to compel them to stop. Naval constabulary operations can also involve ADF personnel boarding a vessel without permission of the master, detaining and searching the crew or others on board, searching the vessel, breaking open compartments to effect the search, seizing weapons or evidential material and taking control of the vessel or its equipment.[166] Even without being fired upon, delays and diversions are potentially expensive for the various commercial interests, such as the owner, operator, cargo owner or crew agent, of a merchant or fishing vessel. Without lawful authority, any of these activities could be criminal offences under the *Crimes at Sea Act 2000* or the *Defence Force Discipline Act*.

Until recently, Australia's practice appeared to have been to legislate for enforcement powers at sea where such powers served a domestic law enforcement purpose, rather than being primarily the conduct of foreign affairs. This included legislating for a range of international maritime law enforcement instruments such as the *Torres Strait Treaty*,[167] the *United*

---

163 *Criminal Code Act 1995* (Cth) div 270 and also *Maritime Powers Act 2013* (Cth) s 17.
164 *Treaty Between the Government of Australia and the Government of the French Republic on Cooperation in the Maritime Areas Adjacent to the French Southern and Antarctic Territories (TAAF), Heard Island and the McDonald Islands*, (signed 24 November 2003) [2005] ATS 6 (entered into force 1 February 2005), arts 3, 4. This is also enforceable under the *Maritime Powers Act 2013* s 19. The *Regional Assistance Mission to Solomon Islands Agreement*, 24 July 2003, [2003] ATS 17, art 1(a) also grants enforcement powers to Australia within the Solomon Islands, which includes within Solomon Islands maritime jurisdiction.
165 Sea Power Centre of Australia, above n 9, xiv and generally.
166 See Royal Australian Navy, above n 10, 65–9; see also M D Fink, 'The Right of Visit for Warships: Some Challenges in Applying the Law of Maritime Interdiction on the High Seas' (2010) 49(1–2) *Military Law and Law of War Review* 7, 17–29.
167 *Treaty Between Australia and the Independent State of Papua New Guinea concerning Sovereignty and Maritime Boundaries in the area between the two Countries, including the Area Known as Torres Strait, and Related Matters*, (signed 18 December 1978) [1985] ATS 4 (entered into force 15 February 1985) being a schedule to, and partially implemented by, the *Torres Strait Fisheries Act* 1984 (Cth) ('*Torres Straight Treaty*').

Nations Fish Stocks Agreement[168] and the *Pacific Fisheries Treaty*.[169] Where there was really no domestic law enforcement purpose, such as with the enforcement of United Nations Security Council Resolutions[170] or the agreement with France, the domestic legal authority for international naval constabulary operations rested primarily upon executive power. Since the enactment of the *Maritime Powers Act 2013* there have been comprehensive statutory powers to enforce international agreements and decisions.[171] There is a risk that these statutory powers will not provide for every eventuality and *Fortuna* may find them wanting. The powers are effectively the same for both domestic and international law enforcement however,[172] and the tasks of stopping vessels, boarding, searching and seizing are common to many maritime law enforcement operations. The risk of *Fortuna* finding the powers wanting therefore is lower than for land-based operations seeking to restore a functional government to a foreign territory and people, as discussed below, where issues of necessity and emergency, and *Fortuna*, are more likely to arise.

2 The Contrast between the Law of Naval Constabulary Operations and the Law of Naval Warfare

It is worth noting at this point the significant contrast between the regulation of naval constabulary operations prior to the *Maritime Powers Act* and the law of naval warfare. Naval operations in war, or armed conflict, are in fact relatively well regulated by the law of naval warfare,[173] in particular with regard to the law of prize, which provides some judicial

---

168 *Agreement for the Implementation of the Provisions of the United Nations Convention on the Law of the Sea of 10 December 1982 Relating to the Conservation and Management of Straddling Fish Stocks and Highly Migratory Fish Stocks* 1995, (opened for signature 4 December 1995) 2167 UNTS 3 (entry into force 11 December 2001) ('*United Nations Fish Stocks Agreement*'), sch 2 of, and partially implemented by, the *Fisheries Management Act 1991* (Cth).
169 *Agreement among Pacific Island States Concerning the Implementation and Administration of the Treaty on Fisheries Between the Governments of Certain Pacific Island States and the Government of the United States of America*, (opened for signature 2 April 1987), [1988] ATS 42 (entered into force 15 June 1988) ('*Pacific Fisheries Treaty*'), sch 1 to the *Fisheries Management Act 1991* (Cth).
170 See Andrew Forbes (ed), *Australia's Response to Piracy: A Legal Perspective* (Sea Power Centre Australia, 2011).
171 s 19.
172 ss 31, 32, 33.
173 See International Institute of International Humanitarian Law, *San Remo Manual on International Law Applicable to Armed Conflict at Sea* 1994.

scrutiny.[174] Prize law regulates the capture of merchant ships and cargos during naval warfare and serves as a means of protecting trade to some extent in spite of the disruption of war.[175] Notably, it actually directly incorporates international law into national law as prize courts are national courts applying international law.[176] This illustrates the relative paucity of the law relating particularly to international naval constabulary operations and raises the question of why war should be more regulated and 'peace' operations less.[177] This lends some weight to the argument that international law, including human rights law, should inform any consideration of the limits of prerogative power in external security operations generally and particularly where the application of Act of State doctrine is in issue.

B Martial Law in Foreign Territories

As to taking over territories under foreign jurisdiction, this first occurred with the previously German territories of Nauru and New Guinea in 1914. Australia subsequently placed New Guinea under civilian control in 1921 as it became the administering power under a League of Nations mandate.[178] It is worth noting that Nauru apparently surrendered to HMAS *Melbourne* in 1914 without fighting and, although under military occupation, then had a civilian administrator responsible to the Colonial Office.[179] The ADF presence in Somalia in 1993 under authority of a United Nations Security Council Resolution amounted effectively to an occupation of the area around Baidoa given the extent to which it substituted for a civil administration.[180] Martial law also effectively occurred when Australia intervened in East Timor in 1999 under the

---

174 *Naval Prize Act 1864* (Imp), 27 and 28 Vic c 25; *Naval Prize (Procedure) Act 1916* (Imp), 6 and 7 Geo 5 c 2; *Prize Act 1939* (Imp), 2 and 3 Geo 6 c 65; *Prize Courts Act 1894* (Imp), 57 and 58 Vic c 39; *Prize Courts Act 1915* (Imp), 5 and 6 Geo 5 c 57; *Prize Courts (Procedure) Act 1914* (Imp), 4 and 5 Geo 5 c 13 in force through the *Australian Capital Territory Self-Government Act 1989* (Cth) s 34, sch 2, pt 3 'Imperial Acts in Force in the Territory'; see Lord Stowell, 'Address to the Maritime Law Association' (Speech to the Annual General Meeting of the Maritime Law Association of Australia and New Zealand–Queensland Branch, November 1998).
175 See Colombos, above n 24, 795–825.
176 *The Tojo Maru* [1972] AC 242, 290–1.
177 Fink, above n 166, 21 also makes this point.
178 A H Charteris, 'The Mandate over Nauru Island' (1923–1924) 4 *British Yearbook of International Law* 137, 138.
179 Ibid.
180 Michael Kelly, *Peace Operations: Tackling the Legal, Military and Policy Challenges* (AGPS, 1997), 8-6–8-7. (NB pages in this book are numbered by page within chapters, in ADF style, rather than sequentially from the beginning to the end of the book.)

authority of a United Nations Security Council resolution.[181] In each of these cases, the Commonwealth's military forces were the effective government of the territory until it handed over to civilian authorities.[182] The term martial law appears to have been eschewed but military control nonetheless amounted to a form of martial law. This chapter will not consider the Australian occupation of Japan post 1945, Iraq post 2003 or Australia's military presence in any other conflict because Australian forces did not actually displace the local civilian governments, even if United States forces did.

The legal basis for the Australian military occupations of German New Guinea, Somalia and East Timor can only have been prerogative power as there was no legislative authority for the takeover of each of these territories. In the case of the former German territories in 1914, although not the conduct of warfare, martial law was clearly a consequence of the exercise of the war prerogative—even if it subsequently became an exercise of the external affairs prerogative once combat operations against the enemy ceased. The King had declared war against Germany on behalf of the British Empire and the occupation and control of the territories occurred as a result of this.[183]

In the cases of Somalia and East Timor it is a little more unclear. There was no declaration of war against Somalia or Indonesia. Australia sent an armed force to Somalia as part of a larger coalition under the authority of a United Nations Security Council Resolution, which engaged in only low-level uses of force in order to maintain control.[184] Australian sent a much larger armed force as the leader of a coalition to occupy East Timor, which engaged in only limited fighting to secure and maintain control there.[185] In Somalia and East Timor the fighting therefore did not amount to armed conflict in factual terms of scale and intensity. Australia at no stage acted or indicated that it viewed itself as being engaged in

---

181 See Michael Kelly, Timothy L H McCormack, Paul Muggleton, Bruce M Oswald, 'Legal Aspects of Australia's Involvement in the International Force for East Timor' (2001) *International Review of the Red Cross* 841.
182 Noting the ADF did not exist as such in the First World War. The force which formed to occupy German possessions in the Pacific was the Australian Naval and Military Expeditionary Force, which was separate to the Australian Imperial Force, which formed to serve in the Middle East and Europe, see Peter Dennis, Jeffrey Grey, Ewan Morris and Robin Prior, *The Oxford Companion to Australian Military History* (Oxford University Press, 2nd ed, 2008) 62–4, 66, 234–5.
183 Commonwealth *Gazette*, No 50, 3 August 1914, 1335, 30.
184 Kelly, 'Peace Operations', above n 180, 10-16–10-21.
185 Kelly, et al, above n 181, 5.

an armed conflict in either place, so the operations appear to have been an exercise of the external affairs prerogative.[186] This would be consistent with the analysis of Arden LJ in *Al-Jedda*,[187] Lord Carnwath in *Smith*[188] and Holdsworth,[189] to the effect that once combat operations have ceased, or if there were no combat operations as in *Bici*,[190] occupation becomes an exercise of the external affairs prerogative rather than the conduct of war.

As to what constitutes occupation of a foreign territory, Kelly reviewed the international law, literature and practice on this in his book dealing with the ADF's involvement in Somalia, *Peace Operations: Tackling the Legal, Military and Policy Challenges*.[191] Key to his analysis is the concept of effective control.[192] Kelly referred to the first modern statement of the laws of war in the Lieber Code. It has had an enduring influence on the international laws of war. Dr Lieber drafted it for the United States in 1863 during the American Civil War.[193] It was meant, therefore, to apply to circumstances of both internal insurrection and war between nation states. Article 1 of the Code addresses martial law in occupied territories directly, which Kelly quotes as follows:

> A place, district or country occupied by an enemy stands, in consequence of the occupation, under Martial Law of the invading or occupying army, whether any proclamation declaring Martial Law, or any public warning to the inhabitants, has been issued or not. Martial Law is the immediate and direct effect and consequence of occupation or conquest. The presence of a hostile army proclaims its martial law.[194]

---

186 See Rob McLaughlin, '"Giving" Operational Legal Advice: Context and Method' (2011) 50 (1–2) *The Military Law and Law of War Review* 99, 112; Bruce Oswald, 'The Corps on Operations: 1987–2000' in Bruce Oswald and Jim Waddell (eds) *Justice in Arms: Military Lawyers in the Australian Army's First Hundred Years* (Big Sky, 2014) 422.
187 *Al-Jedda* [2011] 2 WLR 225, 253.
188 [2013] UKSC 41 [187].
189 Holdsworth, 'The History of Acts of State in English Law', above n 38, 1318.
190 [2004] EWHC 786, [98]–[101].
191 Kelly, *Peace Operations*, above n 180, chs 3–6.
192 Ibid 3–6. Note also the use of the test of 'effective control', as a question of fact, by the European Court of Human Rights in determining the human rights obligations of the United Kingdom in Iraq in *Hassan v United Kingdom* [2014] (Application No. 29750/09), 39, citing its own judgment in *Al-Skeini v United Kingdom* [2011] [138]–[139].
193 United States Adjutant General's Office, *Correspondence, Orders, Reports, and Returns of The Union Authorities From January 1 To December 31, 1863 – General Order No 100*, 'The Lieber Code of 1863'.
194 Kelly, *Peace Operations*, above n 180, 3-8.

Civil and criminal laws were to remain in effect unless altered by order of the commander although all governmental functions—administrative or legislative—ceased unless continued by the commander.[195] On martial law in such situations, Holdsworth stated that:

> When martial law is a fact of international law, the existence and duration of the state of war are matters of state which the Crown alone can determine; and the acts done in the exercise of martial law in an enemy's country are a series of acts of state.[196]

He then quotes the United States *Opinions of the Attorney-Generals*, cited in Chapter 3, thus:

> The commander of an invading, occupying, or conquering army rules the invaded country with supreme power, limited only by international law and the orders of the sovereign government he serves or represents.[197]

1 The Historical Examples

The historical examples bear this out. In the case of German New Guinea between 1914 and 1921, Somalia in 1993 and in East Timor between 1999 and 2000, the scope of military control in these territories was wider than the military control exercised in areas under Australian jurisdiction between 1942 and 1946.[198] Australian laws did not apply to those territories upon occupation even if Australian forces themselves were subject to some Australian laws.

(a) German New Guinea in the First World War

In the case of the German territories, German law continued in force until the *Laws Repeal and Adopting Ordinance 1921* (New Guinea) and the *Laws Repeal and Adopting Ordinance 1922* (Nauru) respectively came into effect. These ordinances ceased the application of German law, whilst preserving the legal status of any acts already done or in progress under that law, and applied various statute laws of the Commonwealth, Queensland and Papua as well as the principles and rules of the common law and equity of England. Prior to that time, however, it appears that

---

195 Ibid 3-9.
196 Holdsworth, 'The History of Acts of State in English Law', above n 38, 1318.
197 Ibid.
198 Both the German colonial and Australian military administrations administered Nauru as part of New Guinea. Nauru entered into separate administration upon the granting of the League of Nations Mandate in 1920, Charteris, above n 178, 137–8; Dennis et al, above n 182, 234–5.

Australian forces issued ordinances,[199] and three Australian Army legal officers sat as Judges of the Imperial District Court, later known as the Central Court, presumably applying German law.[200] They dealt with a full range of matters including crime, probate, debts, guardianship, marriage and divorce and native labour regulation.[201] As Australian law did not apply to the territory however, with respect to Australian legal authority, the military judges could only have operated under the authority of British imperial prerogative power effected by the Australian military presence. In this case there does not seem to have been the same reticence with respect to the administration of justice occurring under military authority as was later the case under the *National Security (Emergency Control) Regulations 1941* (Cth) discussed in Chapter 3 on martial law.

The other important point here is the extent of administrative activity exercised under military control, as reflected in the records held in the National Archives of Australia. It included regulating taxation and public expenditure, property transactions, running a government store, native affairs, labour recruitment, shipping and customs, receivership of businesses, liquor licensing and immigration as well as dealing with the German population.[202] This list is not exhaustive but indicative of the range of routine governmental functions which the military administration took control of as well as being an occupying force. This provides another interesting contrast to the *National Security (Emergency Control) Regulations 1941* regime in that there was no sense of emergency in these arrangements post 1914. The local German military forces were defeated and other German forces posed only a negligible further threat.[203] The situation in the German territories seems, then, to have been one of transition, with military control filling the governmental vacuum until the postwar status of the territory became clear.[204]

---

199 Dupont, above n 21, 413 n 14.
200 Colonel Jim Waddell, 'From Federation to Armistice: The Earliest Army Legal Officers' in Oswald and Waddell, *Justice in Arms*, 25.
201 Peter Nagle, *Papua New Guinea Records* (National Archives of Australia, 2002) 13–19.
202 Ibid.
203 On the strategic situation see Stephen Webster, 'Vice-Admiral Sir William Creswell: First Naval Member of the Australian Naval Board, 1911–1919' in D M Horner (ed) *The Commanders* (George, Allen & Unwin, 1984), 44, 51–2.
204 As to the details of the granting of the postwar mandates over the former German colonies, see Charteris, above n 178, 138–9.

(b) Somalia in 1993

In 1992, *United Nations Security Council Resolution* 774 empowered the Unified Task Force Somalia (UNITAF) 'to secure the environment for the distribution of humanitarian relief'.[205] Under this authority, in January 1993 the ADF took control of a Humanitarian Relief Sector (HRS) which was essentially a province of Somalia known as the Bay area, based around the major regional centre of Baidoa. UNITAF was the sole occupying military force. The only other armed forces were unofficial militia and bandit groups which did not represent the then-collapsed former Somali government. The ADF was, therefore, the sole authority capable of enacting government functions and proceeded on this basis.[206] The Commanding Officer of the 1st Battalion, Royal Australian Regiment group, Lieutenant Colonel Hurley,[207] was the HRS Commander and stated: 'In the absence of any form of civil government at any level and the failure of the UN to provide resident local UN political officers, HRS commanders became military governors'.[208]

The Army legal officer on this deployment, Major Kelly,[209] focused on the occupation regime under the law of armed conflict but in doing so indicated that the ADF effectively exercised martial law in its sector by virtue of the defined area of control and lack of any other governmental authority within it.[210]

As to the extent of martial law in Australia's sector in Somalia, the ADF's control extended well beyond the direct protection of humanitarian relief. The ADF acted on the basis that establishing conditions for relieving the humanitarian crisis required reestablishing the rule of law.[211] To this end, it created a new Somali police force for the sector and reestablished a functioning judiciary, court and prison system.[212] These new institutions operated under the authority of Somali law as it stood in 1962 on the advice of Somali jurists that the Somali government and laws after this

---

205 SC Res 774, UN SCOR, 3145th mtg, UN Doc S/RES/774 (3 December 1992).
206 Kelly, *Peace Operations*, above n 180, 8-2–8-3, 8-6.
207 Subsequently General Hurley, Chief of the Defence Force and then Governor of New South Wales.
208 Kelly, *Peace Operations*, above n 180, 8-6 n 24.
209 Subsequently Member for Eden-Monaro and Parliamentary Secretary for Defence in the Commonwealth Parliament.
210 Kelly, *Peace Operations*, above n 180, 8-2–8-3, 8-6; Michael Kelly, *Restoring and Maintaining Order in Complex Peace Operations: The Search for a Legal Framework* (Kluwer Law International, 1999), 227.
211 Kelly, *Peace Operations*, above n 180, 8-5.
212 Ibid 8-11–8-22.

date were unconstitutional.[213] This system dealt with criminal, civil and family matters.[214] An appeal court even sentenced one warlord, Gutaale, to death. The Somali police carried out his execution in the prison grounds virtually immediately in accordance with Somali law.[215] Whilst these were Somali institutions relying upon Somali law, it is apparent that the ADF instigated, funded and directed their creation or revival as part of its control of the Bay area.[216]

There is no Australian case law to support an assertion that these actions were lawful under prerogative power. There might have been some criticism of the ADF supporting the execution of Gutaale contrary to Australia's position on international abolition of the death penalty.[217] There has been debate as to whether the law of occupation regime under the international law of armed conflict was applicable de facto or de jure.[218] Despite this, there has been little serious questioning of whether the ADF's actions in exercising martial law were regulated in any direct way by Australian, as opposed to international or local, law. In the exercise of martial law in occupied foreign territories, it might arguably be lawful, as well as being an international law obligation, to establish a system of law and order where none is operating based upon the existing laws and legal institutions of the foreign territory, but this is certainly not clear.

---

213 Ibid 8-15–8-16.
214 Ibid 8-18.
215 Ibid 8-25–8-33. See more detailed description in Oswald, 'The Corps on operations: 1987–2000' in Oswald and Waddell, above n 422, 411–12.
216 Kelly, *Peace Operations*, above n 180, ch 8.
217 *Second Optional Protocol to the International Covenant on Civil and Political Rights, Aiming at the Abolition of the Death Penalty*, (opened for signature 15 December 1989) 1642 UNTS 414 (entered into force 11 July 1991) art 1, 'No one within the jurisdiction of a State Party to the present Protocol shall be executed'. See Oswald, 'The Corps on operations: 1987–2000' in Oswald and Waddell, above n 422, 411–12. Australia accepted that this obligation may apply extraterritorially where Australia had the power to 'carry out sentences imposed by courts'. Human Rights Committee, *Replies to the List of Issues (CCPR/C/AUS/Q/5) to be Taken Up in Connection with the Consideration of the Fifth Periodic Report of the Government of Australia (CCP/C/AUS/5)* UN Doc CCPR/C/AUS/Q/5/Add.1 (21 January 2009) 5.
218 There is an international law debate as to whether the *Fourth Geneva Convention* on occupation applies in such situations de jure (Kelly's view, *Peace Operations*, above n 180, 8-6) or whether occupations under authority of a United Nations Security Council Resolution are not belligerent and therefore incapable of attracting the application of the *Fourth Geneva Convention*, (opened for signature 12 August 1949), 75 UNTS 287 (entered into force 21 October 1950), schs 1 to 4 of the *Geneva Conventions Act 1957* (Cth). International human rights law would be the applicable international law instead, Boss, above n 3, 340–4; see also Oswald, 'The Law of Military Occupation', above n 2, 316. It is not necessary for this book to prefer a view on this but it is relevant to note that the nature of the obligations in occupation of foreign territory under UN authority is disputed in international law also.

The Somalia precedent was significant for subsequent operations in East Timor however, particularly as Kelly had a key role as a legal adviser in both operations.[219]

(c) East Timor in 1999–2000

The more recent example of military control by the ADF is similarly one of filling a governmental vacuum during the INTERFET period in East Timor (now Timor-Leste). As stated above, this period was from late September 1999 until February 2000.[220] The ADF intervened as the lead of a UN-authorised military coalition, a first for Australia, to restore peace and security in East Timor under *United Nations Security Council Resolution* 1264.[221] There had been widespread violence and destruction once it became clear that the East Timorese had voted overwhelmingly to reject an Indonesian offer of special autonomy within the Republic of Indonesia, which effectively meant secession.[222] Indonesian military-sponsored militias were responsible for most of the chaos.[223] Whilst Indonesia agreed to the deployment and was meant to have continuing responsibility for peace and security, by early October the Indonesian police had effectively withdrawn from the territory.[224] The judiciary and court system collapsed.[225] Most other civil governmental services ceased and much infrastructure suffered damage.[226] Indonesia formally renounced sovereignty over East Timor on 20 October 1999.[227]

INTERFET needed to assume the responsibilities of civil government in order to achieve its mission.[228] The United Nations Transitional Administration in East Timor was meant to assume some very limited governmental functions relatively early in the intervention, such as through the United Nations Civilian Police, but this was practically constrained by the security situation and the lack of United Nations resources in East

---

219 See Kelly et al, above n 181.
220 Ibid, see also Felicity Rogers, above n 158, 566.
221 See Commonwealth, *Parliamentary Debates*, House of Representatives, 21 September 1999, 10047–51 (Alexander Downer) reproduced in Kemp and Stanton, above n 9, 280–4.
222 Ibid.
223 Bruce Oswald, 'The INTERFET Detainee Management Unit in East Timor' (2000) 3 *Yearbook of International Humanitarian Law* 347, 348.
224 Kelly, et al, above n 181, at nn 12, 13; Oswald, ibid 350–1.
225 Oswald, 'The INTERFET Detainee Management Unit in East Timor', above n 223, 350–1.
226 Felicity Rogers, above n 158, 569.
227 *Declaration of the People's Consultative Assembly of Indonesia*, 20 October 1999, cited in Rogers, ibid 571.
228 Michael Smith and Maureen Dee, *Peacekeeping in East Timor: The Path to Independence* (Lynne Reiner Publishers, 2003) 421–2.

Timor at that stage. Reportedly, there were only two United Nations civilian police officers in East Timor when INTERFET arrived.[229] Many matters, therefore, clearly required the control of the military force. General security was a priority and, within hours of arrival, INTERFET detained people carrying weapons.[230] There were other less obvious, but still important, functions which sovereign governments normally perform but which only INTERFET could perform in this situation. These included control of the port for naval and civilian shipping, the control of the airports as well as control of the land border with West Timor.[231]

(i) The Detainee Management Unit

Perhaps the most significant action of the ADF in East Timor from a martial law perspective was the exercise of legislative and judicial power in the establishment of the Detainee Management Unit (DMU). In the absence of any judiciary or legislature, the Commander of INTERFET, Major General Cosgrove, promulgated an ordinance establishing the unit and the rules under which it would function.[232] Significantly, the ordinance applied the law of Indonesia as it had applied to East Timor, with some exceptions. This was controversial but arguably necessary. It was controversial because Australia was one of very few countries which recognised Indonesian sovereignty over East Timor. Most nations saw Indonesia's occupation of East Timor from 1975 to 1999 as unlawful. Australia's main partner in INTERFET, New Zealand, among others, therefore took the view that Portuguese law as it applied to East Timor in 1975 should still apply.[233] It became practically necessary to apply Indonesian law as it had been the de facto applicable law in the territory for the previous 24 years.[234]

The Commander of INTERFET's Ordinance was therefore a significant legislative act which has had an enduring effect. The United Nations Transitional Administration in East Timor in its Regulation 1 of 1999 (27 November 1999) applied the law as it stood in East Timor on 25 October 1999, thereby accepting the Ordinance as law as well as

---

229 Kelly, et al, 'Legal Aspects of Australia's Involvement in the International Force for East Timor' above n 181 n 39. See also Oswald, 'The Corps on Operations: 1987–2000' in Oswald and Waddell, above n 621, 426.
230 Oswald, 'The Law of Military Occupation' above n 2, 311.
231 Kelly, et al, above n 181, 3. See also Felicity Rogers, above n 1434, 573–8.
232 Oswald, 'The INTERFET Detainee Management Unit in East Timor', above n 223, 352.
233 Felicity Rogers, above n 158, 571–3.
234 Oswald, 'The INTERFET Detainee Management Unit in East Timor', above n 223, 353.

continuing the application of Indonesian law.[235] This regulation is still part of the law of Timor-Leste and, with it, effectively the Commander of INTERFET's Ordinance.[236] As an exercise of prerogative power in a situation of martial law this legislative act has not been questioned.

The DMU itself exercised judicial power. In the absence of a judiciary there was a need to provide a substitute form of due process for those arrested for serious crimes. The DMU acted effectively as a bail court.[237] Where INTERFET detained a person for alleged criminal behaviour, there was a process whereby such persons came before the DMU. There was a military judicial officer, a military prosecuting officer and a military defending officer. After taking paper submissions, the military judicial officer could order continued detention of the person for handing over to the future civilian judicial system, or for a fixed period of time, conditional release (akin to bail) or unconditional release.[238] The DMU heard matters against 60 persons, of whom it released 21 without conditions.[239] INTERFET also ran a Force Detention Centre, for which the DMU exercised an oversight role in the form of a Visiting Officer. This was effectively the East Timorese prison system for the duration of INTERFET and its detainees subsequently became the detainees of the civil judicial system at the end of the INTERFET period.[240] As an exercise of prerogative power, this form of martial law also has not been questioned.

(ii) East Timor Post INTERFET

The ADF retained a role in maintaining security after the INTERFET period, which continued until 2013.[241] It is unclear the extent to which this has extended at various times beyond exercising powers like any ordinary citizen could exercise in Australia,[242] such as self-defence, arrest and so on as discussed in Chapter 4. The prerogative for the control and

---

235 Ibid 352.
236 *Constitution of the Democratic Republic of Timor-Leste 2002* s 165.
237 Oswald, 'The Law of Military Occupation', above n 2, 312–13.
238 Oswald, 'The INTERFET Detainee Management Unit in East Timor', above n 223, 356–8.
239 Ibid 351, 358.
240 Ibid 359–61. See Oswald, 'The Corps on operations: 1987–2000' in Oswald and Waddell, above n 422, 422–3, including praise from UN human rights special rapporteurs on the treatment of the detainees.
241 Department of Defence, *Timor-Leste* <www.defence.gov.au/operations/pastoperations/timorleste/>.
242 These powers could be available by virtue of Timor-Leste's own law or by virtue of *Defence Force Discipline Act* s 61 applying the criminal law of the Jervis Bay Territory to the conduct of ADF members. Although, as discussed in Chapter 4, this would not be the same as an ordinary citizen exercising these powers.

disposition of the forces would have authorised the armed presence of the ADF on the streets in Timor-Leste.[243] The maintenance of vehicle checkpoints would have had to rely upon the external affairs prerogative, possibly together with the authority of local law, as it would have been beyond the power of any ordinary citizen to do this. Other than that, the ADF does not appear to have exercised coercive powers, so this chapter will not address this period any further.

2 Observations on the Limits of Martial Law in Occupied Foreign Territories

In some respects the DMU represents a modern form of martial law court martial in that it was a military means of affording due process to civilian detainees in a foreign territory where no other system of justice existed. The Duke of Wellington's comments would have been equally applicable to the DMU:

> Martial law is neither more nor less than the will of the general who commands the army. In fact martial law means no law at all, therefore the general who declares martial law, and commands that it should be carried into execution, is bound to lay down distinctly the rules and regulations and limits according to which his will is to be carried out.[244]

On one view, as far as prerogative power is concerned, the history of the ADF's practice of martial law in foreign occupied territories could suggest that there are relatively few limits on powers of the ADF in such circumstances. Statute law, as discussed above in the form of the *Defence Force Discipline Act* and the *Criminal Code*, for example, will primarily provide a distinct limit to the powers exercisable but does not purport to regulate explicitly the conduct of a military occupation or martial law. Prerogative power could, arguably, authorise any act that is related to the mission of the ADF in the foreign territory. The application of martial law in territories outside of Australia, whether so called or not, would appear from even recent history to be virtually unchallenged. So long as the ADF's actions relate to its mission, its assumption of civilian government functions overseas is arguably not directly restricted by Australian law. There are alternative possibilities however, to which this chapter will return.

---

243 *Nissan* [1970] AC 179, 195.
244 *Hansard*, Third Series, 17 March–10 April, 1851 cited in H P Lee, *The Emergency Powers of the Commonwealth of Australia* (Law Book Company, 1984) 213; Mark Neocleous, 'Whatever Happened to Martial Law? Detainees and the Logic of Emergency' (2007) 143 *Radical Philosophy*, 13 n 4; W S Holdsworth 'Martial Law Historically Considered' (1902) 18 *Law Quarterly Review* 117, 137.

It is important to note that the ADF operations in Somalia and East Timor were less than six months. There was local law which the ADF sought to apply, even if there was no functioning government. In this sense, unlike the situation in *Serdar Mohammed* where British forces did not directly apply Afghan law,[245] ADF actions arguably relied for their authority upon the local law. The exception to this is that ADF members were not officials appointed under that law. Given the collapse of government in both situations, arguably the external affairs prerogative as informed by the relevant United Nations Security Council resolution remedied this deficiency for the purposes of Australian law. General Cosgrove's ordinance creating the DMU was the only means of legislating within East Timor at that time. If the operations had extended into years rather than months, the requirement stated in *Serdar Mohammed* for the government to seek legislative authorisation from the Australian Parliament may have been a consideration.[246]

The ADF experience is quite unlike the contemporaneous scrutiny which British forces have undergone in the English courts as discussed above. This seems to have a connection to jurisdiction under the *Human Rights Act 1998* (UK), which was a central concern in *Al-Jedda*,[247] *Smith*[248] and *Serdar Mohammed*[249] and also possibly to the greater extent of British involvement in external security operations generally, which might explain *Nissan*,[250] *Thring*[251] and *Bici*.[252] It is only if comparable cases come before Australian courts with respect to the ADF that it can really be seen if the practice does reflect the law. This chapter will argue below that, should a comparable case arise, Australian courts should follow the approach in *Serdar Mohammed*.[253]

---

245 [2015] EWCA Civ 843. This was not a direct issue in *Al-Waheed* [2017] UKSC 2 but did arise in *Rahmatullah (No 2) v Ministry of Defence; Mohammed v Ministry of Defence* UKSC 1 ('*Rahmatullah (No 2)*'), in which the Government successfully argued Act of State doctrine.
246 *Serdar Mohammed* [2015] EWCA Civ 843, [363].
247 [2011] 2 WLR 225.
248 [2013] UKSC 41.
249 [2015] EWCA Civ 843.
250 [1970] AC 179.
251 Court of Appeal (Civil Division) (Unreported, Pill, Clarke, Bennett LJJ, 20 July 2000).
252 [2004] EWHC 786. Adam Tomkins, 'The Struggle to Delimit Executive Power in Britain', in Paul Craig and Adam Tomkins (eds), *The Executive and Public Law: Power and Accountability in Public Perspective* (Oxford University Press, 2006) 16, 47 speculated that the *Human Rights Act* may have this effect. Thomas Tugenhadt and Laura Croft, *The Fog of Law: An Introduction to the Legal Erosion of British Fighting Power* (Policy Exchange, 2013) 14–21, attribute this to the *Human Rights Act*. They describe a state of 'legal siege' and express concern that the military values upon which operational success rely are being replaced by legal values which derive from human rights instruments originally intended for application in 'stable European contracting states' and not military operations in countries 'far beyond its original design'.
253 [2015] EWCA Civ 843. Reassuringly, *Rahmatullah (No 2)* [2017] UKSC 1 was consistent with the position argued for in this book.

IV Limitations

A Occupation of Foreign Territories as Martial Law

It seems fairly clear that when Australian forces take over a foreign territory that the traditional factors for the imposition of martial law, discussed in Chapter 3, are in place. These are that the military exercises some or all of the executive, legislative or judicial functions in part or all of that territory. This could be the case even if some elements of the previous administration remain effective, such as was initially the case in German New Guinea,[254] but the sovereign authority has been displaced and with it the authority for the residual elements of the previous administration to act. Martial law applies as a matter of fact, if not law. Two further questions arise, then. One question is the substance of that law, which this chapter will address below. The other question is the duration of martial law.

1 Duration

To deal first with duration, as stated in the case of East Timor, this was for as long as it took to establish a civilian administration under United Nations authority.[255] In the case of the occupied German territories, this lasted for the duration of the war and for some time afterwards, until the League of Nations mandates clarified the postwar status of those territories.[256] The continuing state of war with Germany appeared to be enough to justify maintaining military control for that period rather than establishing a civilian administration, even though Nauru had Colonial Office civilian administration during the same period.[257] The situation was not apparently subject to legal challenge. The much shorter occupations in Somalia and East Timor were both less than six months and there was no legal challenge to the Australian occupation of these territories at any stage. As a matter of policy, the duration of martial law in occupied foreign territories would appear to be until a civilian administration can take over. It is not possible to discern from these diverging examples that this is a rule of law though, nor that there is a limitation of necessity as there would be in a case of martial law within the realm.

---

254 Nagle, above n 201, 6.
255 Kelly, et al, above n 181.
256 Charteris, above n 178, 137–8.
257 Ibid.

2 What is the Substance of Martial Law Applied outside Australia?

As discussed in Chapter 5 on war, historically and currently, the doctrine of extraterritoriality means that only limited Australian law applies to the conduct of operations by the ADF outside Australia and the most relevant statutory regime since 2002 is div 268 of the *Criminal Code Act 1995* (Cth) together with the *Defence Force Discipline Act*. The regulatory aspects of the international law of occupation do not apply by force of statute though. There are some specific offence provisions of the *Criminal Code Act 1995* which might relate to occupation, such as not unjustifiably appropriating property,[258] forcibly transferring the population[259] or torture[260] but most of the *Fourth Geneva Convention*,[261] which might regulate an occupation, and which only applies de jure after an armed conflict to which the occupier is a party, remains in the realm of international law only.

Interestingly, although a property law case, *Mabo*,[262] has some bearing on the question of the applicable law in foreign territories which come under the control of the Crown. Reflecting the same concern which appears to underlie s 268.29 (unjustifiably appropriating property) of the *Criminal Code Act 1995*, Brennan J considered the significance of private property rights in such situations and stated:

> [T]he true rule as to the survival of private proprietary rights on conquest to be that 'it is to be presumed, in the absence of express confiscation or of subsequent expropriatory legislation, that the conqueror has respected them and forborne to diminish or modify them'.[263]

His Honour also considered that the authorities meant that this applied to situations of cession as well as conquest.[264] The significance for this book is that in situations where there is no purported acquisition of sovereignty, as in East Timor and Somalia, there would appear to be less of a basis to argue that the Crown could disregard local private property rights. This is consistent with the view of the House of Lords in *Nissan*[265] discussed above. It is also consistent with the position discussed in Chapter 5 that executive

---

258 s 268.29.
259 s 268.11.
260 ss 274.2, 268.13, 268.25, 268.73.
261 *Fourth Geneva Convention*, 21 ATS 1958, (opened for signature 12 August 1949), 75 UNTS 287 (entered into force 21 October 1950).
262 *Mabo (No 2)* (1992) 175 CLR 1.
263 Ibid 55, citing Lord Sumner in *In re Southern Rhodesia* (1919) AC 233.
264 Ibid 55.
265 *Nissan* [1970] AC 179.

power could not acquire property on other than just terms if it is beyond the power of the Commonwealth Parliament to do so. Section 51 (xxxi) of the *Constitution* is not on its face limited to actions within Australia as it refers to acquisition from 'any State or person for any purpose in respect of which the Parliament has power to make laws'. In the case of conquest, as in German New Guinea, even though de jure sovereignty was ultimately subject to a League of Nations mandate, it appears that the Crown respected private local property rights through its conduct of property cases and land administration.[266] This is a limitation upon the prerogative power of the Crown in an occupation. It would not prevent acquisition or requisition of property in the occupied territory but this would have to be done with due regard to local property law and on just terms.

Arguably this reasoning extends beyond private property rights to all existing law within the occupied territory, which would apply until such time as the military commander explicitly changed it. Clode was of this view, stating:

> With regard to such Crown Colonies as are acquired by conquest, except in so far as rights may have been secured by any terms of capitulation, the power of the Sovereign is absolute … Such possessions keep, it is true, their own laws for the time; but subject to … the absolute power of the Sovereign … to alter those laws in any way …[267]

This would be consistent with international law and Australian practice in each of the historical examples. The emphasis in *Serdar Mohammed*[268] on the significance of local law discussed above, and the need for compelling public policy considerations to justify not relying upon that law,[269] point strongly towards a requirement generally to respect all local law and also to take into account Australia's international human rights obligations.[270] The emphasis on the principle of legality in *Williams*, *CPCF* and *M68* also discussed above would support this. As to whether there is a common-law obligation on the Crown to enforce law and order, through martial law, in an occupied territory is another question again.[271]

---

266 Nagle, above n 201, 13–19.
267 Clode, *Military Forces of the Crown*, above n 33, 175.
268 [2015] EWCA Civ 843.
269 Ibid [364].
270 On this point and its uncertainty in 1906, see Harrison Moore, above n 7, 78–83.
271 For a discussion of the related issue of the obligation in Dutch and international law of UN troops to afford protection to local civilians see Otto Spijkers, 'The Netherlands' and the United Nations' Responsibility for Srebrenica Before the Dutch Courts' (2011) 50 (3–4) *The Military Law and Law of War Review* 517.

While the ADF remains accountable to the Parliament and the courts in Australia for its actions overseas, as far as the local jurisdiction is concerned, as discussed above, Australia's constitutional arrangements for subordination of the military to civilian control, the separation of powers and the responsibility of the States for general policing have no direct application. This is a matter for international law and whatever arrangements might be made between the Commonwealth Executive and the local jurisdiction. This means, effectively, that the ADF is less constrained in its lawful activities overseas. There is no impediment in Australian law then to the ADF becoming the de facto government of East Timor in 1999, for example. A similar action in the future would not directly offend div 268 of the *Criminal Code Act* or the *Defence Force Discipline Act*. There would appear however to be a specific requirement to respect local property law and a more general obligation to assume the application of all local law unless explicitly changed by a legislative act, taking into account Australia's international human rights obligations.

B Use of Force and Contrary Statutes

As discussed above, some ADF actions in external security operations could amount to offences against persons, such as through arrest, detention and so on, and there is applicable statute law which would proscribe such action. As discussed in Chapter 5, the *Defence Force Discipline Act* and the *Crimes at Sea Act 2000* apply to ADF operations outside of Australia.[272] The *Criminal Code Act 1995* also applies, although, as discussed above, fewer of its provisions are relevant to ADF operations outside of an armed conflict. With respect to the use of force, the operations considered above indicate that ADF external security operations essentially have a law enforcement character. The force required is that necessary for mission accomplishment, such as stopping, searching and detaining people, vehicles and vessels, as well as self-defence.[273] While actions in self-defence are consistent with the applicable statutes, the absence of statutory authority for the use of force for mission accomplishment actions raises similar questions as those relating to the use of force in war discussed in Chapter 5. It is arguable that, as with war, as a matter of statutory interpretation, the Parliament would not legislate to abolish the prerogative with respect

---

272 *Crimes at Sea Act* 2000 (Cth) s 6; *Defence Force Discipline Act 1982* (Cth) s 9.
273 See Oswald, 'Detention of Civilians on Military Operations', above n 112, 532 on the relevance of domestic criminal law to detention in military operations and, generally, on issues with detention in international law.

to external affairs without express words.²⁷⁴ The applicable statutes are of general application and do not explicitly regulate the use of force under the external affairs prerogative, apart from relevant sections of div 268 of the *Criminal Code* (relating to crimes against humanity such as torture,²⁷⁵ and forcibly transferring the population).²⁷⁶ Therefore an ADF use of force clearly pursuant to an exercise of the external affairs prerogative could be lawful, but this would have to be despite the existence of a contrary statute.

1 The State of the Authorities

The difficulty is that the war prerogative, while having virtually no authority for its substance, is well recognised. However, the authority to conduct coercive external security operations has very little authority to support it. The authorities most on point are *Buron v Denman*,²⁷⁷ *Thring*,²⁷⁸ *Al-Jedda*²⁷⁹ and *Serdar Mohammed*.²⁸⁰ As discussed above, there are Australian cases which create some uncertainty as to the strength of these authorities. With this in mind, as for war, it is still possible to argue on the basis of statutory interpretation that apparently contrary statutes do not proscribe the use of force in ADF external security operations. This argument cannot be made as strongly as it can be for the war prerogative, however, given the state of the authorities. Still, there does not appear to be any other way to reconcile the practice of ADF external security operations with the existence of apparently contrary statutes. This is problematic.

There is a problem with relying upon practice alone to determine the legality of ADF operations. As Heydon J firmly stated in *Pape*:

---

274 *Barton v Commonwealth* (1974) 131 CLR 477, 508; *Tampa Case* (2001) 110 FCR 491, 540; see Pearce and Geddes, above n 152, 181.
275 ss 274.2, 268.13, 268.25, 268.73.
276 s 268.11.
277 (1848) 2 Ex 167; 154 All ER 450.
278 Court of Appeal (Civil Division) (Unreported, Pill, Clarke, Bennett LJJ, 20 July 2000).
279 [2011] 2 WLR 225.
280 [2015] EWCA Civ 843. Lady Hale is more emphatic however in *Rahmatullah (No 2)* [2017] UKSC 1, 'We are left with a very narrow class of acts: in their nature sovereign acts – the sorts of things that governments properly do; committed abroad; in the conduct of the foreign policy of the state; so closely connected to that policy to be necessary in pursuing it; and at least extending to the conduct of military operations which are themselves lawful in international law (which is not the same as saying that the acts themselves are necessarily authorised in international law)' [37].

> Executive and legislative practice cannot make constitutional that which would otherwise be unconstitutional. Practice must conform with the *Constitution*, not the *Constitution* with practice. The fact that the executive and legislative practices may have generated benefits does not establish that they are constitutional ...[281]

In the absence of any specific authority, practice may provide a guide as to what is accepted as lawful. If a matter is not a subject of legal controversy or specific statutory regulation then this may indicate lawfulness. This is not in any way conclusive, merely indicative. The High Court considered practice as a guide in *Williams*[282] and *Pape*[283] so it might be appropriate to look to practice when there is no law that is specifically applicable. Past practice however does not justify any past unlawfulness by the ADF in external security operations. It merely prompts a consideration of what justification there may be in law for such practice. The alternative is that the practice is unlawful. If there is no authority for the use of coercive measures under the external affairs prerogative then practice will not make it lawful. As Kiefel J stated in *Williams*, consistent with the principle of legality, 'actions of the Executive must fall within the confines of some power derived from the *Constitution*'.[284]

Given the emphasis on the principle of legality emerging from *Williams*, *CPCF* and *M68*, an argument based only upon past practice, statutory interpretation and an uncertain prerogative is unlikely to be enough. This needs to be taken together with the considerations in *Serdar Mohammed* regarding not relying upon local law, such as the direct authority of a United Nations Security Council Resolution or the objectionable nature of local law allowing a practice such as slavery.[285] The effect is that the use of force in external security operations should find authority in local law, Australian law or an international law instrument such as a United Nations Security Council Resolution. The external affairs prerogative may justify the high-level policy decisions to commit the ADF to an operation with

---

281 *Pape v Commissioner of Taxation* (2009) 238 CLR 1, 230, ('*Pape*').
282 (2012) 248 CLR 156, 340 (Crennan J on parliamentary appropriations practice), 361, 369 (Kiefel J on parliamentary appropriations practice and responsible government respectively).
283 (2009) 238 CLR 1, 24–25 (French J on parliamentary appropriations practice) 74 (Gummow, Crennan and Bell JJ on parliamentary appropriations practice) 122 (Hayne and Kiefel JJ on delineation of roles of executive and legislature).
284 (2012) 248 CLR 156, 373–4.
285 *Serdar Mohammed* [2015] EWCA Civ 843 [364]. *Al-Waheed* [2017] UKSC 2, even though giving more scope to the authority of sovereign acts in the conduct of the foreign policy of the state (Lady Hale) [37], does not change this conclusion in respect of Australia.

the intention of using force. Beyond that, authority should be sought in directly applicable law. This is because actions involving the use of force are likely to be justiciable in an Australian court, both because the executive is always subject to the jurisdiction of Australian courts as discussed, and also because a court would likely be quite capable of adjudicating on such actions as if they had occurred in Australia. The defence of Act of State in such a proceeding may well rest only upon a directly applicable United Nations Security Council Resolution. This position is consistent with McLachlan's argument in *Foreign Relations Law* that such questions fundamentally concern choice of law, whether it be local law, the law of the nation sending the armed force, or international law.[286]

(a) Use of Lethal Force

This raises a key difference between external security operations and war, which is the presence of an enemy and, therefore, when it is lawful to use lethal force. If there is no enemy in an external security operation then there can be no basis to use lethal force for the purpose of the operation, unless it becomes an armed conflict as a question of fact and then a question of the war prerogative. This does not affect the right to use force in self-defence or the defence of others, as the applicable statute law provides for this. This is consistent with the principle of legality in *Shaw Savill Albion & Co Ltd*,[287] in that members of the ADF enjoy combat immunity only when engaged in actual operations against an enemy.[288] If there is no enemy, there is no combat immunity, and so the use of lethal force is subject to the ordinary law applicable to the ADF which limits the use of lethal force to situations of self-defence. The concept of mission essential property advanced by Kelly and others, which is that it is lawful to use lethal force to protect certain mission essential property even without a direct threat to life, is not sustainable on this view.[289] Any other, nonlethal, use of force would have to be consistent with the external affairs purpose of the ADF operation, which would most likely be that required only to enforce or carry out a United Nations Security Council Resolution or bilateral or regional agreement. Even then, the authority for even nonlethal uses of force is scant.

---

286 McLachlan, above n 21, 278, and more broadly 276–93.
287 *Shaw Savill Albion & Co Ltd v Commonwealth* (1940) 66 CLR 344, 354 ('*Shaw Savill Albion & Co Ltd*').
288 Rob McLaughlin, 'The Use of Lethal Force by Military Forces on Law Enforcement Operations – Is There a "Lawful Authority"?' (2009) 37(3) *Federal Law Review* 441, 442–46.
289 See Kelly et al, above n 181, 9. See Oswald, 'The Corps on operations: 1987–2000' in Oswald and Waddell, above n 422, 423–4, which outlines the arguments, and their protagonists, for and against.

As to contrary statutes and the dearth of authority overall, it is open to consider whether this is a situation which requires further regulation by statute. The Court in *Serdar Mohammed* strongly indicated to the Parliament that it should look at legislation,[290] and it is a matter that has been under consideration by the House of Commons as indicated by its Defence Committee report titled *UK Armed Forces Personnel and the Legal Framework for Future Operations*.[291] It is not the direct aim of this book to explore statutory reform as it is to find the limits of executive power as it relates to the ADF. However, it is worth considering briefly whether there are alternatives to the current uncertain state of the authorities. From the perspective of the Commonwealth seeking to maintain maximum flexibility in highly uncertain situations outside Australia, which do not directly intrude upon the limitations upon executive power within Australia discussed above, it could likely be attractive to keep external security operations on an executive power basis. This could avoid unintentionally constraining the powers available. This still leaves ADF members in an uncertain position, an issue to which the conclusion to the book will return. This approach may also not provide much protection to those foreigners subject to the coercive use of power by the ADF in external security operations either. The operation of the *Human Rights Act* (UK) has provided an example of how statute might provide greater protection. It was not drafted for the purpose of regulating external security operations by British forces however and, given the concerns raised by Tugenhadt and Croft on this point, there could be better ways of approaching the issue.[292] This is a point worthy of further exploration, although not here.

C Act of State Doctrine

It comes now to return to Act of State and this chapter's argument for its place in the law relating to ADF external security operations. As discussed, as opposed to war, there is no combat immunity in external security operations and any interference, loss or damage could give rise to a claim against the Commonwealth. For example, a ship or cargo owner or a crew member could have sued the Commonwealth for loss or damage, much as occurred in *Shaw Savill & Albion Co Ltd*,[293] arising from

290 [2015] EWCA Civ 843 [363].
291 Paper No HC 931, Session 2013–2014 (2013) 47.
292 Above n 252, 31–2.
293 (1940) 66 CLR 344, 354.

a boarding operation by the RAN to enforce a United Nations Security Council Resolution.[294] This could have been the case, for example, even if a detained vessel was clearly engaged in 'inward and outward maritime shipping'[295] from the country in question in the terms of a United Nations Security Council Resolution. The remedy is likely to be a diplomatic one but it is possible that the ship owner could have commenced proceedings against the Commonwealth over the delay caused to the vessel. The Commonwealth could then have pleaded Act of State doctrine.

The question is whether an Australian court would accept this plea and determine the matter to be nonjusticiable or, alternatively, justiciable but subject to immunity. Following *Habib*[296] and *M68*,[297] it is unlikely that an Australian court now would apply *Buron v Denman*[298] or *Thring*[299] and state that actions in accordance with the mission are nonjusticiable. It could apply *Bici*,[300] *Nissan*,[301] the reasoning in *Ali*[302] as well as the reasoning in *Al-Jedda*[303] and *Serdar Mohammed*[304] and see the actions of the ADF as justiciable and scrutinise them for consistency with the relevant international law instrument. The latter approach of justiciability subject to a defence of Act of State is perhaps more likely given the approach taken in *Hicks*,[305] *Habib*[306] and *Ali*,[307] as well as *Williams*,[308] *CPCF*[309] and *M68*.[310] This is, arguably, preferable in international law enforcement operations to an approach which would relieve such operations of the scrutiny of the courts. It would serve to support the purpose of such operations as themselves supporting the international rule of law. This

---

294 Possible claims under admiralty jurisdiction may be limited as most actions for loss or damage arise under contracts, the main exception being for collisions—an occurrence unlikely to be authorised by an enforcement treaty or United Nations Security Council Resolution, see Martin Davies and Anthony Dickey, *Shipping Law*, (Lawbook, 3rd ed, 2004) 409–42.
295 SC Res 665, UN SCOR, 2938th mtg, S/RES 665 (25 August 1990).
296 (2010) 183 FCR 62.
297 [2016] HCA 1.
298 (1848) 2 Ex 167; 154 All ER 450.
299 Court of Appeal (Civil Division) (Unreported, Pill, Clarke, Bennett LJJ, 20 July 2000).
300 [2004] EWHC 786.
301 [1970] AC 179; see Lindell, 'Judicial Review of International Affairs', above n 60, 191.
302 [2004] VSC 6 (Unreported, Bongiorno J, 23 January 2004).
303 [2011] 2 WLR 225, 253.
304 [2015] EWCA Civ 843. See now *Rahmatullah (No 2)* [2017] UKSC 1.
305 (2007) 156 FCR 574.
306 (2010) 183 FCR 62.
307 [2004] VSC 6 (Unreported, Bongiorno J, 23 January 2004).
308 (2012) 248 CLR 156.
309 [2015] HCA 1.
310 [2016] HCA 1.

is not to argue that an exercise of the external affairs prerogative is only lawful if it conforms to international law. As discussed earlier in this chapter this is not necessarily required. However, consistency with the international law instrument, including Australia's relevant international human rights obligations, could inform a consideration of whether an action by the ADF is actually a lawful exercise of the prerogative with respect to external affairs. If the ADF's actions were consistent with the relevant international law instrument, the court could determine that they were a lawful exercise of the prerogative and, therefore, protected by the defence of Act of State. It could also find them to be negligent or intentionally wrongful actions, whether under local or Australian law, or actions inconsistent with the relevant international instrument and, accordingly, not protected by this defence. It would be consistent with *Shaw Savill Albion & Co Ltd*[311] to take this approach and make Act of State a companion doctrine for external security operations to the combat immunity doctrine for operations in war.[312]

V Conclusion

United Nations Security Council Resolutions and other international enforcement instruments should inform the content of Act of State doctrine. Even though the doctrine is uncertain, if it is to have worthwhile meaning, the relevant international law instruments should provide some substance to it. They could limit the defence which Act of State doctrine provides or define the authority protected by that defence. From a policy perspective, it is undesirable that any coercive action in a United Nations or other peace operation by the ADF, of itself, should ground a claim against the Commonwealth. To repeat Arden LJ's point in *Al-Jedda*:

> If courts hold states liable in damages when they comply with resolutions of the UN designed to secure international peace and security, the likelihood is that states will be less ready to assist the UN achieve its role in this regard, and this would be detrimental to the long-term interests of the states.[313]

---

311 (1940) 66 CLR 344, 354.
312 Lindell notes the connection between the two doctrines, *The Coalition Wars*, above n 44, 37 n 140; Renwick sees the answer to these questions lying in Act of State doctrine and nonjusticiability (without elaborating further as to the extent of that nonjusticiability), James Renwick, 'Detention Without Trial – The Relevance for Australia of the US Supreme Court Decisions in *Hamdi, Rasul* and *Rumsfeld*' (Speech to Judicial Conference of Australia, 3 September 2005) 10.
313 [2011] 2 WLR 225, 253.

Where actions within an external security operation do have a clear link to the authorising treaty or Security Council Resolution and other relevant international law, the common law could recognise such international law as being the lawful limits of an Act of State, where it is contrary to local law, and so give greater certainty to the doctrine. It could be a form of international law being a 'source' or 'a legitimate and important influence on the common law',[314] especially when international law declares the existence of universal human rights'.[315] Although the Australian authorities simply do not extend this far at present, the relevant international law is the only place to look for the substance, and therefore the limits, of the prerogative with respect to external affairs and the extent to which Act of State doctrine might provide a defence to actions under it. It would be consistent with the principle of legality at both international and national levels.[316] Should a suitable case come before it, an Australian court should follow *Serdar Mohammed* and find actions directly pursuant to the international law authority which prevent reliance on local law,[317] or an Australian statute, protected by the defence of Act of State to the extent to which the relevant international law requires action contrary to that law.

Despite this uncertainty, there has been a clear preference in Australian practice for external security operations to remain under the authority of executive power. Except recently under the *Maritime Powers Act 2013* (Cth), there has been no attempt to place such operations on a statutory footing,[318] which stands in contrast to the detailed statutory arrangements for ADF domestic security operations. Another interesting feature of such operations is that they are a product of the post *Charter of the United Nations* world which Australian law has not incorporated to anything like the same extent it has incorporated the international law of war. For example, the lack of applicable law stands in contrast to the elaborate constraints in the law of prize, which provided some protection for commercial shipping interests from the vicissitudes of naval warfare prior to the United Nations era. What does this say about the limits of this external prerogative power? Outside of Australia, the limits to prerogative power would appear to be applicable statute law, arguably interpreted

---

314 *Chow Hung Ching v R* (1948) 77 CLR 449, 477.
315 *Mabo* (1992) 175 CLR 1, 55.
316 For a note of caution on courts having too much regard to policy see Jim Evans, 'Questioning the Dogmas of Legal Realism', (2001) *New Zealand Law Review*, 145.
317 [2015] EWCA Civ 843, and now *Rahmatullah (No 2)* [2017] UKSC 1.
318 *Charter of the United Nations Act 1945* s 6.

in accordance with the purpose of the particular exercise of that power, local law, particularly property law, and the defence of Act of State. This is uncertain but international law, such as a United Nations Security Council Resolution, should provide a guide as to whether a particular action is protected by this defence or not. Until there is clear authority to support this proposition however, it remains only arguable.

Conclusion: What are the Limits?

Is it possible to limit the indefinable? The uncertainty of executive power combined with its great potential depth and breadth has a spectral quality which begs caution. Executive power can preserve an order based upon the rule of law or destroy it. To underscore that this tension remains an enduring aspect of constitutional law, which requires a conservative approach, this book has referred a number of times to the following statement of French CJ in *Pape v Commissioner of Taxation*:

> Future questions about the application of the executive power to the control or regulation of conduct or activities under coercive laws, absent authority supplied by a statute made under some head of power other than s 51(xxxix) alone are likely to be answered conservatively. They are likely to be answered bearing in mind the cautionary words of Dixon J in the *Communist Party Case*: 'History and not only ancient history, shows that in countries where democratic institutions have been unconstitutionally superseded, it has been done not seldom by those holding executive power. Forms of government may need protection from dangers likely to arise from within the institutions to be protected.'[1]

The meaning within these words are amplified when placed in the context of the military power of the ADF.

The aim of this book has been to find the sources of, and limits upon, the exercise of executive power by the ADF. This is a difficult exercise because of the tension between the need to have a power which can respond to *Fortuna* and yet remain subject to the principle of legality. This tension is at the heart of the judgments of Dixon J and Starke J in *Shaw Savill & Albion Co Ltd v Commonwealth*.[2] How does the law reconcile the need to respond to the fortunes of war, as in that case, with the need to keep the

---

1   (2009) 238 CLR 1, 24.
2   (1940) 66 CLR 344.

executive power subject to the law? Theories of executive power recognise that it is designed to respond to contingencies, the unpredictable, or *Fortuna*. There are only identifiable powers, which in this book relate to martial law, war, internal security and external operations, but it is not possible to have a case authority for every possible eventuality to which they might apply. Given the lack of litigation on some of these powers, there is little authority at all.

Instead, the limits of executive power within Australia turn on two key concepts, the written *Constitution* and necessity. As to necessity, the circumstances of the case dictate the limits of the power, which can temporarily displace the written law, as with martial law, or provide a standing exception to it, as with war. This is not the common law doctrine of necessity available to any citizen. Within the realm, this is a concept of necessity which operates upon those identifiable powers which only the Crown can exercise. In this book, they are the prerogative powers with respect to martial law, internal security and war, or nationhood power insofar as it relates to protection of Commonwealth interests in the States. As discussed below, necessity is not such an important aspect of operations outside the realm.

Additionally, the prerogative as to the control and disposition of the forces provides the conduit for executive power to flow to the ADF and on to the exercise of command within it. It provides the authority to organise, arm, equip, move or deploy the ADF as required. The fundamental principle which limits this prerogative is the subordination of the military to the civilian government.

As to the *Constitution,* the exercise of these various executive powers is also limited by the broader constraints on Commonwealth executive power. Within the realm, executive power can never effect an enduring change to the *Constitution*, alter the constitutional offices such as those of the Queen and the Governor-General, or otherwise exceed the limits of Commonwealth legislative power. Executive power can only derive from one of the sources identified in *Williams v Commonwealth*; those most relevant to this book being prerogative power, nationhood power and the powers ADF members may exercise by virtue of being citizens, in addition to statutory power.[3]

---

3 (2012) 248 CLR 156, 184-185 (French CJ), 342 (Crennan J), 373-374 (Kiefel J).

CONCLUSION

Further, executive power is subject to the requirements of the separation of powers and federalism. Arguably it also should not operate where Parliament has provided power in statute law which 'covers the field'. The exceptions to these requirements arise where necessity would justify relying upon executive power because the extreme circumstances are present to which the recognised prerogative powers relate, such as the collapse of civilian government, a serious threat to internal security which threatens life, or war. In the examples of such situations in this book, necessity often arises because the alternative to executive power is no law at all. A resort to executive power supports the rule of law rather than undermines it because, as quoted from Blackstone in Chapter 1, these are circumstances which require 'those extraordinary recourses to first principles, which are necessary when the contracts of society are in danger of dissolution, and the law proves too weak a defence ...'[4]

Beyond the realm, the exercise of executive power by the ADF in external security operations is less constrained because it does not normally intrude directly upon the principle of military subordination to civilian government or the jurisdiction of the States or Parliament. The main limits are those statutes which apply extraterritorially, although this requires arguing that prerogative power should operate where it has not been expressly curtailed or extinguished, and local law. Act of State as a defence could operate to cover any action by the ADF sufficiently connected to the purpose of its mission. The law is unsettled in this area, however, and this is only an arguable view of it. International law may be an essential guide here, although it is not necessarily a limitation in itself.

It is possible, therefore, to identify sources and limits to the exercise of executive power by the ADF. There cannot always be precise limitations because it would never be possible to define precisely in advance what circumstances might require of the ADF. *Fortuna* would never permit this. As stated at the beginning of Chapter 1, in the 1988 case of *Davis v Commonwealth*, Mason J said of the executive power that it is potentially very broad yet 'its scope [is not] amenable to exhaustive definition'.[5] Even so, immutable aspects of the *Constitution* provide a means to limit any action by the ADF. Blackstone's previously quoted conviction that the

---

4   *Blackstone's Commentaries with Notes of Reference, to the Constitution and Laws, of the Federal Government of the United States; and of the Commonwealth of Virginia* (1803, Hein Online reproduction) 251.
5   *Davis v Commonwealth* (1988) 166 CLR 79, 93.

political constraints embedded within it will limit the power of the Crown, manifest through the principle of responsible government, therefore still has resonance:

> [T]he king is irresistible and absolute, according to the forms of the constitution. And yet, if the consequence of that exertion be manifestly to the grievance or dishonour of the kingdom, the parliament will call his advisers to a just and severe account. For prerogative consisting (as Mr Locke has well defined it) in the prerogative power of acting for the public good, where the positive laws are silent; if that discretionary power be abused to the public detriment, such prerogative is exerted in an unconstitutional manner.[6]

This constraint may have done more than anything to limit executive power and create a political and military culture that does not accept that executive power is limitless. As much as this culture values the qualities of 'unanimity, strength, and dispatch' in order to respond to *Fortuna*,[7] it also values constitutionalism, legality and military subordination to the civilian government and resists arbitrariness and despotism. The tension between these values is an enduring feature of executive power, which is as much a political issue as a legal one. Therefore, provided that the Parliament retains its ability to call the executive to account, this political accountability should limit executive power.

Even so, the principle of legality applies to the ADF as well, and those who wish to wield executive power through it must keep this in mind. Before and quite apart from any political accountability through the principle of responsible government, those who exercise executive power remain subject to the law. Executive power provides only limited and uncertain authority to depart from the ordinary laws of the land. This demands a requirement to make the justification to rely upon executive power, as quoted from *Entick v Carrington* throughout this book, as 'clear in proportion as the power is exorbitant'.[8] This means that justifications to exercise a prerogative or other executive power based upon necessity, rather than positive authority, must be clear and strong. This book has discussed many examples of where this has occurred, but if an ADF

---

6   *Blackstone's Commentaries with Notes*, above n 4, 252.
7   Ibid 250.
8   (1765) 19 St Tr 1030, 1066.

member exceeds that justification, even in the performance of duty, that ADF member bears liability for that breach personally. To repeat Starke J's statement in *Shaw Savill & Albion Co Ltd* in 1940:

> If any person commits … a wrongful act or one not justifiable, he cannot escape liability for the offence, he cannot prevent himself being sued, merely because he acted in obedience to the order of the Executive Government or any officer of State.[9]

Even where this limitation might not be foremost in the minds of the elected members of the civilian government, it should always remain foremost in the minds of those in the ADF who execute its will.

From the point of view of protection from prosecution and suit for ADF members it might be better to have some sort of defence of superior orders provided in the *Defence Act 1903* (Cth) for all purposes, like that provided in s 14 of the *Defence Force Discipline Act 1982* (Cth) for disciplinary purposes:

> A person is not liable to be convicted of a service offence by reason of an act or omission that:
> (a) was in execution of the law; or
> (b) was in obedience to:
>   (i) a lawful order; or
>   (ii) an unlawful order that the person did not know, and could not reasonably be expected to have known, was unlawful.

The wording of the provision would need to expand to include protection from criminal liability and civil suit. This would shift the burden of any legal liability to the Commonwealth, any minister who gave an unlawful direction or any ADF member who gave an unlawful order, and away from ADF members acting in obedience to apparently lawful orders. Although statutory reform is another debate and the aim of this book is to find the limits of executive power as exercised by the ADF, it is a logical next step to consider.

The tension between the need to respond to *Fortuna* and the principle of legality is inherent in the exercise of executive power. This tension is at its most profound in the case of the more extreme potential exercises of executive power by the ADF. There are limits on the exercise of this power

---

9   *Shaw Savill & Albion Co Ltd* (1940) 66 CLR 344, 353 citing *Raleigh v Goschen* (1898) 1 Ch 73, 77.

and it might be desirable to be certain as to what they are in every case. Apart from those limits in the *Constitution* which it cannot exceed, such limits are inherently and unavoidably uncertain. The exercise of executive power by the ADF is limited by law yet remains indefinable.

Bibliography

Articles/Books/Reports

Abbott, Ernest, 'Law, Emergencies and the Constitution: A Review of *Outside the Law: Emergency and Executive Power*' (2010) 7 *Journal of Homeland Security and Emergency Management* 1, doi.org/10.2202/1547-7355.1717

Allard, Tom, Alexandra Smith, Jordan Baker and David Braithwaite, 'Cessna Pilot Flew into Dogfight with RAAF', *Sydney Morning Herald* (10 September 2007) <http://www.smh.com.au/news/national/cessna-pilot-flew-into-dogfight-with-raaf/2007/09/09/1189276546264.html>

Appleby, Gabrielle and Stephen McDonald, 'Looking at the Executive Power through the High Court's New Spectacles' (2013) 35(2) *Sydney Law Review* 253

Aronson, Mark, 'Private Bodies, Public Power and Soft Law in the High Court' (2007) 35 *Federal Law Review* 1

Aronson, Mark, Bruce Dyer and Matthew Groves, *Judicial Review of Administrative Action* (Lawbook, 4th ed, 2009)

Australian Digest (Lawbook, 2nd ed, 1968) vol 2

Australian Government, *Responding to the 2020 Summit* (2009) <www.tda.edu.au/resources/2020_Summit_paper.pdf>

Baker, J H, *An Introduction to English Legal History* (Butterworths, 2nd ed, 1979)

Barker, Ernest (ed), *Social Contract: Essays by Locke, Hume and Rousseau* (Oxford University Press, 1946)

Barrie, George, 'Judicial Review of the Royal Prerogative' (1994) 111 *South African Law Journal* 788

Barry, John V, KC and Department of External Territories, *Report of the Commission of Inquiry into the Circumstances Relating to the Suspension of Civil Administration of the Territory of Papua in February, 1942* (Australia: s.n., 1945) ('*Barry Report*')

Beasley, Richard, 'Duty of Care on the Battlefield' *Bar News* (Summer 2011–2012) 53

Bingham, Lord, 'The Rule of Law' (2006) 66(1) *Cambridge Law Journal* 67

Blackshield, A R, 'The Siege of Bowral—the Legal Issues' [1978] 4(9) March *Pacific Defence Reporter* 6

Blackstone's Commentaries: with Notes of Reference, to the Constitution and Laws, of the Federal Government of the United States; and the Commonwealth of Virginia (Hein Online reproduction, 1803) vol 5

Blake, Robert, 'Great Britain: The Crimean War to the First World War' in Michael Howard (ed) *Soldiers and Governments: Nine Studies in Civil–Military Relations* (Eyre & Spottswoode, 1957) 25

Boss, B C, *Law and Peace: A Legal Framework for United Nations Peacekeeping* (PhD thesis, University of Sydney, 2006)

Boyce, Peter, *The Queen's Other Realms: The Crown and its Legacy in Australia, Canada and New Zealand* (Federation Press, 2008)

Brazil, Patrick and Bevan Mitchell (eds), *Opinions of Attorneys-General of the Commonwealth of Australia, Volume 1: 1901–14* (1981)

Brereton, Justice Paul, 'Commentary on Military Justice and Chapter III: The Constitutional Basis of Courts Martial' (Paper presented at the Australian Association of Constitutional Lawyers Seminar, Sydney, 8 May 2013)

Bronitt, Simon, 'Balancing Security and Liberty: Critical Perspectives on Terrorism Law Reform' in Miriam Gani and Penelope Matthew (eds) *Fresh Perspectives on the 'War on Terror'* (ANU E Press, 2008) 65 <press-files.anu.edu.au/downloads/press/p54191/pdf/ch059.pdf>

Bronitt, Simon and Bernadette McSherry, *Principles of Criminal Law* (Thomson Lawbook Co., 3rd ed, 2010)

Bronitt, Simon and Dale Stephens, '"Flying under the Radar": The Use of Lethal Force against Hijacked Aircraft: Recent Australian Developments' (2007) 7(2) *Oxford University Commonwealth Law Journal* 265

Burmester, Henry, 'The Rise, Fall and Proposed Rebirth of the Australian Military Court' (2011) 39(9) *Federal Law Review* 195

Calwell, C E, *Small Wars: Their Principles and Practice* (HMSO 3rd ed, 1899)

Campbell, Tom, 'Emergency Strategies for Prescriptive Legal Positivists: Anti-terrorist Law and Legal Theory' in Victor Ramraj (ed) *Emergencies and the Limits of Legality* (Cambridge University Press, 2008) 201

Cane, Peter, 'Prerogative Acts, Acts of State and Justiciability' (1980) 29(4) *International and Comparative Law Quarterly* 680

Cartledge, G J, *The Soldier's Dilemma: When to Use Force in Australia: An Examination of the Laws which are Likely to Affect Australian soldiers Operationally Deployed in Australia* (AGPS Press, 1992)

Charteris, A H (Archibald Hamilton), 'The Mandate over Nauru Island' (1923–1924) 4 *British Yearbook of International Law* 137

Chesterman, Simon, Thomas Franck and David Malone, *Law and Practice of the United Nations: Documents and Commentary* (Oxford University Press, 2008)

Chitty, Joseph, *A Treatise on the Law of the Prerogatives of the Crown; and the Relative Duties and Rights of the Subject* (Butterworths, 1820)

Chordia, Shipra, Andrew Lynch and George Williams, '*Williams v Commonwealth* – Commonwealth Executive Power and Australian Federalism' (2013) 37(1) *Melbourne University Law Review* 189

Chordia, Shipra, Andrew Lynch and George Williams, 'Case Note: *Williams v Commonwealth [No 2]*: Commonwealth Executive Power and Spending after *Williams [No 2]*' (2015) 39(1) *Melbourne University Law Review* 306

Chrimes, S B, *English Constitutional History* (Oxford University Press, 4th ed, 1967)

Churchill, E F, 'The Dispensing Power and the Defence of the Realm' (1921) 37(October) *Law Quarterly Review* 412

Clark, Chris, 'The Statute of Westminster and the Murder in *HMAS Australia*, 1942' (2009) 179 *Australian Defence Force Journal* 18 <http://search.informit.com.au/documentSummary;dn=200910940; res=IELAPA>

Clark, David, *Principles of Australian Public Law* (Lexis Nexis Butterworths, 2nd ed, 2007)

Clode, Charles, *The Military Forces of the Crown: Their Administration and Government* (John Murray, 1869)

Clode, Charles, *The Administration of Justice under Military and Martial Law: As Applicable to the Army, Navy, Marines and Auxiliary Forces* (John Murray, 2nd ed, 1874)

Colombos, C J, *International Law of the Sea* (McKay, 6th ed, 1967)

Commonwealth, *Royal Commission on the Constitution of the Commonwealth, Report of Proceedings and Minutes of Evidence* (Canberra, 22 September 1927)

Commonwealth of Australia, *Air Raids on Darwin, Interim Report* (1942)

Commonwealth of Australia, *Manual of National Security Legislation* (1943)

Commonwealth of Australia, *Inquiry into Certain Australian Companies in Relation to the UN Oil for Food Programme* (2006)

Commonwealth Parliament, Senate Foreign Affairs, Defence and Trade Legislation Committee, *Report on Australia's Military Justice System* (June 2005)

Constitutional Commission, *Advisory Committee on Executive Government: Issues Paper* (Constitutional Commission, 1986)

Corn, Geoffrey, Victor Hansen, Richard Jackson, Christopher Jenks, Eric Talbot Jensen and James Schoettler, *The Law of Armed Conflict: An Operational Approach* (Wolters Kluwer, 2012)

Cowan, Zelman, 'The Armed Forces of the Crown' (1950) 66 *Law Quarterly Review* 478

Cox, Noel, '*Black v Chretien*: Suing a Minister of the Crown for Abuse of Power, Misfeasance in Public Office and Negligence' [2002] *Murdoch University Electronic Journal of Law* 26

Craig, Paul and Adam Tomkins, 'Introduction' in Paul Craig and Adam Tomkins (eds), *The Executive and Public Law: Power and Accountability in Public Perspective* (Oxford University Press, 2006) 1

Craig, Paul and Adam Tomkins (eds), *The Executive and Public Law: Power and Accountability in Public Perspective* (Oxford University Press, 2006)

Craven, Greg, *Conversations with the Constitution: Not Just a Piece of Paper* (University of New South Wales Press, 2004)

Creyke, Robin, 'Executive Power – New Wine in Old Bottles: Foreword' (2003) 31 *Federal Law Review* iv

Creyke, Robin and John McMillan, *Control of Government Action: Text, Cases & Commentary* (Lexis Nexis Butterworths, 3rd ed, 2012)

Crowe, Jonathan and Suri Ratnapala, 'Military Justice and Chapter III: The Constitutional Basis of Courts Martial' (2012) 40 *Federal Law Review* 161

Dahl, Arne Willy, 'Military Assistance to the Police in Situations Requiring the Use of Armed Force' (Keynote Address at the New Zealand Armed Forces Law Conference, Trentham Army Camp, Upper Hutt, New Zealand, 9 February 2007)

Davies, Martin and Anthony Dickey, *Shipping Law* (Lawbook, 3rd ed, 2004)

De Smith, Stanley and Rodney Brazier, *Constitutional and Administrative Law* (Penguin, 7th ed, 1994)

Deakin, Sir Alfred, 'Channel of Communication with Imperial Government: Position of Consuls: Executive Power of Commonwealth' in Patrick Brazil and Bevan Mitchell (eds) *Opinions of Attorneys-General of the Commonwealth of Australia, Volume 1: 1901–14* (1981) 129

Dean, Eric, 'New Zealand Requisition of Ships in Time of War or other like Emergency' (1987) 4 *Maritime Law Association of Australia and New Zealand Journal* 21

Dennis, Peter, Jeffrey Grey, Ewan Morris and Robin Prior, *The Oxford Companion to Australian Military History* (Oxford University Press, 2nd ed, 2008)

Department of Defence, *Commonwealth War Book* (1956)

Department of Defence, *Submission to Senate Legal and Constitutional Committee Inquiry into Defence Legislation Amendment (Aid to Civilian Authorities) Bill* (2005)

Department of Defence, *Operation DELUGE* (9 May 2007) <http://www.defence.gov.au/opdeluge/default.htm> (Site discontinued)

Department of Defence, *Inquiry Officer's Report into the Death of Lance Corporal Jared William MacKinney* (6 January 2011) <http://www.defence.gov.au/Publications/COI/reports/IOI%20Report%20into%20death%20of%20LCPL%20MacKinney%20in%20AFG%20on%2024%20Aug%2010%20scanned%20for%20release.pdf>

Department of Defence, *White Paper 2013*

Department of Defence, 'Operation Slipper' 2012 <http://www.defence.gov.au/op/afghanistan/info/factsheet.htm> (accessed 30 July 2013. Site discontinued)

Department of Defence, *Timor-Leste* (30 July 2013) <http://www.defence.gov.au/Operations/PastOperations/timorleste/>

Devereux, John, 'Discipline Abroad: Re Colonel Aird; Ex Parte Alpert' (2004) 23 *University of Queensland Law Journal* 485

Dicey, A V, *Introduction to the Study of the Law of the Constitution* (Macmillan, 10th ed, 1959)

Dodd, Cyril, 'The Case of Marais' (1902) 18 *Law Quarterly Review* 145

Downer, Alexander, 'Australian Troops in East Timor' in Rod Kemp and Marion Stanton (eds) *Speaking for Australia: Parliamentary Speeches that Shaped Our Nation* (Allen and Unwin, 2004) 280

Dupont, Jerry, *The Common Law Abroad: Constitutional and Legal Legacy of the British Empire* (Rothman, 2001)

Dyzenhaus, David, *The Constitution of Law: Legality in a Time of Emergency* (Cambridge University Press, 2006)

Dyzenhaus, David, 'The Compulsion of Legality' in Victor Ramraj (ed), *Emergencies and the Limits of Legality* (Cambridge University Press, 2008) 33

Dyzenhaus, David, 'Review Essay: Emergency, Liberalism, and the State: Outside the Law: Emergency and Executive Power by Clement Fatovic' (2011) 9(1) Perspectives on Politics 69

Eburn, Michael, 'Responding to Catastrophic Natural Disasters and the Need for Commonwealth Legislation' (2011) 10(3) *Canberra Law Review* 81

Edson, Elise, 'Section 51(xxix) of the Australian *Constitution* and "Matters of International Concern:" Is there Anything to be Concerned About?' (2008) 29(2) *Adelaide Law Review* 269

Evans, Jim, 'Questioning the Dogmas of Legal Realism' (2001) *New Zealand Law Review* 145

Evans, Simon, 'The Rule of Law, Constitutionalism and the MV Tampa' (2002) 13(2) *Public Law Review (The Tampa Issue)* 94

Evans, Simon, 'Continuity and Flexibility: Executive Power in Australia' in Paul Craig and Adam Tomkins (eds), *The Executive and Public Law: Power and Accountability in Public Perspective* (Oxford University Press, 2006) 89

Evatt, H V, *The Royal Prerogative* (Law Book Co, first presented as a doctoral thesis 1924, with commentary by Leslie Zines, 1987)

Fatovic, Clement, *Outside the Law* (John Hopkins University Press, 2009)

Fink, M D, 'The Right of Visit for Warships: Some Challenges in Applying the Law of Maritime Interdiction on the High Seas' (2010) 49(1–2) *Military Law and Law of War Review* 7

Finlason, W F, *Treatise on Martial Law as Allowed by the Law of England in Time of Rebellion: With Illustrations Drawn from the Official Documents in the Jamaica Case, and Comments Constitutional and Legal* (Stevens, 1866)

Finlason, W F, *Commentaries upon Martial Law, with Special Reference to Its Regulation and Restraint* (Stevens, 1867)

Finlason, W F, *Report of the Case of The Queen v Edward Eyre on his Prosecution in the Court of Queen's Bench containing the Charge of Mr Justice Blackburn* (Stevens, 1868)

Finn, Chris, 'The Justiciability of Administrative Decisions: A Redundant Concept?' (2002) 30(2) *Federal Law Review* 239

Fisher, Humphrey, 'Book Review: Johnson U J Asiegbu, *Slavery and the Politics of Liberation 1787–1861: A Study of Liberated African Emigration and British Anti-slavery Policy*' (1971) 34(1) *Bulletin of the School of Oriental and African Studies*, University of London 188, doi.org/10.1017/S0041977X00142041

Forbes, Andrew (ed), *Australia's Response to Piracy: A Legal Perspective* (Sea Power Centre Australia, 2011)

Fox, G Richard and Jodie E Lydecker, 'The Militarisation of Australia's Federal Criminal Justice System' (2008) 32(5) *Criminal Law Journal* 287

Fraser, Malcom and Margaret Simons, *Malcolm Fraser: The Political Memoirs: Commemorative Edition* (Melbourne University Press, 2015)

French, Chief Justice R S, 'The Executive Power' (Inaugural George Winterton Lecture, Sydney Law School, University of Sydney, 18 February 2010) (2010) May *Constitutional Law and Policy Review* 5

French, Chief Justice Robert, 'Constitutional Review of Executive Decisions – Australia's US Legacy' (Speech to the Chicago Bar Association and the John Marshall Law School, 25 and 28 January 2010) (2010) 35(1) *University of Western Australia Law Review* 35

French, Chief Justice Robert, 'Oil and Water? International and Domestic Law in Australia' (The Brennan Lecture delivered at Bond University, 26 June 2009) published in Mary Hiscock and William van Caenegem (eds), *The Internationalisation of Law: Legislating, Decision-making, Practice and Education* (Edward Elgar, 2010) 211

Gageler, Stephen, 'Common Law Statutes and Judicial Legislation: Statutory Interpretation as a Common Law Process' (2012) 37(2) *Monash University Law Review* 1

Gaggioli, Gloria, *Report of the Expert Meeting of the Use of Force in Armed Conflicts: Interplay Between the Conduct of Hostilities and Law Enforcement Paradigms* (International Committee of the Red Cross, 2013)

Galligan, Brian, *The Politics of the High Court: A Study of the Judicial Branch of Government in Australia* (University of Queensland Press, 1987)

Gately, Warwick and Cameron Moore, 'Protecting Australia's Maritime Borders: The Operational Aspects' in Ben M Tsamenyi and Christopher Rahman (eds), *Protecting Australia's Maritime Borders: The MV Tampa and Beyond* (Centre for Maritime Policy, 2002) 37

Gerangelos, Peter, 'Parliament, the executive, the Governor-General and the Republic' in H P Lee and Peter Gerangelos (eds), *Constitutional Advancement in a Frozen Continent: Essays in Honour of George Winterton* (Federation Press, 2009) 190

Gerangelos, Peter, 'The Executive Power of the Commonwealth of Australia: Section 61 of the *Commonwealth Constitution*, "Nationhood" and the future of the Prerogative' (2012) 12(1) *Oxford University Commonwealth Law Journal* 97, doi.org/10.5235/147293412803188838

Gillingham, John, 'The Early Middle Ages 1066–1290' in Kenneth Morgan (ed), *The Oxford Illustrated History of Britain* (Oxford University Press, 1984) 104

Gladman, Mark, 'Comment: *Re Residential Tenancies Tribunal of New South Wales and Henderson; Ex Parte Defence Housing Authority* (1997) 190 CLR 410: States' Power to Bind the Commonwealth' (1999) 27 *Federal Law Review* 151

Goldsmith, Andrew and Bob Lowry, 'Security Sector Reform' in the 'Australian Strategic Policy Institute Special Report' (2008) March (12), *Australia and the South Pacific: Rising to the Challenge* 29

Gross, Oren, 'Extra-legality and the Ethic of Political Responsibility' in Victor V Ramraj (ed), *Emergencies and the Limits of Legality* (Cambridge University Press, 2008) 60

Gross, Oren and Fionnuala Ni Aolain, *Law in Times of Crisis: Emergency Powers in Theory and Practice* (Cambridge University Press, 2006), doi.org/10.1017/CBO9780511493997

Groves, Matthew, 'The Civilianisation of Australian Military Law' (2005) 28(2) *University of New South Wales Law Journal* 364

Guilfoyle, Kate, 'The Relationship Between the Crown and the Subject: Changes to the Position of the Crown as a Consequence of the Judicial Process' (1998) 17 *Australian Bar Review* 13

Hackett, General Sir John, *The Profession of Arms* (Macmillan, 1983)

Haden, Jack D, 'Nauru: A middle ground during World War II' in Pacific Islands Development Program, East-West Center for Pacific Island Studies, University of Hawai'i at Mānoa, *Pacific Islands Report* (2011) 3

Hale, Sir Matthew, *The History of the Common Law of England* (E and R Nutt and R Gosling, 1739)

Hale, Sir Matthew, *The Prerogatives of the King* (Selden Society, written between 1640 and 1664 but unpublished, D E C Yale (ed) (1976 ed)

Handford, Peter, 'Edward John Eyre and the Conflict of Laws' (2008) 32(3) *Melbourne University Law Review* 822

Hannan, Brigadier Mike, 'Defence Support to US President's Visit' (Transcript of official interview by Defence Spokesperson, 21 October 2003)

Harrison Moore, W, *Act of State in English Law* (Dutton, 1906, Rothman reprint 1987)

Harrison Moore, W, *The Constitution of the Commonwealth of Australia* (Maxwell, 2nd ed, 1910)

Hartnell, Air Vice Marshal Geoffrey, *Canberra Papers on Strategy and Defence No 27* (The Australian National University, Canberra 1983)

Hawke, Bob, 'The First Gulf War' in Rod Kemp and Marion Stanton (eds), *Speaking for Australia: Parliamentary Speeches that Shaped Our Nation* (Allen and Unwin, 2004) 253

Head, Michael, 'The Military Call-out Legislation – Some Legal and Constitutional Questions' (2001) 29(2) *Federal Law Review* 273

Head, Michael, 'A Victory for Democracy? An Alternative Assessment of *Fiji v Prasad*' (2001) 2(2) *Melbourne Journal of International Law* 535

Head, Michael, 'Calling out the Troops – Disturbing Trends and Unanswered Questions' (2005) 28(2) *University of New South Wales Law Journal* 479

Head, Michael, 'Australia's Expanded Military Call-out Powers: Causes for Concern' (2006) 3(2) *University of New England Law Journal* 125

Head, Michael, *Calling out the Troops: The Australian Military and Civil Unrest* (Federation Press, 2009)

Henckaerts, Jean-Marie and Louise Doswald-Beck, *Customary International Humanitarian Law: Practice* (Cambridge University Press, 2005) vol II, doi.org/10.1017/CBO9780511804700

Hill, Graeme, 'Will the High Court "*Wakim*" Chapter II of the Constitution?' (2003) 31(3) *Federal Law Review* 445

Hill, Robert, Defence Minister, 'Defence Minister, Senator Robert Hill, Outlines the Contribution of the Australian Defence Force Towards Security for the Forthcoming CHOGM meeting' (Press Release, 22 Feb 2002)

Holdsworth, W S, 'Martial Law Historically Considered' (1902) 18 *Law Quarterly Review* 117

Holdsworth, W S, 'The History of Acts of State in English Law' (1941) 41(8) *Columbia Law Review* 1313

Hope, Justice Robert, *Protective Security Review* (Parliamentary Paper 397, Parliament of Australia, 1979)

Horan, Chris, 'Judicial Review of Non-statutory Executive Powers' (2003) 31(3) *Federal Law Review* 551

House of Commons Public Administration Select Committee, *United Kingdom, Taming the Prerogative: Strengthening Ministerial Accountability to Parliament: Fourth Report* (2004)

Human Rights Committee, *Replies to the List of Issues (CCPR/C/AUS/Q/5) to be Taken Up in Connection with the Consideration of the Fifth Periodic Report of the Government of Australia (CCP/C/AUS/5)* UN Doc CCPR/C/AUS/Q/5/Add.1 (21 January 2009)

Hume, David, *The History of England from the Invasion of Julius Caesar to the Revolution of 1688 (Continued to the Death of George the Second by T. Smollett M D)* (Joseph Ogle Robinson, 1833)

Hussain, Nasser, *The Jurisprudence of Emergency* (University of Michigan Press, 2003)

International Committee of the Red Cross, *Report of the 31st International Conference of the Red Cross and Red Crescent on International Humanitarian law and the Challenges of Contemporary Armed Conflicts* (2011)

International Institute of International Humanitarian Law, *San Remo Manual on International Law Applicable to Armed Conflict at Sea* (1994)

Jefferson, Thomas, 'Letter LXXI to Doctor James Brown, Washington, October 27, 1808' in Thomas Jefferson Randolph (ed), *Memoirs, Correspondence and Miscellanies from the Correspondence of T Jefferson* (F Carr, 1829) vol 3, 115

Jones, Mitchell, 'Judicial Review of Administrative Action against Members of the Australian Defence Force: Can a Warrior Win in Court?' (2005) 13(1) *Australian Journal of Administrative Law* 8

Jones, Mitchell, 'The Governor-General as Commander-in-Chief' (2009) 16(2) *Australian Journal of Administrative Law* 82

Kaye, Stuart, 'Tampering with Border Protection: The Legal and Policy Implications of the Voyage of the *MV Tampa*' in Martin Tsamenyi and Chris Rahman (eds), *Protecting Australia's Maritime Borders: The MV Tampa and Beyond* (Centre for Maritime Policy, 2002) 59

Kelly, Michael, *Peace Operations: Tackling the Legal, Military and Policy Challenges* (AGPS, 1997)

Kelly, Michael, *Restoring and Maintaining Order in Complex Peace Operations: The Search for a Legal Framework* (Kluwer Law International, 1999)

Kelly, Michael, Timothy L H McCormack, Paul Muggleton and Bruce M Oswald, 'Legal Aspects of Australia's Involvement in the International Force for East Timor' (2001) *International Review of the Red Cross* 841 <https://www.icrc.org/eng/resources/documents/article/other/57jqz2.htm>

Kiefel, Justice Susan, 'Proportionality: A Rule of Reason' (2012) 23 *Public Law Review* 85

Kittichaisaree, Kriangsak, *International Criminal Law* (Oxford University Press, 2001)

Kemp, Rod and Marion Stanton (eds), *Speaking for Australia: Parliamentary Speeches that Shaped Our Nation* (Allen and Unwin, 2004)

Kennett, Geoffrey, 'The Constitution and Military Justice after *White v Director of Military Prosecutions*' (2008) 36(2) *Federal Law Review* 231

Kerr, Duncan, 'The High Court and the Executive: Emerging Challenges to the Underlying Doctrines of Responsible Government and the Rule of law' (2009) 28(2) *University of Tasmania Law Review* 144

Kevin, Tony (Rapporteur), *Report of the Australians for War Powers Reform Public Seminar 23 October 2015: Legislating Reform of the War Powers*. <http://www.warpowersreform.org.au/wp-content/uploads/2016/04/AWPR-Public-Seminar-Consolidated-Final.pdf>

Kingsbury, Howard Thayer, 'The "Act of State" Doctrine' (1910) 4(2) *American Journal of International Law* 359

Kostal, Rande W, *A Jurisprudence of Power: Victorian Empire and the Rule of Law* (Oxford, 2005)

Lagassé, Phillippe, 'Parliamentary and Judicial Ambivalence toward Executive Prerogative Powers in Canada' (2012) 55(2) *Canadian Public Administration* 157, doi.org/10.1111/j.1754-7121.2012.00222.x

Lake, Marilyn, 'Introduction: What have you done for your country?' in Marilyn Lake, Henry Reynolds, Mark McKenna and Joy Damousi (eds), *What's Wrong with Anzac? The Militarisation of Australia's History* (University of New South Wales Press, 2010) 1

Lake, Marilyn, Henry Reynolds, Mark McKenna and Joy Damousi (eds), *What's Wrong with Anzac? The Militarisation of Australia's History* (University of New South Wales Press, 2010)

Lee, H P, *The Emergency Powers of the Commonwealth of Australia* (Law Book Company, 1984)

Lee, H P, '*Salus Populi Suprema Lex Esto:* Constitutional Fidelity in Troubled Times' in H P Lee and Peter Gerangelos (eds), *Constitutional Advancement in a Frozen Continent: Essays in Honour of George Winterton* (Federation Press, 2009) 53

Lee, H P and Peter Gerangelos (eds), *Constitutional Advancement in a Frozen Continent: Essays in Honour of George Winterton* (Federation Press, 2009)

Lee, Ricky, 'Applicability of State Laws to Commonwealth Land and Activities' (2002) 6 *University of Western Sydney Law Review* 39

Lendrum, S D, 'The "Coorong Massacre": Martial law and the Aborigines at first settlement' (1977) 6(1) *Adelaide Law Review* 26

Lepsius, Oliver, 'Human Dignity and the Downing of Aircraft: The German Federal Constitutional Court Strikes down a Prominent Anti-terrorism Provision in the New Air-transport Security Act' (2006) 7(9) *German Law Journal* 761

Lim, Brendan, 'The Normativity of the Principle of Legality' (2013) 37(2) *Melbourne University Law Review* 372

Lindell, Geoffrey, 'Judicial Review of International Affairs' in Brian Opeskin and Donald Rothwell (eds), *International Law and Australian Federalism* (Melbourne University Press, 1997) 160

Lindell, Geoffrey, 'Authority for War [Iraq war.]' (2003) 16 (May–June) *About the House* 23. <http://search.informit.com.au/documentSummary;dn=200305909;res=IELAPA>

Lindell, Geoffrey, *The Coalition Wars Against Iraq and Afghanistan in the Courts of the UK, Ireland and the US: Significance for Australia* (Centre for International and Public Law Policy Paper 26, Federation Press 2005)

Lindell, Geoffrey, '*Williams v Commonwealth*: The Shrinking Scope of the Executive Power of the Commonwealth and the Increased Role of the Australian Parliament in Authorising its Exercise' (Parliamentary Briefing Paper No 1, Commonwealth Parliament, 6 December 2012)

Locke, John, 'An Essay Concerning the True, Original, Extent and End of Civil Government (1690)' in Sir Ernest Baker (ed), *Social Contract: Essay by Locke, Hume and Rousseau* (Oxford University Press, 1946) 137

Locke, John, *Two Treatises of Government* (Mobilereference.com, first published 1689, 2008)

Loughlin, Martin, *The Idea of Public Law* (Oxford University Press, 2003)

Loughlin, Martin, *Foundations of Public Law* (Oxford University Press, 2010)

Lynch, Philip, 'Juries as Communities of Resistance: Eureka and the Power of the Rabble' (2002) 27(2) *Alternative Law Journal* 83

Machiavelli, Niccolò, *The Prince* (W K Marriott trans, Encyclopedia Britannica Great Books, 1952 [first published in Italian in 1513 and in English 1640])

Maitland, F W, *The Constitutional History of England* (Cambridge University Press, 1955)

Manual of Military Law (UK) (1899)

Marshall, Geoffrey, *Constitutional Conventions: The Rules and Forms of Political Accountability* (Clarendon Press, 1984)

McKeown, Deirdre and Ray Jordan, 'Parliamentary Involvement in Declaring War and Deploying Forces Overseas' (Background Note, Parliamentary Library, Commonwealth, 2010)

McLachlan, Campbell, *Foreign Relations Law* (Cambridge University Press, 2014)

McLaughlin, Rob, 'The Use of Lethal Force by Military Forces on Law Enforcement Operations – Is there a "Lawful Authority"?' (2009) 37(3) *Federal Law Review* 441

McLaughlin, Rob, '"Giving" Operational Legal Advice: Context and Method' (2011) 50(1–2) *The Military Law and Law of War Review* 99

McLaughlin, Rob, 'Legal-policy Considerations and Conflict Characterisation at the Threshold Between Law Enforcement and non-International Armed Conflict' (2012) 13(1) *Melbourne Journal of International Law* 94

McLaughlin, Robert and Bruce Oswald, '"Wilful Killing" During Armed Conflict: Is there a Defence of Proportionality in Australia?' (2007) 18(1) *Criminal Law Forum* 1

McMillan, John, 'Comments on the Justiciability of the Government's Tampa Actions' (2002) 13(2) *Public Law Review* 89

McNamara, Joe, 'The Commonwealth Response to Cyclone Tracy: Implications for Future Disasters' (2012) 27(2) *The Australian Journal of Emergency Management* 37

Mead, Lieutenant Colonel Lachlan, 'We are more Concerned with the Good Soldier than the Bad one in War: The Australian Army Legal Department 1939–1942' in Bruce Oswald and Jim Waddell (eds) *Justice in Arms: Military Lawyers in the Australian Army's First Hundred Years* (Big Sky, 2014) 77

Mead, Lieutenant Colonel Lachlan, 'Not Exactly Heroic but still Moderately Useful: Army Legal Work during the Second World War 1939–1945' in Bruce Oswald and Jim Waddell (eds) *Justice in Arms: Military Lawyers in the Australian Army's First Hundred Years* (Big Sky, 2014) 127

Meagher, Dan, 'The Common Law Principle of Legality in the Age of Rights' (2011) 35 *Melbourne University Law Review* 449

Melzer, Nils, *Interpretive Guidance on the Notion of Direct Participation in Hostilities Under International Humanitarian Law* (International Committee of the Red Cross, 2009)

Michaelsen, Christopher, 'Reforming Australia's National Security Laws: The Case for a Proportionality-based Approach' (2010) 29(1) *University of Tasmania Law Review* 31

Military Board, *Australian Edition of Manual of Military Law* (CAGP, 1941)

Ministry of Defence, *Manual of the Law of Armed Conflict* (Oxford University Press, 2004)

Mitchell, Andrew and Tania Voon, 'Justice at the Sharp End – Improving Australia's Military Justice System' (2005) 28(2) *University of New South Wales Law Journal* 396

Montesquieu, Charles de Secondat, Baron de, *The Spirit of the Laws* (Anne Cohler, Basia Miller and Harold Stone trans and eds, Cambridge University Press, 1989) [trans of *De L'Esprit de Lois* (first published 1748)]

Moore, Cameron, '"To Execute and Maintain the Laws of the Commonwealth" The ADF and Internal Security – Some Old Issues with New Relevance' (2005) 28(2) *University of New South Wales Law Journal* 523

Morgan, D G, *The Separation of Powers in the Irish Constitution* (Sweet & Maxwell, 1997)

Morgan, Kenneth (ed), *The Oxford Illustrated History of Britain* (Oxford University Press, 1984)

Murray, Sarah, 'Back to ABC after XYZ: Should we be Concerned about "International Concern"?' (2007) 35(2) *Federal Law Review* 315

Nagle, Peter, *Papua New Guinea Records* (National Archives of Australia, 2002)

Neocleous, Mark, 'Whatever Happened to Martial Law? Detainees and the Logic of Emergency' (2007) 143 *Radical Philosophy* 13

O'Cinneide, Colm, 'Strapped to the Mast: The Siren Song of Dreadful Necessity, the United Kingdom *Human Rights Act* and the Terrorist Threat' in Miriam Gani and Penelope Matthew (eds), *Fresh Perspectives on the 'War on Terror'* (ANU E Press, 2008) 327. <press-files.anu.edu.au/downloads/press/p54191/pdf/ch151.pdf>

Office of the Judge Advocate General, Canadian Forces, *The Crown Prerogative* <http://www.forces.gc.ca/en/about-reports-pubs-military-law-strategic-legal-paper/crown-prerogative-guide.page>

Omar, Imtiaz, *Emergency Powers and the Courts in India and Pakistan* (Kluwer Law International, 2002)

Oppenheim, L, *International Law: A Treatise: Vol II: War and Neutrality* (Longmans, 2nd ed, 1912)

Oswald, Bruce, 'The INTERFET Detainee Management Unit in East Timor' (2000) 3 *Yearbook of International Humanitarian Law* 347, doi.org/10.1017/S1389135900000696

Oswald, Bruce, 'The Law of Military Occupation: Answering the Challenges of Detention During Contemporary Peace Operations?' (2007) 8(2) *Melbourne Journal of International Law* 311

Oswald, Bruce, 'Detention of Civilians on Military Operations: Reasons for and Challenges to Developing a Special Law of Detention' (2008) 32(2) *Melbourne University Law Review* 524

Oswald, Bruce, 'The Corps on Operations: 1987–2000' in Bruce Oswald and Jim Waddell (eds) *Justice in Arms: Military Lawyers in the Australian Army's First Hundred Years* (Big Sky, 2014)

Oswald, Bruce and Jim Waddell (eds) *Justice in Arms: Military Lawyers in the Australian Army's First Hundred Years* (Big Sky, 2014)

Papua New Guinea Constitutional Planning Committee, *Report* (1974) <http://www.paclii.org/pg/CPCReport/main.htm>

Pearce, D C and R S Geddes, *Statutory Interpretation in Australia* (Lexis Nexis Butterworths, 7th ed, 2011)

Pejic, Jelena, 'Procedural Principles and Safeguards for Internment/Administrative Detention in Armed Conflict and Other Situations of Violence' (2005) 87(858) *International Review of the Red Cross* 375, doi.org/10.1017/S1816383100181408

Penhallurick, Catherine, 'Commonwealth Immunity as a Constitutional Implication' (2001) 29(2) *Federal Law Review* 151

Ponce de Leon, Lorenzo, 'The Coming of Age of Military Law and Jurisdiction in the English-speaking Countries' (2010) 49 *Revue de Droit Militaire et de Droit de La Guerre* 263

Porter, Bernard, *The Lion's Share: A Short History of British Imperialism 1850–1983* (Longman, 2nd ed, 1984)

Powell, Alan, *The Third Force: ANGAU's New Guinea War, 1942–1946* (Oxford University Press, 2003)

Pringle, Helen and Elaine Thompson, 'The Tampa Affair and the Role of the Australian Parliament' (2002) 13(2) *Public Law Review (The Tampa Issue)* 128

Quick, John and Sir Robert Garran, *Annotated Constitution of the Australian Commonwealth* (Legal Books, first published 1901, 1995 reprint)

Ramraj, Victor, 'No Doctrine More Pernicious: Emergencies and the Limits of Legality' in Victor Ramraj (ed), *Emergencies and the Limits of Legality* (Cambridge University Press, 2008) 3

Ramraj, Victor (ed), *Emergencies and the Limits of Legality* (Cambridge University Press, 2008)

Reid, Kiron and Clive Walker, 'Military Aid in Civil Emergencies: Lessons from New Zealand' (1998) 27 *Anglo-American Law Review* 133

Renfree, Harold, *The Executive Power of the Commonwealth of Australia* (Legal Books, 1984)

Renwick, James, 'Detention Without Trial – The Relevance for Australia of the US Supreme Court Decisions in *Hamdi*, *Rasul* and *Rumsfeld*' (Speech to Judicial Conference of Australia, 3 September 2005)

Reynolds, Henry, 'Are Nations Really Made in War?', in Marilyn Lake, Henry Reynolds, Mark McKenna and Joy Damousi (eds), *What's Wrong with Anzac? The Militarisation of Australia's History* (University of New South Wales Press, 2010) 1

Richards, H Erle, 'Martial Law' (1902) 18 *Law Quarterly Review* 133

Robertson, Justice Alan, 'Commentary on the Boundaries of Judicial Review and Justiciability: Comparing Perspectives from Australian and Canada' (Paper presented at the Australian Institute of Administrative Law (NSW Chapter) Seminar, Sydney, 22 July 2013)

Rogers, A P V, *Law on the Battlefield* (Manchester University Press, 2nd ed, 2004)

Rogers, Felicity, 'The International Force in East Timor – Legal Aspects of Maritime Operations' (2005) 28(2) *University of New South Wales Law Journal* 566

Rose, Dennis, 'The Nature of the Commonwealth: A Comment' (1998) 20 *Adelaide Law Review* 101

Rosenthal, Newman, *Sir Charles Lowe: A Biographical Memoir* (Robertson and Mullens, 1968)

Rothwell, Donald, 'The High Court and the External Affairs Power: A Consideration of its Inner and Outer Limits' (1993) 15 *Adelaide Law Review* 209

Rothwell, Donald, 'The Law of the Sea and the MV Tampa Incident: Reconciling Maritime Principles with Coastal State Sovereignty' (2002) 13(2) *Public Law Review* 118

Rothwell, Donald and Tim Stephens, *The International Law of the Sea* (Hart Publishing, 2010)

Rowe, Peter, *Defence: The Legal Implications: Military Law and the Laws of War* (Brassey's, 1987)

Rowe, Peter, 'The Soldier as a Citizen in Uniform: A Reappraisal' (2007) 7 *New Zealand Armed Forces Law Review* 1

Rowe, Peter, 'Is there a Right to Detain Civilians by Foreign Armed Forces during a non-International Armed Conflict? (2012) 61 *International and Comparative Law Quarterly* 697, doi.org/10.1017/S0020589312000292

Royal Australian Air Force, *Operations Law for RAAF Commanders* (Australian Air Publication 1003, 2004)

Royal Australian Navy, *Australia's Maritime Doctrine: RAN Doctrine 1 2000* (Defence Publishing Service, 2000)

Rubenstein, Kim, 'Citizenship, Sovereignty and Migration: Australia's Exclusive Approach to Membership of the Community' (2002) 13 *Public Law Review* 102

Rubin, Gerry, 'Why Military Law? Some United Kingdom Perspectives' (2007) 26(2) *University of Queensland Law Journal* 353

Sampford, Charles and Margaret Palmer, 'The Constitutional Power to Make War' (2009) 18(2) *Griffith Law Review* 350, doi.org/10.1080/10383441.2009.10854646

Saunders, Cheryl, 'Intergovernmental Agreements and the Executive Power' (2005) 16(4) *Public Law Review* 294

Saunders, Cheryl, 'The Scope of Executive Power' (Speech delivered at Senate Occasional Lecture, Parliament House, 28 September 2012, Papers on Parliament No 59) <http://www.aph.gov.au/About_Parliament/Senate/Research_and_Education/pops/~/link.aspx?_id=C8C131542382464EB28135A33F9EA201&_z=z>

Schmitt, Carl, *Political Theology: Four Chapters on the Concept of Sovereignty* (G Schwab trans, University of Chicago Press, 2005)

Sea Power Centre of Australia, *Database of Royal Australian Navy Operations, 1990–2005 – Working Paper No 18* (Seapower Centre Australia, 2005)

Sealy, Leigh, '"Adrift on a Sea of Faith": Constitutional Interpretation and the School Chaplain's Case' (Paper presented at the Gilbert and Tobin Centre Constitutional Law Conference, Sydney, 15 February 2013)

Selway, Bradley, 'The Nature of the Commonwealth: A Comment' (1998) 20 *Adelaide Law Review* 95

Selway, Bradley, 'All at Sea – Constitutional Assumptions and "the Executive Power of the Commonwealth"' (2003) 31(3) *Federal Law Review* 495

Selway, Bradley, 'Horizontal and Vertical Assumptions within the Commonwealth Constitution' (2001) 12 *Public Law Review* 113

Selway, Bradley, 'Of Kings and Officers – The Judicial Development of Public Law' (2005) 33(2) *Federal Law Review* 187

Shearer, I A, 'The Relationship Between International Law and Domestic Law' in Brian Opeskin and Donald Rothwell (eds), *International Law and Australian Federalism* (Melbourne University Press, 1997) 49

Smith, H A, 'The Nature of Our Constitutional Law' (1920) 36 *Law Quarterly Review* 140

Smith, H A, *The Law and Custom of the Sea* (Stevens, 3rd ed, 1959)

Smith, Hugh, 'A Certain Maritime Incident and Political-Military Relations' (2002) 46(6) *Quadrant* June 38

Smith, Michael and Maureen Dee, *Peacekeeping in East Timor: The Path to Independence* (Lynne Reiner Publishers, 2003)

Smith, Stephen, Minister for Defence, 'Afghanistan – Detainee Management' (Ministerial Statement and Paper, 16 May 2013)

Snow, Deborah and Cynthia Banham, 'Calling Shots in Defence' *Sydney Morning Herald* 28 February – 1 March 2009

Sossin, Lorne, 'Case Comment: The Rule of Law and the Justiciability of Prerogative Powers: A Comment on *Black v Chretien*' (2002) 47 *McGill Law Journal* 435

Spankie, Captain Thomas, 'The Siege of Delhi – 1857' in William Robson, *The Great Sieges of History* (Routledge, Warne & Routledge, 1859) 633

Spigelman, James, 'The Principle of Legality and the Clear Statement Principle' (2005) 79 *Australian Law Journal* 769

Spijkers, Otto, 'The Netherlands and the United Nations' Responsibility for Srebrenica Before the Dutch Courts' (2011) 50 (3–4) *The Military Law and Law of War Review* 517

Stavsky, Mark, 'The Doctrine of State Necessity in Pakistan' (1983) 16(2) *Cornell International Law Journal* 341

Stephen, Sir Ninian, 'The Governor-General as Commander in Chief' (1983) 14 *Melbourne University Law Review* 563

Stephenson, Carl and Frederick George Marcham (eds and trans), *Sources of English Constitutional History: A Selection of Documents from AD 600 to the Present* (Harper and Brothers, 1937)

Stephenson, Peta, 'Fertile Ground for Federalism: Internal Security, the States and s 119 of the *Constitution*' (2015) 43 *Federal Law Review* 289

Stowell, Lord, 'Address to the Maritime Law Association' (Speech to the Annual General Meeting of the Maritime Law Association of Australia and New Zealand – Queensland Branch, November 1998)

Thom, Graham, 'Human Rights, Refugees and the MV Tampa Crisis' (2002) 13(2) *Public Law Review* 110

Thomson, Mark, 'Serving Australia: Control and Administration of the Department of Defence' (2011) June 41 *Australian Strategic Policy Institute Special Report* 1

Tomkins, Adam, 'The Struggle to Delimit Executive Power in Britain' in Paul Craig and Adam Tomkins (eds), *The Executive and Public Law: Power and Accountability in Public Perspective* (Oxford University Press, 2006) 16

Tracey, Richard, 'The Constitution and Military Justice' (2005) 28 *University of New South Wales Law Journal* 426

Tugenhadt, Thomas and Laura Croft, *The Fog of Law: Study of the Law of the Constitution Legal Erosion of British Fighting Power* (Policy Exchange, 2013)

Twist, Peter, 'Limits to the Supreme Command, Government and Disposition of the Armed Forces: *Attorney-General for England and Wales v R*' (2002) *New Zealand Armed Forces Law Review* 43

Twomey, Anne, 'Geographic Externality and Extraterritoriality: *XYZ v Commonwealth*' (2006) 17 *Public Law Review* 253

Twomey, Anne, 'Pushing the Boundaries of Executive Power – *Pape*, the Prerogative and Nationhood Powers' (2010) 34(1) *Melbourne University Law Review* 313

United Kingdom, House of Commons Defence Committee, *UK Armed Forces Personnel and the Legal Framework for Future Operations* Paper No HC 931, Session 2013–2014 (2013)

United States Adjutant General's Office, *Correspondence, Orders, Reports, and Returns of The Union Authorities From January 1 To December 31, 1863 – General Order No 100,* 'The Lieber Code Of 1863'

Vattel, Emer de, *Droit des Gens* (London, 1798)

Waddell, Colonel Jim, 'From Federation to Armistice: The Earliest Army Legal Officers' in Bruce Oswald and Jim Waddell (eds) *Justice in Arms: Military Lawyers in the Australian Army's First Hundred Years* (Big Sky, 2014)

Wall, Jason, 'The Validity of Military Courts after *Lane v Morrison*' (2009) 9 *New Zealand Armed Forces Law Review* 130

War Office (UK), *Land Warfare: An Exposition of the Laws and Usages of War on Land for the Guidance of Officers of His Majesty's Army* (1912)

Ward, Elizabeth, 'Call out the Troops: An Examination of the Legal Basis for Australian Defence Force Involvement in Non-defence Matters— Update of a Background Paper issued 5 September 1991' (1997) *Commonwealth Parliament Bills Digest*

Watt, Nicholas, 'Paratrooper Lee Clegg cleared of last charge over death of teenagers' *Guardian* (online), 1 February 2000 <http://www.guardian.co.uk/uk/2000/feb/01/northernireland.nicholaswatt3>

Webster, Stephen, 'Vice-Admiral Sir William Creswell: First Naval Member of the Australian Naval Board, 1911–1919' in D M Horner (ed), *The Commanders* (George, Allen & Unwin, 1984) 44

Weedon, Lord Alexander of, 'Iraq, the Pax Americana and the Law' (Justice Tom Sargant Memorial Annual Lecture, London, 14 October 2003)

Wheeler, Captain Owen, *The War Office: Past and Present* (Methuen, 1914, Taylor and Francis Reprint, 2009)

Wheeler, Fiona, 'Judicial Review of Prerogative Power in Australia: Issues and Prospects' (1992) 14 *Sydney Law Review* 432

Wheeler, Fiona, 'Original Intent and the Doctrine of the Separation of Powers in Australia' (1996) 7(2) *Public Law Review* 96

Wheeler, Fiona, 'The Separation of Judicial Power and Progressive Interpretation' in H P Lee and Peter Gerangelos (eds), *Constitutional Advancement in a Frozen Continent: Essays in Honour of George Winterton* (Federation Press, 2009) 237

Wheeler, Fiona, 'Parachuting In: War and Extra-judicial Activity by High Court Judges' (2010) 38(3) *Federal Law Review* 485

White, Douglas QC and Graham Ansell, 'Review of the Performance of the Defence Force in Relation to Expected Standards of Behaviour, and in Particular the Leaking and Inappropriate Use of Information by Defence Force Personnel' (Report to the State Services Commissioner, 20 December 2001)

White, Justice Margaret, 'The Constitution and Military Justice: *Re Colonel Aird; Ex parte Alpert*' (Paper presented at the Constitutional Law Conference, Sydney, 24 February 2006)

White, Margaret, 'The Executive and the Military' (2005) 28(2) *University of New South Wales Law Journal* (Australian Military Law Thematic Edition) 438

White, Michael, 'Tampa Incident: Some Subsequent Legal Issues' (2004) 78 *Australian Law Journal* 249

Whitington, R J, 'Case Comment: Act of State – *Attorney-General v Nissan*' (1970) 3(4) *Adelaide Law Review* 522

Wicks, Elizabeth, *The Evolution of a Constitution: Eight Key Moments in British Constitutional History* (Hart, 2006)

Williams, George, 'Feature – *Republic of Fiji v Prasad*' (2001) 2(1) *Melbourne Journal of International Law* 144

Williams, George, 'The Case that Stopped a Coup? The Rule of Law and Constitutionalism in Fiji' (2001) 1(1) *Oxford University Commonwealth Law Journal* 73

Williams, George, Sean Brennan and Andrew Lynch, 'Supplement to Chapter 11' (2012) to Tony Blackshield and George Williams, *Australian Constitutional Law and Theory* (The Federation Press, 5th ed, 2010)

Wilson, Robert, *International and Contemporary Commonwealth Issues* (Duke University Press, 1971)

Winterton, George, *The Parliament, the Executive and the Governor-General* (Melbourne University Press, 1983)

Winterton, George, 'The Prerogative in Novel Situations' (1983) 99 *Law Quarterly Review* 407

Winterton, George, 'Extra-constitutional Notions in Australian Constitutional Law' (1986) 16 *Federal Law Review* 223

Winterton, George, 'The Limits and Use of Executive Power by Government' (2003) 31(3) *Federal Law Review* 421

Winterton, George, 'The Relationship between Commonwealth Executive and Legislative Power' (2003) 25(1) *Adelaide Law Review* 21

Winterton, George, 'Who is Our Head of State?' (2004) 48(4) *Quadrant* September

Winterton, George, 'The Evolving Role of the Governor-General' (2004) 48(3) *Quadrant* March 2004

Zines, Leslie, 'The Growth of Australian Nationhood and its Effect on the Powers of the Commonwealth' in Leslie Zines (ed), *Commentaries on the Australian Constitution: A Tribute to Geoffrey Sawer* (Butterworths, 1977) 24

Zines, Leslie (ed), *Commentaries on the Australian Constitution: A Tribute to Geoffrey Sawer* (Butterworths, 1977)

Zines, Leslie, 'Commentary' to H V Evatt, *The Royal Prerogative* (Lawbook, first presented as a doctoral thesis 1924, with commentary by Leslie Zines, 1987)

Zines, Leslie, 'The Nature of the Commonwealth' (1998) 20 *Adelaide Law Review* 83

Zines, Leslie, 'The Inherent Executive Power of the Commonwealth' (2005) 16 *Public Law Review* 279

Zines, Leslie, *The High Court and the Constitution* (Federation Press, 5th ed, 2008)

Zelinka, Marley, '*Hicks v Ruddock* versus *The United States v Hicks*' (2007) 29(3) Sydney Law Review 527

Cases

A v Hayden (1984) 156 CLR 532

Adelaide Company of Jehovah's Witnesses v Commonwealth (1943) 67 CLR 116

Ali v Commonwealth of Australia [2004] VSC 6 (Unreported, Bongiorno J, 23 January 2004)

Al-Jedda v United Kingdom (2011) 53 EHRR 23

Al-Jedda v Secretary of State for Defence [2011] 2 WLR 225 ('*Al-Jedda*')

Al-Jedda v Secretary of State for the Home Department [2012] EWCA Civ 358

Al Kateb v Godwin (2004) 219 CLR 562

Al-Skeini v United Kingdom [2011] ECHR

Al-Waheed v Ministry of Defence; Mohammed v Ministry of Defence [2017] UKSC 2

Andrews v Howell (1941) 65 CLR 255

Attorney-General (Vic) v Commonwealth (1935) 52 CLR 533 ('*Clothing Factory Case*')

Attorney-General (Vic) ex rel Dale v Commonwealth (1945) 71 CLR 237 ('*Pharmaceutical Benefits Case*')

Attorney-General for Northern Ireland's Reference [1977] AC 105

Attorney-General v De Keyser's Royal Hotel Ltd [1920] AC 508 ('*De Keyser's Royal Hotel*')

Attorney-General v Nissan [1970] AC 179 ('*Nissan*')

Australian Capital Television Pty Ltd v Commonwealth (1992) 177 CLR 106

Australian Communist Party v Commonwealth (1951) 83 CLR 1 ('*Communist Party Case*')

Bank of New South Wales v The Commonwealth (1948) 76 CLR 1

Barratt v Howard (2000) 96 FCR 428

Barton v Commonwealth (1974) 131 CLR 477

Barwis v Keppel (1766) 95 ER 831; 2 Wilson, KB 314

Beckwith v R (1976) 135 CLR 569

Belhaj v Straw; Rahmatullah (No 1) v Ministry of Defence [2017] UKSC 3

Bici v Ministry of Defence [2004] EWHC 786 ('*Bici*')

Blunden v Commonwealth (2003) 218 CLR 330

Blom v Commonwealth (1917) 24 CLR 189

Bradley v Commonwealth (1973) 128 CLR 557

British Broadcasting Corporation v Jones [1965] Ch 32

Bromet v Oddie (2002) 78 ALD 320

Bundesverfassungsgericht (BVerfG – Federal Constitutional Court) 59 *Neue Juristische Wochenschrift* (NJW) 751 (2006)

Burmah Oil Co Ltd v Lord Advocate [1965] AC 75 ('*Burmah Oil*')

Burns v Ransley (1949) 79 CLR 101

Buron v Denman (1848) 2 Ex 167; 154 All ER 450

Cadia Holdings Pty Ltd v NSW (2010) 242 CLR 195 ('*Cadia*')

Carter v Egg & Egg Pulp Marketing Board (Vic) (1942) 66 CLR 557

Case of the King's Prerogative in Saltpetre (1606) 12 Co Rep 12

Chandler v Director of Public Prosecutions [1964] AC 763

Charge to the Bristol Grand Jury on a Special Commission 5 C & P 254

China Navigation Company Ltd v Attorney-General [1932] 2 KB 197 ('*China Navigation*')

Chow Hung Ching v R (1948) 77 CLR 449

Chu Kheng Lim v Minister for Immigration, Local Government and Ethnic Affairs (1992) 176 CLR 1

Clifford v O'Sullivan [1921] 2 AC 570

Clough v Leahy (1904) 2 CLR 139

Commonwealth v Colonial Combing, Spinning and Weaving Co (1922) 31 CLR 421 ('*Wooltops Case*')

Commonwealth v Mewett (1997) 191 CLR 471

Commonwealth v Quince (1944) 68 CLR 227 ('*Quince*')

Commonwealth v Tasmania (1983) 158 CLR 1 ('*Tasmanian Dam Case*')

Commonwealth v Welsh (1947) 74 CLR 245

Commonwealth v Yarmirr (2001) 208 CLR 1

Commonwealth v Zachariassen and Blom (1920) 27 CLR 552

Council of the Civil Service Unions v Minister for the Civil Service [1985] AC 374

Coutts v Commonwealth (1985) 157 CLR 91

CPCF v Minister for Immigration and Border Protection [2015] HCA 1 ('*CPCF*')

Curtis v Minister of Defence [2002] 2 NZLR 744 ('*Curtis*')

Davis v Commonwealth (1988) 166 CLR 79

DPP (SA) v B (1998) 194 CLR 566

Donohue v Schroeder and Kabutz (1916) 22 CLR 362

Dudley v Stephens (1884) 14 QBD 273

Egan v Willis (1998) 195 CLR 424

Entick v Carrington (1765) 19 St Tr 1030, (1765) 2 Wils KB 275, 291 [95 ER 807, 817]

FAI Insurances v Winneke (1982) 151 CLR 342

Farey v Burvett (1916) 21 CLR 433

Federal Commissioner of Taxation v Official Liquidator of EO Farley Ltd (in Liq) (1940) 63 CLR 278

Fletcher v Nott (1938) 60 CLR 55

Grace Bros Pty Ltd v Commonwealth (1946) 72 CLR 269

Grant v Gould (1792) 2 HBL 69; 126 ER 434

Gratwick v Johnson (1945) 70 CLR 1

Habib v Commonwealth (2010) 183 FCR 62

Haskins v Commonwealth (2011) 244 CLR 22

Hassan v United Kingdom [2014] ECHR (Application No. 29750/09)

Hicks v Ruddock (2007) 156 FCR 574

Horta v Commonwealth (1994) 181 CLR 183

In re Southern Rhodesia [1919] AC 233

In the Matter of an Application by Paul Tupuru [2005] PGNC 162

James v The Commonwealth (1939) 62 CLR 339

Jarratt v Commissioner of Police for New South Wales (2005) 224 CLR 44

Johnson v Kent (1975) 132 CLR 164

Johnston, Fear & Kingham & The Offset Printing Company Pty Ltd v Commonwealth (1943) 67 CLR 314 ('*Johnston, Fear and Kingham*')

Joseph v Colonial Treasurer (NSW) (1918) 25 CLR 32

JT International SA v Cth (2012) 86 ALJR 1297

Jumbunna Coal Mine NL v Victorian Coal Miners' Association (1908) 6 CLR 309

Lane v Morrison (2009) 239 CLR 230

Little v The Commonwealth (1947) 75 CLR 94

Mabo v Queensland (No 2) (1992) 175 CLR 1 ('*Mabo*')

Marais v General Officer Commanding the Lines of Communication [1902] AC 109 ('*Marais*')

Marks v Commonwealth (1964) 111 CLR 549

Martincevic v Commonwealth [2007] 96 ALD 576

Millar v Bornholt (2009) 117 FCR 67

Minister for Arts, Heritage and Environment v Peko-Wallsend Ltd (1987) 15 FCR 274

Minister of State for the Army v Dalziel (1944) 68 CLR 261

NSW v Commonwealth (1975) 135 CLR 337 ('*Seas and Submerged Lands Case*')

Nulyarimma v Thompson (1999) 96 FCR 153

Operation Dismantle v R [1985] 1 SCR 441

Pape v Commissioner of Taxation (2009) 238 CLR 1 ('*Pape*')

Petrotimor Companhia de Petroleos SARL v Commonwealth (2003) 126 FCR 354

Phillips v Eyre (1870) LR 6 QB 1

Pirrie v McFarlane (1925) 36 CLR 170

Plaintiff M68 v Minister for Immigration and Border Protection [2016] HCA 1 ('*M68*')

Polyukhovich v R (1991) 172 CLR 501

Prosecutor v Tadic 105 ILR 419

R (Garde) v Strickland [1921] 2 IR 317

R (On the Application of Al-Jedda) v Secretary of State for Defence [2008] 1 AC 332

R v Adjutant General of the Provisional Forces [1923] 1 IR 5

R v Allen [1921] 2 IR 241

R v Bevan; Ex parte Elias and Gordon (1942) 66 CLR 452

R v Bernasconi (1915) 19 CLR 629

R v Bottrill; Ex parte Kuechenmeister [1947] KB 41

R v Burgess; Ex parte Henry (1936) 55 CLR 608

R v Cox; Ex parte Smith (1945) 71 CLR 1

R v Davey; Ex parte Freer (1936) 56 CLR 381

Re Debs 158 US 564 (1895)

R v Duncan; Ex parte Australian Iron and Steel Pty Ltd (1983) 158 CLR 53

R v Eyre (1867–68) LR 3 QB 487

R v Foster (1949) 79 CLR 43

R v Hughes (2000) 202 CLR 535

R v Kidman (1915) 20 CLR 425

R v Kirby; Ex parte Boilermakers' Society of Australia (1956) 94 CLR 254

R v Loughnan [1981] VR 443

R v Nelson and Brand; Frederick Cockburn's Special Report of the Charge of the Lord Chief Justice of England to the Grand Jury at the Central Criminal Court in the Case of The Queen against Nelson and Brand (2nd ed, 1867) ('*Frederick Cockburn's Special Report*')

R v Pinney (1832) 3 B & AD 349

R v Sharkey (1949) 79 CLR 121

R v Secretary of State; Ex Parte Thring, Court of Appeal (Civil Division) (Unreported, Pill, Clarke, Bennett LJJ, 20 July 2000) ('*Thring*')

R v Secretary of State for the Home Department; Ex Parte Northumbria Police Authority [1989] 1 QB 26 ('*Northumbria Police Case*')

R v Toohey; Ex parte Northern Land Council (1981) 151 CLR 170

Rahmatullah (No 2) v Ministry of Defence; Mohammed v Ministry of Defence [2017] UKSC 1

Raleigh v Goschen (1898) 1 Ch 73, 77

Re Aird; Ex parte Alpert (2004) 220 CLR 308

Re Ditfort; Ex parte DCT (1988) 19 FCR 347

Re Refugee Review Tribunal; Ex parte Aala (2000) 204 CLR 82

Re Residential Tenancies Tribunal of NSW v Henderson; Ex parte Defence Housing Authority (1997) 190 CLR 410 ('*DHA Case*')

Re Tracey; Ex parte Ryan (1989) 166 CLR 518 ('*Re Tracey*')

Re Wakim; Ex parte McNally (1999) 198 CLR 511 ('*Cross-vesting Case*')

Reference by His Excellency the Governor-General (under s 213 of the Government of India Act, 1935) PLD 1955 FC (Pak) 435

Republic of Fiji Islands v Prasad (Unreported, Fiji Court of Appeal, Casey J (Presiding), Barker, Kapi, Ward and Handley JJA, 1 March 2001) ('*Prasad*')

Ruddock v Vadarlis (2001) 110 FCR 491 ('*Tampa Case*')

Ruddock v Vadarlis (No 2) (2001) 115 FCR 229

Serdar Mohammed v Secretary of State for Defence [2015] EWCA Civ 843 ('*Serdar Mohammed*')

Shaw Savill & Albion Co Ltd v Commonwealth (1940) 66 CLR 344 ('*Shaw Savill & Albion Co Ltd*')

Silk Bros Pty ltd v State Electricity Commission of Victoria (1943) 67 CLR

Smith v Ministry of Defence [2013] UKSC 41 ('*Smith*')

State v Dege [2002] PGMCJ 1

State v Enuma [1997] PGNC 171

State v Singirok [2004] PGNC 253

Stenhouse v Coleman (1944) 69 CLR 457

Sutton v Commonwealth [2011] FCA 14 (14 January 2011)

The Rolla (1807) 165 ER 963, 6 C Robinson 364

The Tojo Maru [1972] AC 242

The Turul [1919] AC 515

The Zamora [1916] 2 AC 77

Thomas v Mowbray (2007) 233 CLR 207

Thorpe v Commonwealth (No 3) (1997) 144 ALR 677

Tilonko v Attorney-General of Natal [1907] AC 570

Transcript of Proceedings, *Sergeant J and Lance-Corporal D*, Australian Defence Force General Court Martial Pre-trial Directions Hearing, Brigadier Westwood, Chief Judge Advocate, 20 May 2011

United States v Pacific Railroad 120 US 227 (1887)

Victoria v Commonwealth and Hayden (1975) 134 CLR 338 ('*AAP Case*')

White v Director of Military Prosecutions (2007) 231 CLR 570 ('*White*')

Williams v Commonwealth (2012) 248 CLR 156 ('*Williams*')

Wolfe Tone's Case (1798) 27 St Tr 614

X v Commonwealth (1999) 200 CLR 177

XYZ v Commonwealth (2006) 227 ALR 495

Zachariassen v Commonwealth (1917) 24 CLR 166

Zecevic v DPP (Vic) (1987) 162 CLR 645

Legislation

Act of Settlement 1701 (Imp)

ACT Self-Government (Consequential Provisions) Act 1988 (Cth)

Administrative Decisions (Judicial Review) Act 1977 (Cth)

Army Act 1881 (Imp)

Australian Capital Territory Self-Government Act 1989 (Cth)

BIBLIOGRAPHY

Australian Constitution 1900 ('*Constitution*')

Australian Federal Police Act 1979 (Cth)

Australian Military Regulations 1927 (Cth)

Bill of Rights 1688 (Imp)

Border Protection (Validation and Enforcement Powers) Act 2001 (Cth)

Charter of the United Nations Act 1945 (Cth)

Charter of the United Nations (Sanctions – Afghanistan) Regulations 2001

Charter of the United Nations (Sanctions – Iraq) Regulations 2006

Charter of the United Nations (Sanctions – Democratic People's Republic of Korea) Regulations 2008

Constitution of the Democratic Republic of Timor-Leste 2002

Constitution of Iraq 2006

Constitution of Solomon Islands 1978

Constitution of the Sovereign Democratic Republic of Fiji (Promulgation) Decree 1990 (Fiji)

Constitution of the United States

Crimes Act 1900 (ACT)

Crimes Act 1900 (NSW)

Crimes Act 1914 (Cth)

Crimes Act 1958 (Vic)

Crimes at Sea Act 2000 (Cth)

Crimes (Aviation) Act 1991 (Cth)

Crimes (Internationally Protected Persons) Act 1976 (Cth)

Criminal Code 1913 (WA)

Criminal Code Act 2002 (ACT)

Criminal Code Act 1995 (Cth)

Criminal Code Act (NT)

Criminal Code Act 1899 (Qld)

Criminal Code Act 1924 (Tas)

Customs Act 1901 (Cth)

Decree No 1 Fiji Constitution Amendment Act 1997 Revocation Decree 2009 (10 April 2007)

Decree No 2 Executive Authority of Fiji Decree 2009 (10 April 2009)

Defence (Personnel) Regulations 2002 (Cth)

Defence Act 1903 (Cth)

Defence Force Discipline Act 1982 (Cth)

Defence Force Regulations (Cth)

Defence Legislation Amendment (Aid to Civilian Authorities) Act 2006 (Cth)

Defence Legislation Amendment (First Principles) Act 2015 (Cth)

Defence of the Realm Act 1914 (UK)

Facilitation of International Assistance Act 2003 (Solomon Islands)

Fisheries Management Act 1991 (Cth)

Geneva Conventions Act 1957 (Cth)

Human Rights Act 1998 (UK)

Immunity (Fiji Military Government Intervention) Promulgation 2007 (Fiji)

Irish Free State Constitution Act 1922 (Imp)

Jervis Bay Territory Acceptance Act 1915 (Cth)

Judiciary Act 1903 (Cth)

Laws Repeal and Adopting Ordinance 1921 (New Guinea)

Laws Repeal and Adopting Ordinance 1922 (Nauru)

Letters Patent Relating to the Office of Governor-General of the Commonwealth of Australia, 21 August 2008

Magna Carta 1215 (Imp)

Marine Pollution Act 1987 (NSW)

Martial Law Indemnity Act 1854 (Vic)

Maritime Powers Act 2013 (Cth)

Migration Act 1958 (Cth)

Mutiny Act 1689 (Eng)

National Security Act 1939 (Cth)

National Security Act 1946 (Cth)

National Security (Aliens Control) Regulations 1940–1943 (Cth)

National Security (Emergency Control) Act 1939 (Cth)

National Security (Emergency Control) Regulations 1941 (Cth)

National Security (External Territories) Regulations 1942 (Cth)

National Security (General) Regulations 1939–1943 (Cth)

National Security (Land Transport) Regulations (Cth)

National Security (Landlord and Tenant) Regulations 1941 (Cth)

National Security (Prisoners of War) Regulations 1943 (Cth)

National Security (Supply of Goods) Regulations 1939–1942 (Cth)

National Security (Subversive Associations) Regulations 1940 (Cth)

Nauru Act 1965 (Cth)

Naval Prize Act 1864 (Imp)

Naval Prize (Procedure) Act 1916 (Imp)

New South Wales Act 1823 (Imp)

Petition of Right 1628 (Eng)

Private International Law (Miscellaneous Provisions) Act 1995 (UK)

Prize Act 1939 (Imp)

Prize Courts Act 1894 (Imp)

Prize Courts Act 1915 (Imp)

Prize Courts (Procedure) Act 1914 (Imp)

Residential Tenancy Act 1987 (NSW)

Statute of Westminster Adoption Act 1942 (Cth)

Tax Bonus Act 2009 (Cth)

Terrorism (Commonwealth Powers) Act 2003 (NSW)

Torres Strait Fisheries Act 1984 (Cth)

Treaties

Agreement Among Pacific Island States Concerning the Implementation and Administration of the Treaty on Fisheries Between the Governments of Certain Pacific Island States and the Government of the United States of America, (opened for signature 2 April 1987), [1988] ATS 42 (entered into force 15 June 1988) ('*Pacific Fisheries Treaty*')

Agreement Between Solomon Islands, Australia, New Zealand, Fiji, Papua New Guinea, Samoa and Tonga Concerning the Operations and Status of the Police and Armed Forces and Other Personnel Deployed to Solomon Islands to Assist in the Restoration of Law and Order and Security, (opened for signature 24 July 2003) [2003] ATS 17 (entry into force 24 July 2003) ('*Regional Assistance Mission to Solomon Islands Agreement*')

Agreement for the Implementation of the Provisions of the United Nations Convention on the Law of the Sea of 10 December 1982 Relating to the Conservation and Management of Straddling Fish Stocks and Highly Migratory Fish Stocks, (opened for signature 4 December 1995) 2167 UNTS 3 (entry into force 11 December 2001) ('*United Nations Fish Stocks Agreement*')

Charter of the United Nations

Geneva Conventions, (opened for signature 12 August 1949) (entered into force 21 October 1950)
- *Geneva Convention I for the Amelioration of the Condition of the Wounded and Sick in Armed Forces in the Field 75 UNTS 31 ('First Geneva Convention')*
- *Geneva Convention II for the Amelioration of the Condition of the Wounded, Sick and Shipwrecked of Armed Forces at Sea 75 UNTS 85 ('Second Geneva Convention')*
- *Geneva Convention III Relative to the Treatment of Prisoners of War 75 UNTS 135 ('Third Geneva Convention')*
- *Geneva Convention IV Relative to the Protection of Civilian Person in Time of War 75 UNTS 287 ('Fourth Geneva Convention')*

International Convention Relating to Intervention on the High Seas in Cases of Oil Pollution Casualties, (opened for signature 29 November 1969) 970 UNTS 212 (entered into force 6 May 1975)

Law of the Sea Convention, (opened for signature 10 December 1982) 1833 UNTS 3 (entered into force 16 November 1994) (*'Law of the Sea Convention'*)

Protocol Additional to the Geneva Conventions of 12 August 1949 and Relating to the Protection of Victims of International Armed Conflicts, (opened for signature 8 June 1977) 1125 UNTS 3 (entered into force 7 December 1978) (*'Additional Protocol I'*)

Protocol Additional to the Geneva Conventions of 12 August 1949 and Relating to the Adoption of an Additional Distinctive Emblem, (open for signature 8 December 2005) [2006] ATNIF 6 (*'Additional Protocol III'*)

Rome Statute of the International Court, (opened for signature on 17 July 1998) 2187 UNTS 90 (entered into force 1 July 2002)

Second Optional Protocol to the International Covenant on Civil and Political Rights, Aiming at the Abolition of the Death Penalty, (opened for signature 15 December 1989) 1642 UNTS 414 (entered into force 11 July 1991)

Treaty Between the Government of Australia and the Government of the French Republic on Cooperation in the Maritime Areas Adjacent to the French Southern and Antarctic Territories (TAAF), Heard Island and the McDonald Islands, (signed 24 November 2003) [2005] ATS 6 (entered into force 1 February 2005)

Treaty Between Australia and the Independent State of Papua New Guinea Concerning Sovereignty and Maritime Boundaries in the Area Between the Two Countries, Including the Area Known as Torres Strait, and Related Matters, (signed 18 December 1978) [1985] ATS 4 (entered into force 15 February 1985) ('*Torres Straight Treaty*')

Other

Bills Digest No 13, 2000–1, Defence Legislation Amendment Bill (Aid to Civilian Authorities) Bill 2000

Commonwealth *Gazette*, No 50, 3 August 1914, 1335

Commonwealth *Gazette*, No 63, 3 September 1939, 1849

Commonwealth, *Gazette*, No 251, 8 December 1941, 1849

Commonwealth, *Gazette*, No 252, 9 December 1941, 2727

Commonwealth, *Gazette*, No 14, 14 January 1942, 79

Commonwealth, *Gazette*, No 104, 7 April 1942, 859

Commonwealth *Gazette*, No 198, 20 July 1942, 1733

Commonwealth, *Parliamentary Debates*, House of Representatives, 16 December 1941, (Dr H V Evatt)

Commonwealth, *Parliamentary Debates*, House of Representatives, 22 June 1943, 56–64 (Eddie Ward)

Commonwealth, *Parliamentary Debates*, House of Representatives, 4 December 1990, 4319–325 (Bob Hawke)

Commonwealth, *Parliamentary Debates,* House of Representative, 21 September 1999, 10047–51 (Alexander Downer)

Commonwealth, *Parliamentary Debates*, House of Representatives, 18 March 2003, 12505–512 (John Howard)

Commonwealth, *Parliamentary Debates*, House of Representatives, 18 March 2003, 13170, Senate, 20 March 2003, 9888

Declaration of the People's Consultative Assembly of Indonesia, 20 October 1999

Henry I, *Coronation Charter*, (1100)

Inter-Governmental Agreement on Australia's National Counter-Terrorism Arrangements, 2002 (24 October 2002)

Inter-Imperial Relations Committee, 'Report, Proceedings and Memoranda' (E IR/26 Series) *Imperial Conference* 1926

Official Record of the Proceedings and Debates of the Australasian Federation Conference, Melbourne 1890

Official Report of the National Australasian Convention Debates, Sydney, 2 March – 9 April 1891

Official Report of the National Australasian Convention Debates, Adelaide, 22 March – 5 May 1897

Official Record of the Debates of the Australasian Federal Convention, Sydney, 2 – 24 September 1897

Official Record of the Debates of the Australasian Federal Convention, Melbourne, 20 January – 17 March 1898

Order-in-Council of the Governor-General, 1 November 1991

SC Res 84, UN SCOR, 476th mtg, UN Doc S/1588 (7 July 1950)

SC Res 665, UN SCOR, 2938th mtg, UN Doc S/Res/665 (25 August 1990)

SC Res 678, UN SCOR, 2963rd mtg, UN Doc S/Res/678 (29 November 1990)

SC Res 1264, UN SCOR, 4045th mtg UN Doc S/Res/1264 (15 September 1999)

SC Res 1546, UN SCOR, 4987th mtg UN Doc S/Res/1546 (8 June 2004)

SC Res 1790, UN SCOR, 5808th mtg, UN Doc S/Res/1790 (18 December 2007)

SC Res 774, UN SCOR, 3145th mtg, UN Doc S/Res/794 (3 December 1992). SC Res 1264, UN SCOR, 4045th mtg, UN Doc S/Res/794 (15 September 1999)

www.ingramcontent.com/pod-product-compliance
Lightning Source LLC
Chambersburg PA
CBHW050849240426
43667CB00032B/2955